LOCAL BABIES, GLOBAL SCIENCE

Gender, Religion, and In Vitro Fertilization in Egypt

MARCIA C. INHORN

D0112065

Routledge
New York   London

To Kirk, Carl, and Justine,

with love

Published in 2003 by
Routledge
29 West 35th Street
New York, New York 10001

Published in Great Britain by
Routledge
11 New Fetter Lane
London EC4P 4EE

Routledge is an imprint of the Taylor & Francis Group.

Library of Congress Cataloging-in-Publication Data

Inhorn, Marcia Claire, 1957–
    Local babies, global science : gender, religion, and in vitro fertilization in Egypt / by Marcia C. Inhorn.
        p. cm.
    Includes bibliographical references and index.
        ISBN 0-415-94416-3 (hc : alk. paper)—ISBN 0-415-94417-1 (pbk. :   )
    1. Fertilization in vitro, Human—Egypt. 2. Social medicine—Egypt. I. Title.
        RG135 .I5835 2003
        618.1'78059—dc21

                                                                2002015868

Contents

Acknowledgments

This book is the result of more than a decade and a half of involvement with the issue of infertility and new reproductive technologies in Egypt, and, over that period, many debts of gratitude have been incurred.

In the United States, I owe thanks to four universities—the University of California at Berkeley, the University of Arizona, Emory University, and the University of Michigan—which provided academic homes, enabling me to carry out my research and, in the last case, write this book. Generous fellowships for two periods of fieldwork in Egypt were provided by the U.S. Department of Education's Fulbright-Hays Research Abroad Grant Program. Additional support for the initial research period was provided by the National Science Foundation and the Fulbright Institute of International Education. During both periods of research, the administrative and bureaucratic assistance provided by the staff of the Binational Fulbright Commission in Cairo was invaluable.

In Egypt, this research would not have been nearly as successful without the help of a delightful research assistant, Tayseer Salem. A bilingual Egyptian English teacher who is herself infertile, Tayseer sat with me through many of the interviews carried out in Nile Badrawi Hospital. Her warm presence made a significant difference, I believe, in my ability to establish rapport with in vitro fertilization (IVF) patients. Tayseer also helped me carefully translate some of the tape-recorded interviews I carried out alone in Arabic, as well as some written documents. Beyond her services as a research assistant, Tayseer was a great friend to me and my family in Egypt, and our relationship has continued over the years and across the miles.

A number of Egyptian physicians also greatly facilitated this research and deserve special thanks. They include Gamal I. Serour, Mohamed Yehia, and Salah Zaki, three leaders in the world of Egyptian reproductive medicine, whose important roles in my study will be made very clear in the chapters that follow. In addition, I would like to thank to Drs. Hamdy and Hosam Badrawi, physician brothers who are co-owners of Nile Badrawi Hospital and who allowed me to base part of my study there; Dr. Abdel-Hamid Wafik, the IVF laboratory director at Nozha Hospital, who provided me with important and interesting information on laboratory aspects of IVF and intracytoplasmic sperm injection (ICSI) in Egypt; and, similarly, the laboratory team at Nile Badrawi Hospital, including Drs. Ashraf Hakam, Ashraf Nasr, and Fouad El-Nahas, who spent many hours with me talking about a variety of IVF-related subjects. Members of the support staff at these two IVF centers, particularly Abeer Zaki and Siham Moukhtar, must also be thanked for their kindness and their ability to introduce me to IVF patients in a nonthreatening manner.

I must express my continuing gratitude to the patients and staff of Shatby Hospital in Alexandria, who, when I conducted research there in the late 1980s, taught me much that I know about the experiences and treatment of infertile women in Egypt. In particular, I want to pay homage to the memory of one of my most impressive and helpful friends, Dr. Mohammed Mehanna, who would have made a great contribution to the practice of Egyptian reproductive medicine if it were not for his untimely and tragic death. Peace be with you in death, Mohammed, as it was not to be in your short life on this earth.

In the United States, Canada, and Europe, there are numerous individuals who have taken an interest in my subject and have helped me by reading parts of my manuscript in different forms, providing me with references, inviting me to contribute to edited collections, or guiding me to new literatures. They include Kamran Ali, Aditya Bharadwaj, Carole Browner, Barbara Herr Hawthorne, Sally Howell, Nancy Rose Hunt, Trudie Gerrits, Gwynne Jenkins, Beth Kangas, Sandra Lane, Linda Layne, Margaret Lock, Lynn Morgan, Laury Oaks, Carla Makhlouf Obermeyer, Lahoucine Ouzgane, Holly Peters-Golden, Helena Ragone, Robert Rubinstein, Andrea Sankar, Carolyn Sargent, Andrew Shryock, Diane Singerman, Frances Winddance Twine, Frank van Balen, and Sjaak van der Geest. I would like to give special thanks to Gay Becker, Susan Kahn, and Rayna Rapp, as well as two anonymous reviewers, who read the manuscript in its entirety and made excellent suggestions. Working with Priti Gress, the anthropology editor at Routledge, as well as her editorial assistant, Paul Foster Johnson, has been a distinct pleasure.

Four of my colleagues at Emory University also deserve special mention: Carla Freeman for introducing me to the fascinating world of globalization/transnationalism studies, Devin Stewart and Carrie Wickham for sharing my interest in Egypt (and, in the case of Devin, for sharing his computer with me while we were both in Cairo in 1996), and Carol Worthman for caring about my project and eventually developing her own field site in Egypt at my urging. I also owe tremendous thanks to my able graduate research assistant at Emory, Tiffany Worboy, who diligently tracked down and compiled a *huge* stack of literature on infertility and the new reproductive technologies.

At the University of Michigan, I am truly grateful to Abigail Stewart and Sherman James, who have enthusiastically supported me during the writing of this book and, in the case of Abby, provided me with a quiet writing space at the Institute for Research on Women and Gender. I also want to thank my excellent administrative assistant, Beth Talbot, for helping me to organize my materials and putting all the finishing touches on the manuscript. Robin and Betsy Barlow, Michael Bonner, Noreen Clark, Gillian Feeley-Harnik, Roberto Frisancho, Nancy Rose Hunt, Michael Kennedy, Alexander Knysh, Conrad Kottak, and Norman Yoffee all played important roles in my decision to join them at this fine institution. Ivan Karp and Cory Kratz of Emory University gave me excellent advice about doing so.

   Special thanks go to Gay Becker, one of my most important intellectual mentors in the world of infertility scholarship. Not only has she been a role model in terms of her path-breaking medical anthropological research on infertility and reproductive technologies in the United States, but she has also been profoundly supportive of my own research and writing projects in this field. Additionally, I want to pay homage to Arthur Kleinman, Margaret Lock, and Rayna Rapp, three intellectual leaders in medical anthropology. Their interests in social suffering and the "local moral"—particularly the ways individual moral actors respond to, and suffer over, the uses of new biotechnologies in their lives—have had a profound influence on my own thinking.

   On a personal note, I must thank the ones closest to me who have given me strength in this project. My parents, Shirley and Stanley Inhorn, have always been the ones to provide logistical support when I have made my excursions to the field. They have also believed in my desire and ability to write ever since I was a child, and they continue to provide encouragement. Over the past six years, I have been fortunate to develop a close and special friendship with fellow medical anthropologist, Robert Hahn, and his geneticist wife, Stephanie Sherman. They have become what every academic mommy needs—like-minded allies in the delicate balancing act of combining an intellectually satisfying career with a committed family life. And finally, there is my family—my husband, Kirk Hooks, and our children, Carl and Justine—who I have missed while I wrote this book, especially on the weekends, but who always make me happy to come home after a day's work. I owe special thanks to Kirk, who puts his own career temporarily "on hold" as he accompanies me (carrying heavy duffel bags) around the globe. His unflagging support of my career and his excellence as a family man are truly extraordinary. With him, I am able to feel the daily joys of parenting children. And, ultimately, it is my own satisfying family life that makes me realize, with special poignancy, the great tragedy and sense of loss experienced by the infertile Egyptian couples whose ardent and often unrequited desires for test-tube babies constitute the theme of this book. To them—the women and men who allowed me into their secret lives as would-be parents of Egyptian test-tube babies—my gratitude is truly profound. *Alf alf isshukr.*

Prologue

Amira

On a hot Thursday morning in late July 1996, I was introduced by Dr. Mohamed Yehia (his real name), one of Cairo, Egypt's most successful and popular IVF doctors, to one of his most persevering and engaging patients, a forty-year-old woman named Amira (not her real name). Over three years of unsuccessful attempts to conceive a child utilizing the latest in new reproductive technologies, Amira and Dr. Yehia had developed a close doctor-patient relationship, marked by candor, admiration, and even humor in the face of adversity. Although Dr. Yehia generally did not accept patients in her condition (reproductively "elderly," with a very infertile husband and thus a poor prognosis), he said he did so in her case because she was unusually self-reflective about her situation and he ultimately enjoyed talking with her so much. Thus, in his ongoing efforts to recruit willing IVF patients for my interview-based study, Dr. Yehia was keen on having me meet Amira, who he affectionately referred to as the "philosopher."

Upon our first meeting, Amira delivered in flawless English, with little direct questioning or probing on my part, this poignant and compelling story of her life and her decade-long search for a solution to her childlessness. Born into a wealthy Egyptian family, Amira spent a lonely childhood as the only child of educated, "broad-minded" parents who did not feel they needed a son in order to secure the family patriliny. Raised by her strict, "suffocating" grandmother while her parents traveled and enjoyed their lives, Amira vowed that, one day, she would marry a very rich man with a big house, in order to have "*so* many children—not one or two or three! I must have a *big, big* family."

Instead, at age eighteen, Amira entered into what was to become a decidedly unsuccessful three-year marriage. Although she had "fought very much" with her parents in order to get married, her infatuation quickly faded, and she knew that she wanted a divorce.

> But I'm an only child . . . and it would have been a shock for my parents to see me asking for a divorce so soon after marriage. And, here, the law is very

difficult. If a man doesn't want to give a woman a divorce, she can spend years in court fighting. Everywhere it's like this, but especially in the Middle East, and especially if she's very young. I was only eighteen or nineteen years old. People would say, "Be patient. Give yourself time. It's too soon to know."

Like most newly married Egyptians, Amira and her husband did not use contraception, and she became pregnant, without his knowledge, four times. She sought and received abortions from four different doctors, despite the fact that abortion is criminalized in Egypt.

Because I didn't have a medical reason, so many doctors refused me. I looked very young at that time, and I finally took off my wedding ring. When I went and told them the truth that I am married and I am unhappy, they all said, "Give the marriage a chance!" They told me, "You are spoiled," and the only way [they would give me an abortion] was with the permission of my husband. Finally, I took off the ring and told them, "I'm not married, and this was a mistake, and my parents will kill me if they know!" Then, it was very much easier. When I twisted the facts, it was easy, but when I told them the truth, it was very difficult.

Fortunately for Amira, she did not experience infectious, infertility-producing complications from the abortions, and she was also lucky when neither her husband nor her parents objected to her eventual divorce. Amira concluded soberly, however, "Here, because we are Muslims, what I'm facing now is punishment from God for what I did." Despite my gentle protestations, Amira reiterated her conviction that the abortions were a sin for which she is now being punished by God. Amira's punishment has come in the form of a barren second marriage to a handsome, wealthy, kind—but nonetheless seriously infertile—man named Emad, with whom she has been unable to have children over a decade of marriage.

Relatively early in her marriage to Emad, after being asked the question, "Why are you not pregnant?," by so many family members and coworkers, Amira decided to undergo a diagnostic laparoscopy, a procedure designed to visualize the condition of her reproductive organs. Despite the fact that laparoscopy involves general anesthesia and minor surgery, the doctors decided to pursue this course first rather than sending Emad for a semen analysis. As Amira explained, "Because we are in Egypt, most doctors, 99 percent, talk to the woman first. They find it difficult to approach the man." Only when Amira's laparoscopic report came back clear did they ask Emad to get tested.

Upon semen analysis, the reason for the infertility become clear: Emad's semen profile showed that both his sperm count and his sperm motility (movement), were "very bad." And, as Amira describes it, "Since then, all these years, we were in hell. No, *I* was in hell, not him." When I asked Amira what that meant for her, she launched into a lengthy discussion of her husband's reluctance to truly confront his serious male infertility problem head on, either in terms of treatment attempts or admission to others that the fertility problem is his.

He's a petroleum engineer. He's traveling a lot. This kind of medicine, these analyses, they all require exact timing—not yesterday, not tomorrow, today! And then, even when he's here, sometimes he says, "I don't feel like it. We are happy, aren't we? Maybe it will come by time. We only need one sperm. The count isn't so bad." And then, other times, he says, "No! No! No! Today, we are going to the doctor! A new one!"

When Emad was offered work with British Petroleum in northern England, he and Amira jumped at the chance to migrate to Europe—but for very different reasons. As Amira explained,

I thought, "What a terrific opportunity to do IVF! We're abroad!" But he said, "No, you're mistaken. They [the doctors] are not Muslim. Maybe they're not frank with us. Maybe this [semen] sample is not mine. This is *haram* [religiously prohibited in Islam], not *hallal* [religiously permitted]." He knows that I'm very afraid of *haram, hallal,* what God says. He appealed to my fears. But I don't think he was sincere. That wasn't really why he didn't want to do it. It will be a very big problem for his career. He just started work, and it was a very good step for him. The next place for him to be was Canada, and he was dreaming of this. So he was just there [in England] for work, *not* for IVF.

Given Emad's reluctance to try IVF, Amira consulted a British IVF doctor clandestinely while Emad was on a trip to Scotland. The university-based physician told her, "It's rare to do this [IVF] at your advanced age [thirty-five]. Even if we have someone of your age, we prefer they be British, not foreign." He went on to try to convince Amira to adopt a child, telling her that, if donor insemination was prohibited to her by her religion, then adoption was the only solution to her case.

"But they're not Muslim," Amira explained. "He was astonished when I told him that Egyptian Muslims usually don't like the adoptive way." She went on to explain that the Qur'an forbids adoption as it is known in the West, for an adopted child in Egypt is not supposed to take the surname of the adopting father. Rather, the Egyptian practice of adoption is more like the permanent legal fostering of an orphan, which is clearly allowed and is even seen as a good deed in the Islamic scriptures. Yet, legal fostering of this kind is very unpopular, especially among elites, as Amira explained clearly.

Yes, it's a *big deal,* inheritance, especially for the rich. If the family is poor, no one will care [if they "adopt" an orphan]. But, for the rich who can afford adoption, adoption is seen as no way at all, because all the sisters and brothers and aunts and uncles will resent that this amount of money is going to an "outsider." So, it's very complicated.

Unlike most of the other wealthy IVF patients at Dr. Yehia's clinic, Amira has tried many times to convince herself to legally foster a child from an orphanage.

I went so many times to orphanages in Cairo and another one in Alex on the desert road to Fayoum. The people at the orphanage in Maadi [an elite suburb of Cairo] maybe thought I was "that crazy lady" who brings toys, clothes, presents to the children. I never told them my real intention, that I was trying to convince myself that I could adopt. But it's just not me—maybe another woman—but not me. *El-hamdu-lillah* [praise be to God], I didn't go forth.

When I asked Amira why not, she reflected,

It's very painful for both of us—me and the child. If I changed my mind, he will suffer a lot. Once you take a child and he thinks you are his mother, you cannot give him back. But I'm not the mother . . . I will feel pity for him [an orphan], and I will love him, but never like my own child. "He's cute, he's nice," I may think this way, but the child will always feel strange, like he doesn't belong here.

When I asked Amira if not having children was a problem in her marriage, Amira replied,

Yes, it's a big problem for our marriage. Not *between* me and him; it's just a problem for me. I can't get along with it. Maybe if you were from the Middle East, you would understand this. The child is, for us, *very* important. Even if you're poor, without a child, why stay married? People here attach everything *for the child*. Working hard, having a good career—it's for the child. The circle always comes back to the child. The satisfaction of working, of being a couple, these are not counted *at all!*

This year, I had a brand new car, and some family, friends, and neighbors, they said, "Why a new car? Two years ago, they had a new one!" What they really want to tell me straightforward is that I'm kind of selfish or maybe crazy. Just now, before I came here [to the IVF center], I met a neighbor. "What's this? You didn't go to Alex on vacation?" I said, "My husband doesn't have vacation." She said, "What vacation! You can go any time, because you don't have children. I have to go now [while her children are out of school]." Sometimes I meet her in the market, and I say, "I don't know what I'm going to cook today," and she says, "Cook anything! You are only two. You can go to McDonald's if you want to." They're not taking us for real. They think you mustn't have a problem if you don't have kids. You have no problems, you're not suffering for the sake of your child. You're not an *usra* [a nuclear family]. There's no concept of the "couple" even.

Amira noted that her sense of purpose in life—and maybe even the perceptions of others—might be altered somewhat if she were working, but she was forced to give up her thirteen-year career as a banker when she followed her husband to England. Amira now spends her days alone in her large apartment in Nasr City, an affluent Cairo suburb. She says that she and her husband are "very good friends," and when he comes home from work, they play computer and board games, which they set up on the dining room table in their large, three-thousand-square-meter apartment. But, during the days while Emad is at work, she feels the profound absence of children in her life.

> I feel that I need a child. I was a lonely girl, no brothers or sisters. And always from the time when I was very little, I've wanted to have lots of children. This is why I'm *very* convinced that this is punishment from God. Yes, really, this is a punishment. Otherwise, I would be living my childhood dream.

Despite feeling punished for her earlier sins, Amira remains faithful to God, hoping for his mercy and compassion. Three years ago, at about the time she began coming to Dr. Yehia's IVF center, she undertook the *hajj* [a religious pilgrimage to Saudi Arabia, recommended for every Muslim who is able], and she decided to don the veil as a sign of her personal relationship with and duty to God. She has also continued, unflaggingly, to search for a medical solution to her childlessness, never giving up hope that God will forgive her and reward her with a child.

For example, upon their return from England in 1990, Amira began almost immediately to visit what at that time was the one and only IVF center in Cairo. There, with Emad's consent, she undertook three trials of IVF, all of which were unsuccessful. She then switched to another newly opened IVF center, where she tried IVF again. But the doctor there—Dr. Salah Zaki, who she described as a "*very* nice person, *very* honest"—told her frankly after yet another failed trial that, because of her advancing age, "you have not so many years ahead of you that you can try." Indeed, he was astonished to witness the rapid pace at which Amira's ovaries seemed to be shutting down during repeated attempts at ovarian stimulation. "It's decreasing *very* fast," he warned her. "In only a few months, your egg production has gone from five to one. It can't be normal, but I don't know why." Cautioning her not to "lose more time," he recommended that she and her husband undergo ICSI, a new variant of IVF that has proven successful in cases of intractable male infertility. But, at that time, ICSI was available at only two IVF centers in greater Cairo. He said, "I'm not worried, because I can always do IVF for you and make money. But the problem is for you. You might have better success if you go elsewhere."

Convinced by his sincerity, Amira made her way to Dr. Mohamed Yehia's even newer IVF center in a private hospital in Heliopolis, an elite suburb on the edge of Cairo. Yet, over the past three years at Dr. Yehia's clinic, Amira's ovaries have responded little to the ovary-stimulating medications typically used prior to IVF or ICSI.

> [Emad] is fifty-five years old and mostly it's been a male infertility problem. But now it's the opposite. I'm forty years old, and it's *my* problem, the age factor, and it's my turn to get treatment. I usually come every month, on the tenth day of my cycle for a *sonar* [ultrasound]. And Dr. Yehia would usually say, "Let's wait for more eggs." But then we realized that, whether I'm taking or not taking treatment, only one egg is produced—the drugs are not stimu-

lating egg production. So, we're always playing together, "Let's try this cycle with treatment. Let's try this cycle without treatment."

After many months of failure to stimulate her ova production, Amira finally underwent a trial of ICSI at age thirty-nine, with only two viable ova retrieved from her body. Amira described the two-week waiting period between the embryo transfer and the early pregnancy test as "very difficult."

You call the lab: "You are a patient of Dr. Yehia? No, you must wait a full two weeks. You never know if it's accurate if you do a pregnancy test earlier." I was calling the lab all the time. You see, I tried IVF four times [at two other IVF centers], and here one time with Dr. Yehia. And I did *talqih istinaᶜi* [artificial insemination using husband's sperm] before that. And all of this meant waiting for two weeks. Every time, the doctor said, "Please. Please be normal. Live your life normally." But I go out after the operation and stay in bed *completely.* I only go to the bathroom; I'm in bed *all the time. Never* do I move!

You see, I live on the eleventh floor. If there is no electricity—which happens very frequently in Egypt—and no elevator, how can I go up? Better to be safe and stay in bed. So during these periods of waiting, I just wait in bed; no one is with me. Sometimes I go forward with the feeling, "It's going to work this time." And sometimes not.

I pray a lot during those periods. I usually pray, but I feel very near to God during these times. I also have to trust very much the doctor. We believe in the importance of the doctor being Muslim. We like to believe in this. If not, we can get crazy. Because if I don't trust the person doing this, I'm lost. I can't see with my own eyes what's going on in the lab. I'm under general anesthesia, and so I have to place my trust in the doctor.

Describing her first meeting with Dr. Yehia, in the very same room in which we were now doing our interview, Amira said,

You can ask Dr. Yehia about it. This was his room, and my husband sat here [pointing to one of the chairs]. I was standing by the wall, and they were talking. Dr. Yehia said, "You are the patient. All of us are talking, and you are not talking." I said, "I wanted to hear you and see, because if I'm not liking you, I won't feel well here. I passed through this with so many doctors, so many experiences. No more."

Although Dr. Yehia told Amira the same bad news—namely, that her chances of success with ICSI were only 5 to 7 percent, "he was honest but in a gentle way. He let me convince him, 'Let's try. It will be great for both of us if we succeed.'"

Most of us have visited the same circle [of IVF doctors]. There are differences who we start with, but we are all playing in the same arena. There are not so many doctors doing IVF here—very few, in fact. And they saw all of us! And even there are doctors who pretend, "I'm going to do something for you to get you pregnant." They try to convince you to give them a chance. They say, "Anyone can treat infertility. It's all the same result. IVF is playing poker." These other doctors are *against* IVF and ICSI, because they don't know how to do it, and they want patients to continue with them so they can make more money. Lots of doctors are not honest. Very few are. So, frankly, for me, it's not only the hospital, it is the doctor that's important.

So far, Amira's only complaint about Dr. Yehia is that he does not really appreciate the physical side effects, including weight gain, nausea, and vomiting, that she has endured as a result of repeated doses of powerful, ovary-stimulating hormones. Amira also complained that these drugs are very expensive.

Not anyone can afford to do this one, two, three times. It's not a question for me of money, but each cycle, I'm spending between LE [Egyptian pounds] 4,000–4,500 [US $1,300–1,500] on the drugs alone. At [one] clinic, I went through more than ten cycles of drugs. On these drugs alone, I've spent maybe LE 40,000 [more than $13,000]. Totally, I've spent probably LE 100,000 [more than $30,000].

El-hamdu-lillah [praise be to God], we have no financial concerns. But very, very few people can do this. . . . Some had to borrow money, sell their jewelry. For some people, it's a luxury for them. They can't tell their parents, "Please loan me money." I heard one story where the woman had to sell her apartment and live with her parents to get the money. So, for *most* people, this is *the* big problem.

Sometimes you pay a lot of money and you get something in return. But in this game, you are *really* gambling, and even it's worse than gambling, because when you gamble, you may be a good player, and you know you are going to win. But in this, you lay down, take anesthesia, and do what you have to do, and the doctor does what he has to do. You don't have a role; you have a *negative* role!

Despite these feelings of relative powerlessness, Amira has no real supportive others with whom to share her plight. Although members of Amira's family know why she is childless, members of Emad's family do not, as they might not "accept" his emasculating condition. Therefore, neither Amira nor Emad talk about his infertility or their treatment attempts openly with other family members or friends. When asked whether an infertility support group would be helpful, Amira shook her head.

Here, support groups are not going to work. It needs people to be frank. When one of us has financial problems and a doctor asks us, we will be truthful, but not when we're sitting around with other people. We believe that if you talk more, you have more problems. I prefer to spend this time to have a solution. To talk about my problem; I never forget my problem! [Talking] won't get me to feel better.

So I don't think it will be in Egypt what we see in American movies—for example, people talking about their drug problems. It's totally different here than in the U.S. or the U.K. In the U.K., I realized that I would have to tell the doctor my whole Middle Eastern background to make him understand me.

Like most Middle Eastern women, Amira desperately wants at least one child. But her biggest fear is that she is running out of time to have any. As she explained,

I'm not that young to have so many pregnancies. Also, they gave me panic in the U.K. "This is serious not only for you, but to have a preemie, or a Magnolian [i.e., Mongoloid, a child with Down syndrome]." That is why I came straight away to IVF when I returned from England. It's very rare for Egyptian Muslim doctors to talk about abnormalities of children. And if you have an abnormal child, you are much better than the woman who doesn't have a child. Allah will take care.

You can say I'm crazy with only one egg and so little chance, but I still have hope. At home, the biggest bedroom I keep empty, with only carpeting. Always my mother [says to me], "I know you have in mind that this will be the baby's room." Even when I try [IVF or ICSI], I go to the O.R., and I'm not feeling that he's just going to take the eggs out. I feel that I'm going out of this O.R. with a child. My husband said I was talking under anesthesia, "Maybe the baby is cold. Please put a blanket on him."

I know my chances are only 5 to 7 percent, and I accept that. But there's a big difference between what I know and what I want. So I'll keep trying. Dr. Wafik [the laboratory doctor] is astonished: "You are going to try again?" But then he says, "But maybe you'll do it—maybe you'll get pregnant this time."

Hope

And, indeed, Dr. Wafik was clearly joyous when, in the days immediately following my interview with Amira, her one viable ovum was retrieved and successfully fertilized through his valiant efforts to perform the "microscopic injection" (ICSI) on a single egg. Dr. Wafik showed me the picture of Amira's developing embryo, and told me that, for some reason beyond his clear understanding, he has very good luck with fertilization in cases where there is only one viable ovum.

Shortly thereafter, I visited Amira in her hospital room after the transfer of this single embryo to her womb. Unfortunately, she was suffering some complications from the general anesthesia given to her two days earlier during oocyte retrieval. One of her eyes was swollen shut, and she had bruising and blistering on her hand and other parts of her body, for which she had received a cortisone injection. I chatted briefly with her and Emad, who had returned from a recent trip to Texas and Oklahoma—preferring, he told me, the friendly Oklahomans over the Texans. Although I was to leave Egypt in three weeks' time, we exchanged telephone numbers and hoped we'd see each other again before my departure. Our greatest wish, of course, was that Amira would be pregnant this time, thereby ending her long and painful "search for a child."

Resignation

Shortly after I left Egypt in August 1996, Amira learned that her sixth attempt to create a precious test-tube baby, using her one aging ovum and her husband's weak spermatozoon was, like the other attempts before it, an expensive and emotionally costly missed conception.

I heard from Amira that Christmas in the form of an Egyptian holiday card that made no mention of this latest ICSI debacle or of her agonizing decision about what to do next. For, as a last resort, Amira still had the option of attempting to retrieve her four frozen embryos from the IVF center she had first visited several years earlier. However, the transfer of biogenetic substances *between* competing Egyptian IVF centers was unprecedented, and Amira feared that the other IVF doctors would object. Although Dr. Yehia and Dr. Wafik believed that, in theory, such an interlaboratory transfer could be made and that maybe one or more of these frozen embryos would finally "take" in Amira's uterus, they knew that the decision to pursue this difficult route was Amira's, not theirs, to make. Without these frozen embryos, future attempts at ICSI in Amira's unresponsive body seemed overly costly and fruitless.

In subsequent email correspondence with Dr. Yehia several months later, in which I asked specifically about Amira and her case, he told me that Amira had finally reached "resolution." After several agonizing months of indecision, she (with Emad's support) finally decided to leave her frozen embryos well enough alone, knowing that, at some point soon, they would be removed from cryopreservation and destroyed. With this decision to "stop all the madness," Amira also stopped being a patient at Dr. Yehia's IVF clinic, where he had seen her go through so much.

Since that time six years ago, Amira and I have exchanged holiday cards, and, one late fall evening, I even astonished her with an overseas telephone call. As of this writing (to my knowledge), Amira has not resumed working, nor has she fostered an orphan, nor has Emad divorced her to try his reproductive luck with a younger, more fecund wife. According to Dr. Yehia, who sees Amira from time to time when she stops by his clinic for conversations now filled with humor, she has gained thirty pounds and recently made the *hajj,* or pilgrimage to Mecca, with her husband. Thus, for all intents and purposes, Amira's life is as normal as it could be, given the circumstances. However, as a now middle-age, perimenopausal woman who never became a mother of test-tube babies, I know that a *truly* normal life for Amira can never be had without those babies—making Amira's resolution less a peaceful conclusion to her story than a painful letting go of her childhood dreams of having a "*big, big* family" with "*so* many children."

CHAPTER 1

Introduction

Amira, the "philosopher" whose poignant story forms the prologue of this book, hoped—but failed—to become an Egyptian mother of a test-tube baby. This book is dedicated to Amira and the other childless Egyptians whose attempts at test-tube baby making will be described in the chapters that follow. My anthropological understanding of the constraints these Egyptians face in their quest to succeed at IVF and the even newer ICSI was only made possible because of the hundreds of hours I spent with them in Egyptian IVF centers in 1996. To all of those brave IVF patients who agreed to come forward—but whose names have been assiduously changed in the pages that follow—I can never truly express my thanks and admiration for making visible to me a world marked by stigma, silence, and suffering.

The often secretive practice of IVF and other new reproductive technologies by infertile women and men in non-Western, "developing" societies such as Egypt is a story that has been little told. It is one that Westerners, often reflecting on the "overpopulation" of the developing world, find difficult to believe. Yet, since the birth in 1978 of Louise Brown, the world's first test-tube baby, new reproductive technologies have spread around the globe, reaching countries far from the producing nations of the West. Perhaps nowhere is this globalization process more evident than in the nearly twenty nations of the Muslim Middle East, where IVF centers have opened in small, petro-rich Arab Gulf countries such as Bahrain and Qatar and in much larger but less prosperous North African nations such as Morocco and Egypt.

This book documents the spread of these technologies to this region of the world, asking what happens to the infertile Middle Eastern women and men who attempt to access IVF and ICSI in their pursuit of conception. In so doing, it sheds light on the nature of globalization and transnationalism, and especially the unevenness of globalizing processes. Although IVF centers now flourish in most of the urban capitals of the Middle East, the reproductive technologies themselves—representing, for the infertile, the potential bounty of globalization—are often either inaccessible or unhelpful in overcoming intractable infertility. Thus, globalizing reproductive technologies bring with them both pregnant rewards and false promises, the latter of which are exacerbated by real-world constraints on the use of these technologies in cultural sites located on the receiving end of global reproductive technology transfer.

This book is intended to provide the first extended ethnographic analysis of these constraints on new reproductive technology practice in a resource-poor, non-Western setting. In so doing, it demonstrates the culturally specific responses and complex, local social arrangements surrounding the importation and use of IVF and ICSI in the predominantly Muslim nation of Egypt. The book diverges considerably from earlier Western accounts of these technologies[1] in that it highlights how local cultural ideologies, practices, and structural forces not found in most Western countries literally reshape the use of these technologies in Egypt and, in turn, how the use of these technologies in Egyptian IVF clinics serves to reshape local culture in various ways. For example, specific Egyptian cultural responses to the use of these Western-generated technologies include indigenous theories of procreation that reject the notion of women producing "eggs" for in vitro fertilization; Sunni Islamic prohibitions on the use of third-party donation (of sperm, eggs, embryos, or uteruses); local shortages of hormonal medications that lead to "suitcase trading" of IVF pharmaceuticals across national borders; and severe moral stigma associated with IVF, which militates against the formation of local support groups for IVF patients or patients' disclosure of their IVF-seeking status to others in their social worlds. This theme of the "local in the global" pervades this ethnography, with Egyptian sensibilities about what constrains them, *as Egyptians,* from successfully using these technologies foregrounded in the analysis. Indeed, the Egyptian IVF patients in this book ponder the many profound constraints facing them as test-tube baby makers, often wondering out loud whether these local constraints are shared by infertile people in the First World nations where these technologies are produced, as well as in other Third World settings where these technologies are being rapidly deployed.

These cross-cultural ruminations are, in part, a product of Egyptian transnationalism. Today, as in the past,[2] many Egyptians are "on the move"—be it as labor migrants or pilgrims to the Arab Gulf, as students and professionals in Western countries, or as peripatetic "medical migrants" engaged in a kind of international reproductive tourism.[3] This book reflects these global movements, taking us from the IVF wards of private maternity hospitals in Cairo, Egypt, to the Arab Gulf, Europe, and the United States, where both infertile patients and physicians migrate, and then return, carrying with them new expertise and cross-cultural experiences. The stories of Amira and others like her reveal the global enmeshment of Middle Eastern Muslim (and Christian) elites in what is now a very transnational world of infertility treatment-seeking and technological progress. By virtue of their global movement and access to global technologies such as the Internet, reproductive physicians and the highly educated patients they serve in Middle Eastern IVF centers are in continuous conversation with—and thus are able to reflect upon—medical, social, and bioethical developments in the West. As they move between these Middle Eastern and Western worlds, their understandings of IVF and its appropriate use in the conception of test-tube babies are continuously shaped by local social, cultural, religious, and scientific traditions "back home" in their Middle Eastern countries of origin. Thus, the practice of IVF in a place like Cairo, a beacon of education, erudition, and religious authority in the Muslim world, is characterized by a particular Egyptian ethos not to be found in the Western IVF laboratories and clinics where these technologies are perpetually being refined, refashioned, and re-envisioned to treat every conceivable type of infertility. The bioethically questionable direction of some of these Western technological developments is often troubling to Egyptians, who bring their own moral worlds to bear on questions of scientific progress. Thus, the examination of ways in which new reproductive technologies are—and are not—accepted and domesticated in places like Egypt can inform much wider debates about the tensions between locality and globalism in the realm of science, technology, and medicine.

Egypt provides a particularly fascinating locus for investigation of the global transfer of new reproductive technologies because of its ironic position as one of the resource-poor, overpopulated Middle Eastern nations. As the fifteenth largest country in the world,[4] Egypt has pursued population reduction goals through family planning and other economic development efforts since the early 1960s, the first Muslim Middle Eastern nation to do so.[5] In a nation of nearly 70 million people, it is perhaps not surprising that infertility has never been included in Egypt's population program as a population problem, a more general public health concern, or an issue of human suffering for Egyptian citizens, especially women. Yet, when Egypt hosted the International Conference on Population and Development in 1994, infertility was officially placed on the global reproductive health agenda.[6] One year later, the Egyptian Fertility Care Society published the results of its World Health Organization (WHO)–sponsored study, placing the total infertility prevalence rate among married Egyptian couples at 12 percent.[7]

Given the substantial size of this infertile population, as well as the strong culturally embedded desire for at least two children expressed by virtually every Egyptian adult, it is not surprising that Egypt provides a ready market for the new reproductive technologies. Despite its regionally underprivileged position, Egypt has been on the forefront of new reproductive technology development in the Middle East—a legacy, perhaps, of its long history with Western colonial medicine.[8] In 1986, Egypt was one of two nations in the region to open an IVF center, and in 1987, Egypt's first test-tube baby, a little girl named Heba Mohammed, was born. By 1996, there were already ten Egyptian IVF centers in full operation or development, out of the approximately thirty-five IVF centers in the Muslim Middle Eastern region as a whole.[9] But, by the end of the decade, the number of centers in Egypt alone had more than tripled to thirty-six, placing Egypt ahead of even Israel, which boasts twenty-four IVF centers (still the highest number per capita in the world).[10] This explosion of IVF services in Egypt in the course of a decade is remarkable when one considers that a single trial of IVF can cost more than LE 10,000, or approximately

U.S. $3,000.[11] In 1999, this would have represented more than three times the annual income of an average Egyptian, and it is clearly a large sum of money for even the most affluent Egyptians. In other words, the new reproductive technologies would seem to be out of reach for most ordinary Egyptians. Yet, infertile Egyptian patients are flocking to IVF centers, which face such a great demand for their services that they are chronically short of the powerful drugs, supplies, and even competent medical personnel necessary to carry out IVF procedures.

A critical question thus becomes: What factors explain this local demand for high-cost, high-tech global reproductive technologies in a Third World Muslim country such as Egypt? Or, put another way, why are infertile Egyptians such as Amira so powerfully motivated to try these costly, potentially risky, and often inefficacious technologies? Certainly, to understand the demand for new reproductive technologies in a society such as Egypt requires an analysis of the forces fueling the new reproductive technology "revolution" in many Third World societies around the globe, including the Muslim nations of the Middle East.

The Global Demand for New Reproductive Technologies[12]

Demography and Epidemiology

To understand the global demand for new reproductive technologies, one must consider the numbers: Infertility is a global health issue that affects millions of people worldwide. In fact, no society can escape infertility; some portion of every human population is affected by the inability to conceive during their reproductive lives. The classic definition of infertility is as follows: "For couples of reproductive age who are having sexual intercourse without contraception, infertility is defined as the inability to establish a pregnancy within a specified period of time, usually one year."[13] Given this definition, WHO estimates that, on average, 8 to 12 percent of couples—or at least one in every ten couples in developing countries—experience some form of infertility during their reproductive lives.[14] Extrapolating to the global population, this means that between 50 and 80 million people worldwide may be experiencing infertility at any give time, including at least one in every ten couples in the developing countries.[15]

Of this global population of infertile people, it is estimated that between 29.4 and 44.1 million, or more than half, are Muslims.[16] Why? Muslims represent a large percentage of the populations living in the so-called infertility belt of sub-Saharan Africa, where rates of infertility reach as high as 32 percent, affecting nearly one-third of all couples attempting to conceive in some populations.[17] Many of these cases of African infertility involve so-called secondary as opposed to primary infertility. Primary infertility means that infertility occurs in the absence of a prior history of pregnancy, while secondary infertility means that infertility occurs *following* a prior pregnancy (whether or not that pregnancy resulted in a live birth). In the most comprehensive epidemiological study of infertility to date—a WHO study of fifty-eight hundred infertile couples seeking help at thirty-three medical centers in twenty-five developed and developing countries between the years 1979 and 1984[18]—Africa stood out as the continent with the highest rates of secondary infertility cases due to preventable causes. Today, women in sub-Saharan Africa continue to remain vulnerable to infertility, both physically and socially, as documented in a recent anthology, *Women and Infertility in Sub-Saharan Africa: A Multi-Disciplinary Perspective.*[19]

Reproductive tract infections (RTIs), including those caused by sexually transmitted gonorrhea or genital chlamydial infections, are the leading preventable cause of infertility.[20] RTIs can lead to pelvic inflammatory disease (PID), which results in scarring and blockage of the delicate fallopian tubes. The end result is tubal infertility, which is often solvable only through new reproductive technologies. Indeed, IVF was developed in the late 1970s largely to bypass the need for healthy fallopian tubes.[21]

In the non-Western world, tubal infertility is highly prevalent and is the major reason for the high rates of secondary infertility. In sub-Saharan Africa, for example, the elevated levels of secondary infertility—affecting as many as one-quarter of all women in some societies—are clearly due to infection, which is thought to account for 85 percent of all cases of infertility, or more than double the rates in other regions.[22] Nonetheless, rates of infection-induced secondary infertility are also high elsewhere in the Third World—for example, 40 percent in Latin America, 23 percent in Asia, and 16 percent in North Africa, including Egypt. Most of this infectious infertility is due to four sets of factors: (1) sexually transmitted infections, (2) postpartum complications, (3) postabortive complications, and (4) unhygienic health care practices carried out in either the biomedical or traditional health care sectors.

Even though Egypt is immediately to the north of the sub-Saharan infertility belt (which begins in Sudan), all of these factors appear to be at work, leading to significant infertility problems in the country. To be more specific, the aforementioned WHO-sponsored study of Egyptian infertility, based on a random sample of married women ages eighteen to forty-nine in twenty thousand rural and urban households, found that 4.3 percent of women suffered from primary infertility and 7.7 percent from secondary infertility.[23] The higher rates of secondary infertility are clearly linked to tubal infertility, which is the single leading cause of female infertility in the country.[24] Pelvic infections leading to tubal infertility in Egypt are attributable to a number of factors, including sexually transmitted diseases (STDs), postpartum and postabortive infections, postoperative infections following reproductive surgeries, pelvic tuberculosis and schistosomiasis (common infectious diseases in Egypt), and a number of harmful traditional and biomedical practices.[25] In a medical anthropological-epidemiological study I carried out among one hundred infertile Egyptian women and ninety fertile controls in the late 1980s,[26] women appeared to be at significant risk for tubal infertility from a number of sources, including traditional female circumcision practices, as well as inefficacious and even iatrogenic biomedical practices (e.g., dilatation and curettage) commonly employed by Egyptian gynecologists, including to purportedly treat infertility. In addition, in a study examining male infertility outcomes,[27] Egyptian men's exposures to heat and chemicals in the workplace, history of schistosomiasis infection, and male smoking (particularly of waterpipes) seemed to place them at risk for male infertility outcomes.

Male infertility is either the sole cause or a contributing factor in more than half of all cases of infertility worldwide, although it is rarely recognized as such.[28] Four of the major types of male infertility include oligospermia (low sperm count), asthenospermia (poor motility), teratospermia (defects of sperm morphology), and azoospermia (lack of sperm in the ejaculate), the etiologies of which are poorly understood.[29] However, it is increasingly being recognized that men in developing countries who are faced with exposure to environmental and occupational toxicants may be at risk of infertility outcomes. Toxicants of concern include arsenic, heavy metals such as lead, solvents, pesticides, and industrial chemicals.[30] In some cases, class-action legal suits have been brought against various multinational corporations by Third World male workers who have been made sterile because of their exposure to synthetic pesticides at their places of work—the most famous case being that of dibromochloropropane (DBCP), which has clearly been shown to cause male infertility.[31] Furthermore, various lifestyle factors—such as heavy smoking and caffeine consumption, which are highly prevalent among men in the Middle East, as well as other parts of the Third World—have been linked to subfertility in males.[32] In Africa, it is also believed that men suffer from high rates of reproductive tract infections, leading to inflammatory lesions of the testes that impair male fertility.[33]

Despite the high prevalence of male infertility around the world, infertility is usually considered to be a "woman's problem";[34] thus, the role of male infertility is vastly underappreciated and even hidden in many societies. Egypt is no exception. Although Egyptian women continue to be blamed for infertility, male infertility is actually the leading reason why childless couples present to IVF clinics in Egypt today. Because male infertility responds poorly to standard treatments (e.g., hormones, testicular surgeries),[35] it, too, must be overcome through resort to new reproductive technologies—either artificial insemination (using husbands' or donor sperm) or the newest new reproductive technology, ICSI, which is a variant of IVF.[36] Indeed, the introduction of ICSI in the early 1990s has created a "revolution" in the treatment of male infertility, including in places like Egypt, where donor insemination is religiously prohibited.

In summary, most cases of tubal infertility and most cases of serious male infertility are virtually impossible to overcome without the special assistance of the new reproductive technologies, namely IVF and ICSI. Given that rates of tubal and male infertility are significantly higher in the developing world than they are in the West, it should come as no surprise that Third World couples who can afford these new technologies will attempt to access them in order to overcome their childlessness. In theory, the demand for these technologies is almost limitless in the non-Western world, given the millions of infertile Third World couples whose childlessness is incurable through any other means. Thus, while Western scholars have focused their attention almost exclusively on the use of new reproductive technologies in Europe and North America, perhaps the most intriguing sites for investigation of the new reproductive technologies lie elsewhere—in societies such as Egypt, Cameroon,[37] India,[38] and China,[39] where the sheer magnitude of the infertility problem, both demographically and epidemiologically speaking, is daunting.

Fertility-Infertility Dialectic and Pronatalism

The major paradox of infertility is that its prevalence is often greatest in those areas of the world where fertility is also the highest—the phenomenon of so-called barrenness amid plenty.[40] However, the explanation for this paradoxical situation is relatively straightforward: Because children are greatly desired in high-fertility, pronatalist societies, women do not regularly contracept, thereby exposing themselves to the risk of sterilizing infections from STDs, unsafe abortions, and postpartum infections following pregnancy. Thus, high fertility exists in a relationship of tension and contrast to high infertility—a situation that I have characterized in my own work as the "fertility-infertility dialectic."[41]

In fact, investigating infertility in resource-poor, high-fertility countries may shed significant light on issues of *fertility*, for infertility provides a convenient lens through which many fertility-related beliefs and behaviors can be explored. These include, inter alia, ideas about conception and how it is prevented both intentionally and unintentionally; understandings of, attitudes toward, and practices of contraception; and perceptions of risk and risk-taking regarding the body. To take but a few examples, anthropological studies from around the world (including Egypt) demonstrate widespread fears of hormonal contraceptives as agents that may actually *cause* infertility;[42] this fear of hormone-induced infertility may actually keep many individuals from participating in family planning programs in pronatalist societies where children are highly desired for numerous reasons.[43] Alternately, these fears of hormonal contraceptives may lead women in places like Egypt to choose intrauterine devices (IUDs) as a preferable form of "modern" contraception. However, recent studies of reproductive morbidity in Egypt have shown how widespread IUD use is partly responsible for the high rates of secondary infertility from IUD-facilitated spread of sterilizing infections.[44] Furthermore, infertile women and men, because they desire procreation, do not use condoms and may engage in sex with multiple partners, thereby exposing themselves to the risk of sterilizing infections, as well as HIV/AIDS. In fact, infertile women are at significantly increased risk of HIV infection in the developing world, especially sub-Saharan Africa,[45] where infertility along with HIV represent twin threats for *depopulation* in some areas.

To fully understand the consequences of infertility and its relationship to high fertility, the notion of pronatalism—beliefs about the importance of motherhood, fatherhood, and the desirability of having children—must be interrogated. In most Western societies, having children or not having them is generally perceived as a matter of choice. Other life goals, such as pursuing a fulfilling professional career, are often given equal weight. Thus, in many Western countries, motivations for having children often lie in the realm of personal happiness and involve notions of the unique parent-child relationship and the possibility of giving and receiving love and affection.[46] In Western research settings, motivations involving continuity and old-age security are rarely mentioned.[47]

In contrast, in other global locations social and economic reasons for having children are often prominent. Frequently cited reasons for having children fall into three general categories: (1) social security desires, or the conviction that children are necessary in a number of ways to secure parents' and families' survival, either through labor contributions or through later support of aging parents (in the absence of pensions, health insurance, nursing homes, and other forms of support for the elderly); (2) social power desires, or the belief that children serve as a valuable power resource, particularly for women confronted with patriarchal social relations within marriage and the family; and (3) social perpetuity desires, or the perceived need to continue group structures, particularly kin-based extended family systems, as well as ancestral "memories" into the future. Increasingly as well, having children may be seen as an important political investment or statement, as various ethnic, nationalist, and religious-fundamentalist movements use children to promote their causes and engage in demographic wars of relative survival vis-à-vis other groups in the political landscape.[48]

For example, among lower-class urban Egyptians, both men and women view children as a route to gaining social power.[49] Among men, this power may be familial, as fathers become family patriarchs and add "strength" and future generations to their own patrilineal extended families. Among poor women, having children with and for one's husband helps to secure a woman's social position within this patrilocal extended family. Furthermore, having children is perceived as securing a woman's marriage by "tying the husband to the wife." Among the urban Egyptian poor, children are seen as creating bonds of love and affection between a husband and a wife, thereby helping to overcome the feelings of estrangement that often accompany spouses as they enter into arranged marriages with relative "strangers." For poor women in particular, children are seen as the major form of prevention against divorce, given that husbands and wives who have failed to develop such bonds of love and affection often stay together "for the sake of the children." Furthermore, for poor women in urban households, children are their "work" and their major prevention against loneliness. The "noise" of children in a household and the time and attention that children require are perceived as welcome additions to the lives of poor urban women, whose lack of education and lack of spousal permission to work outside the home keep most of them within the domestic sphere as *sittat il-bait*, or housewives.

In addition, among the Egyptian poor, children are a major form of social security for aging parents, who are taken in and cared for by their adult children as they become elderly and dependent. In many poor households, elderly parents are cared for with respect and dignity; indeed, many infertile women pamper their aging parents and in-laws as if they were the children who were "missing" from their lives. Furthermore, for elderly Egyptian men and women, their children are often their only form of immortality—the ultimate memory of an individual's having "left a trace" on this earth. For poor men in particular, who have nothing to leave their children after their deaths, their children are a form of social patrimony—that which they have contributed to society upon their deaths. The oft-cited expression "The one with children is not dead" bespeaks the concerns of both poor men and women to achieve a kind of personal perpetuity after death. But this is particularly true for men, who become immortalized as their children and grandchildren carry their names to future generations.

Among the educated middle to upper class in Egypt, needing children to achieve social power and perpetuity, marital and old-age security, and a meaningful existence is much less pronounced, although occasionally mentioned. Instead, the need for children expressed by elites often has to do with wanting heirs to family businesses and fortunes, and this is particularly true for men, who wish for offspring to inherit from them. For elite women, on the other hand, the oft-cited need for children has less to do with passing on one's patrimony than with achieving a sense of personal satisfaction and fulfillment in lives that are otherwise quite meaningful and complete. Although many middle- to upper-class women in Egypt express satisfaction in their careers, their marriages, and their other accomplishments (e.g., special hobbies, membership on college athletic teams), most also argue that their lives are "incomplete" without the experience of motherhood.

The expression in Egypt, and in many other non-Western societies, of such powerful rationales for having children does not mean that child desire, or pronatalism, stems entirely from a perceived *need* to have children. To be more specific, *wanting* children, in Egypt and elsewhere, involves aspects of both "desire" and "need." Although Egyptian couples of all social classes seem to need children for a variety of social, economic, and even political purposes, they also *desire* children because of the joy, affection, and tenderness that children are perceived as bringing to marriage and family life. Indeed, the notion that children might be less loved, valued, and treated with affection in non-Western places such as Egypt is not only ethnocentric but also belies much evidence to the contrary. Loving, committed, highly affectionate parenting styles can be found throughout the world and are often abundantly evident in non-Western settings, including the Muslim Middle East.[50]

Given the multifaceted nature of child desire in many non-Western societies, not having children is seldom viewed as "voluntary"—a true reproductive "choice" or "lifestyle" option. Children are often desired soon after a couple becomes sexually active (usually through marriage but increasingly through nonmarital consensual unions in some parts of the world). And the failure to produce a child—especially a son in some societies—is readily recognized by the couple themselves, as well as by all those around them, as a major problem with enormous implications. Childlessness in most non-Western societies may not be politely hidden as it is in the West (where any given case of childlessness may be assumed to be voluntary). And it is often the source of much painful and direct derision and gossip.[51] Thus, it comes as no surprise that infertile couples living in such pronatalist societies are under intense pressure to "do something" about their childlessness, which increasingly involves resorting to the new reproductive technologies as these technologies rapidly spread around the globe.

Gendered Suffering and Social Stigma

Given the social, economic, and political pressures to have children in many societies, it is not surprising that infertility leads to mental, physical, and social suffering.[52] Individuals who are infertile, particularly in pronatalist societies such as Egypt, experience profound human suffering and are often willing to do anything, even risking their own lives in the pursuit of physically taxing remedies, in their efforts to conceive. Although men may suffer acutely over their infertility in ways that will be described in this book, the burden of suffering generally rests on the shoulders of women such as Amira, whether or not they are the infertile partner.[53] Indeed, women worldwide appear to experience the major onus of infertility, in terms of blame for the reproductive failing; emotional responses such as anxiety, frustration, grief, and fear; marital duress, abuse, divorce, polygamous remarriage, or abandonment; and social stigma and community ostracism. As noted by Sciarra, past president of the International Federation of Gynecology and Obstetrics (FIGO), the social stigma of infertility can have lifelong consequences, "affect[ing] a woman for the remainder of her life, preventing subsequent marriage, and making her economically vulnerable."[54]

Anthropological studies from around the world have increasingly demonstrated the highly gendered stigma and suffering accompanying infertility, particularly when motherhood is the only way for women to enhance their status within the family and community.[55] Ethnographic studies demonstrate, quite compellingly, that infertility is one of the most stigmatizing health and social conditions for women, in societies ranging from China and India in the "East" to sub-Saharan Africa and Latin America in the "South." To take but a few examples, in People's Republic of China, a woman who cannot conceive is called *bu xia dan de mu ji*—"the hen that can't lay an egg"—and is expected to overcome this stigmatizing status through treatment seeking, even with high-tech methods such as IVF.[56] According to medical anthropologist Lisa Handwerker, the "one-child-only" policy in China is locally interpreted by women as the "you-must-have-one-child" policy, such that no Chinese woman is expected to remain childless. Similarly, in the Kerala region of South India, poor infertile women are sometimes called *machi*, a Malayalam word that has no English equivalent, but which refers to a farm animal that cannot breed.[57] According to medical sociologist Catherine Kohler Riessman, infertile women in Kerala, who deviate from the "ordinary and natural" life course and are thus deeply discredited, nonetheless attempt to resist their stigmatization, in part by fashioning meaningful lives apart from motherhood. However, as Riessman is quick to point out, the ability to "destigmatize" oneself is class and age dependent; thus, poor village women of childbearing age are devalued in ways that affluent and professional women are sometimes able to avoid. In northern Botswana, part of the central and southern African infertility belt, infertility is profoundly stigmatizing for women, who are blamed for the infertility and accused of either witchcraft or violating social taboos.[58] Thus, according to anthropologist Rebecca Upton, infertile women are rendered "socially invisible" in northern Botswana, where they are pejoratively called *moopa,* the term for a cow or other animal that cannot reproduce.

In societies ranging from Mozambique[59] to Laos,[60] infertile women's stigmatization may be experienced as outright community ostracism when they are excluded from the everyday social events and ceremonies typically involving mothers and children. For example, in some societies including Egypt, infertile women are even suspected of harming others' children through their uncontrollable envy and casting of the "evil eye." Thus, they may be avoided by fertile women who fear for their own children's safety. Furthermore, childless women are particularly vulnerable to such community ostracism in their old age; in many societies, the elderly rely on other community members, including their grown children, to support and nurse them until death.

In *Infertility and Patriarchy: The Cultural Politics of Gender and Family Life in Egypt,* I documented what happens to poor urban Egyptian women who are unable to conceive in an emphatically pronatalist, child-desiring society. Framing my findings under the rubric of patriarchy as defined by Middle Eastern feminist theorists,[61] I examined how patriarchy, or systematic gender oppression, is "lived" by poor urban infertile Egyptian women. Infertility casts doubt upon a woman's gender identity, preventing her from achieving full status as an adult woman and marring her personhood in various untoward ways. Infertility also complicates marital dynamics, leading to marital instability in many cases and, occasionally, divorce or polygamous remarriage. However, the stigmatization and ostracism of infertility are often experienced by poor women most profoundly in their relationships with female in-laws and community members, who may harass infertile women and pressure them to seek treatment, especially if they happen to reside in the same household. Because motherhood is a mandatory status for married Egyptian women—even those who are highly educated and professionally successful— women who are unable to conceive experience their infertility profoundly in the forms of social isolation, loneliness, and despair. These social effects, furthermore, appear to be increasing with the rise of Islamism, or so-called fundamentalism, in the country. As Islamically inspired pronatalism and public support for women's domesticity become more and more pronounced in Egypt,[62] Egyptian women who are unable to contribute to the "Islamic multitude" experience their barrenness amid plenty even more acutely.

Adoption Restrictions

Although Westerners often tout adoption as the "natural" solution to childlessness, adoption restrictions, both formal and informal, are found throughout many societies of the world, including the Muslim Middle East. The *shari'a* (the body of Islamic law) contains specific injunctions against adoption based upon the Qur'an, considered by Muslims to be the word of God as delivered to the prophet Muhammad. Official adoption, whereby an orphaned child becomes a legal son or daughter through adoption of the parents' (usually the father's) surname as well as their acknowledged heir, is not recognized by Islamic law.[63] Although the Qur'an encourages kind treatment, generosity, and charity in the upbringing of orphans—who are available in many Muslim countries for permanent, Islamically sanctioned, legal fostering arrangements[64]— widespread cultural resistance to bringing up a "stranger" in the family nonetheless persists, including in Egypt. Resistance to adoption often has less to do with religion than with numerous deep-seated cultural anxieties biasing Egyptians of all social classes against this practice. These include fears that (1) illegitimate children, who can be assumed to be of "bad blood," are innately immoral and dangerous beings; (2) birth parents will come to reclaim the adopted child; (3) feelings of emotional affinity between adoptive parents and children will never emerge; (4) erotic attraction will develop between adoptive parents and children or between "real" children and adopted siblings; (5) adopted children will be perpetually stigmatized within the family and community; (6) adoptive parents, and particularly mothers, will be stigmatized for being unable to produce a real child; (7) adopted children do not have legitimate rights of inheritance and effectively "steal" a family's money after the adoptive parents' death; and (8) adoption is not available to poor people (although this is not true).[65]

In other parts of the non-Muslim world, adoption also meets with a mixed reception. For example, in India, most infertile couples would rather undertake secretive donor insemination to overcome male infertility than broadcast the reproductive failure through adoption of a nonbiologically related child.[66] Even in parts of sub-Saharan Africa and Oceania where informal fostering arrangements, usually of relatives' children, is a customary practice,[67] legal adoption per se is relatively uncommon and is rarely viewed as a permanent solution to a couple's infertility. Furthermore, in Africa, the number of AIDS orphans has now exceeded the supply of foster parents— including infertile ones, who may themselves be dying of AIDS—leading to a surfeit of literally unparented orphans in many central and southern African countries. In other parts of the world, including Latin America and Asia, "excess" babies—born out of wedlock to teenaged mothers, born to poor families, exceeding state-mandated birth quotas, or undesired because they are female—are "marketed" at high costs to infertile Western couples,[68] who are sometimes accused of being greedy exploiters of disadvantaged Third World women. Furthermore, in many of these countries, infertile couples who themselves wish to adopt a child from within the country may face bureaucratic and legal entanglements that delay their court cases for many years.[69]

Thus, as with the fertility-infertility dialectic, problems of infertility are intricately related to problems of adoption, preventing many Third World infertile couples from adopting orphans altogether, and effectively quashing the desire in many other cases. Given the legal, religious, social, and emotional difficulties surrounding adoption, it is not surprising that many infertile couples in places like Egypt view biological parenthood as their only option. Because the new reproductive technologies have been designed to facilitate biological parenthood, they are rapidly gaining popularity among infertile couples in societies where adoption restrictions, both formal and informal, effectively prevent the parenting of orphans as a real solution to involuntary childlessness.

Health Care Seeking

Given the suffering experienced by infertile women and the restrictions that prevent them from adopting, it is not surprising that women typically embark upon relentless quests for therapy,[70] involving both "traditional" and "modern" forms of treatment. Studies from around the globe have shown that infertile women—and increasingly infertile men—are massive users of health care services.[71] For example, in Nigeria, infertility is estimated to be the leading reason for gynecological consultations.[72] Similarly, in Egypt, most gynecologists estimate that one-third or more of their patients are seeking infertility services.[73] Among Egyptian andrologists, or physicians who treat male reproductive health complaints, male infertility accounts for 50 to 60 percent of all patients visits.[74]

In addition to health care seeking in the biomedical realm, infertile individuals may seek help from a variety of traditional healers. These include, among others, lay midwives, herbalists, spiritual healers, diviners, and healers associated with various religious sects. As noted in a recent essay on the global infertility problem, "Regarding traditional healers ... it is sometimes said that they have some advantages over Western style medical and paramedical personnel. They use traditional, long-established medicines, know the people of the area, are often famous and trusted persons, speak the local language, and live according to the same culture."[75] Thus, infertile individuals may seek help from such healers rather than, or in addition to, Western-style biomedical specialists, who often distance their patients in various ways.

Such is the case in Egypt, where simultaneous resort to both traditional and modern forms of infertility therapy is typical for most poor urban Egyptian women. In *Quest for Conception: Gender, Infertility, and Egyptian Medical Traditions,* I documented the five-thousand-year history of shifting medical traditions in Egypt, which continue today in the form of a rich corpus of "ethnogynecological" beliefs and practices. Egyptian women, especially of the lower class, draw upon these traditions at the same time that they pursue remedies in the world of contemporary Egyptian biomedicine. Unfortunately, much of the contemporary "biogynecology" practiced in Egypt—which is rooted in British colonial medical traditions[76]—is outdated and even iatrogenic, or productive of further infertility problems in female patients seeking infertility treatment. Thus, many infertile Egyptian women who are "searching for children"—as they call their quest for conception—actually suffer at the hands of biomedical practitioners. As we shall see in the chapters that follow, such iatrogenesis crosses class boundaries in Egypt, leaving many Egyptian women permanently scarred as a result of their biomedical quests. Such biomedical iatrogenesis has been documented at other sites in sub-Saharan Africa as well,[77] revealing "how little formal health services have to offer to the majority of the infertile people in developing countries."[78]

Furthermore, few Ministries of Health in non-Western countries have formulated systematic state policies and guidelines for the treatment of infertility.[79] In most Third World countries, the management of infertility has yet to be incorporated into programs of population control, family planning, or reproductive health. As a result, infertile patients may drain resources from government health care systems that are unprepared to help these patients with what are often complicated infertility problems. Egypt is a case in point. Although Egypt has an extensive system of government-sponsored maternal and child health clinics, these clinics do not offer routine infertility diagnosis or treatment services. With the exception of one or two government-sponsored infertility clinics at urban, university-based, teaching hospitals, infertility care remains entirely in the private sector—suffered in private by those who are unable to conceive, who must place their fertility and reproductive futures in the hands of private physicians, who view infertile patients as "money-makers" for their practices and often do not have the best interests of these patients at heart.[80]

Given the lack of coordinated infertility treatment services in Egypt, it is no wonder that private IVF clinics have come to flourish in this setting, where they cater to the thousands of Egyptian couples who have been unable to overcome their infertility by any other means. Such couples form a ready market for both the First World manufacturers and local providers of new reproductive technologies, who may literally prey on the desperation of many of these couples.[81] Thus, in Egypt—but also in China,[82] India,[83] Latin America,[84] and many other global sites—demand for new reproductive technologies among a large and overeager population of desperate infertile consumers is serving to fuel the rapid global spread of these technologies, with local implications that are potentially profound.

The Local in the Global

It is the "local in the global" that forms the major concern of this ethnography on the uses of new reproductive technologies in Egypt. As will be argued throughout this book, new reproductive technologies are not transferred into cultural voids when they reach places like Egypt. Rather, local considerations, be they cultural, social, economic, or political, shape and sometimes curtail the way these Western-generated technologies are both offered to and received by non-Western subjects. In other words, the assumption on the part of global producer nations that these new reproductive technologies—as value-free, inherently beneficial medical technologies—are "immune" to culture and can thus be "appropriately" transferred and implemented anywhere and everywhere is subject to challenge once local formulations, perceptions, and actual consumption are taken into consideration.

Indeed, the global spread of new reproductive technologies provides a particularly salient but little discussed example of what anthropologist Arjun Appadurai has termed a "technoscape," or the "global configuration, also ever fluid, of technology, and the fact that technology, both high and low, both mechanical and informational, now moves at high speeds across various kinds of previously impervious boundaries."[85] Appadurai reminds us that this movement of technologies around the globe is both a deeply historical and inherently *localizing* process. In other words, globalization is not enacted in a uniform manner around the world, nor is it simply culturally homogenizing—necessarily "Westernizing" or even "Americanizing"—in its effects.[86] The global is always imbued with local meaning, such that local actors, living their everyday lives at particular historical moments in particular places, mold the very form that global processes take.[87] As noted by Akbar Ahmed and Hastings Donnan in their volume *Islam, Globalization and Postmodernity,* "It is the cultural flows between nations which above all else seem to typify the contemporary globalization process (or its current phase)."[88] Thus, "Even though the same cultural 'message' may be received in different places, it is domesticated by being interpreted and incorporated according to local values."[89]

This acknowledgment of the importance of locality in the global dispersion of modern biotechnologies has been a theme of much recent work on the medical anthropology of reproduction and global reproductive health policy.[90] For example, Margaret Lock and Patricia Kaufert, coeditors of *Pragmatic Women and Body Politics,* call for a "semiotic return" to "local sites of research in order to understand better how globalization affects body politics."[91] In particular, they are concerned with how women in disparate local sites know about and respond to "body technologies of various kinds."[92] They argue, ultimately, that "ambivalence coupled with pragmatism"[93] may be women's dominant mode of response to morally contentious technologies such as IVF; but to understand this requires ethnographic investigation that situates women's subjectivity and agency within the context of their lived experience.

Similarly, in *Conceiving the New World Order: The Global Politics of Reproduction,* coeditors Faye Ginsburg and Rayna Rapp remind us that the global technoscape through which new reproductive technologies spread is an uneven terrain, in that some nations and regions within nations (e.g., major metropolises) have achieved greater access to these fruits of globalization than others. Moreover, even in the West—and then on magnified terms in the Third World—lines of demarcation between gender, race, and class have been brought into sharp relief vis-à-vis access to these technologies. Thus, Ginsburg and Rapp (following Colen[94]) have employed the term "stratified reproduction" in an attempt to get at these transnational inequalities, whereby some are able to achieve their reproductive desires, often through recourse to globalizing technologies, while others—usually poor women of color around the globe—are disempowered and even despised as reproducers.[95] However, Ginsburg and Rapp are quick to point out that the power to define reproduction is not necessarily unidirectional—flowing from the West, with its money and technology, to the rest of the world. Rather, "people everywhere actively use their local cultural logics and social relations to incorporate, revise, or resist the influence of seemingly distant political and economic forces."[96] Indeed, a growing number of studies asserting the voices and agency of non-Western peoples have challenged the image of Third World subjects, particularly women, as passive and powerless in the face of global forces.[97] It is useful instead to ask how Third World recipients of global technologies resist their application, or at least reconfigure the ways they are to be adopted in local cultural contexts.[98]

In this book, I pose that very question: How do local actors living in a rapidly urbanizing, postcolonial society both accommodate and resist the incorporation of globalizing new reproductive technologies into the Egyptian cultural landscape? Although demand for new reproductive technologies has grown dramatically in Egypt over the past decade, the case of Egyptian test-tube baby making clearly demonstrates how the "local" confronts the "global": how local cultural factors reshape and sometimes curtail how global technologies are to be used in particular local sites. In Egypt, the use of new reproductive technologies involves not only a particular postcolonial history, but also unique cultural understandings of the body; the limits of science and technology; the meanings of marriage, kinship, and family life; and the local "moral worlds"[99] in which the recipients of such global technologies and their high-tech offspring must live.

These culturally and historically salient aspects of locality in Egypt are borne out in two ways. On the one hand, those who actually use the new reproductive technologies, both Egyptian IVF doctors and their patients, imbue the practice of test-tube baby making with a particular Egyptian sensibility—one not to be found in the IVF laboratories and clinics of London, Los Angeles, Sydney, or other First World sites where these technologies have been studied. On the other hand, the local terrain of Egyptian test-tube baby making is riddled with what I have come to think of as "arenas of constraint," or various structural, social-cultural, ideological, and practical obstacles and apprehensions that may detract or deter local Egyptian actors altogether from using the new reproductive technologies. I would argue that examining such arenas of constraint facing the infertile wherever these technologies spread is an extremely useful exercise, for it serves to deconstruct the myth that new reproductive technologies are some sort of panacea for infertility wherever it occurs. Such critical deconstruction stands in sharp contrast to the various pro-technology modernist narratives found in both popular and medical discourse, which argue that the new reproductive technologies are a great boon to infertile couples around the world—providing them with an opportunity to overcome their stigma and childlessness through the use of a modern technology representing the cutting edge of advances in Western science and medicine.[100] By using such technologies, the infertile would therefore seem to be agents of their own reproductive futures, and issues of human suffering would be alleviated.

Yet, as many feminist authors have argued quite forcefully,[101] such utopian scenarios are unrealistic and even dangerous, for they not only ignore the myriad obstacles and risks that consumers of these technologies face but also fail to interrogate the notion of "reproductive choice," particularly in pronatalist societies such as Egypt, where motherhood, and thus infertility therapy seeking, are rarely if ever viewed as optional. In fact, the problem with the proposition of reproductive choice—and more specifically, the notion that provision of new reproductive technologies in Third World countries gives women (and men) new choices about how to shape their reproductive futures—is that this concept rests on "a bourgeois notion of freedom that neglects the extent to which women's lives (and 'choices') are constrained by external social and economic contingencies."[102] As pointed out by Lock and Kaufert,[103] the constraints under which many women must operate to make their choices and to maximize their control over their own reproductive lives give very little room for maneuver, significantly narrowing women's abilities to be either agentive or resistant actors. The notion of reproductive choice, then, over-privileges reproductive agency, underestimating the lack of free will and lack of free choice that so often characterize women's lives as they operate within multiple sets of structural and cultural constraints.

I would argue that many medical anthropologists, myself included, who work in Third World settings have been guilty of "romanticizing" reproductive agency at the expense of constraint.[104] In our efforts to show that "subordinated people are not unreflecting automatons,"[105] but rather are actors who demonstrate resolve, struggle, and problem solving in their quests to control their reproductive lives, we have sometimes overlooked, or at least underemphasized, the severe constraints that effectively limit reproductive choices, including the often painful decisions about whether and how to use new reproductive technologies. Thus, on the one hand, I am in complete agreement with scholars who argue that "looking out" for the agency of the infertile is an important scholarly endeavor,[106] particularly given the many stereotypical representations of (almost always female) infertility patients as either "helpless and saved by the technologies" or "victimized by them."[107] As much as I hope to demonstrate the agency of the infertile Egyptian women and men whose stories are told in the pages that follow, I also believe that the time has come to seriously ponder the profound constraints facing many infertile people, particularly in Third World settings where these technologies are being rapidly deployed. In Egypt, the site of my own research over two decades, it is the constraints—and not the happy stories of reproductive agency and "take-home babies"—that characterize most people's narratives of test-tube baby making, be they the infertile patients themselves, the physicians who treat them, the media who report the successes and failures of the IVF industry, and the public who digests these media reports. For the infertile actors themselves, their childlessness, a socially intolerable condition, provides them with little choice in the matter; rather, they feel obligated, or forced to try every possible cure, which, if they can afford it, now means test-tube baby making—the "last resort" in a long line of treatments to make their unyielding, barren bodies produce a child. Thus, "assisted conception" (as IVF is often termed) has, in fact, created new dilemmas of agency for infertile Egyptian couples, who must confront the decisional complexities surrounding IVF and its variants, wagering an opinion on "what's in it for them."

Because these new reproductive technologies are so expensive for many Egyptians, economic barriers to access constitute one of the most fundamental arenas of constraint on the practice of IVF, a reality that is surely repeated in many other parts of the Third World. In the local test-tube baby making scene in Egypt, we see the tension between structure and agency enacted in the lives of infertile couples, many of whom are simply barred by poverty from setting foot in an IVF clinic. On the other hand, arenas of constraint in Egypt are not only structural in nature. As this book attempts to lay out chapter by chapter, there are eight major arenas of constraint facing would-be Egyptian IVF consumers, including the elites who end up at IVF clinics. These range from local understandings of the human reproductive body and its physiology to the gender politics that privilege infertile Egyptian men in their marriages to the local versions of Islam (and Coptic Christianity) that legislate the appropriate use of new reproductive technologies, thereby restricting who may benefit from them. Through careful ethnographic exegesis of each of these eight arenas of constraint, I hope to achieve my primary goal of illuminating the locally significant factors that prevent many infertile Egyptians from making a *tifl l-anabib*—literally, a "baby of the tubes," as the English term "test-tube baby" translates into Arabic—even if they are highly motivated by virtue of their infertility to do so.

Local Actors in Moral Worlds

This book is written from the perspective of these local actors: the childless Egyptian women who, by virtue of their own or their husbands' infertility, would like to become mothers of test-tube babies; the infertile Egyptian husbands who would like to become the fathers of such children; and the Egyptian physicians who practice IVF and ICSI on these women's and men's bodies. Although the book attempts to foreground their perspectives and narratives, it is also necessarily infused with my own "etic" interpretations and analyses, which I attempt to distinguish from local "emic" ones when such distinctions become necessary. Furthermore, I am much less interested in this book in any universalizing claims about the biomedical successes of these technologies[108] than in *local* Egyptian medical discourses surrounding the practice of IVF. This includes Egyptian IVF physicians' commentary on the local IVF industry as a whole, as well as their thoughts about the many local specificities of test-tube baby making as practiced in their home country. Throughout this book, I attempt to present physicians' perspectives—including their sometimes potent indigenous criticisms of the local field of reproductive medicine—in part to show

how biomedical practitioners themselves can become engaged in reflexive, even subversive, auto-critique of a new biotechnology and its uses in a particular local setting. Thus, this book weaves back and forth between patients and practitioners, including their reflections about each other, which I found to be an extremely important dimension of my study. Whereas the physicians who allowed me into their practices said they hoped to learn from my findings so that they could better serve their patients, the patients themselves often wanted to talk about these physicians—what they liked about some, what they did not like about others, and ultimately, why having a strong relationship with a physician matters when making a *tifl l-anabib,* or "baby of the tubes."

Throughout the book, I also use the terms "baby of the tubes," "test-tube baby" and "test-tube baby making"—rather than the more formal medical terms, "assisted conception," "medically assisted conception," or "assisted reproduction"—because the English-language formulation of "test-tube baby making" has been adopted in Egyptian parlance as the synonym for IVF, reflected in the name *atfal l-anabib,* "babies of the tubes," which is the way IVF is locally described per the standard Arabic grammatical (*idafa*) construction. Indeed, one Egyptian physician working in an IVF laboratory lamented the local adoption of the English term "test-tube baby." In his view, it inaccurately conjured up popular notions of babies being "artificially" created and gestated in giant test tubes, thereby further stigmatizing these children and their long-suffering parents.

This book takes as one of its major themes the profound suffering of infertile Egyptian IVF patients such as Amira, who experience physical pain, emotional despair, marital turmoil, moral uncertainty, and social stigma as part of the quotidian experience of infertility and test-tube baby making. In this book, I attempt to represent this multilayered suffering as much as possible from the vantage point of the infertile themselves, believing that they, as "narrating sufferers"[109] or "wounded storytellers,"[110] are in the best position to be the interlocutors of their own lives. This approach to the narrativizing of suffering—where attention is paid to the interpersonal and intersubjective dimensions of suffering through the use of ethnographic stories and interview texts—is in line with the "experience-near" ethnography of illness advocated by Arthur and Joan Kleinman.[111] The "ethnography of experience" they propose is a strategy to grapple with and legitimize the physical pain and emotional suffering occurring within the "local moral worlds" to which the ethnographer has privileged access. Indeed, the narration of "local moral worlds"—or "moral accounts [which] are the commitments of social participants in a local world about what is at stake in everyday experience"[112]—is one of my primary objectives in this ethnographic account of new reproductive technologies in Egypt. At the beginning of each chapter, I attempt to show "what is at stake" for particular Egyptian social actors through the use of their own "morally charged" stories.[113] Then, within each chapter, I attempt to highlight, through generous provision of interview excerpts, topics that seemed to generate animated discussion and passionate moral commentary among my informants.

The importance of the "local moral" pervades this Egyptian ethnography. In Egypt, new reproductive technologies are extremely morally contentious, for reasons that will become abundantly clear in the ethnographic details that follow. The importance of local moralities in shaping the application of new reproductive technologies at other global sites has been noted by a number of medical anthropologists,[114] including Margaret Lock, who states:

> Biotechnologies will only escape from the laboratory, with its particular forms of debate, and be naturalized if a good number of the public actively supports their use, if their artifice is judged as facilitating individual and familial aspirations in connection with reproduction without causing harm. However, . . . if the outcomes of the application of reproductive technologies do not coincide rather closely with widely shared societal values, they may well be judged as disruptive to the moral order, no matter how well packaged and promoted.[115]

Ethnographic literature emerging from a number of developed societies (the United States, England, Israel, and Japan) shows that new reproductive technologies are often viewed as morally threatening, disrupting not only notions of personhood, parenthood, and family formation, but also the moral fabric of society as a whole. Interestingly, however, these moral disruptions are not culturally invariant. If there is one finding that has emerged most clearly from this recent comparative ethnography in First World settings, it is that new reproductive technologies can evoke varying moral responses from one society to the next.

To illustrate this point, I would like to draw briefly upon the two most recent book-length ethnographic accounts of IVF, one coming from the United States and the other from Israel, then compare them to the Egyptian ethnographic scene. In *The Elusive Embryo: How Women and Men Approach New Reproductive Technologies,* Gay Becker takes us into the world of American test-tube baby making, asking how both women and men respond to the new reproductive technologies to overcome their infertility. In her account, religion never surfaces, as most infertile Americans engaged in the actual practice of IVF and its variants do not seem to draw upon their religions to make moral judgments about the inherent "rightness" or "wrongness" of these technologies. Becker's account is in keeping with other earlier ethnographies from the United States[116] and England,[117] where religious convictions and theodicies are never invoked by study subjects to help them overcome the "meaning-threatening" aspects of infertility or to make sense of these technologies from a moral framework.[118] Instead, Becker's account highlights the ways in which American test-tube baby making now operates on a very secular-materialist "consumer model,"[119] whereby savvy IVF patients see themselves as intelligent consumers with ample "choice" in a "free market" that offers them "eighteen ways to make a baby."[120]

Becker's account provides a striking contrast to Susan Kahn's ethnography, *Reproducing Jews: A Cultural Account of Assisted Conception in Israel.* In this book,

Kahn takes us into the often arcane world of Jewish Halakhic law, where male rabbis legislate on the appropriate uses of new reproductive technologies for their followers. Kahn carefully describes how these rabbinical decisions affect the actual practice of Israeli test-tube baby making—including whether Jewish or non-Jewish donor sperm should be used in the practice of gamete donation, whether surrogacy should be allowed for infertile couples using single or married surrogates, and, ultimately, whether and how Jewishness is to be conferred in the offspring produced through "test-tube" means. Although the rabbinical arguments regarding morally appropriate and inappropriate reproduction are sometimes dizzying, they bespeak the importance of local religious moralities in the contemporary world of Israeli assisted conception. There, doctors in many clinics attempt to practice IVF according to the moral dictates set forth by religiously conservative rabbis. But, among more secular Jewish IVF patients, their decisions regarding third-party donation, surrogacy, and the like often reflect their own choices regarding appropriate reproduction. Although Kahn is explicit in stating that the American "consumer model" of free-market reproductive medicine has yet to take hold in Israel, it is clear that infertile Israeli women—as well as single career women who want to make a baby "on their own"—have much greater freedom to do so than in neighboring Egypt.

Egypt is geographically contiguous with Israel, but the gulf between the two nations on a number of scores, both religious and political, could not be wider. Much of what goes on in Israeli IVF clinics today will never find acceptance in Egypt, where all forms of third-party donation are strictly prohibited. In Egypt, furthermore, IVF patients of all backgrounds—from the most devout to the most secular, both Muslim and Coptic Christian—care deeply about making their test-tube babies in the religiously acceptable fashion. As will be seen in their stories and interview excerpts in Chapter 4, religion is, in their view, one of the most important dimensions of test-tube baby making in Egypt—setting Egypt apart from most First World countries and even Catholic Latin America, where secularism appears to have pervaded the IVF industry.[121]

Egyptian patients in IVF centers know this—that they are more "religious" than most Westerners—and they compare their own local moral world to the moral corruption that they see taking place "outside," especially in the West. As will be revealed in Chapter 4, the highly educated Egyptian elites presenting to IVF clinics today have much to say about the immorality of Western IVF practices—even though they delivered their critiques gently to an American, non-Muslim anthropologist. For Western readers, this indigenous Egyptian critique about the ways in which the West has gone awry in its no-holds-barred pursuit of morally questionable reproductive technologies takes on new meaning in the light of recent historical events. In my opinion, September 11 and its aftermath have only served to highlight my argument about the need to understand and take more seriously the varying religious moralities and "local moral worlds" in which Western technologies—to make life and to take it away—are being exported and ultimately deployed around the world. Indeed, this book is a testament to the ways in which the Muslim Middle

East is now globally connected to Western technological developments, but with ramifications that have been little studied and hence are poorly understood.[122]

Time, Place, and People

The research upon which this book is based encompasses two distinct time periods and research settings, thereby capturing the fast-paced historicity of the global spread of new reproductive technologies to Egypt. The first period is 1988–1989, or the "early IVF period" in Egypt, when the new reproductive technologies were neither widely available nor widely understood. The first Egyptian IVF center had just opened in 1986 in Maadi, an elite suburb of Cairo, and the first Egyptian baby of the tubes, a little girl named Heba Mohammed,[123] was born in 1987. In these early days of new reproductive technology transfer to Egypt, I conducted fifteen months of anthropological fieldwork on the general problem of infertility in the country, basing my research in Alexandria, Egypt's second largest city of nearly 5 million people. Working through the University of Alexandria's large, public, ob/gyn teaching hospital, popularly known as "Shatby," I conducted in-depth, semi-structured interviews with one hundred infertile women and a comparison group of ninety fertile ones. Eventually, I made my way through invitations and the development of friendships into the homes of many of these women—homes that were generally located in poor urban and peri-urban neighborhoods in and around Alexandria and several provincial cities in the northwestern Nile Delta region. There, I participated in daily life, including many delicious meals, and also conducted less formal interviewing with women, their husbands, other family members, and traditional healers to whom they introduced me.

With few exceptions, these women were poor, uneducated, illiterate or only semi-literate housewives, who were not employed in wage labor and were economically dependent upon their unskilled, laboring husbands. It is extremely critical to note here that many of these poor urban women were seeking treatment at Shatby Hospital not only because the infertility services there were free, but specifically because of the hospital's widely publicized claims in 1988–1989 to the development of a "free," government-sponsored IVF program. Yet by the end of the 1980s, when I completed this initial fieldwork, it had become apparent to all of my poor, IVF-seeking informants that an IVF program at this public hospital might take months, even years, to arrive. Furthermore, it appeared likely that IVF, even in a government charity hospital, was no "freebie." Many of the costs of the procedure—simple things like test tubes and syringes—were passed onto patients, who were asked to purchase these materials and the expensive hormonal medications on the open market in preparation for future IVF trials.[124] Given that these women came from poor households—where annual household incomes ranged from a meager $240 to $960—it was not surprising that many of these poor IVF-hopefuls ultimately became program "dropouts," despite the fact that most still entertained dreams of making a test-tube baby of their own. Ultimately, because of both medical disqualifications and economic barriers, only a small number, 15 percent to be exact, actually entered the incipient IVF program there as potential candidates.

Shortly after I left Egypt at the end of 1989, Shatby Hospital did, in fact, open its own public IVF center in 1991, and the first Alexandrian baby of the tubes was born ten months later in 1992, with much fanfare in the Egyptian press. However, since those early publicity-driven days of purportedly free, government-sponsored IVF, fewer and fewer test-tube babies have been born to poor Egyptian women. As Egypt's one and only state-subsidized IVF program, the Shatby Hospital IVF clinic continues to operate, but on such a low volume that very few patients receive treatment and success rates are compromised. Instead, the academic physicians charged with running this public "poor people's" IVF clinic put their energies into their *private* IVF practices—which, as is typical for Egyptian physicians working in the public sector, they run "on the side" after putting in brief morning appearances at their government jobs. Indeed, when I revisited the Shatby IVF unit in the middle of a weekday morning in August 1996, the place was entirely deserted—although it should have been literally brimming with summertime IVF patients as were the other busy private practices in Alexandria and Cairo. In short, public, government-sponsored new reproductive technology services in Egypt are moribund, if not completely defunct.[125] And, in all likelihood, the necessary "political will" to revivify public IVF in the country will not be mustered anytime soon.

Moving ahead, the second period of research is the late 1990s, or what may be characterized as the "IVF boom period" in Egypt. To wit, by 1995, Egypt was in the midst of massive reproductive technology transfer, with new urban IVF centers cropping up in private hospitals and clinics on a regular basis. In the midst of this IVF explosion, I spent the summer of 1996 in Cairo conducting in-depth, semi-structured interviews with sixty-six mostly middle- to upper-class women; nearly all of them (sixty-one out of sixty-six, or 92 percent) were either contemplating or undergoing a new reproductive technology procedure at two of the major IVF centers in Cairo, Egypt's largest city of more than 10 million inhabitants.[126] These two private IVF clinics, located in Nile Badrawi and Nozha International hospitals in the elite suburbs of Maadi and Heliopolis, respectively, were among the most established and respected IVF clinics in the city. As a result, they received a daily influx of new patients, especially during the summer months, which were the busiest and were therefore ideal for my research.

In addition, I interviewed five infertility patients in the private clinic of Dr. Gamal Serour, one of the founders of IVF in Egypt and a professor of obstetrics and gynecology at Al-Azhar University in Cairo. Dr. Serour was the official sponsor of my research through his directorship of the Al-Azhar University International Islamic Center for Population Studies and Research. Because of his excellent reputation and many connections in the world of Egyptian IVF, he was able to secure an informed theological supervisor for my study, Dr. Mohammed Rufaat Osman, also of Al-Azhar University,[127] as well as permission for me to conduct my study out of the Nile Badrawi and Nozha IVF centers. In short, without Dr. Serour's support and way in to the Egyptian IVF community, this study would never have taken place.

Similarly, my research could not have been accomplished without the intellectual and logistical support of two very committed and impressive Egyptian IVF physicians. Dr. Mohamed Yehia, director of the IVF unit at Nozha Hospital, and Dr. Salah Zaki, director of the IVF unit at Nile Badrawi Hospital, were generous supporters of my study. Without their permission to locate my research efforts in the midst of their busy IVF practices, I would not have gained access to actual patients—patients who they quietly and diligently recruited for me. They would ask their female patients whether they would mind being interviewed, confidentially, by an American anthropology professor. To my knowledge, no patient ever refused such a request, but I am sure that the gentle suasion of these patients by their physicians was necessary, given the "top secret" nature of the subject. Because these two physicians are nearly uniformly revered by their patients, I believe that many of these patients agreed to talk to me because of their feelings of loyalty and gratitude to these two doctors. As will be seen in the chapters that follow, particularly Chapter 5, much of the discourse in my interviews gravitated toward the importance of these two doctors in their IVF patients' lives. As a result, Dr. Yehia and Dr. Zaki, whose real names will be used throughout this text, are major characters in this story.

Through physician-mediated access to informants at three different sites, I was able meet infertile women at many different stages of the IVF decision-making process. For example, a few women in my study had been absolutely barred by insufficient funds or recalcitrant husbands from trying IVF, even though they desired this technology to overcome their childlessness. A few additional women had not yet "reached the stage" of IVF or ICSI, as they were being "treated" for male infertility in IVF centers with artificial insemination (using husbands' sperm) in the hopes of achieving pregnancy without resort to the much more expensive and complicated ICSI. In some cases, I interviewed women soon after they had been advised by IVF physicians that they should undertake IVF or ICSI; thus, during interviews, we sat and pondered the many implications of the doctors' advice.

However, the majority of my interviews were with women "in the thick of it"— namely, women beginning the hormonal stimulation stage of their first IVF or ICSI trial, women recovering from their embryo transfers in private hospital beds, women repeating an IVF or ICSI trial after the first trial (or multiple trials) had failed, women repeating a trial after miscarrying a test-tube baby, and much happier women who were repeating a trial after already giving birth to a test-tube baby or twins. Although most of the women I interviewed (sixty out of sixty-six, or 91 percent) had not yet become Egyptian mothers of test-tube babies, I did meet quite a few women (thirteen out of sixty-six, or 20 percent) who were in various stages of successful test-tube pregnancies. These included jubilant women who had just received their first ultrasound verification of healthy fetuses, women who were coming to the IVF center for later pregnancy follow-up and care, and women who had just delivered IVF singletons or twins and were recuperating and nursing their offspring in their private hospital rooms.

Who were these women? They were generally well-educated, professional, comparatively affluent career women, who ranged in age from mid-twenties to early forties (twenty-four to forty-three, with a mean age of thirty-four). Because of their advanced educations, many of them spoke fluent, even flawless English—even employing a Western argot—and they were happy to conduct the interview with me in English in order to use their second language.[128] Indeed, because of the high level of English proficiency in this IVF clinic population, I conducted nearly half of the interviews in English (with thirty out of sixty-six women, or 46 percent).[129] These interviews could last anywhere from one to several hours, depending upon the willingness of the informant, her degree of loquacity, and the time pressures she was under. Although I used a semi-structured interview schedule to guide our discussions, interviews were often free-flowing and open-ended, with the list of questions serving more as a reminder to me than as a formal research agenda.

The rest of the interviews—of thirty-six women, or 54 percent—were conducted in the Egyptian dialect of Arabic, the language in which I conducted all of my interviews in the first study. In the initial stages of my second study, when I was attempting to revive my Arabic after six years of disuse, I invited my infertile research assistant, Tayseer Salem, to accompany me to interviews at Nile Badrawi Hospital, where she served as an unobtrusive listener and translator when I needed her. Thus, at Nile Badrawi Hospital, where I interviewed twenty-six women in the initial stage of my study, my research assistant was present with me in nineteen of these interviews. In addition, a very kind young IVF physician, Dr. Ashraf Nasr, sat in on five of these initial interviews (with permission of informants), largely to reassure the IVF clinic directors there that I was carrying out my research in an ethical fashion.

In most cases, and particularly in the latter half of my study at Nozha Hospital, I conducted interviews by myself, in either English or Egyptian Arabic. I tape-recorded some of my Arabic-language interviews for later verbatim transcription with my research assistant, but only when informants were comfortable enough to let me use the tape-recorder. Because of the "top secrecy" and stigma surrounding IVF, which will be explored at length in Chapter 9, I was sensitive about using a tape-recorder and thus only employed one when informants spoke so rapidly that I had difficulty following them. In each case, I asked women's (and husbands') permission, and none ever refused me. However, in most cases, I used my own method of rapid, short-hand note-taking, developed through years of earlier training as a journalist, to record almost word-for-word what women told me, particularly in the English-language interviews.

Although my interviews focused on infertile women's lives and perceptions of test-tube baby making, it is very important to note that husbands were present with their wives in almost 40 percent of all cases. Because many of the women in my study were actually interviewed while recuperating in a hospital room after some stage of an IVF or ICSI trial, their husbands were often there to support them, and I was loathe to ask these men to leave the rooms.[130] Many of the husbands sat quietly and reflectively as I talked to their wives, occasionally adding a brief comment or answering a direct question. However, most of the men proved to be enthusiastic informants in their own right, adding an important (although initially unintended) dimension to the interviews. It soon became clear that many of these men had never had a chance to "open up" about their own male infertility problems, for reasons that will be examined in this book. For these reproductively troubled men, I was a captive audience; talking with me—a knowledgeable and sympathetic "outsider" who would take their "secrets" far away—often seemed cathartic for them.

As a result of this male participation in my study, twenty-four of my sixty-six interviews (36 percent) were true couple interviews, in which both husbands and wives participated in our discussions. In fourteen of these interviews, husbands and wives spoke about equally, with the interviews having a true give-and-take quality. However, in about ten of these interviews, husbands literally overwhelmed the interviews, either because they spoke better English (in interviews that began in English), because their personalities were dominant, or because they had more to say about the experience of male infertility and ICSI. Whatever the case, these couple interviews were often as enjoyable, animated, and intriguing as my interviews with women alone. Thus, I have decided to include them, in the form of stories and interview excerpts, as a vital part of this book on the Egyptian test-tube baby making experience.

Given the high cultural value in Egypt placed on good conversation punctuated with levity and wittiness, I found most of my informants, both women and men, to be talkative and engaging, once they realized (via informed consent forms that I asked them to read and sign) that our interviews were confidential and ultimately anonymous. Although all but one of the IVF patients I met agreed to speak with me, they did so under the condition that their identities remain anonymous. The only Egyptian woman who refused to participate in my study (after being introduced to me by Dr. Mohamed Yehia) used the English term "top secret" as the rationale for her resistance. Those who did agree to be interviewed spoke to me (and sometimes my research assistant, if she happened to be accompanying me) in a private room in the clinic, and only *after* they had been assured of the confidentiality of their interviews via written informed consent forms. While most anthropologists have railed against the use of written informed consent forms—arguing that these official forms may increase informants' discomfort and thereby severely limit the building of natural rapport between anthropologist and informant—I have found that my own research has benefited tremendously from the informed consent process. For infertile informants in both my studies, informed consent forms seemed to put them at ease once they realized that the interviews were private, confidential, and ultimately anonymous. In fact, many informants expressed their gratitude for an opportunity to speak to me confidentially, in the hospital rather than in their homes, about an often painful and private subject that cannot be openly discussed in public, even with close family and friends.

At the beginning of each interview, I introduced myself to informants, showing them the two books I had already written about infertility in Egypt and sharing with them the story of my own reproductive misfortunes (the loss of stillborn twin daughters, followed by a miscarriage). Although I told all of my informants that I was not a physician, many of them considered me to be a *duktura*, a highly educated and also personally knowledgeable "insider" in the world of infertility. As a result, I was asked many medical questions during interviews. When I could answer a question with some degree of accuracy according to the biomedical model, I would do so. If not, I referred them back to their physicians. However, unlike my first study, where I served as an informal patient educator for many of my illiterate informants (who desired biomedical information in order to understand their infertility diagnoses and treatments), I had relatively little to offer these highly sophisticated IVF patients other than my empathy and my desire to hear their stories. I was reminded of this only by Amira, who told me frankly during our interview that she wished I could do more for her in terms of actually overcoming her childlessness.

Although I exchanged local phone numbers with many of these women, I was ultimately invited to very few of their homes, which initially surprised me. Basing my expectations on my first study—where even the poorest of the poor were often proud to bring me, their first foreign acquaintance, to their homes for meals and conversation—I expected to socialize regularly with these IVF patients outside of the clinic. However, I soon realized that I might, in fact, be a social liability to these women and their husbands, who would be forced to explain to family members and neighbors how they had met me, an American infertility researcher in an Egyptian IVF clinic. As will be shown in Chapter 9, few IVF patients admit to anyone, even their closest family members and friends, that they have ever visited an IVF clinic. Thus, bringing me home was risky and could have potentially "blown their covers." This is not to say, however, that these women were not friendly and kind. Several of them gave me rides and brought me small gifts before my departure for America, and I have continued to correspond regularly with a few of them, including one who has subsequently emigrated to the United States.[131]

My inability to participate in the lives of these women outside of the walls of the IVF clinic was thus a major limitation of my study—one also reported by Aditya Bharadwaj in his study of the secret lives of Indian IVF patients.[132] What I came to know about these women and their husbands was revealed to me during interviews; thus, I had no opportunity to corroborate information shared by them through observation of their daily lives at home. Having said this, I must reiterate that the interviews I conducted were generally quite rich and evocative, full of personal disclosure and reflection. Many women, and several husbands, wanted to tell me their personal stories, stories that are reflected in the infertility narratives that begin each chapter of this book. Even among informants who did not share their infertility stories from beginning to end, most still spent several hours talking with me. On average, I was only able to interview one woman (or couple) a day during the normal 9 A.M. to 1 P.M. operating hours of these clinics.

The second major limitation of this study is that I spent much less time observing the day-to-day operations of these clinics than talking to patients and physicians within them. Several recent ethnographic studies of reproductive technologies—most notably Susan Kahn's forays into Israeli IVF laboratories and operating rooms and Rayna Rapp's participant observation in cytogenetics laboratories where prenatal diagnostic tests are carried out[133]—have provided vivid, evocative descriptions of

the innermost sanctums of reproductive medicine. The participation of these anthropologists in laboratories and operating rooms, where, in the case of Kahn and
Rapp, they were either called upon or made an effort to learn the actual medical
procedures, is quite remarkable and exemplary. In my own case, I never pursued
these avenues in Egypt, asking whether I might observe the ultrasound scanning,
oocyte retrievals, laboratory fertilizations, or embryo transfers that are part and parcel of the IVF medical procedure. In part, this was due to my own lack of foresight,
as I never included this kind of observational strategy in my proposals to carry out
this research. Nor did it ever occur to me to ask for these kinds of permissions once I
reached Egyptian IVF centers. Clearly, the ethos of privacy that pervaded patient
care at these elite IVF centers influenced the kind of "private ethnography" I carried
out alone with informants, either in their private hospital rooms or in a private office designated for that purpose. To have attempted something more public and am-
bitious in this secretive setting might have been viewed as quite suspect and ethically
problematic. Nonetheless, if I had been more persistent, I certainly could have observed the workings of the IVF laboratories themselves, where physicians manipu-
lated patients' gametes in petri dishes under high-powered microscopes. At both
Nozha and Nile Badrawi hospitals, I was invited to do so, and my failure to follow
through by actually setting up appointments to don medical garb and visit the labs
is something I now regret in retrospect.

Having said this, I learned a great deal by talking with the laboratory physicians
at both of these centers, particularly the laboratory directors, Dr. Ashraf Hakam of
Nile Badrawi and Dr. Abdel-Hamid Wafik of Nozha Hospital. I conducted many informal interviews with these physicians, as well as more formal ones with the clinical directors, Dr. Mohamed Yehia of Nozha Hospital and Dr. Salah Zaki of Nile
Badrawi. Altogether, there were eight Egyptian IVF physicians with whom I spoke
regularly during the course of my research, all of them adding valuable insights into
the local world of test-tube baby making.

Over the past six years since this research was conducted, I have maintained an
ongoing collegial relationship only with Dr. Yehia, who has kept me up to date on
new developments in the Egyptian IVF scene. Although the research for this book
took place at a point in time in which the world of reproductive medicine was
changing with dizzying speed, my intention is for this book to reflect at least some of
these changes as they have carried over into the new millennium. Nonetheless, it is
important to bear in mind that the stories told here might have been quite different
had they been reported to me in 2003 rather than 1996. In the world of IVF at least,
new stories become old news quite quickly, which is why the typical lag time between research and publication is a very problematic one indeed. Although this
book is written more or less in the "ethnographic present," readers are forewarned
that certain aspects of the narrative may now be dated. Nonetheless, I have made attempts to update material from 1996 through ongoing email conversations with Dr.
Yehia, who is pictured in chapter 5 with Egypt's first ICSI triplets. Clearly, Dr. Yehia
continues to be invested in my research and in "getting the story out" about the ac-

complishments of Egyptian IVF centers such as his—even though I must emphasize that all the arguments put forward in this book and any errors of commission or omission are entirely my own.

It was my initial association with Dr. Yehia and his clinic that opened my eyes to the newest new reproductive technology, ICSI, which Dr. Yehia imported to Egypt in 1994. By 1996, when I arrived on the scene, Dr. Yehia and his laboratory codirector Dr. Abdel-Hamid Wafik were in the midst of an Egyptian "ICSI revolution" of their own making, having by then brought 150 healthy Egyptian ICSI babies to life. This book reflects the palpable excitement of that important historical moment, when Egyptian IVF centers began to be flooded with men who were suffering from male infertility and who were hoping to achieve a cure with *talqih maghari,* or "microscopic insemination," as ICSI is now called in Egypt.[134] The vast majority of couples in my study—a full 70 percent—were attending either the Nozha or Nile Badrawi IVF centers hoping to use ICSI to overcome serious, often long-term cases of male infertility. Thus, by 1996 when this study was conducted, male infertility, the hidden reproductive failing, was beginning to emerge from behind its veil of secrecy.

This book examines the complex gender dynamics that occur when infertile Egyptian women and infertile Egyptian men attempt to make a test-tube baby with either IVF or ICSI. The findings are based largely on my second period of research in Egyptian IVF centers, but they are clearly informed by insights gained through the initial, longer period of research on the general problem of infertility and poor women's desires to gain access to these new reproductive technologies. Thus, my work on this subject incorporates both a longitudinal dimension and a class-based comparison of infertile women seeking treatment in the two largest cities of Egypt. It reveals how a time span of less than a decade has dramatically altered the local infertility treatment landscape and how the treatment experiences of poor and elite infertile women fundamentally differ by virtue of education, economic resources, and power within their marriages. Even more strikingly, my work demonstrates how elite infertile women (and men) in Egypt suffer from the many arenas of constraint on IVF that have little to do with class-based barriers to access—throwing into question the degree to which structure alone limits reproductive agency. On the most fundamental level, this book is about the limits of agency in a class-stratified, resource-poor, Third World society on the receiving end of global reproductive technology transfer.

In its focus on local constraints surrounding the use of globalizing reproductive technologies, this book empirically elucidates the importance of anthropology to studies of globalization. Although I draw inspiration in the chapters that follow from many different sources—including feminist studies, science and technology studies, medical sociology and psychology, medical journalism, bioethics, and Middle Eastern studies—this book is firmly based in the theory and ethnographic tradition of (medical) anthropology. Through its attention to culture, its concern with history, and its serious commitment to the ethnographic details of people's lives as they live them, anthropology has much to offer to current discussions and debates about the importance of the local in an increasingly global world. By sharing this ethnographic account of test-tube baby making in contemporary Egypt, I hope to contribute to this larger scholarly enterprise. Ultimately, I hope to open a window of understanding into a world that has been shuttered from our view—a place where brave "moral pioneers"[135] experience both the profound suffering and the occasional life-altering joys that are at the very heart of Egyptian test-tube baby making.

CHAPTER 2

Class

The Coptic Merchants

When I met Mikhail and Georgette on a hot July morning, thirty-eight-year-old Georgette had just returned from embryo transfer and, recovering from both the anesthesia and the "operation," was lying quietly in her hospital bed in the maternity ward of Nozha Hospital. Mikhail, her forty-six-year-old husband, was waiting patiently beside her and was pleased to meet me, an American anthropologist, with whom he could "pass the time." In fluent English, he insisted that I would not be disturbing them during Georgette's two-hour recovery period. As I was to learn in a lengthy interview conducted mostly with him, he and Georgette had been through this many times before, and neither of them were looking forward to the upcoming fifteen-day period of waiting and wondering about the outcome of this most recent attempt at ICSI.

As he explained in the story of their seventeen-year marriage, he and Georgette are first cousins (a common marital practice in Egypt), who remained childless after two years of marriage. As members of the minority Coptic Christian population in Egypt (who constitute somewhere between 5 and 10 percent of all Egyptian citizens, depending on the estimate), they first visited a Coptic hospital, where most of the doctors were also Coptic Christians. When treatment efforts at the hospital failed, a Coptic doctor offered to accompany Georgette and Mikhail to England, where IVF "started." As Mikhail explained,

> This was maybe fourteen years ago. Even there was no ultrasound here [in Egypt] at that time. All this equipment had not reached to Egypt, or even an idea about it. He told us [about it], and said he would accompany us to England to make IVF. But, in that period, I had a shop. I'm a merchant. I could not let my shop go, and it's difficult to stay in England for one month. So he told us, "You must go to a Muslim doctor in the faculty at Al-Azhar University. They have more equipment and tools than we do. Maybe you have a chance."

The Muslim gynecologist whom Georgette subsequently visited diagnosed an ovarian problem known as polycystic ovarian syndrome (PCOS),[1] explaining this infertility-producing condition in a kind of popular parlance as "fat on the ovaries." Although PCOS has nothing to do with fat, Mikhail and Georgette thus came to understand Georgette's infertility problem as "ovaries that are coated with some fat" that has "blocked the eggs." Unfortunately, Georgette underwent a surgical operation to "remove the fat" that proved to be iatrogenic, or productive of further infertility problems. Although her fallopian tubes were once patent, or open, the surgery itself produced scarring, or adhesions, which has led to tubal blockage. Thus, Georgette now suffers from two forms of infertility—ovarian and tubal. And, after many years of normal semen production, Mikhail himself now suffers from relatively serious male infertility (a common pattern of decline found among Egyptian men, perhaps due to heavy male smoking and other lifestyle and environmental factors). In Mikhail's case, his male infertility may be related to a recently developing medical condition in which he no longer produces sweat. Thus, as seen in many long-term cases of intractable infertility in Egypt, together Georgette and Mikhail suffer from multiple-factor infertility, for which ICSI now seems to be their only hope.

Although Georgette and Mikhail have contemplated undertaking IVF outside of Egypt, for the past four years they have been patients of Dr. Mohamed Yehia at Nozha Hospital's IVF center. "We are old patients here," Mikhail explained. "[The owner of the hospital] knows us very well. He told us many times, 'You are the eldest patients here.'"

For Georgette and Mikhail, "eldest" has a double entendre. Not only are they among the earliest cohort of IVF patients at the clinic, but they are now also a reproductively elderly couple, given Georgette's advancing age. Mikhail stated bluntly,

> Honestly, she has only two years, and then she will turn forty [when IVF success rates begin to diminish precipitously]. We have only a chance to make another four trials. If we can make a trial every six months, we calculate that we can make four more trials before she reaches the age of forty. This is the most essential point and the basis of our calculation—the age of forty.

So far, Georgette has undergone two trials of IVF and two trials of ICSI over a two-year period—but without success. Because Mikhail and Georgette are repeaters, they receive a 10 percent discount on the cost of the ICSI operation.

> Here, with Dr. Yehia, he takes approximately LE 5,000 [$1,471];[2] he makes a 10 percent discount for us because we repeat many times. We also take injections, Pergonal or Humagon, for approximately LE 2,000 [$588]. So, the total operation costs about LE 10,000 [$2,941]. So far, we've spent LE 40,000 [$11,765].

Then Mikhail added, jokingly, "Still another LE 40,000 would buy one Mercedes! Dr. Mohamed Yehia, he has now taken one half of a used Mercedes car from us!"

When asked if the expenses were a problem for them, Mikhail remarked,

It's not too hard, because we're merchants. LE 40,000 is our profit for one year. But for others, this is very difficult. You can find people trying for one chance [of IVF] and that's it. And, if you come to the hospital for a long time like we have, you see people who try one time and just go.

LE 10,000 [nearly $3,000] is *a lot* of money for Egyptian people. The salaries here make this very difficult. A government engineer's salary per month is maybe $100—or LE 340—and that's a *big* salary. For many people, it's not more than LE 100 to 150 [$29–44] a month. So, for most people, they couldn't collect enough money to even do one time. It's *very* expensive. They would have to go without eating and drinking to do it.

But we are merchants. I'm a chemical engineer, but now I'm a merchant because I took over my father's business. I'm the eldest and I have my own shop. I opened my own shop while my father was still living. I import spare parts for big buses and also spare parts for cars. Georgette, she is working with me in my shop. She keeps all the calculations—not like other women, who are only keeping house. She is working and she has no time to think! Now we're making faxes, everything! We have a big office at home with a computer and faxes. And she has a company under her name as well. I have and she has. Hers is importing and mine is government contracts for the Egyptian bus companies. It's a good business.

In fact, it is Mikhail and Georgette's good business that makes their need for a child even more pressing. Mikhail explained,

> I know here in Egypt, the most important thing is that you *must* have a child. It's not like Europe, where they don't care about this, I think. Here it's very important, and this [infertility] is a big problem. All our sisters and brothers, they're all pregnant and having children, and they're "pressing on us" to do the same. Especially because we are merchants and we take our father's business. It's important to have a child for this reason.

Mikhail went on to point out, however, that, personally, he didn't feel he "needed" his own child and that he would consider adoption, which is allowed for Egyptian Copts but not for Muslims. But, Georgette, who was listening to and understood most of our conversation in English, chimed in in Arabic that her "feelings" would keep her from adopting: "He will not be my own son! He will belong to me—or to another? It's an inner feeling. The idea is not to raise a child; the idea is to have my own child, not to take care of someone else's." Mikhail then added, "I think God creates this in women more than men. I think we don't feel just like you." However, he added, for men of wealth in Egypt, the pressure not to "waste" one's money and inheritance on an "outsider" was considerable. "And it's very difficult when we see that we've become an old man and we find nothing [no children to stand by them]."

Thus, for Georgette and Mikhail, adoption as allowed by their religion is still not a viable option for them. As a well-to-do Coptic couple, they hope to pass on their wealth and their family business to their own future offspring. Thus, they will continue to place their hopes in God, in Dr. Yehia, and in the ICSI technology—believing that, this time, with God's permission, the "microscopic injection" just might work for them.

The Enactment of Stratified Reproduction

Although different by virtue of their minority religious status, Mikhail and Georgette are in every other way typical Egyptian IVF patients: They are well-heeled—if not fabulously wealthy—elites, who are able to afford the expensive, high-tech therapies offered at Egyptian IVF centers. Private entrepreneurs who collaborate as business partners in an international automotive importing business, Mikhail and Georgette are members of the small but growing Egyptian upper class, whose lifestyles, consumption practices, and orientation make them, in some senses, more similar to Western elites than to their lower- and middle-class Egyptian country(wo)men. Not only have their financial resources allowed Mikhail and Georgette to undertake multiple IVF and ICSI trials in Egypt—at nearly $3,000 per trial—but they can afford to repeat the procedure several additional times until age begins to work against them. And, if their money does not buy them success, they, like most other Egyptian elites, will consider traveling abroad—perhaps accompanied by an internationally sophisticated Coptic physician who considers them his social peers—in order to undergo the procedure in a European IVF center. For Mikhail and Georgette and the many others like them who attend Egyptian IVF centers today, their class position in this markedly class-stratified society allows them to consume quite freely the fruits of globalization. In this case, globalization comes in the form of Western-generated medical technologies "purchased" from internationally sophisticated Egyptian doctors. Patients such as Mikhail and Georgette view these physicians as their social and class equals, and thus they deem them worthy of the Western *accoutrements* (for example, the Mercedes-Benzes and BMWs) reaped through their provision of new reproductive technologies to desirous Egyptian infertile couples.

It is fair to say that for many, although certainly not all, of the patients attending Egyptian IVF centers, money is not the main object that would prevent them from actually pursuing these costly therapies. Instead, for couples like Mikhail and Georgette, their concerns revolve around the costs of failure, including their inability to secure heirs to whom they can pass down their accumulated patrimony. Yet, for the rest of the Egyptian infertile—meaning poor folk and those in the middle—money is everything, for without it, they are absolutely barred from pursuing the single medical technique that may offer their only hope for reproductive salvation. Thus, social class—and its relationship to economic resources and power—is arguably the most fundamental arena of constraint operating in the realm of Egyptian test-tube baby making today. Whether one can afford the high price tags attached to the medications and operations surrounding IVF and ICSI serves to stratify potential Egyptian consumers of these new reproductive technologies (NRTs) into three distinct tiers: those who can afford these procedures without significant limitation (i.e., the upper class), those who can afford them but under limited circumstances (i.e., the middle class), and those who can never afford these procedures without a miracle of physician charity (i.e., the lower-class Egyptian majority). Thus, Egyptian test-tube baby making provides an example par excellence of what Ginsburg and Rapp (following Colen)[3] have called "stratified reproduction," or the inequitable privileging of the reproductive trajectories of elites over those of the poor and disempowered, whose "right" to reproduce may be called into question and even despised.

In this chapter, we will explore how this kind of stratified reproduction is enacted in the world of Egyptian test-tube baby making—reinforced by class stratification that is unlikely to be overcome in Egypt without a radical (and very unlikely) transformation in the economy and social welfare system. Although stratified reproduction is certainly at play in the Western world of test-tube baby making—such that economic constraints also pose barriers to uninsured, low-income and minority patients[4]—these constraints become truly magnified in resource-poor, lower-income countries such as Egypt, which, like much of the rest of the developing Third World, is positioned on the receiving end of global reproductive technology transfer. Speaking about the state of infertility services in Africa in general, Friday E. Okonofua, a Nigerian professor of obstetrics and gynecology and a reproductive health activist, comments in an article entitled "The Case Against New Reproductive Technologies in Developing Countries":

> It is conceivable that the large number of women with tubal occlusion in developing countries would benefit from the procedure [IVF-ET]. Reports from Nigeria and Egypt indicate that new reproductive technologies can be performed successfully with the existing clinical competence and infrastructure in some African countries. . . . [This] raises several fundamental questions that relate mostly to the appropriateness of institutionalising the technology in an African country, in view of the peculiar health problems in Africa. Particularly pertinent issues that relate to such a programme in Africa include considerations of priorities in health resources allocation, costs, feasibility, quality control and sustainability and how to ensure equity of access in a country with glaring inequity in health matters.[5]

Concluding that these new reproductive technologies benefit "only a small proportion of infertile women," are "extremely expensive per live birth," and would limit the availability of government funds for "other high priority public health projects,"[6] Okonofua ultimately argues that the new reproductive technologies have only a limited place in the current health scene in Nigeria and in most developing countries with similar health, fertility, and economic conditions.[7]

The Public-Private Divide

Okonofua's fundamental assertion that new reproductive technologies are inappropriate for the developing world—a controversial editorial opinion that was published in the *British Journal of Obstetrics and Gynaecology* during 1996, the year this study in Egypt was being conducted—has fallen on deaf ears, both on the producing and receiving end of global reproductive technology transfer. As shown in Chapter 1, the number of centers for IVF in Egypt (and the Middle East more generally) has grown exponentially over a very short time period, with manufacturers in Western countries such as the United Kingdom actively promoting their reproductive wares in developing countries, many of which (like Egypt) are ex-colonies. Yet, part of Okonofua's warning—namely, that Third World governments cannot afford to support these technologies through state-sponsored programs, particularly given all of the other dire public health problems facing nations such as Nigeria and Egypt— seems to have been heeded. Not surprisingly, very few Third World governments have committed funds or demonstrated the necessary "political will" to support the treatment of their infertile citizens through government-sponsored IVF programs.

The Muslim Middle East is a case in point. Of the more than thirty-five IVF centers in the region at the time of the 1996 study, only two—one at the University of Alexandria's Shatby Hospital and one at King Faisal Hospital in Saudi Arabia—were public units, according to Dr. Mohamed Yehia, the director of IVF services at Nozha Hospital where Georgette and Mikhail were private patients. Dr. Yehia, a professor of obstetrics and gynecology at Ain Shams University in Cairo, had pressed the administrators of his own university to start an IVF program in Ain Shams's Maternity Hospital in Cairo's famous Abbassiya Square. As he explained it, this public, "poor people's" maternity hospital is the largest in the Middle East, with twelve hundred total beds and a semi-private specialized hospital unit *within* the larger hospital comprised of five hundred beds reserved for ob/gyn cases. According to Dr. Yehia, the hospital is *extremely* well-equipped, hosting a laparoscopic unit that was in place even before similar units in the West, as well as a center for the early detection of cancer through colposcopy and mammography (in a country where cancer prevention efforts are extremely rudimentary or nonexistent). The hospital was built under the direction of an Ain Shams ob/gyn professor who was once a very influential minister of family planning in the country. As Dr. Yehia noted, "Things in Egypt work by influence and politics. The only thing that is not present in this hospital is infertility. Although there is an infertility clinic, there is no IVF, and this is 'politics only.'" He added that money to fund an IVF unit in this public hospital "can always be found," and Western drug companies and manufacturers are more than happy to provide the equipment at no (or low) cost. "But this hasn't happened," Dr. Yehia lamented, "and so there is presently no IVF unit at a public hospital in Cairo serving the poor."

This is in stark contrast to neighboring Israel—a non-Muslim country with a much different political history than Egypt and a much clearer Western orientation (as well as much more generous political and economic support from Western backers). Israel is the only nation in the Middle Eastern region offering a program of government-subsidized new reproductive technologies to its citizens. All Israeli citizens—regardless of income level, religion, or marital status—are entitled to unlimited rounds of IVF treatment free of charge, up to the birth of two live children, in the twenty-three *public* IVF clinics designated for this purpose.[8] This generous program of government-sponsored IVF in Israel clearly reflects the state's pronatalist desires to "reproduce Jews," including with the "assistance" of new reproductive technologies that are offered quite freely in these public clinics. Israel is also proud of the "cutting-edge" nature of its assisted conception services—positioning it closer to Western producer nations of new reproductive technologies than non-Western consumer nations such as Egypt. Yet, ironically, Israel and Egypt are positioned geographically side by side, serving to highlight the "public-private divide" in IVF services *across* nations with markedly different social, economic, and political histories.

The Three-Tiered System

But where does this leave hopeful IVF patients *within* Egypt, where the internal public-private divide in IVF services is also pronounced? As noted earlier, the mostly private nature of IVF services in Egypt has quickly engendered a three-tiered, class-based system of IVF accessibility, in which only the country's wealthy (as well as affluent Arabs from neighboring petro-rich nations) have unfettered access to the new reproductive technologies now available in the country. For middle-class and lower-class infertile Egyptians, having enough money to afford IVF or ICSI treatment is perhaps *the* fundamental arena of constraint limiting their ability to utilize these technologies—despite, in many cases, their ardent desire to do so.

It must be noted here that the very concept of "class" in the Middle East is a contentious issue. This region of the world has often been represented as an area so fundamentally different from the capitalist West that classes cannot be recognized, thereby making class analyses seem irrelevant.[9] Yet, clearly, there *are* classes in the Middle East, including in Egypt. If class can be understood in the Marxist sense as determined by employment—specifically one's position in relation to ownership or control of the means of production—then it is quite clear that a number of different social classes have traditionally existed in the Middle East, and do so today.[10] Although Middle Eastern classes have been variously described, sociologist Saad Eddin Ibrahim—who was recently imprisoned for his views that challenged the Egyptian government—has provided a somewhat dated but nonetheless enduring description of the multilayered class divisions present in Cairo, Egypt.[11] Using the components of income, occupation, education, and durable goods (lifestyle), he distinguishes between six class strata in Cairo, providing population estimates for each stratum as follows: (1) the lowest stratum—the destitute (11.2 percent); (2) the low stratum—the poor (10.3 percent); (3) the low-middle stratum—the borderline (26.5 percent); (4) the middle stratum—the upwardly mobile (36.1 percent); (5) the upper-middle stratum—the secure (15.3 percent); and (6) the upper stratum—the rich (1.0 percent).

Certainly, Ibrahim's very exacting percentage estimates have shifted over time as the Egyptian middle class (now the largest in the Middle East) continues to grow through access to public education. However, Ibrahim's original estimates—showing that approximately half of all Cairenes live in or on the margins of poverty—seem to be upheld by more recent survey research undertaken by Egyptian scholars. A 1994 nationwide survey of twenty-four hundred households showed that 27 percent of the Egyptian population was living in poverty.[12] By 1999, the percent of households that fell below the poverty line had increased to 33 percent, or exactly one-third.[13] Furthermore, some analysts argue that both the depth and the severity of poverty have increased in Egypt over the past two decades (1981–1997).[14] For example, Nagi argues that 37.3 percent, or more than one third of the Egyptian households he surveyed in 1995, were objectively poor.[15] Similarly, Assaad and Rouchdy argue that half of Egypt's population now lives in either dire poverty (25 percent) or on the margins of poverty (25 percent).[16]

Although poverty rates in Egypt are continuously debated,[17] it is nonetheless clear that a very pyramidal class structure exists in urban Egyptian society. At the top of the pyramid is a relatively small upper- and upper-middle class elite, composed of traditional wealthy families and nouveau riche Egyptians, some of whom have made the most of labor migration opportunities in the wealthy Arab Gulf; an educated middle class with aspirations for a better life, but whose class position may actually be slipping as a result of economic factors and inflation beyond their control; and "the masses," the marginally educated, poorly paid working people, who face economic uncertainty and the threat of unemployment and underemployment in their government and informal-sector jobs.

Not surprisingly, these three tiers—the elites, the middle class, and the masses—are differentially represented in Egyptian IVF clinics based on the degree to which their finances constrain them. Visits to IVF clinics—and all of the extraordinary expenses incurred there—are paid for by patients on an immediate, fee-for-service basis, as health insurance is a newly developing concept in Egypt and is not at all widespread.[18] Similarly, most Egyptian Muslims do not own or use credit cards, as Islam explicitly prohibits usury, or the taking of interest on a loan (including a credit card loan), which is considered an unfair expropriation of a person's capital.[19] Thus, without the economic strategies of insurance coverage or credit-card payment plans, the amount of money one has "in one's pocket" at any given time determines whether or not a trial of IVF or ICSI can be undertaken. Those with such excess cash—particularly the large amounts needed at the time of an IVF or ICSI cycle—are generally upper middle to upper class. For the middle class, garnering such financial resources can be a real struggle and can lead to deferments or one-shot attempts at baby making. And, for the lower classes, the absolute lack of such resources imposes a fundamental constraint for most. Although this mapping of class status onto economic constraint in the arena of Egyptian test-tube baby making may be rather crude and inexact, it nonetheless serves as a relatively useful heuristic device for portraying the nature of the contemporary Egyptian IVF treatment scene, including the three groups of patients who do—or do not—show up for treatment in Egyptian IVF clinics today.

The Lower Class

Poor infertile Egyptian women—and those in the lower-middle class stratum just above them—do, on occasion, appear at private Egyptian IVF centers with or without their husbands. But they are relatively rare and remarkable by their presence. Some may make initial visits to IVF centers, often traveling long distances from rural areas, only to realize that the procedures and drugs are absolutely unaffordable. Others attend IVF centers only to undergo artificial insemination, which is a less invasive and, hence, *significantly* less expensive reproductive technology. Others present to IVF centers hoping to undergo one trial, having either sold off everything they own (e.g., jewelry, household goods, small pieces of land) or borrowed substantial sums from better-off relatives. Still others are the lucky charity cases—usually a woman whose reproductive tragedy has elicited sympathy from a noble IVF physician and who has been taken on as a gratis patient or has been charged only minimal fees.

During my 1996 study, I met six of these women in Egyptian IVF centers (11 percent of the total sample). Two were charity cases taken on at the Nile Badrawi Hospital IVF unit. In one of these cases, the husband had suffered a war-related injury that had made him impotent, and the hospital administrators had decided to take the couple on as an ICSI charity case, given the husband's heroic military record. In the other case, Dr. Salah Zaki, director of the IVF unit, had taken pity on a very young, impoverished, but beautiful woman who suffered irreparable tubal blockage. Under his care, she had produced twin daughters by IVF, and her undying devotion and gratitude to Dr. Zaki were profound.

In three of the remaining cases, lower-middle-class women were being treated at the Nile Badrawi IVF center, but they were receiving only artificial insemination at a fraction of the cost of IVF or ICSI. In each case, Dr. Zaki had assessed the patient's financial status, and realizing that IVF or ICSI was out of the question, he had offered the woman the only other available therapeutic option.

In only one case did I meet a poor woman in an Egyptian IVF center who was actually attempting to go forward with an ICSI trial. She was a rural woman, from the governorate of Menoufia, who had traveled with her husband to Cairo's Nile Badrawi Hospital numerous times. Her husband suffered from azoospermia—complete absence of sperm in his semen—due to a botched varicocelectomy, a testicular surgery to supposedly repair a varicocele, a varicose enlargement of the veins of the spermatic cord. Given her husband's diagnosis, ICSI constituted their only hope of ever conceiving a child. As the woman explained,

> We were happy to find *anything*—even the eye of a needle. Every time we went to a doctor, he says something, and we became hopeless. All the doctors told us, "Leave it to God. Leave it to God." After twenty-two years [of marriage], we're happy to find the eye of a needle.

At the time of the interview, this woman had sold all of her gold bracelets in order to buy the expensive medications to prepare her for the ICSI procedure. When

I asked her how she would pay for the actual operation, she replied, "It's very diffi-cult. God only knows how we will pay. Our family can't help. Maybe we will sell everything—our refrigerator, everything."

In addition, during my 1996 study, I met two poor infertile women who would never make it to an Egyptian IVF center, although they knew themselves to be candi-dates for the procedure and were under the care of an infertility specialist. In these cases, the physician, Dr. Gamal Serour, hoped to spare these women the "embarrass-ment" of a referral to his IVF center, given his realization that they were poor and could never afford the costs of the procedures and medications being offered there. But one of these women, who, as a poorly paid nurse's aide, was well aware of IVF, stated bluntly,

> IVF is only for the rich. I'm sure. How will I ever be able to get LE 10,000, or even LE 5,000? From where do I pay for two or more trials? And I'm sure I will not succeed from the first time. If I had the money, I *would* try. Since I've tried many treatments, why don't I take the step that will give me hope?

That poor Egyptian women such as these are essentially barred from undertak-ing IVF is not lost on Egyptian elites, including both the doctors and patients such as Georgette and Mikhail who frequent Egyptian IVF centers. Many of the upper-middle to upper-class patients I interviewed in 1996 commented on the economic exclusion of lower-class patients from the Egyptian IVF treatment enterprise. Often their comments were made apologetically, reminding me (and themselves) that they were comparatively fortunate to be unconstrained by economic factors. I was often told that "not many can afford this operation," or that "not all people can pay for this." As one wealthy woman said,

> When I come here, I'm always in a hurry. I don't like to sit, but I see these people, and I feel very sorry for them. I see a man in slippers; he's very poor. How can he spend [his money] on this when he needs money for food, for clothing, an apartment, and living?

Others were less troubled by the misfortune of class stratification and the subse-quent exclusion of "poor ones" from test-tube baby making. In a thinly veiled, neo-eugenic discourse captured in interviews with at least a few Egyptian elites in this study,[20] it was made clear to me that new reproductive technologies are "not for everyone" in Egypt—the "everyone" in this case tacitly meaning poor women, who are often known to wealthy women only in their capacity as domestic servants. Stated another way, the new reproductive technologies to combat infertility *should not* be "for everyone," because, as the equation goes, those who cannot afford these technologies certainly cannot afford children. To wit, poor women do not deserve to be mothers—and especially not mothers of test-tube babies. And any reproductive technology directed at them should be to inhibit—not facilitate—their fertility.

This sentiment—one that I have heard many times in both Egypt and the United States when I have declared my research interests in infertility and new reproductive technologies among poor Egyptians—is, in my view, what "stratified reproduction" is all about. Elites deserve to reproduce, with whatever assistance they can muster. The poor do not, and are in fact despised for trying to bring more babies into this world. In Egypt, a poor country with the oldest, most heavily subsidized (through Western aid) population control program in the Muslim Middle Eastern region,[21] it comes as no surprise that test-tube baby making is off limits for the infertile masses, who will never be served by the kind of effective, government-subsidized, new reproductive technology program found in neighboring Israel. Instead, test-tube baby making in Egypt will remain the province of "worthier" elites—whose test-tube offspring, privately made in exclusive IVF clinics, are deemed better potential contributors to the future Egyptian state.

The Middle Class

But where does this leave the Egyptian middle class, whose numbers are growing unsteadily in an economy that remains unstable? Unlike the poor, whose access to new reproductive technologies remains extremely limited, middle-class Egyptian patients are well represented at Egyptian IVF centers today, although in most cases their concerns over the cost of treatment are profound. In my very first meeting with Dr. Yehia—who quickly outlined for me what he saw as the major problems for patients undergoing IVF or ICSI—the number one problem he described was the exorbitant expense, "especially for middle-class patients who put all of their resources into IVF." Dr. Yehia's assertion could not be more accurate. For the middle class, having enough money to conduct IVF or ICSI, especially multiple times, is the most fundamental arena of constraint, even though this constraint is not as absolute as it is for the poor. For many middle-class patients, IVF remains a one-time proposition, while for others who are able to repeat the procedure, IVF proves financially devastating over time.

It is important to note that middle-class Egyptians are often highly educated, but typically their salaries are relatively low, particularly if they work in the public sector. Per capita annual income in Egypt in 1997 was estimated at exactly $1,200,[22] making a government engineer who is paid $100 per month a typical Egyptian wage-earner. Unfortunately, the 1997 annual income estimate for Egypt of $1,200 is a *per capita*—or per person—estimate, suggesting that an average Egyptian engineer would have great difficulty supporting a family of, say, four on an annual *household* income of only $1,200. In short, government salaries in Egypt—even among the educated middle-class intelligentsia of doctors, lawyers, and engineers—are paltry and make a middle-class lifestyle very difficult to sustain, especially as the cost of living in Egypt (e.g., the cost of purchasing an apartment) grows ever steeper. As one cynical ICSI patient put it, comparing Egyptian salaries to those abroad, "A salary in the U.S. is something like LE 7,000 [$1,892] a month. A salary here is LE 300 [$88] a month—and that's if he's 'something' [e.g., a professional]!"

Of the fifty-eight middle- to upper-class women patients I met in Egyptian IVF clinics in 1996, I estimated that seventeen of them and their husbands (29 percent) were solidly middle class, based on information I gathered from them regarding wife's and husband's occupations, history of labor migration, and frank discussions of financial matters in interviews. Virtually all of these members of the middle tier lamented the economic constraints facing infertile Egyptian couples in Egypt, who must spend all of their available resources on treatment. And many of them blamed the poor salary structure in Egypt, which they believed was out of step with contemporary economic realities in the country. In an interview with one highly educated woman, who spoke perfect English and worked as a computer programming analyst for a private insurance company, she discussed the economic constraints facing Egyptian couples who need to do IVF:

> Because it costs much money, it stops many people from doing it. Egyptians are not rich. Our salaries are lower than people in other countries. My mother and sister both offered to help, but I said "Thank you very much" [i.e., she did not want to accept their offers]. But I've ended up using some money my mother gave me, and some inheritance from my stepfather, and some savings. It's expensive.

As in this woman's case, cash-generating strategies among middle-class patients attempting a trial of IVF or ICSI often involved drawing upon savings, selling jewelry and other valuables, and borrowing money, particularly from family members. In nine cases in this study, parents were helping to finance their children's IVF/ICSI attempts, which in several cases would not have been possible without such parental aid.

Most middle-class women and their husbands were quite candid about the "very expensive" nature of IVF/ICSI, and how paying for even one trial was both a major expenditure and a major source of anxiety. They described IVF/ICSI as "*very* expensive," "*very* difficult financially," "*so* costly," and, ultimately, a huge "sacrifice" of their precious resources. Many questioned how they would ever "raise all this money," especially if they needed to undergo repeated trials. Of the sixty-six women in the 1996 study, thirty-two of them—or nearly half—described the expenses of IVF/ICSI as a problem. This even included women from the upper-middle class, who said they could afford repeated trials only with difficulty. For middle-class women, however, repetition was often out of the question, and thus they found themselves "gambling" all of their money on one-time attempts to get pregnant.

For example, one woman whom I met at Nile Badrawi Hospital after she had just delivered an ICSI daughter by cesarean section described her one and only attempt at test-tube baby making. Both she and her husband were accountants who had undergone many failed treatment attempts for his serious male infertility problem. They had once sought IVF in the United States, where her brother lived and had taken them to two IVF clinics on the East Coast. Appalled by the high cost of even one trial of IVF in the United States—$15,000 at an IVF center in Delaware and $9,000 at a center in New Jersey—they returned to Egypt despondent, having wasted their time and a significant amount of money (about LE 10,000, or nearly $3,000) on the travel. Eventually, they found the Nile Badrawi IVF center through an advertisement in the newspaper and were told that ICSI, the most appropriate technology for their particular case, was now available. With their remaining savings, they underwent one ICSI trial and were incredibly fortunate to succeed on the first attempt. Expressing her profound gratitude to the Nile Badrawi IVF team, the woman exclaimed,

> Thank God, the expenses are not too bad here! But all of the money we had is gone. All of our life savings went into trying to have a child. This money stopped us from buying a car, or any other thing. Considering how people here in Egypt live, this [IVF] is considered very expensive, and not everyone can do it.

In several cases (seven to be exact), the only reason why middle-class couples were able to afford IVF/ICSI was because of money earned through labor migration to the Arab Gulf states, where salaries are much higher than in Egypt. Extended periods of labor migration are common among Egyptians of all social classes, although middle- to upper-middle-class Egyptians are more likely to migrate as families (as opposed to solo male migration, which is more common among the Egyptian poor). In fact, Egypt, with the largest population in the Middle East but with relatively small oil reserves, has been the major sending country—supplying approximately 60 percent of the foreign Arab labor (mostly in construction, services, and manufacturing) for the richer countries of the Middle East, particularly prior to the Gulf War.[23] Although post–Gulf War return migration has been considerable, Egypt continues to send thousands of workers—from all spectrums of social life—to the Arab Gulf each year, where, now 3 million strong, they make significant amounts of money that are returned to Egypt as remittances that boost the Egyptian economy.

The importance of such labor migration to many of the IVF-seeking couples in this study cannot be underestimated, and it is one of the local features of test-tube baby making in Egypt that makes it very different from the West. For example, one Egyptian couple whom I interviewed together described how repeated, annual attempts to make a test-tube baby would have never occurred without fourteen years of labor migration to Qatar, where he worked as an accountant and she as a nursery school teacher. Returning home on annual, two-month vacations to Egypt, they finally succeeded with a twin pregnancy on their third trial of ICSI—a pregnancy that would have never occurred without Qatari money. According to the wife, "Altogether, we've spent about LE 24,000 [$7,059]. Nobody in our position has LE 7,000 [$2,059]—if no work in Qatar!"

This tale—no labor migration, no money for IVF—was one I heard repeatedly, among both the middle-class and even among the upper-middle-class couples who had become relatively affluent as a result of extended periods of work outside of the country. Of the sixty-six women patients I interviewed in 1996, eighteen of them had labor-migrant husbands, and in most of these cases, the wives lived with their spouses abroad, sometimes also working there as Egyptian expatriates. The primary host country was Saudi Arabia (ten of the eighteen total), but a number of couples lived in the smaller Gulf countries of Oman, the United Arab Emirates, Qatar, and even Yemen (which, unlike the other countries, is not known for its exceptional wealth). In some cases, the labor migration had preceded the discovery of the couple's infertility. But in other cases, couples had chosen to become expatriates precisely to generate the money needed for infertility treatment, including IVF. This was true even among a number of physician couples I interviewed, who had decided to join ranks of the large expatriate Egyptian medical community working in the Gulf in order to generate the cash reserves they knew would be needed to undertake IVF "back home."

But this begs the question of why Egyptian labor migrants to the Gulf—and especially to Saudi Arabia, where there were at least ten IVF centers as of 1996—feel the need to return home to undertake test-tube baby making. There seem to be three major reasons. The first might best be called (in a play on words) "ex-patriotism"—namely, most of these Egyptian expatriates feel a kind of patriotic attachment to their home country and prefer to return to Egypt for something as momentous as creating a "baby of the tubes." Often, this attachment to home was couched during interviews in the language of "psychological comfort." But several patients pointed out that, because new reproductive technologies in the Middle East arrived in Egypt first, IVF was bound to be more "professional" and "advanced" in Egypt, where these technologies had a longer history and the doctors were more "experienced." A second concern (although I was unable to confirm whether this was true or not) had to do with Egyptian expatriates being turned away at IVF centers in the Gulf, given the prioritization of Arab Gulf nationals as patients on waiting lists that had developed at some centers there. Finally, Egyptian expatriates were savvy about costs, and virtually all of them had concluded (rightly so) that IVF was significantly less expensive in Egypt than in the Arab Gulf. Summing up many of these concerns, an Egyptian couple who had lived in Abu Dhabi for fifteen years but had come back to Egypt to undergo their first trial of ICSI described their feelings as follows:

> He: They said in Abu Dhabi that ICSI is newly introduced. ICSI, for LE 25,000 [$7,353]. It's a very new center. We just heard about it.
>
> She: But we trust more here. We believe in Egypt more.
>
> He: All the doctors in Abu Dhabi, most are Egyptians or different nationalities. But they are not very experienced there. Only one or two years ago they started this IVF center. How many cases do they get? The total population is only 1 million in the United Arab Emirates, and Abu Dhabi is only twelve thousand. So here [in Egypt], there are 60 million, which means they are much more experienced.
>
> She: You read about [IVF and ICSI] here in Egypt. A lot of details in magazines and newspapers, on the TV, all the time.
>
> He: It's cheaper here, and much more professional. Because the period they started here was about five years ago.

Another Egyptian couple, living in Riyadh, Saudi Arabia, for ten years, argued that because test-tube baby making is "older in Egypt than in Saudi Arabia," its success in Egypt is probably greater. Furthermore, they explained that the closest IVF center in Saudi Arabia was in Jiddah, one thousand kilometers away from their home in Riyadh. Ultimately, the logistics of getting across the desert to Jiddah were just as, if not more, complicated than getting back to Cairo. Given considerations of cost, professional experience, and the logistics of treatment, they surmised that most Egyptians working in the Gulf would prefer to return directly to Egypt, rather than explore the possibility of undertaking IVF in the host country.

These considerations—reduced costs, professional experience, and the logistics of travel—are the same reasons why many Gulf Arabs decide to take their own IVF trials in Egypt, where they are prominent in IVF clinics by virtue of their distinctive national garb. Among Gulf Arabs, Egypt is a frequent destination of summer travel, where the air-conditioned luxury hotels and apartment complexes in places like Cairo and Alexandria are known to cater to wealthy Middle Easterners from other countries. However, Egypt is also a frequent destination of Arab patients who come to Egypt to seek treatment, as well as Arab physicians who come to Egyptian universities for advanced medical training.[24] Because of a long tradition of Egyptian medical education and because of the concomitant availability of resources and facilities, "Egyptian medicine is highly valued by people in other Arab countries."[25]

Not surprisingly, then, Cairo, Egypt, has become known as an excellent destination for IVF treatment seeking among infertile Arab Gulf couples, for many of the same reasons expressed by expatriate Egyptians. As one Kuwaiti woman in this study explained,

> Egypt has a very good reputation in IVF. IVF succeeds in Egypt more than in Kuwait. All the people in Kuwait know that, and one who becomes pregnant while in Egypt, they know it's a "baby of the tubes." Most [Kuwaiti] people would try IVF in Kuwait, but they have only one center in Kuwait City, and you have to wait three to four months for an appointment. So some people went to America, sometimes they go to London, and some to Egypt. People who are infertile try any way they can. But here is better [than London]. Here you don't feel strange *at all*, and the cost is less.

This transnational movement of IVF-seeking infertile couples—both Arab Gulf nationals and Egyptian expatriates—back and forth from the Arab Gulf has engendered some interesting dynamics and complications. For one, it has made the hot summer months of May, June, July, August, and September—when most Egyptian expatriates also take their one- to two-month annual vacations to escape the truly blistering heat of the Arabian peninsula—the busiest period at most of the established IVF centers in Cairo. When I first set foot in an Egyptian IVF center in late May 1996, I was amazed to see the large number of patients, including some distinct foreigners, squeezed like sardines into the available seats lining the walls of the clinic waiting room. Although other IVF centers had more seating space and hence less

congestion, the two centers in which I worked in the summer of 1996 were perpetually busy with both local patients and the overload of patients flocking in from the
Gulf. When I asked Dr. Yehia about this, he told me that, in his clinic, he encourages
his local Egyptian patients to delay their trials until after the summer months, if at
all possible, until the Egyptian expatriates and Gulf Arabs have a chance to return to
the Gulf. This had engendered a surprising finding in his clinic—November 1995
had been the "busiest month" in the prior year, probably because of all of the Egyptian locals who had delayed their IVF/ICSI trials until the fall.

For Egyptian expatriates, however, annual IVF vacations back home were far
from restful holidays with family and friends who had been missed over the previous year. Instead, these IVF vacations were periods of high stress. Adding to the financial burden of treatment were the logistical pressures of being able to complete
an IVF or ICSI trial in record time. Many of these patients described how they prepared themselves in advance of the vacation—contacting Egyptian IVF centers in
the spring, faxing their medical records to Egyptian IVF doctors, and often buying
the required hormonal medications from pharmacies in the host country. In some
cases, Egyptian IVF doctors even requested that the woman begin taking the hormonal medications while still in the Gulf in order to expedite matters back in Egypt,
where time would be very limited. Furthermore, many patients described making an
almost direct beeline to the IVF center once they set foot in Cairo. And each subsequent day of the vacation involved trips to the pharmacy for injections or to the IVF
center for ultrasound monitoring and the IVF and ICSI procedures themselves. If
there was failure at any step along the way, this meant canceling or ending the trial—
but without enough vacation time left over to try again until the following year. In
other words, for many couples, the brief window of opportunity afforded by a one-
month vacation back in Egypt was simply not long enough, serving to severely limit
their opportunities for undertaking IVF. One couple described it as our "once a year
chance." Another compared it, more bluntly, to "having sex once a year."

For the lucky few expatriates who did become pregnant during an IVF holiday,
they were then faced with the decision about what to do during the following nine
months. Some decided to quit their jobs and stay in Egypt, in order to have the pregnancy monitored and the baby delivered there. Others decided to remain apart during the pregnancy, so that the husband could return to his job in the Gulf. Although
the pregnant woman was usually surrounded by family back in Egypt, the separation of the couple during this period of uncertainty (usually involving intense fears
about the well-being of the precious fetus) was considered far from ideal. Or, in a
decision that was usually very uncomfortable for those who had literally waited
years for a child, they felt "forced" to return together to their jobs in the Gulf—placing themselves in the care of a physician in the Gulf and ultimately birthing their
test-tube babies abroad. In some cases, couples returned to the Gulf together for the
duration of the pregnancy, but then requested an "emergency vacation" so that they
could return to Egypt to have the baby delivered by their IVF physician.

All in all, the logistics of labor migration, and the ensuing complications of
transnational test-tube baby making, take their toll on the middle-class couples for

whom expatriatism is a financial necessity. In my study, this was revealed most clearly in the case of a couple who had returned to Egypt from Yemen in order to be present at the birth of a test-tube baby belonging to his brother and sister-in-law. The husband was a physician and the wife a nurse, and they had worked together as a health care team in a remote Yemeni town for nearly nine years. When his brother, also an expatriate physician in Saudi Arabia and also suffering from male infertility, underwent a successful trial of ICSI during a holiday back in Egypt, his brother convinced him to try the procedure under the care of Dr. Yehia at Nozha Hospital. Thus, when I met this couple at Dr. Yehia's clinic, they were in the middle of an ICSI trial, and they were also assisting some infertile friends (also expatriates in Yemen) whom they had persuaded to come back to Egypt. In other words, by talking with only one couple, I was ultimately able to learn the labor migration stories and treatment trajectories of three separate infertile Egyptian couples—all of them middle-class expatriates and all of them deeply immersed in the world of test-tube baby making.

In the case of my direct informants, the physician and his wife living in Yemen, they were at odds over what they should do next. The husband wanted to return to Yemen where, after only a year, he could obtain Yemeni nationality.

> Maybe this will benefit us. Because I can get private work, get good money for us. Now, I'm on a fixed salary, which is not good. There's not a lot of money in Yemen, but it's better than Egypt. It's also a poor country, not like Saudi Arabia. But I was recently married when I first went there—no good house, not a good car—and I wanted to emigrate to get more money.

After nearly a decade in a remote Yemeni outpost, he realized that his Egyptian wife, who had successfully secured a nursing position at Nozha Hospital, was loath to return to their foreign home. When she stepped out of the room, he explained,

> She is insisting about doing IVF here. She doesn't want to return to Yemen. But I want to travel back to Yemen. I'm losing lots of money, staying here to finish IVF. Maybe even if she gets pregnant, I'll return to Yemen. In Yemen, there is money, but no good doctors. In Egypt, there is education about medicine, but no money.

Indeed, if there *were* more money in Egypt—and hence better salaries for middle-class professionals like this physician and his nurse wife—then the Egyptian "brain drain" described in this section would certainly abate dramatically. But until that time, infertile middle-class Egyptian professionals will be forced to make complex decisions about the importance and value of a test-tube baby in their own lives and to assess which costs of making that baby they are able to endure.

The Upper Class

Given the economic exclusion of both the poor and much of the nonmigrating middle class from the Egyptian IVF treatment scene, it should come as no surprise that test-tube baby making is widely perceived in Egypt as being "only for the rich." As one poor woman, an ICSI charity case, explained it, "None of the lower classes reach this hospital. Only rich people reach here. It's only for rich people, or people able to spend money. It's not even for the middle class." But, she added, insisting that I express her own gratitude through the book I would write, "They [the doctors at Nile Badrawi Hospital] sympathize with people from the middle class, and people like us who are not able to pay the whole cost."

This commonly held conviction—that IVF is limited to the affluent in a country where the costs of IVF are unbelievably expensive for the average Egyptian—is, in fact, an accurate one. It serves to explain why the typical IVF patient presenting to the Egyptian IVF clinics in which I worked in 1996 was an upper-middle to upper-class woman whose husband had consented to the procedure. Again, judging by accounts of women's occupations, educations, lifestyles, and financial matters disclosed during interviews, I would estimate that twenty-four of the sixty-six women I met in Egyptian IVF centers in 1996—or more than one-third (36 percent)—were at least upper-middle class if not truly rich by Egyptian standards. And the remaining seventeen women—or one-quarter (26 percent)—were clearly members of the upper class, estimated by Ibrahim to constitute only 1 percent of Egyptian society as a whole.[26] Thus, taken together, elite women—both the secure and the rich, to use the terms of Ibrahim's Cairene class stratification scheme described earlier—represented, based on my admittedly unscientific economic classification scheme, nearly two-thirds (62 percent) of those women trying to become Egyptian mothers of test-tube babies in my study. Clearly, then, the rich *are* significantly overrepresented in Egyptian IVF centers, given that the upper tip of the Egyptian class pyramid is a small one indeed.

Although many of these well-to-do women had wealthy professional or entrepreneurial husbands, as in the case of Georgette and Mikhail, the vast majority did not derive their class position exclusively from marriage to a rich man. Instead, most of them were high-class professional women in their own right. In marked contrast to my earlier study at Shatby Hospital, where 80 percent of the one hundred poor infertile women I interviewed described themselves as housewives, only three of the thirty-six women who discussed their occupations with me in my 1996 study described themselves as such. Instead, these women were currently or recently employed (only five women described themselves as unemployed, largely because of employment disruptions due to labor migration). And, as a group, their jobs were impressive. They included accountants, physicians, pharmacists, dentists, lawyers, professors, engineers, architects, bankers, private school teachers, international travel agents and tour guides, translators, personnel directors, senior auditors, several employees of American institutions in Cairo (e.g., USAID and American University in Cairo), several private business owners, one maker of Tiffany lamps, and even one movie star. Not surprisingly, these women were highly educated—some having taken their degrees at Cairo's exclusive American University—and more than half of them spoke English, often fluently and rapidly, even employing Western idioms. (Several women also spoke French.) When I encountered elite women such as these at their appointments in IVF centers, they were usually dressed quite fashionably—including in flattering "Islamic" outfits with color-coordinated veils (actually just headscarves covering the hair and neck). Many of them also wore what would be considered by American standards to be ostentatious amounts of jewelry, including diamond rings and significant numbers of gold bracelets, necklaces, and earrings.

Although career satisfaction was not a focus of our interviews together, several of these women volunteered how much their own careers meant to them, and in at least a few cases, these women had gone against strong Egyptian norms by delaying childbearing until their careers were well established. As one thirty-eight-year-old architect, married for nine years, explained,

> At first I didn't think at all about children. On the contrary, I didn't want a child for the first four years, so we used the "safe period.". . . At that time, I was working for a French company, which completed [two major architectural projects in Egypt]. These two big projects for my firm were ending, so I had no work in Egypt. The company offered me work in France, but that was impossible because my husband has his own private [architectural] firm in Cairo. So I've been "on vacation" since February 1. My husband said, "You were working too much. Maybe you didn't become pregnant from your way of living." Maybe because I was always very tired. But I loved my career.

Other women told how their careers provided them with a valuable outlet—and a sense of self-esteem—in the face of the demoralization of infertility. As one woman, also married for nine years, stated,

> I have a career. I'm a senior auditor in a private company. I have a beautiful house and a loving husband. Of course, we were longing for children, and sometimes he felt demoralized [over his serious male infertility problem], but I rarely discussed this with him. I said, "It's God's will, and it will not change anything by feeling depressed. It will only increase the problems."

As revealed in this woman's comments, being a successful professional did not mitigate her "longing for children." And this represents one of the most crucial differences between the lives of infertile women in Egypt, including those of the upper class, and the lives of infertile women in the West. Although infertile Western women may also long for children, Western women in general have the "option" to remain "child-free," or what is sometimes referred to as "voluntarily childless," by pursuing meaningful careers *instead of* motherhood.[27] On the contrary, in Egypt—as in much of the rest of the pronatalist, developing world—motherhood is culturally compulsory, even for educated professionals. And, in the Muslim Middle East, such motherhood always goes hand in hand with marriage, the institutional vehicle through which women attempt to achieve entrance into what Bouhdiba has called, appropriately, the "cult of motherhood."[28] Thus, no matter a woman's career aspirations, or even her inherent desire for children, she has little choice *but* to pursue motherhood, including through the assistance of new reproductive technologies if she has the financial means to do so.

Without question, the forty-one upper-middle-class to upper-class women in this study had the financial means to participate in the world of test-tube baby making, both in and outside of Egypt. Whereas the middle-class Egyptians described in the previous section were forced to migrate outside the country *in order to obtain the means* to make a baby of the tubes back home, many upper-middle-class and upper-class Egyptians in this study were migrating to Europe and the United States *in order to actually make* test-tube babies, often returning to Egypt only when transnational treatment attempts had failed them. Indeed, this kind of "therapeutic transnationalism"—international, boundary-crossing treatment seeking that has been relatively poorly studied by medical anthropology scholars—is one of the most typical features of test-tube baby making among Egyptian elites, and is part of a larger Middle Eastern phenomenon of international medical migration in the face of extraordinary health problems.[29] As transnationally sophisticated individuals who may have lived, studied, or worked in the West, the therapeutic vistas of infertile Egyptian elites extend well beyond the borders of Egypt—where, they fear, infertility treatment may not be as "advanced" as in Western countries. As a result, many of them have used their own assets to make sometimes extensive international medical migrations for the sole purpose of undertaking repeated treatment attempts, including IVF. Those who have not made such medical pilgrimages to European or American IVF centers have usually considered doing so, and they have often inquired about the logistical details from friends or family living abroad, or from other wealthy acquaintances who have tried IVF outside the country.

To be more specific, of the forty-one elite patient couples in this study, one-third (fourteen, or 34 percent) had either undertaken some sort of infertility-related treatment, including the use of new reproductive technologies, in Europe or the United States, or had come very close to doing so on trips to Europe for that purpose. For example, in one case, a couple affected by very severe male infertility began in the mid-1980s to make regular trips to London for both diagnostic tests (including testicular biopsies) and hoped-for treatment. However, the husband's case was considered "very severe," with no chance for treatment "even by IVF." With the introduction of ICSI in Europe in the early 1990s, the couple eventually returned to England to undertake ICSI at a hospital in Nottingham. Unfortunately, by this point, the wife had turned forty, and when she attempted to become a patient at the British hospital, she was refused on account of her advanced age (and the low likelihood of ICSI success). In despair, the couple returned to Egypt, where they had "lost all hope until last year." Then, they learned of the introduction of ICSI at Nile Badrawi Hospital. Although the wife had already turned forty-one, she was accepted as an ICSI patient at Nile Badrawi, where, at the time of my interview with her, she had spent LE 40,000 ($11,764) on four unsuccessful ICSI attempts.

Several of the other elite couples in my study—nine to be exact—had considered trying IVF or ICSI abroad or had friends or acquaintances who were encouraging them to do so. But, like the Coptic merchants Georgette and Mikhail, most of these couples were reluctant to actually make such a medical pilgrimage, for reasons ranging from the logistical to the moral. As with middle-class labor migrants whose Egyptian patriotism emerged in their desires to return to Egypt for test-tube baby making, many upper-class Egyptians also spoke of the increased "psychological comfort" of test-tube baby making in their own country. One Egyptian woman, married to a German man, had considered undergoing ICSI in his home country. But, she complained, "In Germany, it's one, two, three. In you go, out you go. Doctors are not understanding in Europe. You're treated more humanely here. I feel comfort here." Another woman, with a cousin living in Wisconsin, stated,

> I will try my third trial [in Egypt], and if it fails, maybe I'll go to England, or to my cousin living in the USA. You know, we sometimes think abroad is always better than Egypt, but really, I told my husband, "I'm satisfied with this place. They're doing their maximum."

Another well-to-do woman, who with her husband ran a successful Egyptian tourist business, relayed multiple doubts about undergoing IVF in Europe.

> When I went to France, the doctor there was surprised we are very developed in infertility medicine in Egypt. I had the possibility to go to England, France, Germany for IVF, but I refused, because in Egypt, we have what we need. My husband prefers to do [IVF] outside Egypt, but I convinced him, if we will have success to have a baby, it will be here in Egypt. First, it's easier to do here. If I think I'm "outside" without my mother, my friends, even my spouse, it would be difficult. Also, I heard a man can "buy his sperms." They can give her donor sperm. Or a couple can give another woman ova and hormones and she can carry the baby for nine months. Surrogacy. These things I'm afraid of, because morals are *very, very, very* important. In an Egyptian hospital, they pay attention to this, the husband and wife and the doctor. Here, we have trust in the doctor. And I know outside Egypt, it's *very, very, very* expensive—three times [as expensive]. For us in Egypt, it's still expensive here, but between the two of us, we can pay.

This kind of comparative cost analysis is a decisive factor in the decision making of even wealthy Egyptian couples, whose wealth is relative in global terms. To take but one example: One upper-middle-class woman, who worked as a banker and whose husband was a sales manager for a private electrical cable firm (and who was also starting his own business in the evening hours), explained how she and her husband's combined monthly income of LE 2,500 was a "huge" salary by Egyptian standards. This money allowed them to afford an upper-middle-class lifestyle (including a large apartment in an affluent suburb, a car, and the services of two maids, one daily and one weekly). But, even with careful budgeting of their monthly income, they were finding it difficult to accrue enough savings to easily purchase repeated trials of IVF, given that the cost of one trial was four times their combined monthly income. Thus, they had turned to family aid to help finance their repeated IVF trials.

> My mother is a wealthy woman, but I can't ask her every time for money. The last time, she paid LE 10,000 [for a trial of IVF]. She has no husband and she lives off her interest, but I can't push her every month. Per trial it is LE 10,000, and you know something, this is my mother's expression, "LE 10,000 is in the toilet" [when the treatment fails].

This woman also realized that her household income, $735 a month, would place them at or below the poverty line in the United States. In other words, many upper-middle-class infertile couples who are well-off by Egyptian standards realize that their wealth may buy them relatively little on the global IVF stage. In the case of this woman, she had assessed the costs of IVF abroad because of her close friendship with another wealthy infertile woman, who had undertaken IVF fourteen times, finally succeeding in delivering a healthy test-tube baby only two months prior to our interview. "She made it here, and in Saudi Arabia, and in London," my informant explained. "She spent—we made an estimate of LE 250,000 ($73,530). So I know how much more expensive it is abroad."

This single factor—the high cost of IVF in the West, and even other parts of the Middle East—is certainly one of the most compelling reasons why many Egyptian elites decide to try their reproductive luck at home in an Egyptian IVF center. In fact, in global terms, new reproductive technologies in Egypt are a real bargain, or, as one grateful patient put it, "the lowest cost in the world," given that the prices of hormonal medications and the procedures themselves have been dramatically adjusted by reproductive technology manufacturers and IVF doctors to make them more realistic for Egyptians. If the price tags for these technologies were any higher, even Egyptian elites might be unable to afford them, putting Egyptian IVF centers out of business. Although comparative global cost estimates have never been compiled or published, the differences in the cost of IVF between Egypt and the United States are striking. In Egypt in 1996, a single trial of IVF, including medications, seemed to average between LE 6,000 ($1,765) and LE 8,000 ($2,353). For ICSI, the cost was between LE 8,000 ($2,353) and LE 10,000 ($2,941). By comparison, a study of 266 American IVF centers published in 1995 found the average charge for an IVF cycle in 1993 (adjusted for the fact that some cycles are never completed) to be $6,233,[30] or more than three times the rate in Egypt. However, in the United States, *unadjusted* charges per IVF cycle, including the costs of medications (at more than $2,000), put the mean cost at $7,861, or closer to four times the Egyptian rate. Moreover, this does not account for the fact that there is wide variation in prices *between* U.S. clinics, some of which may charge well over $10,000 per cycle. In the United States, furthermore, the computed cost of a single live birth from IVF treatment (given the need for repeated cycles) was in excess of $40,000, or the equivalent of LE 136,000. While such costs are increasingly being covered by the United States insurance industry, thereby allowing middle-class and even working-class American women to access new reproductive technologies,[31] an Egyptian woman who could afford to travel to the United States to undertake IVF would pay for these services directly—and dearly—without the benefit of insurance coverage. For most Egyptians, even the ultra wealthy, such costs are prohibitive and make many of them think twice before they become reproductive actors on the global stage. In short, even members of the upper echelons of Egyptian society experience economic constraints that limit their ability to "choose" new reproductive technologies freely in the global marketplace.

Nonetheless, back home in Egypt, many elites also deem test-tube baby making to be very expensive, given the likelihood of repeated trials. In fact, I was impressed by the unexpected candor of elite women, who were more than willing to "talk money" with me. In my interviews with fifty-one women, mostly of the upper-middle to upper class,[32] I was provided with amazingly precise details of how much money these women (and their husbands) had already spent on test-tube baby making, both the medications and the IVF/ICSI procedures themselves. Of this group, only four women had, to date, spent less than LE 5,000. The majority (twenty-seven women to be exact) had spent between LE 5,000 and LE 9,999, usually on a single trial. Nine others, mostly women who had undergone the more expensive ICSI, had spent between LE 10,000 and LE 14,999. But then there were the "repeaters": the five women who had spent between LE 15,000 and 24,000 on two to four trials, and the six women, such as Georgette, who had spent between LE 40,000 and LE 100,000 on four to six trials of IVF or ICSI.

Furthermore, many informants contextualized these high costs in terms of how much they'd already spent on other forms of "useless" infertility treatment. And many women expressed their "shock" and dismay over the high price of the imported medications that they were forced to purchase (often with considerable difficulty, as will be seen in Chapter 7) at LE 1,000–LE 2,000 per IVF trial. Patients who had visited more than one Egyptian IVF clinic also compared the prices they had paid or were quoted at different centers, and those who had undergone more than one trial described how the prices charged for IVF and ICSI had continually increased in Egypt over time. Yet, many women were grateful for the small discounts they were given for being repeaters (e.g., 10 percent at Nozha Hospital) or for using already frozen embryos (and thereby avoiding ovulation induction costs and laboratory fees). As one woman, who had undergone IVF three times over a four-year period, explained to me in the kind of detail that was quite typical in my discussions with women at IVF centers:

> It's not a problem of money for me, because I worked before marriage, and my husband has a good job. But not everyone can do [IVF]. The hospital now charges LE 3,000 [for IVF]. The Pergonal [a hormonal medication] costs LE 900. I spent more than LE 100 per day on Pergonal. LE 36 per injection times twenty-five injections over fifteen days. I spent LE 250 on Superfact [another hormonal medication]. The total comes to LE 4,186. This is very expensive! Not everyone can do [it]. And every time is more expensive

than before. In 1992, Pergonal was only LE 25 per injection. The hospital was LE 2,000, and that was because they made a discount for me because I repeated. This time, they made a discount from LE 3,500 to LE 3,000 because of my repeating.

Indeed, if there was one factor that separated upper-middle-class couples from upper-class ones in this study it was the degree to which they could sustain repeated trials of IVF or ICSI. In virtually all of my interviews, I asked women (and those husbands who were present) whether money was an issue for them. Among the twenty-four upper-middle-class women, two-thirds of them complained, sometimes bitterly, about the expenses surrounding IVF and ICSI, and many worried about their personal ability to pay over time for repeated trials. This was in marked contrast to the sixteen truly wealthy women in this study, who may have viewed IVF and ICSI as expensive, but who said they could afford to repeat the operation many times, including overseas if necessary. Thus, the degree to which subtle differences in class status affected even elite Egyptians' utilization of new reproductive technologies was striking and was reflected in the stories and comments of upper-middle-class versus upper-class women.

For example, one upper-middle-class physician, who conceived twin sons naturally following six unsuccessful trials of IVF, described how she eventually "ran out of money" and was forced to finance her final trial of IVF, at about LE 11,000 ($3,235), through the sale of all of her gold jewelry. Another upper-middle-class lawyer described how she could only afford three trials of IVF, then she would have to stop in order to rebuild her savings. Fortunately for her, she became pregnant on her second trial of IVF, and joked, "He'll be the most precious child. I'll tell him, 'You don't know how I suffered for you, and you cost us a lot!'"

Upper-class women, on the other hand, often prefaced their remarks with "*El-hamdu-lillah*" (praise be to God) when they went on to describe how "money was no problem" for them personally. Many of them were frank about their affluence, commenting on their "good jobs," "good businesses," and "families with money." As one upper-class woman described her situation, in a self-consciously comparative manner,

> It's not expensive for me, but it's expensive for a poor one. It may reach LE 1 million ($294,118) before I'm done, because every time, they [the doctors] take LE 5,000 to LE 10,000. Not everyone can do this, but for me and my husband, there are no problems. My husband has very good work.

Likewise, the wealthy women and men in this study, such as Georgette and Mikhail, sometimes justified their need for repeated trials of IVF or ICSI by virtue of their need for heirs to whom they could pass on family businesses and fortunes. One woman, whose husband was a wealthy building contractor, asked me pointedly during a lengthy interview: "Do you believe there are *very* rich people here in Egypt?" When I shrugged my shoulders to indicate my uncertainty, she replied,

There *are* very rich people here in Egypt. Do you see all these Mercedes? People who come to such centers don't like to have children *just* to have children. They care to have children *from their wives* [i.e., biological children], because they care to leave money to them—*not* to be taken by just anybody from the family. *All* wealthy people care very much about inheritance, especially here when they're in this situation [of needing IVF or ICSI].

One wealthy husband, who had accompanied his wife to the IVF center, drew upon an oft-cited Qur'anic passage to justify his "need" for children:

In the Qur'an, it is said that "Money and children are the most precious thing in the world." Since we have money, we are able to search for children. It's not reasonable to have money and be deprived from having children. So we don't think of the money at all.

Conclusion

Those IVF patients who "don't think of the money at all" are the privileged few—the wealthy upper crust of Egyptian society for whom the costs of IVF are not at all constraining. For the rest, the financial costs of test-tube baby making are among the major limitations, preventing the infertile poor from undertaking IVF altogether, forcing the middle-class infertile to migrate in order to undertake one-shot attempts at IVF, and even limiting the upper-middle class in their ability to repeat the procedure indefinitely or to go abroad if Egyptian IVF clinics fail them.

As such, test-tube baby making in Egypt is an exclusive and exclusionary business, serving to prevent many Egyptian test-tube babies from ever being made. That the babies of the affluent *do* get made—and I doted over many of these babies in Egyptian IVF centers during 1996—is a reality that has not been lost on infertile Egyptian "poor folk." Although their needs for children have nothing to do with passing on family fortunes, poor Egyptians have both ardent desires and ardent love for children and are able to articulate often quite poetically the multilayered meanings and joys of having children in their lives.[33] Yet, their legitimate needs for test-tube babies are rarely if ever met in Egyptian IVF centers today, which are private affairs, intended for the privileged few who can afford to have children by any means.

Thus, test-tube baby making in Egypt serves as an example par excellence of the limits on reproductive agency posed by class structures in a truly class-stratified, resource-poor, Third World society. In the world of Egyptian test-tube baby making, the only ones who are financially able to receive the largesse of globalization are Egyptian elites, who often resemble elites of other societies more than their own Egyptian brethren. And though these elites may take pity on those who have been excluded from the ranks of would-be test-tube baby makers, their pity has never been turned into activist attempts or private philanthropic efforts to somehow increase access to IVF services in the country. Thus, when all is said and done, economic structures impinge emphatically upon reproductive agency in Egypt, posing perhaps the major arena of constraint in the world of Egyptian test-tube baby making. As one poor woman, without a prayer in the world of ever overcoming her tubal blockage through IVF, concluded sadly:

> As IVF becomes more expensive, it will not be widespread. Because it is becoming more and more expensive, it is limited to a few, mostly the affluent. Of course, the *biggest problem* with IVF is economic. See how crowded this [infertility] clinic is? There are *many* infertile people in Egypt. But, like me, it's out of the question for them to do IVF. In my opinion, [IVF] *must* be made more available. When someone wants to have a family, they'll sell even their own clothes. So, if [IVF] were more available, just try to count how many happy people there would be.

CHAPTER 3

Knowledge

The Oasis Dwellers

Mabruka is a plump, veiled woman from the Egyptian oasis community of Fayoum. For most of her five and a half years of marriage, she has been trying to figure out the *real* reason why she cannot become pregnant. Mabruka wants to know, but feels she lacks knowledge of her "case," including the various hormonal treatments and reproductive technologies that have been tried out on her recalcitrant, "weak" body.

As Mabruka tries to reconstruct the history of her problem, she recounts how, in the early part of her marriage, she had "some infections," for which she underwent cervical electrocautery (an outdated and even dangerous procedure that is nonetheless widely performed by Egyptian gynecologists). She also suffered from an irregular period, which the doctors she visited in Fayoum could not seem to fix. After two years of ineffective therapies, Mabruka boldly embarked on the first of what was to become a regular, three-year stint of monthly, bimonthly, and even weekly trips to Cairo, a city within a day's roundtrip of Fayoum, where Mabruka hoped she would find some answers and a solution to her childlessness.

The gynecologist she consulted, Dr. Mohammed Fayad, requested a semen analysis from Mabruka's husband, Ragab, and performed hormonal assays and ultrasound scans on Mabruka's reproductive body. No male infertility problem was detected in Ragab's semen profile. However, Dr. Fayad diagnosed ovulatory-factor infertility in Mabruka, namely, lack of regular ovulation. Not completely understanding Dr. Fayad's medical explanation for the infertility, Mabruka translated his message into the more familiar cultural idiom of "weakness." As is common among lesser-educated Egyptians, Mabruka glossed her problem as "weak ovaries" and believed that even the eggs in her ovaries (as shown to her on ultrasound scans) were "weak" and defective.

When Mabruka's ovulatory problem proved intractable, Dr. Fayad referred her to Dr. Salah Zaki, the chief attending physician at Nile Badrawi Hospital's IVF center. Mabruka is now a regular patient of Dr. Zaki's, and although she says she trusts him completely, Mabruka remains convinced that there *must* be something more seriously wrong with her reproductively defective body. Otherwise, she would have become pregnant during her five-and-a-half year marriage to Ragab.

"I was just speaking to him [Dr. Zaki] about my problem," Mabruka commented to me during an interview in a consulting room adjacent to Dr. Zaki's office.

> And I asked him if it was *really* weakness. He said, "I keep telling you [that] it's *only* weakness in your ovaries. Do you want me to swear?" And he told me there's improvement after he doubled my treatment this month. But my husband's sister doesn't believe that it's *only* weakness after five years [of marriage]. They don't believe me.

"They," in this case, refers to Ragab's family members, who are beginning to doubt that Mabruka's infertility problem will ever be solved and constantly remind Mabruka that Ragab wishes to have children. Ragab himself has started to act differently toward Mabruka and, on occasion, has exploded in anger over his frustration with the situation and the large amounts of money Mabruka seems to be wasting on futile treatment attempts. Like most other lower-class Egyptian men, Ragab does not participate actively in Mabruka's treatment quest and, in fact, has often proven to be an obstacle to that quest—particularly when Mabruka was referred to an IVF unit, where he feared his own sperm might be "mixed" with that of other men. As Mabruka explained:

> At first, he refused *completely*. He said, "It [the sperm] may not be mine." This was his way of thinking. Then I convinced him. I told him some people did it, and they became pregnant—many people who suffered from this [infertility]. How would the doctors do this mixing of sperm with everyone?
>
> Most people here are afraid of artificial insemination. Everyone has his own way of thinking, but most people are afraid of mixing, mistakes being made. It is possible to mix sperm from different men, which is why, of course, you must trust the doctor. Here [at Nile Badrawi Hospital], they are very good and kind, and I feel comfortable with them.
>
> I also heard Dr. Attia Sa'a on TV. He's very famous for giving *fatwas* [religious opinions on the permissibility of various practices]. One of the women asked him about the religious opinion on artificial insemination. And I heard the answer. He said that if the injection is from the husband, it is not *haram* [sinful]. That's what made *me* convinced. It was on a Friday morning show, but my husband wasn't watching.

Eventually, however, with gentle persuasion and the intervention of Ragab's only educated sister, Mabruka finally gained Ragab's permission to undergo artificial insemination using his own sperm. He even made the unusual sacrifice of missing a day's work in order to accompany Mabruka from their oasis community to the Cairo hospital for semen collection prior to artificial insemination using his own sperm (AIH). Unfortunately, however, two attempts at AIH have failed, for reasons that Mabruka does not clearly understand.

The next step, Mabruka knows, is IVF—a procedure that is not accepted by members of Mabruka's oasis community, where most adults are poorly educated and of lower-class status. What information they do have tends to be *mis*information, which is why Ragab, for one, will not allow his wife to even consider what he believes would be an "out-of-body" pregnancy. Mabruka explained,

> I've heard about IVF. But once I mentioned it in front of my husband and he said, "No. Since [the baby's] not in your *buton* [stomach], it's not yours." I tried to prepare my husband for this, in case Dr. Salah [Zaki] recommended it for me. . . . And when I told my husband this, all he said was "No, this is not for us."
>
> I, myself, have no idea how IVF is done. I don't know what it is. I told him, "I think they take a sample from you and a sample from me, and they put them together, then they'll have an embryo." But I don't really know how they do it. He also doesn't know anything about IVF. And, frankly, I don't want to think about it, because it will be a bullet!

Mabruka considers her husband to have a "locked brain" on the subject of IVF. And, even if he would agree to it, Mabruka, who, like her husband, is a poorly paid government employee (with a salary of only LE 100 [$30] a month), doubts that they could ever afford the expense of even one trial, unless she were offered a deep discount as a charity case. Already, her husband is very angry over how much money he has spent on hormonal medications and transportation for Mabruka to and from Cairo (LE 25 per roundtrip).

> At the beginning, he was giving me this money easily when I would ask him. But now, he says he doesn't have any. He couldn't afford all of this money. I estimate I've spent about LE 5,000 altogether, and [motioning to her arm] I've sold off all of my [gold] bracelets.

Mabruka continued, sadly,

> In front of me, he tells me that he will support me until the last day of his life. But behind my back, he says, "I wish to have a baby." He doesn't want to embarrass me, but with his friends and those he feels close to, he says, "I wish to have a baby." He's the kind of man who adores children.
>
> When we married each other, he used to love me. But now it became very difficult because of this. I don't think of anything else [these days]. Only that I *need* to have a child, because I don't want to fight or be divorced. I'll take only one! Only one child to have a happy life.

The Problem of Knowledge

Mabruka suffers from intractable infertility, but she also suffers from significant problems of knowledge, including perceived lack of knowledge about her own infertility case, uncertain understandings of her reproductive biology, fragmentary knowledge of the reproductive technologies utilized in infertility cases such as hers, and the self-recrimination and doubt accompanying the knowledge that something "wrong with her" has held up her marital fertility and happiness. Yet, her own problems of knowledge seem, somehow, more tractable than those of her poorly educated, "traditional" husband, Ragab, who accepts neither Mabruka for who she is (with or without children) nor the new reproductive technologies that have become necessary to overcome her infertility. Ragab, whose misgivings about and misunderstandings of the new reproductive technologies are pronounced, is, according to Mabruka, fairly typical of their lower-income social class in a rural oasis community, members of whom remain deeply opposed to the morally questionable new reproductive technologies being tried in "big cities" like Cairo. Despite the medical and clerical authorities who have posed on television to publicly condone the use of these new reproductive technologies under limited circumstances such as Mabruka's, these public opinion leaders have yet to unseat deeply entrenched local systems of knowledge, which leave no room for reproductive technologies that disrupt so fundamentally notions of human procreation. Thus, knowledge itself—including its imbrication in class structure and its moral valence in Egypt—poses one of the most fundamental arenas of constraints on the utilization of new reproductive technologies among large segments of the rural and urban Egyptian underclass.

It is to this arena of knowledge that this chapter attends. Following recent debates and discussions in science studies, I hope to forward four main arguments in this chapter. First, despite the massive globalization of new reproductive technologies themselves, the accompanying science of assisted conception has not so easily spread around the world, including to the Middle East. In other words, in places like Egypt, there is potentially a profound disjuncture between the Western scientific knowledge system in which new reproductive technologies are wholly based and what might best be described as "local scientific knowledge systems," deeply embedded in Egyptian history, that are at odds with Western scientific orthodoxy.

This problem of "conflicting knowledge systems" has been well described in the anthropological anthology Naked Science, which provides several cogent examples of "clashing" belief systems. As the editor, Laura Nader, points out,

> During most of human history, there have been different ways of knowing and an enormous range of ways of understanding the world. Because the modern Western idea of science is a contemporary fact, the process of its demarcation, its construction, its dress, and how it fits as part of the dynamics of power are crucial to a critical understanding of the basis for modern knowledge about the world. For science is not only a means of categorizing the world, but of categorizing science itself in relation to other knowledge systems that are excluded.[1]

She goes on to argue that, despite the "extraordinary expansion of Western science" over the past three centuries, different scientific traditions, even among supposedly "scientifically illiterate," non-Western cultures, have not been displaced and, in fact, have much to offer to Westerners willing to engage in "different ways of looking at the world." Thus, even though modern Western science has a "silencing effect" by virtue of its claim as "universally applicable knowledge," its power to supplant site-specific, local knowledge systems has not been unchallenged. Local peoples have often resisted the global expansion and supposed omnipotence of Western science, which has operated on a core-periphery model whereby the spread of Western science to the world's margins is imagined as a "one-way street."[2] What anthropologists in particular have offered to technoscience studies are revealing portraits of how Western scientific hegemony itself has been resisted in local settings. Such challenges serve to demonstrate how science is both socially and culturally situated— deeply "influenced by its surroundings."[3]

In the particular case of the new reproductive technologies, it is imperative to recognize how these technologies are based in very Western notions of human reproductive biology—notions that have been assumed by Westerners (including, surprisingly, generations of Western anthropologists)[4] to be universal. Nonetheless, as shown in a number of recent, compelling anthropological studies from the Middle East,[5] notions of human procreation may take forms quite distinct from the Western version of dual biogenetic inheritance—or what anthropologist Emily Martin has called, so evocatively, the Western "romance of egg and sperm."[6] In Egypt, as in a number of other Middle Eastern societies including Israel,[7] popular scripts of human procreation do not necessarily involve this "romance," and may even be thought of as "egg free." That divergent theories of procreation introduce confusion and uncertainty into the world of test-tube baby making in Egypt should become clear in this chapter, helping to explain why men like Ragab argue that new reproductive technologies are "not for us."

A second major point of this chapter, one that follows from the first, is that current Western definitions of "scientific literacy" are inadequate on a number of counts. In *Science Matters: Achieving Scientific Literacy*, science literacy is defined as "the knowledge you need . . . to put new [scientific] advances into a context that will allow you to take part in the national debate about them."[8] However, as pointed out by Martin and her colleagues, this seemingly unproblematic definition is fundamentally flawed, especially when one considers the extremely "narrow and technocratic content of the knowledge" contained in *Science Matters* and most other (Western) books about science literacy.[9] They argue that the definition of scientific literacy needs to be broadened to include the existential, metaphysical, moral, political, and social knowledge that is *already* embedded in people's talk about science, and particularly their health and their bodies. By listening to "nonscientists"—"at all educational levels and from a variety of ethnic and socioeconomic settings"[10]— much can be learned about the imagery, metaphors, and the ways in which people use scientific "facts" in very different ways, making them "work with their particular local circumstances as well as express their most overarching views of the world."[11]

Furthermore, as argued by the feminist science critic Sandra Harding, we are all "inside" science, even those who appear to be "outside" its practice.[12] This would include women, racial and sexual minorities, and inhabitants of the least privileged parts of the globe. She argues that we must "start from the lives" of excluded others, for example, the lives of women, in order to understand how meanings are negotiated in specific ways, even in understanding science. Thus, definitions of science literacy that privilege the knowledge claims of a small minority (Euro/American, mostly male scientists) or that assume that acquisition of science literacy means absorption and mastery of a prescribed set of Western scientific "facts" must be challenged if science is to be "democratized."

Heeding this call for the democratization of science, Lynda Birke and Rosalind Whitworth, scholars studying Asian Muslim women in Britain, have argued forcefully through examples drawn from their own research that "women's attitudes toward, and understandings of, science and of what scientists do, is shaped by their gender, by their 'race,' and by many other cultural influences . . . [including] Islamic teachings in their local context. The *meanings* of scientific information are thus negotiated through their understandings of local culture and religious mores."[13] Birke and Whitworth go on to describe "epistemological communities," or local "communities of knowers," who, in the case of the women they studied, utilized their Muslim identity to negotiate the meanings of scientific information presented to them. These Asian Muslim women desired scientific information that they deemed relevant to their own lives (e.g., in the area of nutrition), but they were also deeply concerned with the ethical implications of modern science, particularly future directions in biotechnology (e.g., cloning).

In Egypt, as in Muslim communities in Britain, scientific knowledge has moral dimensions that appear to cut cross the divides of social class, educational level, and even religious affiliation. Thus, no matter one's degree of purported Western "scientific literacy" in the narrow sense of that term, Egyptians tend to contemplate new scientific developments in moral terms, often referring to their religion for guidance in the bioethical realm. Certainly, Egyptians such as Mabruka and Ragab, who are forced to contemplate the uses of new reproductive technologies in their own lives, make such moral judgments over whether such "assisted" forms of human conception are ethical. The importance of religion to the bioethical practice of new reproductive technologies is the subject of the next chapter. However, in this chapter, discussions of science knowledge and morality presage some of the predicaments posed by the new reproductive technologies for both religiously observant Muslims and Coptic Christians in Egypt, whose ethical dilemmas will be explicated more fully in Chapter 4.

A third main point of this chapter involves the acquisition of scientific literacy in the realm of test-tube baby making—namely, how Egyptians come to acquire knowledge about these technologies and how this knowledge affects their decision making. As I will argue, Egypt is a "mass-mediated" society[14] in which multiple forms of media have played a major role in introducing the new reproductive technologies to the public. As argued by Walter Armbrust in *Mass Culture and Modernism in Egypt*, "In the twentieth century, mass media has been an important means for disseminating modernist ideology in Egypt."[15] Yet, as Armbrust also points out, the "blind adoption of Western culture has never been an unambiguous or uncontested feature of modern Egypt."[16] In the realm of the new reproductive technologies, the Egyptian media have, at times, promoted the use of these technologies—thereby highlighting one of the ways in which "science is always advancing" in modern-day Egypt. But, at the same time, the media have warned of the dangers coming from the unfettered use of these technologies in the West. The moral discourse and cautionary tales about new reproductive technologies widely disseminated in the Egyptian media, including through popular cultural formats such as TV mini-series, leave many potential Egyptian consumers of these technologies both uneasy and misinformed in ways that may inhibit their utilization of these technologies.

Finally, this chapter demonstrates how consumers of new reproductive technologies, such as Mabruka, search for knowledge, just as they search for technologies to help them overcome their infertility problems. As infertile Egyptian Muslims are quick to explain, God creates illnesses, but he also creates solutions for these maladies, under the expectation that true believers will seek solutions to their suffering. Similarly, Islam enjoins believers to seek knowledge "from cradle to grave."[17] Thus, infertile women such as Mabruka are ardent consumers of information and often feel frustrated when they are impeded from acquiring knowledge about their medical conditions and treatments. This "desire to know" cuts across social classes, characterizing poor, illiterate women as much as it does elite, educated ones. However, as we'll see in this chapter, elite women are clearly advantaged in the multiple ways in which they acquire knowledge—and hence scientific literacy—about the nature of test-tube baby making itself. Nonetheless, even among elites, technical understandings of high-tech reproductive procedures are sometimes partial and incomplete. This then leads to questions about what "informed" really means when Egyptian patients sign informed consent forms, and it suggests that infertile patients may be particularly vulnerable to unrealistic and unfounded expectations about the ease and success of test-tube baby making.[18]

Problems of Procreative Knowledge

To begin with the first point—the problem of conflicting procreative knowledge systems—I would argue that in Egypt, one of the most fundamental constraints on the acceptance of IVF and the other new reproductive technologies has to do with major differences in knowledge about the human body and its procreative processes. This problem of procreative knowledge goes hand in hand with class constraints: Members of the urban and rural Egyptian lower class, such as Mabruka and Ragab, are often prevented by *both* their lack of access to capital and their deeply held beliefs about human reproduction from pursuing the new reproductive technologies to overcome their infertility. In other words, class-based knowledge in Egypt may conflict rather directly and profoundly with supposedly global—or at least rapidly globalizing—Western versions of reproductive biology that are assumed in the West to be self-evident and hence are taken for granted as "right" and "natural."

But why does local knowledge get in the way of IVF in Egypt? The very notion of duogenetic inheritance through equal contributions of eggs and sperm—a fairly recent scientific "fact" that did not emerge until the development of the microscope—is not the cultural script of procreation imagined by most lower-class Egyptians such as Mabruka and Ragab. Instead, among the often illiterate Egyptian masses, views of procreation are decidedly "monogenetic," a term first coined by anthropologist Carol Delaney in her work with Turkish villagers.[19] In rural Turkey, as in lower-class rural and urban areas of Egypt, it is men—and not men *and* women—who are thought to bring life into this world, a one-sided view of procreation that has been reported as well by other anthropologists working throughout the Middle Eastern region.[20] This notion that men create life—and, hence, that only fathers (and by extension, father's relatives) are the true "blood" relatives of their children in societies where blood lines and lineage are profoundly important cultural concepts—certainly serves to give men, and not women, biological "ownership" of their children. It also provides strong ideological support for the nearly universal presence of patrilineal kinship systems in this region of the Muslim world.[21]

In Egypt, such monogenetic theories of procreation can be shown to date back literally five thousand years to the pharaonic period.[22] Although a number of hegemonic medical traditions have come and gone in Egypt since that time, notions of monogenesis have been remarkably stable, receiving support within most of the literate medical traditions that existed in Egypt over thousands of years. Today, monogenetic models are alive and well among the Egyptian masses, who view men as literally creating life vis-à-vis preformed fetuses that they carry in their sperm and ejaculate into women's waiting wombs. Such "preformation models" hark back to early European biomedicine, when debates flared over whether preformed humans—sometimes referred to as "homunculuses," or "little men"—were carried in the woman's ovum (as declared by the "ovists") or in the man's sperm (as charged by the "animalculists").[23] Thus, at the time that European colonial biomedicine (first French and then British) was entering Egypt in the early part of the nineteenth century, preformation models were widely accepted in Europe; their arrival in Egypt lent considerable support to monogenetic models that had already existed in the country for thousands of years under pharaonic and *Yunani* (Greek) medical systems.[24]

Given this long history, the monogenetic preformation models forwarded by most lower-class rural and urban Egyptians today make sense. They also make these lesser-educated citizens "scientifically literate" in their own right. Indeed, the versions of procreation that they espouse have emerged from literate scientific traditions, including European ones, which have existed in Egypt since nearly 2000 B.C.[25]

Among lower-class Egyptians today, models of procreation are slowly changing as a result of increasing access to education, Western-style biomedicine, and exposure to health messages in the media. The model of procreation that is beginning to gain ground envisions women as "egg producers." Whereas "eggs" were absent in the popular versions of procreation just described, this newer duogenetic version of human procreation involves "eggs," or *buwaidat.* From this perspective, then, sperm alone are not sufficient to produce the fetus; eggs are also necessary. However, it is important to note that this expanding discourse of procreative eggs in Egypt receives varying expression, depending largely on educational and class background. Educated Egyptians from the lower-middle to upper classes, whose first exposure to Western-style human reproductive biology usually comes in junior high schools, are often well-versed in the duogenetic sperm-ovum union theory and are able to recite it in some detail. On the other hand, lesser-educated Egyptians—in a society where about 60 percent of all women and 38 percent of men remain illiterate[26]—are much less likely to espouse this view of women as egg producers. And even if they do conceive of procreation as a union of egg and sperm, they are likely to deem women's eggs as much less important, either contributing "less than half," little, or nothing at all to conception itself. Lower-class women such as Mabruka who demonstrate some knowledge of eggs often situate this knowledge within other, more monogenetically inspired, procreative discourses, leading to artfully blended, conceptually consistent theories in which fetus-laden sperm, menstrual blood, various "fluids," and eggs may all play some role in the creation of the fetus.

Ironically perhaps, the acceptance of women's eggs in procreative discourse has only served to heighten the pre-existing level of blame placed on women for reproductive failures. Although Egyptians are willing to entertain the possibility of male infertility when a couple is childless, they tend to view most infertility problems as problems of female *reception* of men's sperm. Thus, rarely is male infertility accepted as the *absolute* cause of any given case. With the widespread advent of semen analysis in Egypt over the past three decades, virtually every Egyptian has heard of the problem of "weak sperm," and most have come to accept the idea that men, too, may be infertile because of sperm that are few in number, slow, sluggish, dead, or even absent altogether. Nonetheless, it is extremely important to note that accepting male infertility in theory is not the same as accepting it in practice. In other words, even when men are acknowledged as having sperm "weakness," their problems are seen as correctable through "strengthening" medications that are thought to enliven dramatically even the most moribund of sperm. That such medications, in fact, fail to solve most cases of male infertility is not widely acknowledged. Nor is it understood that, from a biomedical standpoint, male infertility cases are among the hardest to overcome.[27]

Instead, women are usually blamed for having more severe, intractable infertility problems, which may involve their eggs in the duogenetic sperm-ovum model now emerging in Egypt. In the realm of infertility in Egypt, the persistence of woman-blaming cannot be overstated. Both infertile women such as Mabruka and *fertile* women who have been given a clean bill of health by numerous physicians may be condemned for the failure to conceive by husbands, husband's family members, and even fertile neighbors.[28] Like Mabruka, they may continue to search for additional diagnoses and treatments under the assumption that there *must* be something else wrong with them. In fact, the internalization of blame seen in cases such as Mabruka's is often quite remarkable and is what motivates, in part, women's relentless quests for therapy, including quests for new reproductive technologies.

But, given the monogenetic model of procreation described here, new reproductive technologies such as IVF are profoundly challenging to lower-class Egyptian couples such as Mabruka and Ragab, producing in them a kind of "cognitive dissonance" that may be difficult or impossible to overcome.[29] This is because IVF and all of its variants are based *completely* on Western duogenetic models of biological inheritance through *equal* contributions of eggs (a.k.a. ova, oocytes) and sperm. In fact, IVF is *all about* eggs and sperm. It is a technology that allows these procreative substances to "meet and romance" each other in couples with various biological impediments to fertilization.

In a typical IVF cycle, a woman first undergoes so-called ovarian stimulation with one or more hormonal medications for the purpose of producing excess numbers of eggs (i.e., rather than the one egg that is produced and released from the ovary during a normal menstrual cycle). Once the eggs have matured in fluid-filled "follicles" within the ovary (which are visible by ultrasound scanning), they are removed from the woman's body—what is often referred to as "egg harvesting"— through a delicate, transvaginal, surgical extraction procedure commonly referred to as "oocyte pick-up." The eggs are then rushed to the IVF laboratory, where they are isolated and combined with sperm (typically ejaculated through masturbation) as soon as possible. This combination of sperm and egg, furthermore, usually takes place in a petri dish, rather than in a test tube, as the name "test-tube baby" implies.

In classic IVF, the eggs and sperm are left to fertilize in a petri dish on their own. But in the newer ICSI procedure, skilled laboratory personnel, who are usually physicians in Egypt, "micromanipulate" these gametes under a high-powered microscope, thereby isolating one viable spermatozoon and injecting it directly into the egg. This microscopic injection is basically a form of forced fertilization—allowing otherwise nonviable sperm to penetrate eggs and fertilize them. Once this combination of eggs and sperm has occurred, the fertilized ova are incubated in the laboratory for a brief period lasting from twenty-four to forty-eight hours, depending upon the exact procedure being subsequently performed. If successful fertilization takes place, then the newly formed conceptuses—either in the form of zygotes, gametes, or embryos, depending upon the degree of cell division—are transferred back into the woman's fallopian tubes or uterus, again, depending upon which variant of IVF is performed. This "embryo transfer"—ideally of at least three and usually not more than five or six embryos—completes the physical part of the IVF cycle. However, women undergoing IVF or ICSI are often required to take additional hormonal medications to "support" the gestational environment of the uterus during the two-week waiting period until pregnancy results are known.

To summarize, IVF involves stimulating *egg* production, removing *eggs* from women's bodies, fertilizing these *eggs* in the laboratory with sperm that have been isolated from masturbated semen, and then returning fertilized embryos back to the woman's waiting womb. Such privileging of women's eggs—particularly in a society where the presence of eggs in human females is not widely accepted—goes against everything most rural and urban poor Egyptians have come to know about their bodies and their procreative processes. Indeed, the disruptions to local procreative knowledge posed by the new reproductive technologies are manifold. Such challenges include (1) that women have eggs that can be removed from and later returned to their bodies in a different form; (2) that women's eggs contribute actual biogenetic substance to the creation of offspring, thereby giving women biological ownership of their children in their own right; (3) that men do *not,* in fact, contribute everything to the procreation of offspring if their sperm are made to combine with women's eggs; (4) that men's sperm and women's eggs may somehow be of equal weight in biogenetic inheritance; and (5) that this combination of eggs and sperm can occur outside of the body, separate from the "bringing" (as in the colloquial English expression "coming") of children through heterosexual, marital, penetrative, male-orgasmic sex, which is what normative sex in Egypt is all about.[30]

Morality and Scientific Literacy

In fact, it is this last point—the separation of procreation from sex, and in this case, marital coitus—that is one of the most deeply disturbing aspects of the new reproductive technologies in Egypt.[31] It is not the disruptions in sexuality per se that are troubling to most Egyptians, although sexual issues are of major concern to a minority of infertile Egyptian couples.[32] Rather, Egyptians of all social backgrounds are troubled by lingering questions regarding what happens to procreative substances during the period in which they are *in vitro,* or outside the body. Indeed, it is what *cannot be known* during this in vitro period that elicits suspicion in Egyptians, and particularly in men like Ragab, who fear for the whereabouts and well-being of the fetuses that they carry in their sperm. And, it is this problem, lack of knowledge about and control over one's own procreative substances once they leave the body, that elicits oppositional moral stances toward IVF/ICSI, particularly among Egyptian men who must never doubt the verity of their own paternity. It is this extracorporeal dimension of IVF/ICSI—and the possibility that some form of advertent or inadvertent "mixing" of substances might occur behind the scenes in IVF laboratories—that represents the true moral trouble spot of the new reproductive technologies in Egypt, evoking widespread fears of these technologies and their resultant stigmatization.

But there are also gendered dimensions to the moral discourses surrounding the extracorporeality of IVF. Among Egyptian women, primary concerns may revolve less around the possibility of "mixing" men's sperm than around the "artificiality" of fetuses created and gestated outside their own wombs. In a Muslim country where adoption is prohibited, parenthood is synonymous with "natural," that is, biological, parenthood. For women, their biological connection to their children is through gestation of their husbands' fetuses inside their own bodies. Fetuses that are viewed as being gestated outside the woman's body, even if produced through the procreative substances of husband and wife, are not only deemed unnatural, but, like orphans, would be viewed as "strangers" by the husband and wife, who would therefore lack appropriate parental sentiments.

This is particularly troubling to lower-class women such as Mabruka, who admittedly have little idea about how IVF is carried out and are unclear about the length of time test-tube babies spend outside the womb. In the study I conducted with poor Egyptian women in the late 1980s, many of them described for me the details of "out-of-body" test-tube pregnancies, which they had learned from a popular televised *tamsiliya,* or soap opera, that had aired throughout the country in 1989. In the soap opera, a woman spent thousands of Egyptian pounds undergoing IVF following years of hopeless infertility. Finally, she made a test-tube baby, which was gestated in a laboratory for a lengthy period, usually described to me as *weeks or months,* only to lose the baby in a dramatic twist of fate. Clearly, this soap opera established in women's minds the notion that IVF involves extracorporeal pregnancies, whereby IVF babies linger for months in giant test tubes, "aquariums," or "glass uteruses." Such futuristic, fantasy visions of babies artificially produced in glass containers and then interned there for months were most disturbing to the Egyptian women in my study, who spoke to me at length of the necessity of "natural," God-given conception, gestation, and childbirth. Many of them, furthermore, suspected that the extracorporeal reality of IVF made it *haram,* or sinful, in Islam. Among these poor women, ultimate fears were of God himself, whose will would be defied if human beings were to attempt to "play God" through the production of such "manmade" babies outside of women's bodies.

As one woman explained to me, "It's not the same as when you carry the child inside you and suffer with it. It's as if you're taking it from someone else. It grows outside the womb of the mother, so it's like going and getting it 'ready-made.'" As reflected in this statement, relatively few poor women are well informed about the mechanics of IVF—and this was as true in 1996 as it was in 1988–1989. The oasis-dwelling Mabruka knew as little about the technical aspects of IVF as most of the women I had encountered in my earlier study. As she told me, "I, myself, have no idea how IVF is done. I don't know what it is." Her husband Ragab was similarly uninformed, believing that a test-tube baby would not be carried in Mabruka's "stomach" and would therefore not be "hers." He also suspected that a test-tube baby would not be "his," due to the potential mixing of the sperm of different men. Thus, for lower-class couples like Mabruka and Ragab, frank lack of technical understanding of IVF clearly fuels moral anxieties about the unnatural, illicit, forbidden nature of the procedure—as an act "going against God." Ragab's decision that IVF is "not for us" reflects these uncertainties.

Clearly, Ragab is not alone in his misgivings. During both periods of my research, curious Egyptians I met outside IVF clinics were both befuddled and awkwardly uncomfortable when I told them that I had come to their country to study infertility *and* in vitro fertilization. Many insisted that IVF was "uncommon," even "rare" in Egypt, and that I would never find an Egyptian willing to admit to having undergone IVF. In other words, even after ten years of IVF in the country, public views of IVF as "bad" and "immoral" were still rampant in the country, including in the most "civilized" urban area of Cairo. This was perhaps best illustrated to me when I hopped into a cab on August 15, 1996—feeling victorious over the near completion of what had been a very successful study of IVF in greater Cairo. The young, male, English-speaking cab driver asked me what I was doing in Egypt. When I told him I was finishing a study of IVF, he replied bluntly, "I don't like that," and then went on to explain that, as a Muslim, he could "never accept" IVF. He continued to tell me that his cousin was married to a woman who was infertile and that, even though he loved her, he was thinking of divorcing her. In the view of this educated, middle-class cab driver, it was better for his cousin to divorce an infertile wife than to make a test-tube baby with her.

This general lack of knowledge and lack of acceptance of IVF in Egypt was a theme that haunted my interviews with infertile IVF patients and drove many of them into the conspiracy of silence to be described at the end of this book. Most of those I interviewed in 1996 thought that IVF was widely misunderstood by most ordinary Egyptians. For example, one woman from a provincial city who had come to Cairo to undertake IVF explained,

> People in the countryside, they don't accept this idea [of IVF]. They say, "It may not be from the same husband. It's against the religion." That's one of the reasons why I told my husband to keep it secret. People in the countryside [where we live] have no awareness—especially the illiterate ones, but also the literate.

In short, knowledge—or lack thereof—as well as local social mores impinge upon the acceptance of new reproductive technologies in this particular cultural setting. Clearly, for most Egyptians not involved in the world of IVF, both their conceptions and *mis*conceptions about the science of test-tube baby making evoke moral questions and uncertainties. In other words, scientific literacy in the realm of new reproductive technologies in Egypt can only be understood within a moral framework. As will be revealed in the next chapter, it is this association of IVF with immorality that effectively precludes IVF acceptance and use among many Egyptians from all walks of life.

Acquiring Scientific Literacy

In the early IVF period, when I conducted my first research on this subject in Egypt, lack of acceptance of IVF was the rule, and fears of its immorality abounded, such that only the most desperate moral pioneers seemed willing to actually enter the brave new world of high-tech reproductive medicine.[33] However, the past decade *has* yielded some dramatic changes in the realm of IVF knowledge and acceptance, as is evident in the fact that IVF centers are flourishing in Egypt at the beginning of the new millennium. In fact, by the time I returned to Egypt in 1996, three things had clearly changed: The number of IVF centers in the country had significantly increased, the number of infertile patients accepting treatment at these centers had increased as well, and the level of expertise among these IVF-seeking Egyptian patients was readily apparent. As I will argue here, these three phenomena are related. Many more infertile Egyptian couples have become willing to enter Egyptian IVF centers as patients because they have come to achieve moral acceptance of these technologies. This increasing acceptance is due, in turn, to the acquisition of scientific knowledge. In other words, knowledge has become a form of power in Egyptian test-tube baby making. Those who acquire the necessary knowledge are much more likely to seek IVF because their scientific literacy has served to allay, in a powerful manner, many of the niggling moral anxieties about the extracorporeality of IVF that continue to haunt lesser-educated Egyptians and prevent them from even contemplating IVF as a form of treatment.

In fact, one of the most striking findings of my 1996 study was the level of expertise apparent among patients in Egyptian IVF centers. Many of these patients were proud of the fact that they had acquired significant knowledge during the relatively short time period, generally perceived as the "five to ten years," that IVF had been available in the country. Furthermore, virtually all of the women and men I interviewed who were undergoing IVF or ICSI understood the basic mechanics of these technologies. By virtue of their college educations and exposure to Western biology over many years of schooling, all of these women and their husbands accepted the duogenetic model of procreation underlying IVF, and hence were well versed in the role of eggs and sperm in human reproduction in general and in IVF specifically. In other words, the problems of procreative knowledge described earlier—and the cognitive dissonance engendered by conflicting procreative models—were simply not present among this middle- to upper-class, highly educated population.

Not surprisingly, then, when I asked women in Egyptian IVF centers about how IVF is performed, I usually received confident, somewhat detailed, and biomedically accurate responses about how eggs and sperm are removed, handled, and replaced in a typical IVF cycle. For example, one woman offered this fairly typical description:

> The drugs are [given] to stop the natural hormonal system through the brain, and these medications increase the ovulation. They [the doctors] make a follow-up of the eggs by ultrasound. When the eggs become ready, the number is suitable, they take them out. (They took eight out of me.) They take the eggs out surgically, then they take the sperm at the same time. Then they fertilize the eggs with the sperm in the laboratory. Then they take the best four embryos and inject them into the uterus—not by anesthesia, but it doesn't hurt. After embryo transfer, they give you injections to "fasten"

the embryo. You stay at home waiting for the results. Sitting at home waiting for the result is the most difficult part.

In addition to the "how to's" of test-tube baby making, women could usually tell me why such technologies are necessary to overcome infertility, and they could often distinguish which form of technology is most useful for which type of infertility problem. For example, at least one-third of the women in my study had undergone repeated trials of artificial insemination with their husbands' sperm (AIH) prior to IVF or ICSI, with one woman undergoing a record number of twenty-four AIH trials. But all of these AIH repeaters were women with open fallopian tubes, and it was generally understood that AIH was not a successful treatment for women whose fallopian tubes were blocked. Instead, IVF was deemed the ideal form of treatment for tubal obstruction, as well as other female infertility problems (e.g., anovulation) that did not respond to treatment.

ICSI, on the other hand, was widely perceived as the new treatment for male infertility. But why it was better for male infertility and how it differed from IVF or AIH were not clearly understood. Because ICSI had only arrived on the scene in Egypt during the previous two years, some of the women in my study had either never heard of it or had heard of it only recently (one to six months preceding our interviews). Most were uncertain what it was. This was true even among some women who had undergone or were scheduled to undergo ICSI, but could not distinguish it from IVF, or had partial, incomplete, and sometime erroneous information about the differences between the two technologies. In other words, whereas IVF had become "famous" among infertile couples in Egypt and was quite well understood by 1996, information about ICSI had yet to take hold, even among the highly educated and savvy clients in Egyptian IVF centers.

Having said this, it was clear from interviews that many infertile Egyptian couples were genuinely interested in understanding the differences between AIH, IVF, and ICSI. Most were willing to venture guesses about why ICSI was "better" for male infertility than IVF. In some cases, their descriptions came close to biomedical representations of these technologies, while in other cases, they did not.

For example, one woman offered this nearly "textbook" characterization of ICSI, which she said she had learned from talking to her physicians:

> They told me that because his sperm are few and weak, the only solution for him is ICSI. They take my eggs and then my husband's sperm, and then they inject my eggs with his sperm. Then they will stay for 48 hours, then they examine it [in the laboratory]. If there is fertilization, they will move it back into my uterus through the vagina. The doctor told me that ICSI is best for me, because my chances will be more. I know that the chance of success of ICSI is more than IVF. The difference is, they take the sperm itself and inject it into the egg. But in IVF, they put the two together and that's it; they let them fertilize on their own. Whether they use IVF or ICSI depends on her problem, or the problems they suffer.

Another woman offered a less certain (and less biomedically precise) version of why ICSI might be preferable to IVF in overcoming their so-called unexplained infertility:

> In ICSI, the egg is fertilized "in its place" [in the woman's ovary]. They do a surgery by laparoscopy to fertilize and inject the egg while it's in its place. Then they sew the wound. This is our information about ICSI; we're not sure whether it is like that or not. But we think that in IVF, the egg is outside, and in ICSI, it is in its place [in the ovary]. The doctor said that IVF is not needed [in our case] because the tubes are not blocked. ICSI is better and the chances of success are more.

Paths to Knowledge

So the question remains: From where do Egyptians acquire this kind of information—as well as *mis*information—about the new reproductive technologies? In contemporary Egypt, there appear to be three main paths to knowledge among IVF-seeking patients: knowledge acquired from reading books and other printed materials written specifically for Arabic audiences to educate them about the uses of the new reproductive technologies, knowledge acquired from doctors themselves and from other forms of patient education provided at Egyptian IVF centers, and knowledge acquired from exposure to many forms of media publicity about the new reproductive technologies in what is a decidedly media-saturated society. In Egypt, the degree to which one acquires knowledge from any of these sources has much to do with one's class position and level of literacy.

To reiterate an earlier argument, class position and knowledge are arenas of constraint that go hand in hand in Egypt: The lower one's social class position in Egypt, the less one likely is to be educated and, hence, literate. In short, most lower-class Egyptians cannot read Arabic (let alone English) and are subsequently barred from acquiring *written* knowledge about the new reproductive technologies, which is now widely available in Egypt. Without literacy as a means to knowledge, lower-class infertile women who seek access to new reproductive technologies must rely entirely on *broadcast* forms of media, including popular cultural forms such as soap operas, which tend to present factual inaccuracies, as described earlier. Or, more commonly, they learn the little they can about these technologies through their brief and often deeply unsatisfying encounters with busy, sometimes brusque Egyptian physicians, who tend to believe that lower-class women are incapable of receiving and absorbing such information.[34]

Such was the case with Mabruka, who remained convinced that the doctors she had visited over many years had failed to tell her something important about her own case. The little information that she had been able to glean from her encounters with physicians had been conveyed to her in a partial and simplistic fashion—a common practice when Egyptian physicians speak to lower-class patients. Thus,

Mabruka had come to understand her problem of recalcitrant anovulation as weakness in her ovaries, and she blamed herself for being weak and unable to bear children for her husband. Nonetheless, what is striking about Mabruka's story, and is typical in the infertility narratives of many lower-class Egyptian women, is her continuing belief in doctors' authority. As Mabruka admitted, "For myself, frankly, if a doctor tells me about anything, I'm convinced, because he's a doctor and he knows everything." However, Mabruka remained frustrated with her own lack of knowledge of her case, and she wished that the physicians *she* trusted would trust *her* with more information.

Among educated, middle- to upper-class infertile women, the situation is quite different. Although physicians and broadcast media may also be important sources of information for these women, the educated clientele of Egyptian IVF centers today are active consumers of printed information, which they seek out before, during, and after they embark on this line of therapy. These women are not only highly literate, but they are proud of the fact that they are "readers" and "self-educators," devouring everything they can get their hands on relating to infertility and the new reproductive technologies. This may include magazine and newspaper articles; books written by physicians or religious authorities for educated, Arabic-speaking audiences; the package inserts accompanying medications; printed information provided by IVF centers; and even original research reports.[35] As one woman, who was described to me by her physician as "very knowledgeable about all these procedures," explained, "I read a lot—periodicals, newspapers, books. Because we are suffering for sixteen years, I'm following up on this." Another woman offered, "I didn't know anything about IVF, but just through reading I educated myself. Magazines, *many* books. I have a library in my house!"

Books, in particular, seem to play a major educational role for some women. Usually written by physicians for educated lay audiences and available in Egyptian bookstores, such books attempt to explain for infertile readers the dynamics of human reproduction, the impediments to reproduction, and the ways in which new reproductive technologies are designed to overcome those impediments.[36] The author of one of these books is the "guru" of Egyptian IVF himself: Muhammad Aboulghar, an Egyptian professor of obstetrics and gynecology at Cairo University and the man widely perceived by infertile couples as the first to bring IVF to Egypt. As one reader of Dr. Aboulghar's book explained to me,

> Now there are *many* books on these subjects. But there's one book, *There Is Nothing Impossible in Infertility*, written by Aboulghar. It's in bookshops. This is the only book that explains *everything* about this operation. Three to four months ago, I bought this book before doing my first cycle. It helped to convince me. It explained *everything*, including ICSI. Now I know everything. The names of the hormones and medications I took, I knew them before I took them. I read that, in IVF, we use it for a woman with many problems in her fallopian tubes. But ICSI is 100 percent for the man, and we

use it if the man's sperm is very weak, and IVF if the sperm are very good and active.

In addition to books written by doctors such as Aboulghar, some Egyptian IVF physicians are aware of the need for patient education and pride themselves on providing it in their clinics. Such doctors spend considerable time talking to patients, not only in initial visits that generally last from forty-five minutes to an hour, but also in later sessions, where they often respond to patient questions. For example, Dr. Mohamed Yehia asks his IVF and ICSI patients to write down any questions that may occur to them between visits; the next time he sees the individual patient or couple, he attempts to respond to every query in a systematic fashion. He also employs a female assistant—a friendly woman who patients call by her first name, Abeer—who serves as an all-purpose health educator, fielding a variety of questions and offering patients advice on issues ranging from medication dosages to the religious opinions on the appropriateness of these technologies. Although such professional health educators are very *uncommon* in Egypt—where there are no schools of public health offering specific degrees in health education—Dr. Yehia considers Abeer's role in his practice to be essential. Although he hired her for her "smileyness" and the comfort she could offer his patients, Abeer has turned out to play a much bigger role than expected in providing information to his patients, and for this he pays her a "good salary" by Egyptian standards. Among patients desiring information, Abeer is extremely popular, and most of the clinic's IVF and ICSI patients raved to me about her during interviews. For example, an infertile male patient coming to the Nozha Hospital clinic with his wife for ICSI commented,

> Abeer is *perfect* about giving instructions. She's always busy, but she's always doing her best, always smiling. After Dr. Yehia explains something, sometimes you feel he doesn't have time to explain it again. So she takes you and explains it one more time or two times, and she says, "Call me if you have any questions." Her role is *very* big. She helps Dr. Yehia *a lot*. We weren't expecting this. The people here are *very* nice, friendly, giving you support. You feel happy about this. Arabs normally like to talk, ask "What is the reason?" But, sometimes we were coming from hospitals, feeling not satisfied, tense. We didn't feel this *at all* here. The role of these people is very important.

In addition to employing the services of a full-time health educator, Dr. Yehia's IVF center is also unique in providing patients with a written report—namely, a treatment discharge summary that is filled out by Dr. Yehia and given to all patients upon completion of an IVF cycle. This report summarizes for patients how much and which type of medication has been given, how many eggs were collected, how sperm were collected (i.e., through regular ejaculation or a surgical procedure), how healthy sperm were on the day of fertilization, how many eggs were successfully fertilized, how many embryos were transferred back into the uterus, and on which day a pregnancy test will be performed. Again, this summary report was of great comfort to patients, some of whom read their reports to me on the day they were leaving the hospital. Furthermore, because of this report, I was able to collect detailed information from many patients on their individual cases, including semen profiles and the number of eggs and embryos that had been collected, fertilized, and transferred. Several couples told me that, if they were to become pregnant, they would save this report for posterity, in order to present it to their IVF child(ren) some day.

In addition, Dr. Yehia's center, as well as the Nile Badrawi IVF center where Mabruka was being treated, requires all patients to sign an informed consent form prior to embarking on either an IVF or ICSI trial. Although not intended as a tool in patient education, this paper, which patients are asked to read, sign, and return to the treating physician (i.e., literacy is assumed), provides some vitally important information for them. Most important, it is this informed consent form that reveals to patients the success rates for the IVF and ICSI procedures. It is this written success rate—for example, 25 percent for IVF and 20 percent for ICSI (the latter amended from an original estimate of 10 percent) at Nozha Hospital—which sticks in patients' minds as a most crucial piece of information.

Despite patients' desire to believe that they are being accurately apprised of their chances of success, these rates may be inflated in some Egyptian IVF centers, which report success rates (e.g., 40 to 50 percent) that are too high, even by Western standards. Furthermore, there is currently no comparative information of this sort *across* centers, to help patients decide *where* they should spend their time and money. As one woman lamented,

> I asked if there is a brochure on IVF centers in Egypt—the success rate of this one, and of that one. If it does exist in Egypt, I don't know about it. I wanted someone to tell me, "Go ahead to [a particular clinic]. It's one of the best in Egypt and has a good percentage of success compared to England and elsewhere."

Thus, a major issue in the informed consent process in Egypt is how well informed patients really are about this expensive and life-altering reproductive technology. Given the misconceptions about IVF and ICSI, as well as success rate inflation in some centers, the term "decisionally impaired," one coined by the National Bioethics Advisory Commission (NBAC) in the United States, seems to characterize many infertile, IVF-seeking Egyptian couples, who constitute a "vulnerable . . . population at risk for inadequately informed consent."[37] These issues will be taken up at greater length in subsequent chapters.

Suffice it to say here that educated, middle- to upper-class patients in Egyptian IVF centers are generally much better apprised of their situations and more prepared to utilize these new reproductive technologies than their lesser-educated, lower-class counterparts. Many are savvy consumers of information who come to their IVF clinic encounters with detailed knowledge of their own medical histories and reproductive complaints, garnered through many years of experience and self-education. Furthermore, these patients are much more likely to be treated by physicians as social equals and are therefore much more likely to be adequately apprised about the details of their cases by their treating physicians. Thus, for elites, physicians can be an important source of valuable information, adding their personal insights and convictions to the book learning that most elite patients do on their own.

Scientific Literacy in a Mass-Mediated Society

In addition, the power of the Egyptian media to provide information and promote acceptance of these technologies cannot be underestimated. The media have served a *major* role in promoting public understandings (qua scientific literacy) of these technologies, among an increasingly educated, literate audience that views itself as "knowledge hungry" and "always on the lookout" for information regarding the latest advances in infertility treatment.

In fact, the role of the Egyptian media in placing these global technologies on the local radar screen has been striking. Ever since the first Egyptian IVF center opened in 1986, the local media have followed test-tube baby making in Egypt very closely, reporting both the successes of these technologies in Egypt and abroad and providing moral commentary on the "excesses" of the infertility treatment industry in Europe and the United States. Some of the media coverage has been educational, while some of it has been for entertainment purposes. But, without a doubt, the Egyptian media have been dogged in their pursuit of new twists and turns in the field of reproductive medicine, with each new development making "headline news" in a variety of media outlets, as well as high drama for Egyptian soap operas and films.

The media interest in new reproductive technologies stems from the fact that Egypt has a large and active journalism profession and the region's most well known and beloved film industry, which has been in place since the 1930s.[38] Egypt is both the "Hollywood" and the "CNN" of the Middle East, creating high-quality, local media productions that are then exported throughout the Arabic-speaking world.[39] As noted by Viola Shafik,

> Egypt still hosts one of the major entertainment industries in the Middle East. With its talk shows, quiz, variety, and TV serials (*musalsalat*) it feeds the numerous channels of other Arab broadcasts, in particular those of the Arabian Peninsula. Moreover, Egyptian movies are screened and aired all over the Arab World.[40]

In addition, Egypt imports many global (qua Western) media productions into the country. Indeed, the Egyptian media and communications industry provides an example par excellence (although one that is inadequately studied[41]) of local-global connections in the production, distribution, and consumption of information and entertainment.

The Egyptian media are noteworthy for their science and health reportage. Television in particular has been used extensively since the 1980s to convey a wide variety of health information to Egyptians. According to medical anthropologist Sandra

Lane,[42] who has studied the use of television mini-dramas in health promotion in Egypt, a number of characteristics of Egypt itself make it particularly well suited for intensive, media-focused health education. For one, Egypt's television industry began in the 1960s to produce serialized dramas, known as *tamsiliyat,* which air nightly all over the Arab world and are an Egyptian national pastime. In addition, the presence of well-established television and film industries means that there is a considerable pool of talent in the technical aspects of film and video production. In addition, because of their relatively long-term exposure to television as a media form, Egyptians themselves comprise a "potentially quite sophisticated" viewing audience.[43] And television reaches nearly every Egyptian: More than 80 percent of Egyptian households, including quite poor ones, own a television, and 75 percent of married women watch television daily.[44] This is especially important for illiterate Egyptians, for whom television is a potentially critical source of health information. The importance of the media, and particularly television, in conveying health information to Egyptians was described by one woman in my study as follows,

> I see nowadays in Egypt a lot of awareness in the media about IVF. Dr. Moustafa Mahmoud [with his television show *Science and Faith*] and the newspapers try to direct women to have such treatment if they suffer from such problems. Maybe because I'm suffering from this problem, I hear more. But, on Thursday, I was watching TV. On the first, third, fourth, fifth—most of the channels—they were showing programs on IVF!

As suggested by this woman's comments, the Egyptian media have played a number of very crucial roles in "spreading the word" about test-tube baby making. First, the media have promoted awareness of the new reproductive technologies, alerting the infertile Egyptian public to the presence of these technologies in their country. Second, the media have served a major role in providing publicity for specific Egyptian IVF centers, in the form of both news coverage and paid-for advertisements. Third, the Egyptian media have covered ongoing developments in the global arena, providing international news service accounts of new uses of the reproductive technologies in other countries. Fourth, the media have created a lively, public, moral debate on the uses of the new reproductive technologies in Egypt and abroad. Finally, because of the ongoing coverage, the media have served to "normalize" these technologies to some degree over time. The stories brought by the media into ordinary homes have certainly served to remind Egyptians that infertility is a real problem in their country and that new reproductive technologies, if appropriately applied, provide a morally acceptable solution to human suffering.

Exactly half of the women in my 1996 study reported that their initial awareness of either IVF or ICSI had come from media coverage, either a newspaper or magazine article, a television or radio broadcast, or, in a few cases, an advertisement for a new IVF or ICSI program. Oft-cited sources of this information included the national daily newspaper, *Al-Ahram;* national magazines, including *Rosel Youssef, Muslimuun,* and the woman's magazine *Nus id-Dunya;* and popular television shows, including Dr. Moustafa Mahmoud's *Science and Faith,* a news show called *Tazeen*

Salaam, and a program called *A Very Special Invitation* allowing viewers inside the exclusive domain of an Egyptian IVF center.

When IVF first became available in Egypt in 1986, all of these media sources covered its introduction. Over the years, they have continued to provide updates on new developments related to this technology. Indeed, just months before my arrival in Egypt in 1996, the "big news" was the birth of ICSI triplets in Egypt under the supervision of Dr. Mohamed Yehia at Nozha Hospital, as pictured in chapter 5. The birth of these multiples was particularly remarkable because their father suffered from a severe form of male infertility in which he did not produce mature spermatozoa. Through aspiration of immature spermatids from the father's testicles, followed by microscopic injection of these spermatids into several of his wife's ova, the doctors at Nozha Hospital were able to produce viable embryos and, ultimately, a healthy pregnancy and delivery of normal triplets. This remarkable birth of ICSI triplets was heralded in both the print and broadcast media. Thus, the media had focused considerable attention on Dr. Mohamed Yehia, the first to introduce ICSI to the country. As one infertile man coming to Dr. Yehia's clinic for ICSI told me,

> I asked *many* people before I made the decision to come here [to Nozha Hospital]. But lately, [Dr. Yehia] became very famous, especially for the "microscopic injection." I saw his picture *many, many* times, on TV, in magazines, newspapers. Especially last year, with the birth of ICSI triplets, I heard about him many times.

Similarly, an Egyptian woman living with her infertile husband in Oman described how she learned about Dr. Yehia and his ICSI triplets:

> I read about Dr. Yehia in a magazine, an Egyptian woman's magazine that we have in Oman called *Nus id-Dunya.* It was about one with the exact same case [as ours]. The husband had no sperm, but three babies were born in January 1996. There was a nice picture of Dr. Yehia; he was carrying the triplets. I read about this in March, but the babies were born in January. So I called Dr. Yehia from Oman and sent my husband's case report by fax, and he said, "OK, you can come and make ICSI."

This initial coverage of ICSI by the Egyptian media had, in fact, prompted the attendance of many long-term infertile couples, particularly those suffering from male infertility, to Dr. Yehia's clinic. In fact, Dr. Yehia, a former actor who maintains ties with specific journalists, is very media savvy and uses the local media to broadcast his clinic's accomplishments,[45] including "big events" such as the birth of ICSI triplets. During the period of my study, Dr. Yehia had begun to contact a number of reporters in order to announce that 150 ICSI babies—all healthy—had now been born in his clinic. Thus, the media "make careers" for some Egyptian IVF doctors— a phenomenon that has been very well described by Bharadwaj for India also[46]— creating fame and fortune through news accounts that become an important vehicle for public relations.[47]

Other centers, with less newsworthy successes, are still media hungry; their strategy is to take out direct advertisements in the Egyptian media, in which they boast their high (probably inflated) success rates and their "consultants" from Europe. As one woman commented,

> There are so many centers advertising in the papers. One in Dokki, one in Muhandiseen, one in Musr Gadida, one in Maadi [all affluent suburbs of Cairo]. They're all advertising for ICSI, saying they're getting experts from European countries. Some centers are claiming rates higher than this one— 30 to 40 percent. We don't know. We don't trust them. We have an Egyptian saying, "What you know is better than what you don't know." So our experience tells us it's better to stay with one you've tried.

In addition to covering the local scene, the Egyptian media bring things global to Egypt, vis-à-vis news stories, documentaries, films, and television series dealing with the theme of new reproductive technology development outside the country. Some of this material is imported directly from abroad. Some of it is produced locally to reflect Egyptian sentiments on the Western use (and abuse) of these technologies.

To take but a few examples, one woman who had just undergone IVF had recently seen a European documentary (of uncertain origin), in which one woman's IVF trial was covered from beginning to end. "They showed *everything!*" my informant exclaimed. "We saw all the steps we did the week we were doing them! But it was frustrating, because at the end of the program, she was not pregnant."

Another couple described a report they had viewed on the "Israeli TV channel" available on Egyptian television. According to the couple, an Israeli IVF doctor put some "sticky adhesive material" into a woman's uterus in order to help the IVF embryos implant. When they asked their Egyptian physician about this—pleading with him to "put this material in to solve our problem"—the doctor denied the existence of any such adhesive material, further confusing the couple. When I asked them who they believed, the Israeli specialist or their own physician, the husband replied, "I think there is [this material]. I think the Israelis are more advanced than us. Or maybe [the Israeli doctor] is just saying this, but it's not true."[48]

Although many Egyptian couples believe that Israel and most of the Western countries are more "advanced" in IVF and ICSI than Egypt, they nonetheless frown on many of the Western practices of reproductive medicine, including surrogacy, sperm banks for donor insemination, IVF in women age fifty and older (including grandmothers carrying their grandchildren for infertile daughters), and the use of frozen sperm and embryos following death or divorce of parents. In most cases, Egyptians have heard of these practices because of exposure to them through the Egyptian media. Some have read or heard news stories taken from Western wire services. However, most Egyptians derive their most lasting impressions from movies—some Western imports, some Egyptian originals—that invoke the evils of Western test-tube baby making. In fact, one of these popular, Egyptian-made movies was entitled *Evil Offers a Solution,* and it dealt with the purported racial implications of donor insemination. As one of my informants described it, "We saw a film, an Egyptian movie, where the husband lied to his wife and didn't say he had [an infertility] problem. He went abroad, and he used a sperm bank. The baby is black and his grandfather had a shock when he saw him." Another Egyptian-made movie, broadcast on television during the early part of my 1996 study, was entitled *One Child Only* and dealt with the theme of surrogacy. Although I did not see the film myself, learning about it only after the fact, my Egyptian research assistant, as well as several informants, described this controversial film to me in animated tones. Interestingly, even though the film had been broadcast very recently, each informant's rendering of the basic plot differed slightly—indicating the considerable heterogeneity of media reception.

According to my research assistant, whose account was most detailed, the movie was based on a true story that took place in Michigan. An older couple with one son paid a surrogate mother $10,000 to carry their baby. But the surrogate produced twins, a boy and a girl. The hiring couple wanted only the girl, since they had a son and the father felt he would be too old to play sports with a young boy. So, they decided to put the male twin up for adoption. The surrogate couple was poor and already had three of their own children to support. But the surrogate mother started having nightmares about the babies crying, and she felt that they were *her* babies. So she and her husband became convinced that they needed to legally adopt the twin boy. As this child grew, he started telling his parents that he missed his sister, so the surrogate couple sued the older couple to get the twin sister back. Because they hired a clever lawyer, who used the older couple's rejection of the boy as grounds for their lack of parental "fitness," the surrogate couple won the case. However, the surrogate couple suffered social rejection from their friends and family for "giving up their babies." The movie concluded by describing a law that was subsequently enacted to prevent "baby making by hire" and limiting surrogacy arrangements to close family and friends.[49] According to my research assistant, this conclusion was "surprising" because it was widely assumed in Egypt that surrogacy was "common and completely accepted" in the United States.

Movies such as these made for Egyptian television audiences provide both entertainment and potent cautionary tales about how babies should be made within proper limits. In the religiously conservative Muslim country of Egypt, these movies invoke moral indignation—or at least thought-provoking moral commentary—on the part of many viewers, serving to convince Egyptians that their own restricted practices of IVF and ICSI are morally superior to the moral corruption occurring in the Christian West. These movies, furthermore, serve to crystallize opinions of the West, and particularly America, which are generated through the importation to Egypt of American television serials, including *Dallas, Dynasty, Falcon Crest,* and *The Bold and the Beautiful,* all of which have been popular nighttime fare over the past two decades. Such television shows reveal to Egyptians the unbridled materialism, alcohol and drug abuse, marital infidelities, and dysfunctional families that many Egyptians now consider to be a normal part of the American cultural landscape. In the next chapter, these issues of comparative moralities—specifically, Egyptian versus

Western—in the realm of test-tube baby making will be taken up at greater length. Suffice it to say here that the Egyptian media have played a major role in promoting such moral discourse and reflection through their offering of Western new reproductive technology realities to fascinated, yet disapproving, local audiences.

In addition, the Egyptian media have promoted moral discourse about these technologies by featuring "religious experts," who are provided the opportunity in print and over the air to comment on the rights and wrongs of test-tube baby making. In an increasingly conservative Muslim country, such religious programming and printed content is becoming increasingly popular. For infertile couples desiring expert religious opinion on the proper uses of the new reproductive technologies, such programming has been extremely helpful. As one informant explained,

> Our *mufti*—the big head of Islam in Egypt, who was at that time [Shaikh] Tantawi—many times he went on TV to discuss people's problems. Women and their husbands asked him [about IVF], and he said it's no problem in the religion if the semen is from my husband and it's my egg. Other *shaikhs* have agreed.

Other women told me that they had read Shaikh Tantawi's *fatwa,* or religious opinion, in the newspaper, and some had heard it on the radio on a channel devoted to the Qur'an and its commentary. In other words, for some infertile Egyptians, including Mabruka, who had witnessed a televised discussion of IVF on the part of a noted Egyptian *shaikh,* the Egyptian media have facilitated their understanding of the religious dimensions of IVF and ICSI by bringing religious opinions to them straight "from the experts." In many cases, these "media clerics" have helped to normalize these technologies and allay potential users' fears.

To summarize, at the same time that the Egyptian media have moralized about the abuses of new reproductive technologies *outside* the country, they have also served as an agent of normalization *inside* Egypt—making these reproductive technologies seem less bizarre, frightening, and unusual. Several women in my study commented on this, telling me how the media were slowly changing public views of IVF toward increasing acceptance and openness. One woman commented,

> I read about IVF and heard about it on radio and television. Since they started treatment with IVF, I've known about it—in Europe and the States. But this was something strange ten years ago. But now it's not so strange. There are thousands in Egypt, *a lot* who did it. It's becoming natural because of progress in science.

This woman's remarks highlight an argument made by anthropologist Walter Armbrust in his study of mass media in Egypt,[50] namely, that the Egyptian media have played a major role in highlighting the country's "modernity," with the media coverage of new reproductive technologies in Egypt being but one excellent example. To wit, by their mere presence in the country—in fact, their sheer proliferation—the new reproductive technologies provide a clear signal of Egypt's scientific advancement and its ability to apply successfully the latest in modern biomedical technology.

Having said this, it is important to point out that the drive to be modern is not a major motivating factor for most Egyptian IVF patients (although it may be for some Egyptian IVF physicians, who pride themselves on being up to date in the latest medical advancements). For the Egyptian infertile, their desire to utilize cutting-edge technologies to overcome their infertility has nothing to do with signaling one's modernity to the rest of the world. Quite the contrary! As will be shown in Chapter 9, most Egyptian IVF patients do everything in their power to hide their treatment attempts from others. In virtually all cases, they utilize these technologies only because they have to, typically after years of duress. Nonetheless, such patients may be *secretly* pleased with their ability to access and utilize the latest technologies and are often proud of the fact that Egyptian medicine is so "advanced." As one woman who had just undergone ICSI for the first time in an attempt to overcome her husband's azoospermia put it, quite aptly,

> Thanks to God, here, medicine has advanced, and there are new techniques to give people a new hope. When I read about ICSI, I knew that this is a great advancement, and it made us optimistic. In our country, there's something new; it makes us happy that our countrymen are able to do things like that.

Conclusion: The Desire for Knowledge

In Egypt, there is a heartfelt belief among many Muslims that God gives humans knowledge to overcome their problems, just as He provides treatments to overcome "diseases" such as infertility. Thus, Islam enjoins believers to be seekers of knowledge "from cradle to grave," in order that they may find solutions to their suffering.

As this chapter as shown, most infertile Egyptians are seekers of knowledge, making every effort to know about their own cases and the technologies to be applied to their infertile bodies. Although this desire to know cuts across class lines, the Egyptian poor—by virtue of their lesser educations, their illiteracy, their conflicting models of procreation, and their unfruitful interactions with physicians—are at a clear disadvantage in coming to terms with their own infertility and the new reproductive technologies that are becoming increasingly available as a treatment modality. In short, because of these multiple impediments, issues of knowledge constitute a fundamental arena of constraint to test-tube baby making among the Egyptian poor, highlighting the ways in which access to knowledge itself is embedded in Egyptian class structures. Thus, lower-class infertile women such as Mabruka, who ardently desire sufficient knowledge to be convinced of the moral acceptability of IVF, face many barriers to achieving scientific literacy, which, in Egypt, cannot be understood without reference to a moral framework.

Because of these constraints among the poor, those who end up at Egyptian IVF centers today are generally scientifically literate, highly educated, middle- to upper-class Egyptians who consume knowledge from many sources—books, discussions with physicians, and varied forms of print and broadcast media. They pride themselves on their aggressive pursuit of information, and it is this information, particularly media coverage of specific scientific achievements such as ICSI, that leads many of them into treatment with new reproductive technologies. Thus, knowledge serves these individuals well in their pursuit to be cured of their childlessness. For them, knowledge *is* power—despite the fact that these technologies provide no guarantee of success.

Yet, on a more sobering note, issues of impaired knowledge also come to the fore even for the infertile elite, particularly in discussions of success rates, which are often presented misleadingly. Furthermore, infertile elites are exposed to local media presentations exposing the global horrors of test-tube baby making when it "runs amok" in the West. That these media portrayals make most infertile couples happy to be in Muslim Egypt is clear. But, as we shall see in the following chapter, they also give Egyptian elites great pause—forcing them to think twice about undertaking a technological innovation whose moral implications are profound.

CHAPTER 4

Religion

The "Americans"

Like most of the couples who attend Egyptian IVF centers today, Dalia and Galal represent the upper crust of Egyptian society—wealthy elites who are able to purchase the fruits of globalization, including high-cost, high-tech medical services such as IVF. When I met Dalia and Galal in July 1996, they were relatively new to the Nozha Hospital IVF clinic, where I interviewed them together in fluent English. As an internationally sophisticated couple, they were already old pros at IVF, which they had tried two years earlier in Los Angeles.

Together, Dalia—modestly veiled, but dressed in a fashionable, vivid pink women's suit, with liberal amounts of gold and diamond jewelry—and Galal—dressed in an expensive, brightly patterned, Western-style sports shirt, slacks, and sandals—recounted the story of their transnational quest to make a test-tube baby.

Dalia had married Galal four years before their first IVF attempt, knowing that Galal, her first cousin,[1] suffered from a surgically irreparable varicocele, or a cluster of dilated veins in his testicles causing him to have a very poor sperm count. Galal's infertility became known to his extended family when, after fathering one son in his first marriage, he was unable to impregnate his wife again. Galal eventually divorced his first wife and fell in love with his attractive cousin, Dalia. Dalia was also smitten with Galal, a kind, handsome, rich factory owner. However, Dalia's parents were deeply opposed to her marrying a man known to be infertile, even if he was her relative. Dalia recalled,

> My mother got sick, crying all the time and making fights with me. She wanted to "see my children." My family made a lot of problems, but I loved him so I married him. When I married him, I thought maybe I won't be pregnant. This was something that made it a little easier; I accepted his infertility.

In part to escape family pressure and in part to seek medical advice, Dalia and Galal decided to emigrate to the United States in 1992, where Galal, an ex-military man, had once received basic training and where Dalia now had a sister living in California. Once settled in Pasadena, they sought treatment for Galal's infertility and were told that, given his poor semen profile, they should undergo artificial insemination using donor semen from a sperm bank. Incredulous, Dalia and Galal explained to the American physician, "We are Muslims and this is forbidden." So he referred them to an Egyptian Muslim physician running his own Los Angeles–based IVF clinic. This was the first time either Dalia or Galal had ever heard of IVF. But once they talked with the Egyptian doctor, they were soon convinced that IVF was allowed within Islam as long as both sperm and eggs came from husband and wife.

Following their consultation with the Muslim doctor, as well as a second opinion from another Los Angeles–based, "religious" Lebanese Christian physician, Dalia and Galal decided to go ahead with one trial of IVF, which cost them $16,300 and which they paid for in a series of four installments. When the in vitro fertilization process produced extra embryos that were not to be transferred to Dalia's uterus, the IVF clinic staff gave Dalia and Galal three choices: freezing, destroying, or donating to another couple. As Dalia explained: "We said, 'Destroy! It is our religion.' If it's from the man and his wife, yes, it is okay [in Islam]. But to donate eggs or sperm, this is *haram* [sinful]!" Galal added,

> There is a *fatwa* [religious opinion] from Al-Azhar [the major religious university in Egypt] about this. If I give someone my sperm, this baby is going to take another [man's] name, and he's going to take [from him] some money, some inheritance, although he's not "from him." Maybe I give another woman my sperm and she gets a son, and another woman and she gets a daughter, and when they grow up, he marries his [half] sister. This [i.e., potential incest] is the main thing [problem].

Although Dalia and Galal acknowledged that laboratory mistakes resulting in "accidental" donation might still be made, even under the best of circumstances, they believed that they had avoided this eventuality by relying on a religiously vigilant, scrupulous, Middle Eastern–born Muslim physician to carry out the actual IVF procedure. However, they were concerned about the general moral decline of American IVF practices, including the frequent donation of sperm, ova, and embryos from third parties. In their view as religiously observant Muslims, such donation practices would inevitably lead to an immoral and genealogically bewildering "mixture of relations." Furthermore, they had heard that one American doctor made approximately twenty babies "from himself"[2]—probably in an attempt "to become successful and famous." Given the morally questionable nature of American IVF practices undertaken by American physicians, Dalia and Galal concluded that, in retrospect, it was better that their trial of IVF did not succeed in the United States. When Galal's real estate ventures in Orange County, California, also soured, they decided to return to Egypt in 1995. There, Dalia opened a successful children's clothing boutique in an affluent suburb of Cairo, where wealthy women clients could purchase the latest children's fashions imported by Dalia from the States.

But, as expected, Dalia and Galal's return to Egypt also meant increased "family interference." Relatives on both sides of their family began urging them to go to doctors in Egypt, where "science is constantly advancing." However, Galal still maintained serious reservations about the ability of Egyptian doctors to carry out IVF with any hope of success. As Dalia explained, "My husband at first didn't want to do it in Egypt. He thought maybe some mistakes would be made. Plus, we heard a lot [of people] say that they make this in Egypt 'for commerce.'"

It wasn't until they read two news articles, one in the major daily newspaper *Al-Ahram* and the other in the news magazine *Nus id-Dunya*, that Dalia and Galal changed their opinion. The media were covering the coming to Egypt of ICSI, in which men such as Galal with serious male infertility problems could finally be helped to have a child. Dalia and Galal decided that ICSI might be the solution to their childlessness, and they proceeded to the clinics of two physicians offering this newest technology. One made Dalia and Galal feel like "he was just in it for the money." So they chose Dr. Yehia, whom they perceived as both a good Muslim and a good doctor. Now, Dalia says,

> Galal is happy to be doing it in Egypt. After what we went through in the U.S., we prefer to do it in Egypt—because they're Muslim here. And you must feel comfortable with the doctor. He must feel what you feel. He must not be doing it just for a job. He must like you to have babies. With Dr. Yehia, he shows you his feelings. From the first time we came here, we felt this. He's not doing it just for the money. He pats you and says, "OK, it will be all right."

Dalia needed Dr. Yehia's reassurance after her first trial of ICSI was canceled. After going to great lengths to obtain the hormonal medications necessary to stimulate her ovaries, including having friends and relatives bring the drugs by car and plane from Alexandria and Saudi Arabia, these agents did not succeed in producing an adequate number of ova for retrieval. As Dalia explained, "It costs your body and your feelings and your money. It's not easy. But my husband always supports me. You feel like you're desperate and after that, he says, 'We will try again.'"

When Dalia told Dr. Yehia that she did not think she could go through the emotional rollercoaster of another failed trial, he told her to remain hopeful, and this time he provided her with the hormonal medications from his own clinic supply. On their second try, the hormones worked to produce a substantial number of mature ova, and Dalia and Galal were therefore able to go forward with the ICSI procedure. Although ICSI is the most expensive new reproductive technology available in Egypt, it cost Dalia and Galal only LE 10,000 ($2,940), or less than one-fifth of what it had cost them to undertake one trial of IVF in the United States.

Luckily for Dalia, she became a mother of a test-tube baby, a beautiful little girl named Deena, in the spring of 1997. Through cards and pictures that Dalia has continued to send me from Egypt and later from Texas, where she and Galal emigrated in 1999, I have watched little Deena grow into a curly-haired child; I have mourned the loss of Dalia's second pregnancy, this one conceived "without the help of any doctors"; and I have rejoiced in the subsequent birth of a healthy ICSI son named Mohammed. As Dalia has explained to me, "Even if they have all these facilities now for IVF and ICSI, after everything, if God wants me to have a child I will, and if not, I won't." Clearly, Dalia is grateful that God has granted her permission to become the mother of two beloved, test-tube babies.

Reproductive Medicine and Religious Morality

The story of Dalia and Galal is a morality tale[3]—one in which an internationally "savvy" but religiously observant Egyptian Muslim couple must confront head on what they perceive to be the immorality of test-tube baby making in a technologically advanced but morally wayward Western Christian society. Indeed, Dalia and Galal experience a clash of local moral worlds: that of God-fearing Muslim Egypt, where leading religious authorities have effectively banned third-party reproductive donation on the basis of its inherent immorality, and that of the secular United States, where organized religion has exerted relatively little influence over the practices of medically assisted conception, leading to an unregulated climate where "anything goes." In short, reproductive medicine and religious morality form an important nexus in Egypt, but one that is hard to detect, if not altogether invisible,[4] in the religiously heterogeneous, technology-worshipping, secular societies of the West, where civil law seems to have replaced religion in monitoring the excesses of the medical profession.

It is to the role of religious morality in Egyptian test-tube baby making that this chapter is devoted. As I will argue here, religion, both Islam and Coptic Christianity in Egypt, represents one of the most fundamental arenas of constraint on the practice and use of new reproductive technologies in Egypt. Why? For one, religion serves to restrict quite effectively how test-tube babies are to be made in local Egyptian IVF clinics—restrictions with which Egyptians wholeheartedly agree and to which they stringently comply. In the process of contemplating religious restrictions and why they are important, however, would-be Egyptian IVF patients are also confronted with a host of moral uncertainties and anxieties, which may serve in many cases to curtail their desire for these technologies. Thus, religion in Egypt has served to reduce both the number of technological options available to infertile Egyptian couples *and* the number of infertile Egyptian couples willing to use the available reproductive technologies for fear of their moral ramifications. Clearly, in Egypt, new reproductive technologies such as IVF and ICSI are morally "loaded" in ways that are rarely seen (or at least reported) in the West, suggesting that these technologies are anything but morally neutral, value-free, and universally applicable.

This view that religion matters in the practice of IVF in Egypt appears to be controversial on two levels. On the one hand, religiously observant Muslim intellectuals who agree with the assertion that religion *is* important sometimes rail against the characterization of religion as a constraint on IVF practice. Clearly, infertile Egyptians pursuing these technologies do not view their religions, either Islam or Coptic

Christianity, as constraining them in any way. Instead, they see the local restrictions on the various forms of IVF and ICSI as a moral good, even as a form of moral discipline that is both appropriate and righteous. In other words, the local exclusions that prevent Egyptians from undertaking the "eighteen ways to make a baby"[5] currently available in the West are never articulated in the language of "constraint" being used throughout this book. This disjuncture between the Egyptian "emic" view of religion and IVF and my own "etic" analysis of this relationship has been pointed out to me several times by observant American and Middle Eastern Muslim intellectuals, some of whom are clearly offended by my depiction of Islam as a constraining force in their lives.

The second controversy engendered by this focus on religion in the world of Egyptian test-tube baby making takes a quite different form. I have been publicly challenged on my position by an Egyptian-born anthropologist who denies that Islam can so profoundly affect high-tech reproductive medicine as I suggest in this chapter. Calling me an "Orientalist"[6] after I delivered a paper on "Infertility, in Vitro Fertilization, and Islamic Patriarchy" at the 1996 annual meeting of the American Anthropologist Association, this Marxist scholar claimed that my description of how Islam affects the practice of IVF in Egypt was tantamount to arguing that Christianity controls the use of reproductive technologies in the West. Telling the audience that I had ignored the importance of "structure" in limiting reproductive agency, she suggested to them that I had grossly overemphasized the importance of the religion-IVF nexus in her country of origin. Perhaps because I am not Egyptian, I was unable to distinguish the difference between what people there *say* they do (to an American non-Muslim anthropologist in a polite interview setting) versus what they *really do* in the "backstage" of their lives where the anthropologist "outsider" is not permitted to enter.

Reflecting these criticisms, others have pointed out to me the paradoxical case of abortion in Egypt: Although abortion is officially criminalized within the civil (as opposed to *Islamic*) legal code in the country,[7] it is nonetheless widely and covertly practiced by both Muslim doctors and their women patients in Egypt. Extrapolating from this example to the case of IVF, it could be that both the public and private religious discourse surrounding IVF in Egypt (on the part of religious scholars, doctors, and patients) is just that—discourse, which does not in any way affect the actual practice of these technologies in Egyptian IVF clinics. As pointed out to me by a Turkish sociologist when I delivered a recent paper on this subject at Harvard University, IVF could be similar in some ways to Egyptian women's entry into the middle-class labor force in the 1980s. Because both women's work and IVF were new and controversial practices in the country during that decade, they were justified through the safety of religious discourse (and, in the case of women workers, the symbolism of the veil).[8] In other words, during periods of moral uncertainty, appeals to religion may provide an important source of moral legitimization for controversial actions. This does not necessarily mean, however, that actors themselves maintain religious convictions that are deeply felt, which would lend support to the aforementioned Marxist critique.

As I have confronted these kinds of intellectual objections over the years, I have always ended up returning to the social scientific evidence, which consists of empirical data from numerous sources. Specifically, these include the pages and pages of interviews and field notes that I personally collected while carrying out ethnographic research on this subject in Egypt; the scholarly writings of Egypt's leading IVF physicians, who attempt to represent the "Muslim viewpoint" on new reproductive technologies to the Middle Eastern and international medical communities; the supporting survey research from other Muslim countries that suggests that the Egyptian case is not unique; and my ongoing conversations with Muslim physicians in both Egypt and the United States regarding the continuing role of religion in the practice of IVF and ICSI. Thus, I continue to argue, through resort to empirical research rather than through ideological polemics, that religion matters deeply to most Egyptians, including both the doctors and patients who are involved in test-tube baby making.

Furthermore, the importance of religion in test-tube baby making may be a reflection of IVF's emergence during the late 1980s and early 1990s, a historical period of heightened religiosity and growing Islamism in Egypt. As noted by anthropologist Lila Abu-Lughod in her essay "The Marriage of Feminism and Islamism in Egypt,"

> Many Egyptian secularist liberals and progressives fear that women's rights are now under threat. They see signs of this in the growing popularity in the last two decades of the new forms of dress called Islamic or modest dress and the adoption in particular of the form of head covering called the *hijab*, institutionalized in the reversion to more conservative personal status laws, and publicized in calls made in Parliament, mosques, and the media for women's return to the home and their "traditional" roles.[9]

Both Abu-Lughod and Egyptian film scholar Viola Shafik describe how Islamist values are perpetuated through the popular Egyptian media, including the film industry.[10] Since the early 1990s, more than twenty famous Egyptian female movie stars and at least two male actors have retreated from show business for religious reasons. These so-called repentant artists have given up their careers, donned the *hijab*, and described their religious awakenings, or what Abu-Lughod calls their "born-again" experiences, through the publication of best-selling books and pamphlets. Both Abu-Lughod and Shafik see these movie stars' renunciations as indicative of a "new morality" in Egypt and of a growing ideological controversy between secular modernism and 1990s' Islamism, which has carried over into the new century.

That secular modernism is not "winning out" in Egypt and in many other parts of the Arab world has been noted in a foreword to the 1994 volume *Islam, Globalization and Postmodernity*:

> One of the best known and most widely held ideas in the social sciences is the secularization thesis: in industrial and industrializing societies, the influ-

ence of religion diminishes . . . [as] the scientific basis of the new technology undermines faith. . . . One thing, however, is clear: The secularization thesis does not apply to Islam. In the course of the last one hundred years, the hold of Islam over the minds and hearts of believers has not diminished and, by some criteria, has probably increased. Moreover, this hold is not limited to some restricted zones of social life: it is not backward or socially underprivileged strata which are specially prone to the preservation of faith, or rustics, or women, or those linked to traditional regimes. The retention of a religious orientation marks the populations of socially radical countries as much as traditionalist ones. Christianity has its Bible belt: Islam *is* a Qur'an belt.[11]

As suggested by all of these scholars, Islamic religiosity appears to be increasing in the Muslim world among many social strata. Thus, understanding how Western-generated reproductive technologies are locally accommodated within this increasingly religious moral environment is a topic worthy of serious inquiry, even though, in my own experience, it is one that generates sometimes well-meaning and at other times fervent oppositional stances. Given these intellectual risks, it is perhaps not surprising that the moral dimensions of reproductive technologies are as poorly understood in the producing nations of the West as they are in the receiving societies of the world.[12] As noted in a recent essay by Tine Gammeltoft,

> Perhaps more than any other kind of medical technology, reproductive technologies give rise to moral controversy, as they touch upon sensitive issues concerning the nature of personhood, the limits to life, and the relations between nature and culture. While the ethical dilemmas arising from technological interventions in human reproduction have spurred lively debates within the field of bioethics, anthropological contributions to these debates have been surprisingly limited. In spite of anthropology's longstanding interest in morally sensitive issues and the values underlying them, few anthropological studies have dealt explicitly with the "ethno-ethics" involved when people make choices concerning the use of reproductive technologies. While several studies examine women's pragmatic uses of technology and the socio-cultural dilemmas raised by reproductive technologies, few have dealt explicitly with the moral deliberations of technology users. An exception is the work of Rayna Rapp which examines pregnant women's moral reflections on amniocentesis.[13]

Gammeltoft makes a number of important points relevant to this chapter—first, that morally sensitive reproductive technologies are rapidly spreading around the world; second, that anthropology has failed to enter into bioethical debates about the uses of these technologies; and third, that amidst a spate of recent ethnographies focusing on women and reproduction in the West, only Rayna Rapp's work seriously engages issues of religion and morality as they affect women's difficult choices surrounding amniocentesis and second-trimester abortions of fetuses with

Down syndrome.[14] Indeed, anthropologists, and particularly medical anthropologists, have missed an important opportunity to reveal local moral discourses surrounding new reproductive technologies, thereby effectively relegating all discussion of this nature to the very Western and Eurocentric field of professional bioethics.[15]

The pitfalls of the Western bioethical approach to medical dilemmas, including the problematic uses of medical technologies, have been spelled out most clearly by the medical anthropologist-psychiatrist Arthur Kleinman in his essay "Anthropology of Bioethics."[16] Kleinman argues that the ethnocentrism characteristic of Western biomedicine is also prominent in the standard bioethical approach to health and health care, based as it is in the Western philosophical tradition. Thus, according to Kleinman, the four "universal" bioethical principles upon which international codes of bioethics are based—respect for autonomy, beneficence, nonmaleficence, and justice—constitute, in fact, a deeply problematic "intellectual commitment, which is reinforced by the deep subjectivism of the Western tradition."[17] Kleinman shows, for example, how the supposedly paramount value of autonomy of the person—or an individuated self, set off from the collective—is quite foreign in many non-Western societies, where "there is usually a paramount sociocentric consensus in which social obligation, family responsibility, and communal loyalty outweigh personal autonomy in the hierarchy of ethical principles."[18] Kleinman goes on to argue that the globalization of Western bioethics—through, for example, the adoption of international bioethical codes—has served only to privilege the deeply subjective Western ethical view of the individual and suggest to other societies that social transformation should occur through a process of "hypertrophic individualization." Kleinman continues,

> Similarly, from an ethnographic perspective, the use of abstract concepts of justice and beneficence as universal ethical principles in decision making is suspect . . . [for] there is a failure to take into account the local worlds in which patients and practitioners live, worlds that involve unjust distributions of power, entitlements, and resources. . . . Thus, there is a deeply troubling question in the philosophical formulation of an ethical problem as rational choice among abstract principles, because that problem is always the burden of a man or woman's particular world of pain and possibility. That social space contains the flows, routines, and everyday practices of moral experience. . . . Intellectualist perspectives that universalize ethical choice are flawed, at least for application to serious conflicts in the human experiences of illness and care, because they are, in a fundamental way, groundless.[19]

From Kleinman's perspective, anthropology, perhaps more than any other single discipline, is positioned to reveal the "local moral worlds" of pain, suffering, and tormented health care decision making as they are experienced "on the ground" by real people in a variety of cultural and treatment settings. Because of its contemporary commitment to ethnography, biography, social history, and political economy,

anthropology offers ways of entering "local social spaces" to reveal the moral landscape surrounding medical dilemmas of all kinds. In the anthropological imagination, a clear distinction needs to be made between the "ethical" and the "moral,"
according to Kleinman. Whereas the former refers to a codified body of abstract
knowledge held by experts about "the good" and ways to realize it, the latter refers to
the "commitments of social participants in a local world about what is at stake in
everyday experience."[20] To wit, everyday life is an inherently moral—as opposed to
ethical—process, one that anthropologists are particularly well positioned to study
and render visible.

That local moral worlds often derive from local religious traditions is a reality
that is similarly underappreciated in Western bioethical discourse. Yet, in the world of
test-tube baby making, the importance of religiously based moral systems is striking—even in the presumably secular West. In one of the few studies of its kind,
Baruch Brody offers a fascinating account of current religious perspectives on the
new reproductive technologies among America's religious communities.[21] In the official teachings of America's Christian, Jewish, and Muslim communities, at least six
major concerns have been expressed: (1) the new reproductive technologies disrupt
the connection between unitive conjugal intimacy and procreative potential that is
required by morality; (2) the new reproductive technologies often introduce third
parties into the process of reproduction, and this is morally illicit; (3) the new reproductive technologies often result in a morally illicit confusion of lineage, since children
are unaware of their (biological) parents; (4) some new reproductive technologies
(e.g., IVF) often involve a failure to implant fertilized eggs, which constitutes a form
of early abortion and is therefore morally illicit; (5) the new reproductive technologies often involve a dehumanization of the reproductive process and are therefore
morally illicit; and (6) some new reproductive techniques, especially surrogacy, involve commercialization and exploitation that make them morally illicit.

As Brody is quick to point out, however, none of these religiously based moral
concerns involves an appeal to the principles of rights, of consequences, and of justice that dominate secular discussions of bioethics. He adds,

> This might lead some readers to conclude that these are not really moral
> concerns, and that these are at most theological concerns. Such a conclusion
> would be a mistake; it would rest upon a much too narrow conception of
> morality. These religious concerns involve appeals to the portion of morality
> that involves deontological constraints. These concerns appeal to the claim
> that certain types of actions are intrinsically wrong, independent of any con-
> sequences they have, independent of any violations of rights they involve,
> and independent of any injustices they produce. It is an important feature of
> most religious moralities—but not just of religious moralities—that they in-
> volve these deontological constraints on morally licit actions.[22]

In other words, in many American religious communities, including the American Muslim community, moral concerns rest on the inherent rightness or wrongness of the new reproductive technologies and have little connection to the four,

supposedly universal, principles of autonomy, beneficence, nonmaleficence, and justice promulgated within Western bioethical discourse. Or to reiterate Kleinman's earlier point, morals and ethics must be distinguished.[23] For even in the United States, considered by many to be the seat of the Western bioethics profession, religious communities view the new reproductive technologies from an inherently "local moral," as opposed to "abstract ethical" perspective.

As we shall see in the rest of this chapter, the degree to which at least some of these moral concerns—and particularly the second and third issues of third-party donation and confusion of lineage—are also shared by the Middle Eastern Muslim community is striking. Indeed, the morally illicit nature of third-party donation and the "mixture of relations" that ensues from such donation have been of paramount concern among Middle Eastern Muslim religious authorities, who have issued repeated proclamations denouncing such donation practices, particularly donation of sperm. Furthermore, research shows that in the Muslim world, including Egypt, there is a strong convergence between official religious doctrine, the practices of the medical profession, and the actions of patients themselves in the domain of test-tube baby making. I would argue that this striking convergence between religious dogma and everyday practice marks the Muslim world as different from the Christian West. To wit, in the Middle Eastern region as a whole, religion seems to matter in the making of test-tube babies, such that religious proclamations are taken very seriously by both doctors and patients at IVF centers. In the West, on the other hand, religious influence has waned to the point where, despite official church teachings, both doctors and patients regularly defy religious doctrine by engaging in new reproductive techniques that can only be viewed as morally questionable and even sinful by those who are religiously observant. Thus, for a religiously devout Egyptian Muslim couple such as Dalia and Galal, a foray into the morally ambiguous world of American IVF is experienced as profoundly disquieting, serving to illustrate some of the ways in which the permissive West has gone awry in its degree of moral latitude and laxity.

In this chapter, we will first examine "official" Islamic discourse on the new reproductive technologies, including the ways in which religious proclamations about these technologies have been put to use by the Egyptian medical profession. However, the bulk of this chapter will be devoted to the local moral worlds of Egyptian IVF patients, who are forced to reflect on the opinions of religious authorities and attempt to implement them as closely as possible in their own lives. That the "unofficial" discourse of Egyptian IVF patients mirrors quite closely the official religious rhetoric will become clear, as will issues of religiosity and theodicy (religious meaning-making) in Egyptian IVF patients' lives. The degree to which infertile Egyptians, including both Muslims and Coptic Christians, attempt to "follow their religion" in making a family will be explored in some detail. But, as I will argue here, it is in these attempts not to "go against the religion" that problems arise—for anxious infertile patients, as well as the doctors who must arbitrate between local religious traditions and the high-tech Western medicine that they offer in their clinics. And it is this contrast between the local and the global—seen first in the opening account of the globe-hopping Dalia and Galal—to which this chapter will return, with comparative reflections by Egyptian IVF patients on their own local moral worlds and the "wrong path" taken by Western countries in their morally abandoned pursuit of technologically assisted conception at any cost.

Fatwas and "Official" Islam

Islam has often been characterized as an "encompassing" or "comprehensive" religion, in that the teachings of Islam cover many fields of human activity, be they spiritual, social, cultural, educational, economic, political, or medical. Instructions that regulate everyday activities—for example, daily prayer, food and alcohol prohibitions, marital relations, and the care of orphans and the elderly—and are meant to be adhered to by observant Muslims constitute the Islamic *shari*c*a*. Muslims consider the primary sources of the *shari*c*a* to be the Qur'an, considered the word of God as delivered to the prophet Muhammad; the *sunna* and *hadith,* a collection of traditions and sayings of the prophet Muhammad as authenticated by Islamic jurists; *ijma*c, which is the unanimous opinion of Islamic scholars; and *qias,* or analogy, which involves intelligent reasoning on issues not mentioned in the Qur'an or *hadith* (usually by examining similar or equivalent issues already ruled upon).[24]

When an action is mentioned in the Qur'an or *hadith,* the correct action to be taken by a devout Muslim is considered to be straightforward. Thus, for example, there is little disagreement among Muslims regarding the prohibition against consuming pork or alcohol. However, when there is no direct mention of a phenomenon such as medically assisted conception in these holy scriptures, then contemporary Islamic scholars must arrive at a religious judgment through interpretation, analogy, and personal reasoning, a process known as *ijtihad.*[25] Such judgments are regularly made by leading religious scholars, who issue *fatwas,* or nonbinding religious opinions, interpreting whether a behavior or action falls into one of these five categories, according to the Islamic *shari*c*a:* obligatory (*wajib*), recommended (*sunna*), permitted (*mubah*), undesirable but not forbidden (*makruh*), or forbidden (*haram*).[26]

Any religious scholar may offer a *fatwa* for the guidance of his followers, and many do.[27] However, in Egypt, the government has mandated that there be only three "official" sources of *fatwas* for the country: those issued by the country's highest-ranking religious figure, the Grand Mufti of Egypt, who was Shaikh Mohammed Sayed Tantawi during the time of my study, but who is currently Shaikh Ahmed Mohammed El Tayeb; those issued by the Grand Shaikh of Al-Azhar University, who is now Shaikh Mohammed Sayed Tantawi, following the death of Shaikh Gad El Hak Ali Gad El Hak in the late 1990s; and those issued by the Fatwa Committee of Al-Azhar University, headed by Shaikh Abdullah Al-Mashad during the time of my study.[28] Because Al-Azhar, one of the oldest universities in the world, is considered by most Muslims to be the center for Islamic education in the Muslim world, the *fatwas* issued from Al-Azhar have great weight throughout the Arab countries as well as non-Arab Muslim world.

Nonetheless, it is also imperative to mention that the Grand Mufti, the Grand Shaikh, and the members of the Al-Azhar Fatwa Committee are all on the Egyptian government payroll. Thus, they are considered by at least some Egyptians to be "mouthpieces for the government"—at worst, government "patsies"—who are viewed with some suspicion as being under the thumb of the Egyptian president, his family members, and associates. Indeed, it is clear that the Egyptian government has used official *fatwas* to support its own policies throughout the years—for example, in 1988, when the Grand Mufti of Egypt published a *fatwa* endorsing family planning. Similarly, the Egyptian government has ignored or downplayed other *fatwas* that do not promote state interests.[29]

Given the rapid development of reproductive technologies that were never mentioned in the Islamic scriptures, it is not surprising that many *fatwas* have been issued, both officially and unofficially, in recent years to cover a wide range of reproductive health issues, including birth control, abortion, sterilization, female circumcision, surrogacy, and the treatment of people with AIDS.[30] Because the Egyptian government has never had a vested state interest in infertility or the new reproductive technologies, the government has neither promulgated, nor prevented, the issuance of an official *fatwa* on the appropriate uses of these technologies. Nonetheless, such *fatwas* have emerged from Al-Azhar over the years, as early as 1980 and as recently as 2001. Presaging the developments that would soon take place in Egypt, the Grand Sheikh of Al-Azhar, Shaikh Gad El Hak Ali Gad El Hak, issued the first *fatwa* on medically assisted reproduction on March 23, 1980, only two years after the world's first test-tube baby was born in England, but a full six years before the opening of Egypt's first IVF center. The full text of the Shaikh Gad El Hak *fatwa* is included in the Appendix to this volume. As noted in my preface to the Appendix, this initial *fatwa* has proved to be truly authoritative and enduring in all its main points. By 1984, the *fatwa* had been reconfirmed by the Islamic Fiqh Council in its seventh meeting held in Mecca, Saudi Arabia, where a nearly identical *fatwa* on medically assisted reproduction was issued.[31] Since then, the original Al-Azhar *fatwa* has been upheld by several of the *fatwa*-issuing centers in the religiously conservative Arab Gulf, and it has received widespread support among the local religious leaders in Egypt, including official leaders such as the Grand Shaikh Tantawi, and popular clerics such as the recently deceased Shaikh Muhammad Mitwalli al-Shaᶜrawi, whose televised broadcasts brought him a large following.

In fact, the basic tenets of the originally issued Al-Azhar *fatwa* on medically assisted reproduction have achieved wide acceptance throughout the Arab world—including, quite importantly, among the Muslim physicians who provide new reproductive technologies to their Muslim (and Christian) patients. With regard to this last point, the degree to which the official Islamic discourse on new reproductive technologies has affected Middle Eastern reproductive medicine, at the level of both discourse and practice, is quite striking. In terms of discourse, the religious opinion on the new reproductive technologies has been made known to the Middle Eastern medical community through the writings of Gamal I. Serour, Mohamed Aboulghar, and Ragaa Mansour, the three founding members of the first Egyptian IVF center. Gamal Serour, in particular, has played an exceptionally active role in disseminating the "Muslim viewpoint" on the new reproductive technologies to Middle Eastern as well as international, medical audiences, through numerous articles published in both regional and international medical journals.[32] As a distinguished professor of obstetrics and gynecology and director of Al-Azhar's International Islamic Center for Population Studies and Research, Serour has been both a prolific scholar and a force behind the development of an official code of ethics in human reproduction research in the Muslim world.[33]

In article after article, Serour describes the original Al-Azhar *fatwa* as the first authoritative statement of the Muslim view toward medically assisted conception. Serour then goes on to spell out the main points of that *fatwa,* including its implications for Muslim physicians. First, he notes that medically assisted conception was not mentioned in the primary sources of the *sharica.* However, both the Qur'an and the *hadith* have affirmed the importance of marriage and family formation through marital procreation, as indicated in the opening paragraphs of the Al-Azhar *fatwa.* Infertility is acknowledged in the Qur'an, and its treatment is encouraged in order to preserve the integrity of the marital union. According to Serour, the prevention and treatment of infertility are of "particular significance" in the Muslim world, as "the social status of the Muslim woman, her dignity and self-esteem are closely related to her procreation potential in the family and in the society as a whole."[34]

As for the techniques of medically assisted conception themselves, the Al-Azhar *fatwa* spells out rather clearly which techniques are *hallal,* or permitted, and which are *haram,* or forbidden. In Serour's recent writings, he has carefully reiterated these points, as well as his own conclusions about the implications of the "Islamic opinion" for the practice of medically assisted conception in the Muslim world.[35] Accordingly, among Muslim physicians and patients participating in medically assisted conception, a number of basic guidelines must be followed:

1. Artificial insemination *with the husband's semen* ("without doubt of its exchange or mixing with that of other couples or species"[36]) is allowed, and the resulting child is the legal offspring of the couple.
2. Since marriage is a contract between the wife and husband during the span of their marriage, no third party should intrude into the marital functions of sex and procreation. In Sunni Islam, no third-party donor of *any* kind is acceptable, whether he or she is providing sperm, eggs, embryos, or a uterus. Such donation is tantamount to *zina,* or adultery. (In Shi'a Islam, the minority branch found primarily in Iran, parts of Iraq, Lebanon, and the Arab Gulf, both donor eggs and donor sperm are now accepted as of the late 1990s.[37] However, the child conceived from donor sperm cannot inherit from his or her social, infertile father.)

3. Extracorporeal (in vitro) fertilization of an egg from the wife with the sperm of her husband and the transfer of the fertilized egg back to the uterus of the wife ("without exchange or mixing with cells from other couples or species"[38]) *is* allowed, provided that the procedure is indicated for a medical reason and is carried out by an expert physician.

4. Adoption of a child from an illegitimate form of medically assisted conception is not allowed. The child who results from a forbidden method belongs to the mother who delivered him or her. He or she is considered to be a foundling (i.e., an illegitimate child, or *walad il-zina*).

5. The physician is the only qualified person to practice medically assisted conception in all its permitted varieties. If he performs any of the forbidden techniques, he is guilty, his earnings are forbidden, and he must be stopped from his morally illicit practice.

6. Establishment of sperm banks with "selective" semen threatens the existence of the family and the race and should be prevented.

7. If the marriage contract has come to an end because of divorce or death of the husband, medically assisted conception cannot be performed on the ex-wife even if the sperm comes from the former husband.

8. An excess number of fertilized eggs (pre-embryos) can be preserved by cryopreservation. The frozen pre-embryos are the property of the couple alone and may be transferred to the same wife in a successive cycle, but only during the duration of the marriage contract.

9. Multifetal pregnancy reduction (i.e., selective abortion) is allowed only if the prospect of carrying the pregnancy to viability is very small. It is also allowed if the health or life of the mother is in jeopardy.

10. All forms of surrogacy are forbidden. This includes gestational surrogacy, which involves extracorporeal fertilization of an egg from the wife with sperm from the husband and transfer of the fertilized egg to the uterus of another woman.

With regard to this last point, the Islamic Fiqh Council, which meets in Saudi Arabia, initially allowed what might best be described as "polygynous gestational surrogacy"—that is, the transfer of the fertilized egg of a man and his wife to the uterus of the second wife of the same husband. However, the Council later withdrew its opinion; its *fatwa* on medically assisted conception is now nearly identical to that of Al-Azhar. Although the Egyptian Coptic Orthodox Patriarchate holds that surrogacy is acceptable, surrogacy is not practiced in Egypt among Copts because the Egyptian Society of Obstetrics and Gynecology's code of ethics for IVF centers also forbids the use of third parties of all kinds, including surrogates. Thus, in Egypt, surrogacy arrangements cannot be officially made.

Serour goes on to state that research and practice in medically assisted conception are issues of "great importance to every Muslim physician and the couple seeking treatment for their infertility."[39] Thus, all potential candidates for new reproductive technologies must be screened by a physician, and as a matter of conscience, the physician must limit access to these technologies under clinical circumstances in which there are significant risks to potential offspring.[40] Furthermore, he notes that "it is assuring to the conscience of the Muslim physician and those patients seeking his/her advice" to observe the aforementioned guidelines.[41]

But to what degree are these religiously inspired medical guidelines, particularly the explicit prohibitions on third-party donation of reproductive materials, followed by physicians in Egypt and the rest of the Muslim world? Or, put another way, to what degree does official religious discourse—translated into medical discourse through the writings of Serour, director of Al-Azhar's International Islamic Center for Population Studies and Research—actually affect medical practice in the realm of test-tube baby making?

A global survey of sperm donation among assisted reproductive technology centers in sixty-two countries in the mid-1990s provides some indication of the degree of convergence between discourse and practice. In all of the Muslim countries surveyed, including the Middle Eastern countries of Egypt, Iran, Kuwait, Jordan, Lebanon, Morocco, Qatar, and Turkey, as well as a number of non-Middle Eastern Muslim countries including Indonesia, Malaysia, and Pakistan, sperm donation in artificial insemination and IVF is strictly prohibited.[42] As the authors of this global survey explain, "In many Islamic countries, where the laws of Islam are the laws of the state, donation of sperm was not practiced. AID [artificial insemination with donor sperm] is considered adultery and leads to confusion regarding the lines of genealogy, whose purity is of prime importance in Islam."[43]

They note that donation of sperm is also prohibited by the three main branches of Christianity—Roman Catholic, Eastern Orthodox, and Protestant. In the Roman Catholic countries, for example, the official position of the church, as enunciated by the pope himself, regards donor insemination and in vitro fertilization as fundamentally wrong because of the separation of the "unitive" conjugal and procreative aspects of normal intercourse.[44] Thus, Catholics are officially prohibited by the Vatican from practicing IVF and other new reproductive technologies.

> However, in most Christian countries the medical legislation and regulations are liberated from religious influence and therefore semen donation is permitted. Even in Italy and Spain, countries which are strongly influenced by the Roman Catholic church, the practice of sperm donation in ART [advanced reproductive technology] is not prohibited. In the Catholic countries of South America sperm donation in ART is not practiced at public ART centers, but since regulations concerning the procedure do not exist, sperm donation in ART is practiced at private ART centers.[45]

The degree to which the Muslim Middle East looks different from its Jewish neighbor Israel is also striking. In *Reproducing Jews: A Cultural Account of Assisted Conception in Israel,* anthropologist Susan Kahn has shown how rabbinical authorities have made numerous rulings on the appropriate uses of the new reproductive technologies for their followers, rulings that have clearly influenced the practices of doctors in Israel's mostly public IVF sector.[46] Although most Israeli rabbis share

Muslim clerics' concerns about the implications of sperm donation—specifically, about adultery, the conception of illegitimate children, and future incest of half-siblings—these concerns matter only when *Jewish donor sperm* is utilized. Thus, many rabbis, including the most ultraorthodox, allow donor insemination with *non-Jewish donor sperm*, a reproductive practice that seems counterintuitive until one considers that a child's essential feature of "Jewishness" is conferred through the mother and not the father. Furthermore, as in the Christian West, many Israeli Jewish women looking for a sperm donor, including single women, who are allowed to reproduce by the rabbinical authorities and the Israeli state, defy these rabbinical rulings, choosing instead to use Jewish donor sperm. In other words, even though the medical and religious establishments are structurally enmeshed in Israel as they are in Egypt and the other Middle Eastern Muslim countries, the opinions of leading rabbis may simply not hold sway as the *fatwa*s do in the neighboring Muslim countries. Furthermore, rabbinical interpretations of what is acceptable in assisted conception are clearly more permissive than the *fatwa*s in the Muslim countries. Thus, many of the practices being employed in Israel today—including donor insemination among unmarried Jewish women, surrogacy arrangements between married couples and single surrogates, and sperm banks for both Jewish and non-Jewish donor sperm—are absent in the neighboring Muslim countries.

In short, what is deemed moral in one country may be considered immoral in the next. Furthermore, what is considered immoral by religious authorities may nonetheless be widely and regularly practiced by physicians and their patients, with or without legal support. Thus, in the world of test-tube baby making at least, the Sunni Muslim Middle East—with its strict, religiously derived prohibitions against third-party donation and surrogacy, which appear to be followed closely by physicians and patients working within Middle Eastern IVF centers[47]—is significantly different from the rest of the world. But the question is: Why? To answer this, we must turn to infertile patients themselves, whose "unofficial" religious discourse about the moral valence of new reproductive technologies and of themselves as moral human beings has much to do with the ways in which these technologies are, and are not, utilized in places like Egypt.

"Unofficial" Discourses of Islam and IVF

In Egypt, as in many other countries in the Middle East, the last two decades have been a period of profound religious revitalization. Islamism—the renewed commitment to Islam that has resulted in political and even militant (qua "fundamentalist") movements in many countries—has shaped not only the macropolitical landscape of the Middle East, but the micropolitics of everyday life as well. As noted earlier, many Muslims in places like Egypt have renewed their personal commitment to Islam, both outwardly in their adoption of Islamic dress and inwardly in their quests for a spiritual relationship with God. On the streets of cities like Cairo and Alexandria, the vast majority of women are now veiled, covering their hair and necks, if not their faces, and men's beards and callused "prayer spots" on their foreheads mark them as religious men.

Over the fifteen years that I have worked in Egypt on the issue of infertility, I have witnessed the growing importance of religion in everyday life. From the standpoint of my research, many Egyptians of all social classes, educational backgrounds, and religious affiliations (Copt or Muslim) have convinced me that their religion—and, more specifically, their personal relationship with Allah, the only God to both Muslims and Christians—matters a great deal to them in determining how they think about their infertility and pursue its treatment. For example, in the late 1980s, the poor women who were both my informants and my friends wanted me and others to think of them as "good Muslims," and although most were illiterate, they could often refer to and repeat important religious scriptural passages with an impressive degree of accuracy. Among the infertile poor, ultimate explanations for infertility that implicated God's will, and particularly his "testing" of a woman's religious faith and patience, provided powerful theodicies that sustained many women, and their husbands, through long periods of childless suffering.[48]

When I returned to Egypt to study the utilization of new reproductive technologies among elites, I assumed, perhaps naively, that religious influences and understandings might be significantly less pronounced among this more educated, worldly, and probably more secular population. What I discovered was quite the opposite. Elites at Egyptian IVF centers were as concerned about their religion, if not more so, than the poor women I had encountered in my earlier study. Clearly, they were more religiously educated, having studied the scriptures and other religious texts directly in many cases. But, in addition to being proud of their religious expertise, these elite women and men were often deeply concerned about being moral persons according to the dictates of their religion. For Dalia and Galal and many others like them, being "good Muslims" and "following the religion" very closely were major themes to which they returned again and again in interviews. In fact, I was told many times by Egyptian IVF patients—both Muslim (87 percent of my sample) and Coptic Christian (13 percent)—that Egyptians are particularly religious, as they live in an "Islamic country" where religious belief is "strong." According to one infertile Muslim woman, "Egypt is good. People are religious and know their religion well. We are controlled by our religion." Similarly, an infertile Coptic man explained, "The Egyptian is very sticky to his religion. We say in Egypt, 'Who is not afraid of God?' And this is a very good point."

Indeed, I was always struck during interviews at how often God's name was invoked—not only in formulaic expressions such as *mash Allah* (thanks to God) and *el-hamdu-lillah* (praise be to God), but in lengthy discussions of the importance of God's will and his control over test-tube baby making. In other words, without much probing on my part, interviews with elite patients in Egyptian IVF centers were typically filled with talk of God and the powerful religious theodicies that provided meaning to the suffering that these long-term infertile couples had endured. This high level of religious discourse among Egyptian IVF patients stands in marked contrast to the West, where ethnographic accounts of the experience of IVF in the

United States and Britain suggest that religious theodicies are rarely invoked.[49] In fact, sociologist Arthur Greil, in his study of middle- to upper-middle-class infertile couples in western New York, has argued persuasively that technological developments in infertility treatment, by making the experience of infertility more "open-ended" than it may have been in previous generations, have served to limit the effectiveness of religious theodicies among infertile Americans. Few infertile couples in his study, and particularly the husbands, were able to "bring religious resources to bear successfully on their attempts to deal with the meaning threatening aspects of the experience of infertility."[50]

This finding that technological developments have superseded the meaning of religion among highly educated, middle- to upper-class northeast coast Americans is not at all surprising. But what might surprise most Americans is that the opposite is true in Egypt: There, highly educated, middle- to upper-class Egyptians are also keen to try the latest infertility technologies, but most do so under the firm conviction that God has made them infertile for good reasons that only He can know; that He expects them to seek treatment to overcome their infertility; and that the new technologies He has created to overcome infertility are firmly under His control. Thus, God ultimately decides whether or not these technologies will succeed in any given case, and His reasons for success or failure must not be questioned. Ultimate outcomes are simply "in God's hands," and Muslims who are faithful realize that they "do what they can," leaving "the rest up to God." In numerous interviews—with both Muslims and Copts, women and men, veiled and unveiled, avowedly "religious" or not—I was told how Egyptians experience this "will of God" in their lives. For example, one infertile woman who had just gone through her first trial of IVF explained,

> We have some religious beliefs, if God intends to give us a baby, He will give us. If we don't have a baby, we are not going to take it against God's will [e.g., through adoption or third-party donation]. We may try to make a test-tube baby, and still we don't have a baby, because this is God's will. But we have changed our opinion a little: It's God's will, but we have to do our best. That is what made us try [IVF] this time. There's a proverb: "Allah told us to try, and we will do our best."

Similarly, an infertile man remarked,

> Medicine has improved, okay? [There are] new things, new methods, and this ICSI is the most advanced thing. But still, such things are very critical and sensitive. It's God's will if they will be successful. The doctor said to us, "Medically, we've done it, and technically everything is very good. But keep praying to God that it will work." You see, the doctors are placing their faith in God, too.

This recurring theme of "God and doctors" was related by another infertile woman as follows:

We believe in God first, and then doctors second. A doctor is only a means for God's will. Who makes the sperm? Who makes the egg? Who makes this small cell to be subdivided? Who controls all this? It's all the science of God. He's controlling it.

This belief that God is "in command" of one's life and one's procreative outcomes was shared by women and men in my study. Virtually everyone I interviewed—from the most religious women completely swathed in black and gray, who removed their facial veils and gloves only in the secluded privacy of the interview room, to the most secular women, who dressed in Western-style clothing, smoked during interviews, and drank alcohol with their husbands in their homes—described for me their personal relationship with God and the ways in which they attempted to bring themselves "closer" to Him, especially during the period of an IVF or ICSI cycle. For some women, this meant reading the Qur'an and other religious material. For others, both Muslim and Copt, this meant undertaking special pilgrimages to holy sites within Egypt and also to Mecca and Medina in Saudi Arabia. The power of prayer, including special prayers asking God to grant a test-tube baby, was also mentioned by many women and their husbands. In fact, women commonly described the intense prayer they undertook before, during, and after an actual IVF or ICSI cycle. Finally, a few women described the "bargaining" they did with God around test-tube baby making: either a promise to call the hoped-for child by a special, religiously meaningful name (e.g., Muhammad or Ahmed), or, in some cases, a promise to adopt the *hijab,* or veil, after a successful IVF cycle. As one woman, about to embark on her first trial of ICSI, described it,

> I've been doing some special prayers, and reading the Qur'an more. Also my mother and all our parents. I'm just praying to God for help. Maybe after [ICSI], in my heart, if it succeeds, I will do the *hajj* [pilgrimage] next year. Maybe I'll also become *muheggaba* [veiled].

For women and men who have made it to an Egyptian IVF center, they are convinced that God wants them to undertake IVF or ICSI—that, in effect, they are "achieving God's will" by undergoing this expensive, difficult, and risky procedure that is not for the faint of heart. However, most have not arrived at this conclusion on their own. As seen in the case of Dalia and Galal, several "religious" physicians played a fundamental role in making them accept IVF. In fact, physicians, who may accentuate their own religiosity, are often crucial arbiters in patients' tortured decisions over whether or not to undertake test-tube baby making—sometimes turning patients "on" to the new reproductive technologies, as in the case of Dalia and Galal, or, in many cases, turning them "off" for reasons that will be explored in some detail in the following chapter.

In many other cases, couples contemplating the uses of new reproductive technologies look directly to their religion for guidance. Both Muslim and Christian IVF patients in my study had consulted spiritual leaders, either local *shaikh*s or Coptic priests, to ask their opinions about whether test-tube baby making conflicted in any way with religious doctrine. One of the five Coptic couples in my study explained,

> He: This was one of our concerns, so we had asked one of the priests in our church. He said as long as it's from both husband and wife and no cells are transferred from, for example, another husband or another woman isn't carrying the baby, then there's nothing against it.
>
> She: We haven't seen anything written, but the priest said, "Our Pope, Father Shenuda, has said this." So it's like a *fatwa*.

Another Muslim woman in the study recounted how she "found comfort" by going directly to Al-Azhar University to seek a religious opinion on IVF.

> I wanted to know if this will be illegal in the religion. So I asked a *shaikh*. I went to a special place for *fatwas* at Al-Azhar. I went to the *mufti* there and asked his opinion. He told me that if it was from the couple themselves [i.e., no third-party donor], it was permitted. Of course, this is supervised by Al-Azhar. They are specialized in taking opinions and then making a decision. I was *very* concerned to do the right thing. I didn't want to do something and then see that it was a mistake afterward.

The reference in both of these descriptions to *fatwas*, even in the case of a Coptic Christian couple, is quite relevant. In fact, there were relatively few women and men in this study who did not talk about *fatwas*, as many had made great efforts to find an authoritative *fatwa* on medically assisted conception before embarking on this course of treatment. Not surprisingly, given the aforementioned role of Al-Azhar University in Egypt, many IVF patients described the Al-Azhar *fatwa* included in the Appendix as being *the* authoritative statement of the Islamic opinion on IVF. Some patients had read about it in books, seen it published in the newspaper, heard it broadcast over radio or television, or seen it posted on IVF clinic walls. Others had gone directly to Al-Azhar to hear the opinion "from the experts." Thus, despite the aforementioned ambivalent feelings of many Egyptians about the relationship between Al-Azhar and the Egyptian government, the considerable credibility still maintained by Al-Azhar University as a beacon of religious education and as a source of official and religiously "correct" *fatwas* was clear in this study. Many IVF patients told me, rather adamantly, that Al-Azhar had "approved" of IVF, that the doctors from Al-Azhar University such as Gamal Serour were the first to "make test-tube babies," and that *fatwa*-issuing institutions in Saudi Arabia and other Muslim countries where they "apply the *shari^ca*" had followed suit in their agreement with the Al-Azhar *fatwa*. Shaikh Tantawi—"our *mufti*" and "the biggest one in Islam"— was also mentioned by some patients as being in full agreement with other Al-Azhar *shaikhs* on the permissibility of IVF. Similarly, among Coptic patients, Father Shenuda, the highest-ranking religious authority in the Egyptian Coptic Orthodox Patriarchate, was said to have accepted the basic premises of the Al-Azhar *fatwa*.

As a result of this religious knowledge among patients, I was told time and time again that IVF is *only* permissible *as long as sperm and egg come from husband and wife,* according to the Al-Azhar *fatwa.* Indeed, Egyptian IVF patients in my 1996 study were "experts" on the official religious opinions regarding third-party donation. And it is to their discourses surrounding donation, particularly why it is religiously unacceptable and morally illicit, that we now turn.

Discourses of Donation

As every patient who visits an Egyptian IVF center knows already or soon finds out, the new reproductive technologies, including artificial insemination, IVF, and ICSI, are *hallal,* or permissible and morally licit, only if procreative substances (i.e., sperm, eggs, embryos) and locations (i.e., wombs) are restricted to the conjugal unit of husband and wife. This is the decision that has been reached by Al-Azhar, confirmed by many other Sunni Muslim religious authorities, instituted in Middle Eastern IVF clinics, *and* adopted by patients at Egyptian (and other Middle Eastern) IVF centers. To reiterate my earlier argument, official religious discourse on the new reproductive technologies has been translated rather exactly into medical practice on the part of both Middle Eastern IVF physicians and their Muslim patients, who seek to "do right" by the religion in the making of a test-tube baby. While religious discourse and medical praxis do not necessarily converge in other areas of reproductive health in the Middle East (e.g., differing opinions on the use of contraception), the degree to which the prohibition against third-party donation in test-tube baby making has "taken hold" in the hearts and minds of infertile Middle Easterners is quite remarkable. Clearly, it is reflected in the passionate discourses among Egyptian IVF patients regarding the moral degradation of third-party donation and the reasons why new reproductive technologies should be restricted to married couples.

To be more specific, the vast majority of women in my study (forty-eight out of sixty-six) specified quite clearly that IVF and its variants are only *hallal,* or religiously permitted, if they are "from the husband and wife." On the contrary, they described third-party donation as *haram,* describing this practice as "against the religion" and a "closed matter." Although many women knew that third-party donation was considered a "medical treatment" in other countries, they argued that this is "not accepted in Egypt" and, therefore, "does not happen." As one woman put it, this is *"the* limitation" on test-tube baby making in Egypt—the major arena of constraint which all Egyptians, Muslim or Christian, must consider and accept.

When I asked Egyptian IVF patients such as Dalia and Galal why third-party donation is a "mistake," I typically received lengthy responses about the many reasons donation is both an immoral and ill-conceived practice. Furthermore, the responses did not seem to differ much whether I was interviewing a woman alone or with her husband. However, I noticed that Egyptian husbands often became very animated during these discussions, due, I would guess, to the many implications of sperm donation for masculinity and paternity.[51] To take but one example, a couple affected by severe male-factor infertility had "sent their papers outside" to both England and the United States, but offered me this litany of excuses about why they had decided against going abroad for treatment:

She: One of the centers told us our only solution is to have donor insemination. This was abroad, not here. It was in England, and also the States. But, of course, no, *never, never*. We are both Muslims. You *must* know the father and mother. For having relatives, for marriage.

He: This is going to be illegal—an illegal child. As if it's from a relationship without marriage—like adultery.

She: In Egypt, we think about incest. I cannot be married to my brother, my uncle.

He: Who's the father of this boy? And in the future, maybe he'll meet his brother or sister from another mother. And we heard about sperm banks. This is forbidden! For sure, there is a *fatwa* on this. Only donation is *haram*. But other sorts of IVF, ICSI, there's no problem so far as it's "from the father and mother," the husband and his wife, and putting the embryo back into the same mother.

She: That's why we never considered [going] outside. As long as [ICSI is] present here, why go outside? I think it's a matter of conscience. We have confidence; I think [the doctors] are straightforward here. But outside, if I want [donation], okay, and if not, okay also.

This couple's response is very typical and very similar to that of Dalia and Galal, who were mortified to learn about donor insemination and sperm banks in America, donation of extra embryos to other couples, and American doctors using their own sperm to impregnate unwitting patients. Dalia and Galal thus were concerned to find a trustworthy Muslim physician who would share their concerns about avoiding a "mixture of relations," thereby preserving the lineage and preventing future incestuous marriages of half-siblings from identical donors. The concerns voiced by Dalia and Galal and many other Egyptian IVF patients revolved around two sets of related issues: first, the moral implications of third-party donation for marriage, and second, the moral implications of donation for kinship and family life.

With regard to marriage, Islam is a religion that can be said to privilege—even mandate—heterosexual marital relations, with "relations" referring to the instrumental, affective, and sexual components of the marital union. Thus, the first paragraph of the Al-Azhar *fatwa* reads, "Lineage and relationship[s] of marriage are graces of Allah to mankind." The *fatwa* goes on to describe reproduction as "marriage's noble objective." As is made clear in the *fatwa*, reproduction outside of marriage—either through premarital or extramarital relations—is considered *zina*, or adultery, which is strictly forbidden in Islam.

Although third-party donation does not involve the sexual "body contact" of adulterous relations, nor presumably the desire to engage in an extramarital affair, it is nonetheless considered by Islamic religious scholars to be a form of adultery, by virtue of introducing a third party into the sacred dyad of husband and wife. Qur'anic rules forbid any kind of sexual association outside formalized, legally sanctioned marriage.[52] Thus, *zina,* or extramarital relations, is considered one of the "great sins," according to the Qur'an and *hadith.*[53]

Apparently, ordinary Egyptians share this view. The term *zina,* which glosses in Egypt as both "adultery" and "prostitution," was one I heard repeatedly when I interviewed IVF patients on the implications of donation. Both Muslims and Christians, the latter of whom are forbidden to divorce, described *zina* as a "big sin." In their view, it matters not *how* "donation" occurs, through extramarital intercourse or through donor techniques. Rather, it is the very fact that another man's sperm or another woman's eggs enter a place where they do not belong (e.g., a wife's womb, when only her husband's sperm rightfully belong there) that makes donation of any kind inherently wrong and threatening to the marital bond. As one husband, who had not yet decided whether he "accepted" IVF, explained to me,

> According to our religion, this is called *iqtilat in-nasab,* "mixing relations." We consider it some kind of *zina,* prostitution. Because there are many *hadith*s from the Prophet Muhammad that confirm this. If you put your sperm in another woman besides your wife, you go to hell. This is adultery. There is a *hadith* on adultery. "If you put your sperm in another woman other than your wife, you are going to commit a sin."

The other aspect of third-party donation that troubles marriage is the potential for incest among the offspring of unknown donors. This is a concern that has been raised by rabbis in Israel, a small, "intermarrying" country of only 6.5 million Jewish citizens.[54] But even in neighboring Egypt, an "overpopulated" country of nearly 70 million, moral concerns have been raised about the potential for a single donor's offspring to meet and marry each other, thereby undertaking the incestuous union of half-siblings. This potential for incest is horrifying to Egyptian couples such as Dalia and Galal, who describe incest as the "main thing" wrong with donation. Most couples who mentioned the possibility of incest were glad that Muslim scholars had anticipated this eventuality, thereby prohibiting donation practices.

The other major moral concern for Muslims is that third-party donation confuses issues of kinship, descent, and inheritance. As with marriage, Islam is a religion that can be said to privilege, even mandate, biological inheritance, which is expressed not in the Western medical language of "genes" and "heredity," but rather in local kinship idioms of "lineage" and "relations." The first paragraph of the Al-Azhar *fatwa* begins, "Lineage and relationship[s] of marriage are graces of Allah to mankind" and ends, "Therefore, origin preservation is a most essential objective of Islamic law." Preserving the "origins" of each child, meaning his or her relationship to a known biological mother and father, is considered not only an ideal in Islam, but a moral imperative. The tie by *nasab* (lineage, or relations by blood) is considered to be one of God's great gifts to his worshippers; thus, the Qur'an established rules to ensure the sanctity of the family and the purity of *nasab.*[55] Knowledge of *nasab* is considered morally significant to Muslims, just as it is in some portions of the Jewish community.[56] The problem with third-party donation, therefore, is that it destroys a child's *nasab*, which is immoral in addition to being psychologically devastating to the child.

Infertile Egyptian IVF patients have clearly adopted this reasoning and use the term *iqtilat in-nasab*, or "mixture of relations," to describe this untoward outcome. Such a mixture of relations, or the literal confusion of lines of descent introduced by third-party donation, is described by Egyptians as being very "dangerous," "forbidden," "against nature," "against God"—in a word, *haram*, or morally unacceptable. According to Egyptian IVF patients, every human being must have *nasab*, relations who are "known." It is argued that donation, by allowing a "stranger to enter the family," confuses lines of descent, and particularly paternity in an emphatically patrilineal society. For men in particular, but for women as well, ensuring patrilineal continuity and the "purity" of lineage through "known fathers" is of paramount concern. Thus, the importance of "knowing" one's "relations," and particularly one's "real" parents, was mentioned time and time again in interviews. I was told repeatedly that every child must have a "known" father and mother—that is, biological ones, even though the term "biological" was never used by Egyptians. Without "known" parents, familial relationships themselves, and particularly the relationship between father and child, will be severely threatened and even irreparably damaged. Many of my informants told me that a child conceived through third-party donation will have an "unknown father" and will wonder who his "real father" is (qua, the problem of "genealogical bewilderment" described for Western adoptees).[57] Egyptian men emphasized the father's perspective on this genealogical disruption—namely, that a child conceived through donor sperm will "not be my own," will "not be my son," will "not be my child." I was told by many husbands, whose wives often agreed with them, that "not being the father of the child" was totally unacceptable to them, "the most important point."

Egyptian men's inability to accept the child made through donor sperm was considered to be inauspicious for family life. Bringing such children into the world was considered unfair to the children themselves, who would never be treated with the love and concern parents feel for their "real" children. Such a child could only be viewed as a bastard—an *ibn haram*, literally "son of sin." Thus, a child of third-party donation starts its life off as an "illegal" child (the term used in the Al-Azhar *fatwa*). It is deemed illegitimate and stigmatized even in the eyes of its own parents, who will therefore lack the appropriate parental sentiments. As one woman put it,

> My baby must be mine, and from my husband. This is logical. A mother will never feel this is her child if it is from another [man's] donated sperm or ova. It's only natural. Everything must occur naturally. If the child is from the father and mother, they will feel this is *actually* our baby. If not, we'll not be a family. You will feel you're acting, making a movie, living a life that's not true.

This firm conviction that social parenthood is an impossibility is clearly linked to the legal and cultural prohibitions against adoption in Egypt. Third-party donation and adoption are associated in Egyptians' minds, just as they are officially linked in the Al-Azhar *fatwa*. As mentioned earlier, the Islamic scriptures, including the Qur'an, encourage the kind upbringing of orphans, but disallow adoption as it is known in the West, whereby the child adopts the social parent's (usually the father's) surname. This kind of legal fiction—that an orphan adopts a family's name and is treated as its own child—is considered *haram,* or morally illicit in Islam. This is why Muslim countries such as Egypt, which adopt Islamic personal status laws, must "get around" the adoption of orphans by allowing only permanent fostering arrangements.[58] In Egypt, couples with proof of infertility can "adopt" a child from an orphanage and raise the child for the rest of his or her life. But, as the legal guardians of the child, they cannot change the child's name on the birth certificate (which is usually created at a police station or in the orphanage). Although some Egyptians are willing to go to court to change the child's name, this is considered tantamount to a public admission of adultery (i.e., that the child is one's own from an illicit relationship) and is considered morally questionable on a number of grounds, particularly for women. So is changing the child's birth certificate in an illegal way, through bribes and falsification of records. The fact that at least some Egyptian foster parents attempt to conceal the origins of their legal ward by falsifying the child's "illegitimate" history is a reflection of the severe stigmatization that still accompanies these children.[59] Indeed, Egyptian adoption scholar Amira el Azhary Sonbol states, "Illegitimate children themselves are regarded as a real stigma, almost a threat, a source of evil."[60]

In short, adoption in Egypt is fraught with great difficulty—legally, religiously, and culturally. This is why infertile couples from the humblest backgrounds to the wealthiest households rarely consider adoption to be a viable solution to involuntary childlessness. But this option seems to be entertained even less by elites than by the poor. To wit, whereas poor infertile women in my first study were sometimes open to the idea of adoption, elites in Egyptian IVF centers considered adoption to be very similar to third-party donation, and they usually dismissed both simultaneously as being *haram,* or "against the religion." In fact, the issue of adoption was raised in nearly half of my interviews conducted in Egyptian IVF centers, and half of those said they were absolutely opposed to this practice, usually on religious grounds. Although adoption was seen as preferable to third-party donation, most of those refusing the idea of adoption argued that adoptive parents, like the parents of third-party donor children, would "lack the feelings" necessary to provide a proper upbringing for an adopted child. Those who said they would consider adopting a child—almost all women, who were often opposed by their husbands—usually deemed adoption a "last resort." They pointed out that adoption was only acceptable if you raised the child without giving it your name, and most of them argued that their husbands would refuse this as a solution. One couple, who like many others moved seamlessly in their interview from a discussion of the pitfalls of donation to adoption, explained,

He: If the sperm and the egg are not from the husband and the wife, there won't be *nasab* [blood relations]. He won't be my son. I don't guarantee it. I want my own son!,

She: Especially the man must know that it is his own son. Unlike the woman who is carrying it, the man needs to have one of his own body. . . . The most important thing is that it must be from the husband and wife. This is nature, which was created by God.

He: Islam also refuses adoption. It is prohibited. When I need to have a child to bring him up [through adoption], I don't give him my name. I must give him his own name.

She: We thought of such an idea [adoption]. But I found that it will cause problems. Besides, there's science and we didn't lose hope completely. If it was not possible for me or for him to have children, we might think of something like that, to adopt a child for the sake of God.

He: But, thanks to God, we have hope that God will be generous to us and give us [a test-tube baby]. But if they said that it was impossible for us to have children, we might adopt a baby. But one thinks of something like that as a last solution—only when he loses hope completely to have children.

That adoption is a problematic last resort done only for the "sake of God" is reflected in a striking finding from my 1996 study of Egyptian IVF patients. Of the sixty-six couples in my study, only one, who happened to be the last couple I interviewed, had actually "adopted" a child. Married for twelve years and now in their late thirties, the wife, a private school math teacher, and the husband, a gastroenterologist, had decided to adopt an infant only when their case, an absence of sperm production, was deemed hopeless by experts they consulted in the West. The wife had initiated the adoption process and had chosen a six-month-old baby girl from a Cairo orphanage. To avoid "religious problems," the couple had no intention of changing the child's name on the birth certificate, which had been issued at the orphanage. Although the couple's family members realized the infant was adopted, their outpouring of love toward the child took the adoptive parents quite by surprise. As the wife exclaimed, "They know she's an orphan, but they accepted her. They love her *so, so, so much*. They can't believe she's not our baby."

Despite the love the adoptive couple also professed for this child, they did not consider her their daughter, and they were subsequently pursuing ICSI at Nozha Hospital in the hopes of having their own offspring. Indeed, they never mentioned the adoption until halfway through the interview, and only in the context of another story about a relative who had emigrated to America and solved his male infertility problem through adoption. In other words, although they vowed to raise this child, giving her a special room apart from the test-tube children they hoped to create, the adopted orphan girl would always, on some level, be an outsider to the family.

Contemplating Immoralities

These deeply felt constraints on adoption in the Muslim world may come as a surprise, even a shock, to Westerners, who consider adoption the "natural" solution to infertility. However, most Egyptian Muslims are equally appalled at the ease with which Westerners seem to solve their infertility problems—through an exploitative international trade in adoptive babies, through "rent-a-womb" arrangements with surrogates, through sperm and embryo banks, and through preternaturally assisted conceptions of postmenopausal women, including grandmothers carrying their own grandchildren. Some Egyptians, such as Dalia and Galal, find out about these practices directly when they are confronted with them in Western IVF centers. Others, as we have seen in the last chapter, learn about them through the Egyptian media, which actively import the latest stories about new reproductive technologies in the form of both news and entertainment. Thus, Egyptian IVF patients are continuously exposed to the latest practices of assisted conception in the West and are in an excellent position to contrast their local moral worlds with the global scene.

In making these local-global comparisons, Egyptians, both Muslim and Coptic Christian, perceive themselves as morally superior to the Christian West, where in their opinion, the "complete freedom" of medically assisted conception has created "many problems." Sometimes prefacing their remarks to me with the apologetic acknowledgment that "each society has its own traditions and customs," many Egyptian IVF patients told me that the West has lost its moral compass in the pursuit of reproductive practices and trajectories that go against God and His will. The vehemence with which Egyptians shared their righteous indignation over the immorality of Western practices was often quite striking. For example, one Muslim woman exclaimed,

> If I go abroad, and I have something wrong [infertility], they take my eggs and his sperm and put [them] in another woman, the "carrier." And they have "the bank of the sperms"—if you want him yellow [blonde], fair, black, dark hair. What is this? Nonsense! No way! For Muslims, this is wrong, and for Christians everywhere, too. But everyone does it there in the U.S. and Europe. I have no idea why, because the punishment of this is horrible. Maybe these mistakes are made abroad, but here, no way! Because all the doctors are Muslims, and it will be *their* punishment. So they are religious, too.

Similarly, a Coptic Christian man asserted,

> The most important point is to make sure if it's your boy or not! We've heard that a doctor in England, he makes transfers from his own self—more than

twenty babies. He's in prison now, because he kept secret the names of families with his babies. He was taking the egg from the woman and injecting
from his own sperm. This made me very afraid. This was maybe one year
ago. A big and intelligent doctor, and when they asked him why, he said: "I
want to make many families happy." But this is a big problem, and it makes
me very surprised. In Egypt, this is *not* going to happen. If they're Muslims
or Christians, they're sticking to their religion very hard. And especially the
Muslims are afraid. But I think there is some "looseness" in Europe and
America. Now they are far away from their religion, even the Christians. I
went to a church in Germany, and I found only three elderly people praying.
Here in Egypt, you'll find lots of people in church, really praying.

As suggested by these comments, one from a Muslim and one from a Christian, the
Western practices that have evoked the most comment from Egyptians include the
presence of sperm banks and the racial implications of sperm donation, surrogacy
and disputes over surrogate offspring, and the most recent practice of egg donation.
Topics that did not evoke much interest or commentary among my Egyptian informants—despite heated debates about these issues in the West—included embryo
preservation, research, and disposal. In one of the IVF centers in which I worked,
embryo cryopreservation was not available; therefore, all unused embryos were disposed of immediately, without concern on the part of either patients or physicians
that feticide was being committed (although at least some patients regretted that
valuable embryos were being "wasted"). However, one Coptic Christian couple told
me that the Egyptian "pope," Father Shenuda, had argued against embryo disposal,
urging Coptic couples to have all of their fertilized embryos transferred back to the
wife's uterus if embryo preservation facilities are not available. In the other IVF center in which I worked, which catered to a large population of Coptic Christians,
cryopreservation facilities were available. Most couples, both Muslim and Christian,
who were offered these services chose to freeze their embryos for future trials and
had no moral compunctions about doing so. Dr. Mohamed Yehia, the director of
this center, told me that "We don't have this problem" of anti-abortion groups
protesting the disposal of unclaimed embryos, as in the United States and Britain.
But he did admit that it was difficult to know what to do with unclaimed embryos in
cases lost to follow-up. Indefinite storage was an impossibility in his clinic, due to
limitations of space, the expense, and problems of record-keeping. Because he
found it difficult to make decisions on a case-by-case basis, he and his partner, Dr.
Abdel-Hamid Wafik, had instituted a five-year cutoff point for the disposal of unclaimed embryos. This was in keeping with Western standards and also made sense
medically, as the quality of cryopreserved human embryos begins to decline after
three or four years.

In short, in Egypt, the Islamic view on embryo disposal does not coincide with
the Roman Catholic view that life begins at the moment of conception; thus, in the
Muslim world, embryo disposal is not considered murder. As a result, American embryo debates—part of the larger anti-abortion rhetoric that has polarized Amer-

ica—were not being played out on Egyptian soil at the time of my study. However, three famous incidents, all true, which had occurred in Western IVF laboratories had been widely publicized in the Egyptian media and were clearly presented as cautionary tales to elite Egyptians who might consider seeking IVF treatment abroad. In one case, a doctor had used his own sperm to impregnate patients. In another, a postmenopausal grandmother had acted as a surrogate for her own daughter (who was missing a uterus). And in the third case, a Dutch white woman bore IVF twin sons, one white and one "black" (actually biracial), due to a careless admixture of semen in the IVF laboratory. Declaring that such practices would *never* take place in Egypt, where patients can trust that their doctors are God-fearing Muslims, Egyptian IVF patients spoke of these Western practices with righteous incredulity and a healthy dose of typical Egyptian humor. For example, one woman told me, "Jane Fonda went to a doctor in Italy—she was over fifty—to make a baby." When I expressed surprise and uncertainty, she continued, "I believe so, she got a baby. Even women over sixty! It's a big story in Italy. Even [if] you don't have to have a uterus; a lot of women get pregnant in their stomachs!"

The influence of the Egyptian media in promoting "sensational" stories of this kind was clear in many interviews. For example, another woman told me that she saw a program on television, in which "in another country, the mother wants a child with green eyes and white skin and yellow hair. It's like a supermarket—like she bought it from a supermarket! You can get tall or fat, strong, a genius! This is refused *completely* in Egypt."

Clearly, one of the sensational elements broadcast by the Egyptian media involved the racial implications of donation, which, according to one man, "scared many people in Egypt." Although Egypt is officially a "color-blind" society, with no explicit concept of "race" or racially based "minorities," veiled and not so veiled racism, especially toward individuals with dark skin and African features, is prevalent among Egyptians. Several elite women in my study made openly racist comments to me during interviews, two of them using the English term "nigger." And such comments particularly surfaced around issues of donation, as women described the racial "surprises" that might be in store for unwitting parents.[61] For example, one woman mused,

I wouldn't like it if someone will tell me, "You can have sperm or semen from this guy." It's not right. How would my husband feel? It's not his baby. It's not correct! And I wouldn't like to have a black child with a big nose! But if he gets a "nigger" nose, then it's not from me, because I'm 100 percent Egyptian!

Another woman had joked with her IVF physician,

I told the doctor, "If he's black, he's not mine!" He told my husband, "Your wife is very beautiful" [i.e., light-skinned]. I was worried about this thing, of course. If I have a black baby, from whom? Also, I heard an Arabian man from the Gulf—you know they are not black, but they have dark skin like Indians—after this operation, he had a European-looking baby, after IVF in Europe. So he and his wife refused to receive him [the baby], because, of course, a mistake was made. They refused to take him, and this was a big problem, of course.

As revealed in these statements, Egyptians are not only shocked by Western donation practices, both intentional and accidental, but they fear them as well. This fear of the immoralities (and racial outcomes) that occur in American and European IVF centers keeps many well-to-do Egyptian couples, including Egyptian Christians, from undertaking treatment attempts abroad, even if they consider the West to be more advanced and successful in the application of these new reproductive technologies. Some couples, such as Dalia and Galal, who have traveled abroad to seek treatment, feel lucky to have "escaped" before making a test-tube baby of questionable origins. And some Egyptian IVF physicians with whom I spoke told me that the nature of Western donation practices prevents them, as Muslims, from considering emigration to the Western countries, where they might be expected, as physicians, to carry out medical practices that are immoral. In short, fear of Western donation practices constitutes a powerful constraint on transnational movement of both Egyptian IVF patients and physicians to the Western countries.

This is not to say, however, that such transnational movements never occur. I was told by a staff member in one Egyptian IVF center that some infertile Egyptian couples have been known to go abroad in order to seek third-party donors who cannot be obtained in Egypt. Similarly, anthropologist Susan Kahn has told me that Palestinian Muslim patients may request donor methods in IVF clinics in Israel. Perhaps most interestingly, Sunni Muslim IVF patients may be traveling abroad in order to access donor methods offered by Shi'ite Muslim IVF providers. As noted earlier, only the Shi'ite sect of Islam has allowed any form of third-party donation, making the Shi'a minority paradoxically much more liberal than the Sunni majority in the realm of test-tube baby making. These Shi'ite rulings on the permissibility of both donor egg and donor sperm have been made by the Supreme Jurisprudent (*faqih*) of the Shi'a branch of Islam, none other than Sayyid ʿAli Khamenei, the successor of the Ayatollah Khomeini in Iran. His *fatwa*, issued and published in 1999, is in keeping with the Shi'ite tradition of *ijtihad*, or jurists' legal reasoning, which makes the Shi'ites often "more adventurous" than the Sunnis, according to scholars of Shi'a.[62] The actual effect of this ruling is that donor technologies are now being applied in Iran—a fact that shocked the Sunni Muslim majority when they heard an Iranian female IVF physician (completely swathed in black) discuss Iranian donor egg practices at a Middle Eastern IVF conference held in Lebanon in 2001.[63]

In short, for the Shi'ite minority, including the substantial diasporic community in the West, third-party donation is now a distinct possibility, one that is forbidden to the millions of the world's Sunni Muslims. The effect of this disparity is that at least some Sunni Muslim IVF patients are now traveling abroad in order to request donor technologies from Shi'ite Muslim IVF providers. According to one such provider,[64] Sunni patients who come to him sometimes reason that third-party donation is now a realistic option, given that at least one branch of Islam has allowed the practice. Thus, at least some Sunni Middle Eastern Muslim patients are moving outside their country, and their own branch of Islam, in order to overcome infertility.

Returning to Egypt, however, none of the infertile elites of my 1996 study, all Sunni Muslims or Coptic Christians, regarded donation as an acceptable alternative in their own lives, and they often reasoned that the indigenous restrictions on donation were a sign of the inherent moral goodness of Egypt when compared to the West. However, such comparative moralizing belied the deep-seated anxieties many infertile patients in my study still harbored regarding the moral standards of IVF *in their home country.* Many of the women and men I interviewed, including those who had tried the new reproductive technologies in Egypt and those who had not, confessed to me their worries about the possibilities of inadvertent "mix-ups" and "mistakes" being made in Egyptian IVF laboratories, leading to what might best be described as "accidental donation." These fears of unintentional "mixing" were a major concern among the poor infertile Egyptian women whom I met in the late 1980s. They opined that a poorly funded, public IVF center could not be counted on to practice IVF without occasional mistakes being made. But I was surprised to see such fears resurface in my 1996 interviews with elite patients in private Egyptian IVF centers. Although no accidents had yet been reported by an Egyptian IVF clinic—not that they would, given the severe recriminations the clinic staff could be expected to suffer in this Muslim country where donation is prohibited—many Egyptian IVF patients retained lingering doubts that unintentional mistakes might be made in private IVF laboratories. These fears were clearly exacerbated by the Egyptian media's reportage of the Dutch case, whereby a careless laboratory admixture of sperm had resulted in the birth of twins of different racial backgrounds. According to my informants, this story compounded the "confusion" and "worry" that mistakes might be made, even under the best of circumstances.

Furthermore, this common belief that unintentional "mixing" may occur in Egyptian IVF laboratories has clearly contributed to the ongoing widespread public disapproval of the new reproductive technologies on the part of ordinary Egyptians. As noted in the last chapter, most Egyptians, and especially the lesser-educated lower class, know relatively little about the new reproductive technologies and believe that, as a group, they are *haram,* or against the religion, due to the "mixing" of procreative substances. Furthermore, even highly educated Egyptian elites attending IVF centers believe that at least *some* unscrupulous Egyptian IVF doctors *intentionally* mix procreative substances in order to improve their clinics' success ratios, thereby ensuring their financial futures. For at least some—and probably many infertile Egyptians who never make it to IVF centers—the moral uncertainty associated with these fears of mixing constitutes *the* major arena of constraint on their acceptance of these technologies. For husbands in particular, the inability to know for certain whether one's sperm has been mixed with that of another man prevents them from accepting this line of treatment altogether; once the products of conception leave one's body, it is impossible to know for certain whether they are being returned to a wife's womb untainted. One husband told me,

I will *never* try IVF. And [my wife's] refusing IVF, also. We are not very sure with IVF if they add, by any way, any other thing—eggs or sperm or any other thing. . . . At least I'll think three hundred times before I try IVF. It's a *very* hard decision. I would *really* have to ask a *shaikh*. We, as Muslims—no offense—when we feel some suspicion, we don't do it, and when we feel relieved, God facilitates us. The Prophet says, "Ask your heart. If you feel relieved, do it, and if not, don't do it."

Indeed, this man was not alone in harboring lingering suspicions that illegal sperm mixing might occur in Egyptian IVF laboratories. In several cases in my study, including that of Mabruka and Ragab, whose story was told in the last chapter, moral uncertainties about the possibility of sperm mixing had led to flat refusal of IVF on the part of husbands, some of whom were eventually convinced to try IVF only after they had established rapport with a particular IVF physician. In fact, many women and men in this study said that they had asked their IVF physician directly about the possibility of mixing and other mistakes being made. In most cases, the doctor had been successful in convincing these patients that their fears were totally unfounded.

For their part, most Egyptian IVF physicians realize that patients are extremely concerned about this eventuality, and they take steps to reassure them. In my very first meeting with Dr. Mohamed Yehia, he reiterated the importance of the "religious aspects" of IVF for most of his IVF patients. In his view, economic barriers to IVF constituted the major obstacle for most infertile Egyptians. But, for those who could afford IVF, the religious implications and the possibility of inadvertent or advertent third-party donation were of paramount concern. Toward the end of my study, I interviewed Dr. Yehia again about what he does to quell patients' moral anxieties. He said,

Well, I'll tell you, if a patient is hesitant, I usually tell them, "Don't do it," because I believe that doubt can cause many problems later on. But, in my experience, most of these cases return after two to three weeks and want to go ahead. I rarely bring the subject up on my own, but if the patient thinks that there may be some accident, with mixing of sperm—and many patients do ask me that—what I usually tell them is, "We are very careful, maybe even more than you, and we don't have any sort of advantage or incentive to mix up. We are quite sure of our reasons—for example, we are not going to do that to get our success rate higher. So we are quite sure of ourselves, and it is you—her eggs and your sperm." This is very important that they feel that you are very sure of whatever results you have, and this is not going to effect whatsoever intentionally mixing up.

And the other thing is: We are making every *human effort* possible to make sure this [mixing] is not being done and the system is tight—foolproof. We don't have this problem [of human error]. Everything is color-coded; we are taking about six or seven steps; every one is being done very cautiously; they are put in different incubators, different groups, different drawers; and Patient A is blue, Patient B is green. And so it's really *very* tight; very, very, tight. I think this is the standard; this should be the standard.

Many of Dr. Yehia's patients had noticed these small details: the importance of labeling of all specimens, the color coding, the informed consent form that mentioned the Islamic *shariᶜa,* and the relatively small number of patients on any given day (thereby reducing the chances of patient confusion). Furthermore, somewhat ironically, the less-than-perfect success rates at Dr. Yehia's (and other Egyptian) IVF clinics were reassuring to patients, constituting one form of "proof" that doctors were not increasing their success rates through tampering with patients' sperm and eggs.

In addition, in Dr. Yehia's clinic, he and his laboratory partner, Dr. Abdel-Hamid Wafik, had instigated a unique method of "witnessing" through videotaping. At the end of a successful round of laboratory fertilization/injection, each couple was given the videotaped version of the actual laboratory procedure that had produced their own embryos. Not only did couples treasure this tape—calling it their first picture of their test-tube babies, which they would show to them when they were grown—but they also felt reassured by the tape and what it captured. Indeed, this tape made visible to couples what was essentially invisible—not only the microscopic process of fertilization itself, but also the inner recesses of the laboratory from which they were otherwise barred admission. Thus, by exposing what was otherwise obscure, the videotape made couples feel that they were, in fact, witnesses to their own laboratory conceptions. And, they reasoned, the videotape also served as a witness to the laboratory doctor himself, ensuring that he would be exceptionally careful in carrying out the procedure with precision and accuracy. Although such videotaping was very expensive for the clinic, Drs. Yehia and Wafik argued that it had been a very successful innovation, and they were proud to be the only ones offering this service at the time of my study.

However, one could argue that because sperm and eggs do not come with patients' names on them, even a videotape does not constitute irrefutable evidence that no mixing has occurred. In fact, one patient questioned me about this, when there was a one-egg discrepancy between the number of fertilized ova reported on her discharge summary and the number shown to her on her videotape.[65] Thus, it was never clear to me how videotaping alone could absolutely prevent mistakes from being made. As noted earlier, such mistakes—including switched embryos or gametes, as well as negligent destruction of embryos—have clearly occurred in Western IVF laboratories, constituting one of the major "legal trouble spots" in assisted reproduction, according to an American law professor who specializes in this subject.[66]

It is interesting to note that, in neighboring Israel, many IVF clinics, and particularly those catering to orthodox Jewish populations, employ orthodox women called *maschgichot,* or "supervisors," who monitor all laboratory procedures involving the handling of reproductive genetic material, in order to ensure that there is no untoward mixing of sperm, eggs, or embryos.[67] To my knowledge, such laboratory witnesses, who literally peer over the shoulders of laboratory technicians while they work, are not routine in most Western IVF centers, nor were they being employed in Egypt at the time of my study. Nonetheless, such "human witnessing" of IVF laboratory procedures has been highly recommended by at least one Al-Azhar theology professor, Dr. Mohammed Rufaat Osman, whose interest in reproductive health and new reproductive technologies made him the logical theological supervisor of my 1996 study. He told me that, in his writings, he had argued that *two doctors* should always be present in an IVF laboratory at any one time, so that one could serve as a witness to the other, thereby preventing any mistakes or wrongdoing from occurring. This practice, he argued, was in keeping with the Islamic tradition of always witnessing important events (e.g., marriage, divorce) with at least two parties. Yet, why this practice of human witnessing had not taken hold in Egypt as in Israel at the time of my study—especially given pronounced Egyptian anxieties about the possibilities of laboratory mistakes— was puzzling. The absence of laboratory witnesses probably had to do with the lack of regulation and monitoring of these clinics (a problem to be described in the following chapter), as well as the costs of employing such additional personnel.

Ultimately, then, patients in Egyptian IVF centers must rely on individual doctors to be trustworthy. Most of them reason that a Muslim doctor will certainly fear the punishment from God that will rest on *his* shoulders—not the patient's—if he makes a mistake. In fact, among Muslim patients, I was told time and time again that it is important to have a Muslim physician as an IVF doctor, and particularly one who is "religious." The perceived need to trust a "good Muslim" physician was apparent in one woman's statement:

> Today, I'm coming to Dr. Mohamed Yehia, [because] I know he's Muslim and knows his God. So he knows [mixing] is *haram,* and he will not do it. But if he did it, it will be *his* responsibility only, not ours. God will not punish us. So [Dr. Yehia] will not come to me and tell me, "I will bring you sperm from another place or an egg from another place," and I'll tell him, "Okay." He will not ask me, and I will not say yes. I am sure he is okay, because he is Muslim. *He* will be afraid of mistakes, because he's afraid of God!

Another patient of Dr. Yehia's, an infertile man, opined,

> We trust in our country, because I'm Muslim and my doctor is Muslim. So he is very . . . he believes in God and knows everything. This is very important: the doctor must be a good Muslim. Dr. Yehia is very famous in Egypt and he's very religious. I think so. He always says, "*bismillah ir-rahman ir-rahim*" [in the name of God, the compassionate] Dr. Wafik—he's religious, too. To me, it is very important that the doctors are Muslims, and this is one reason not to go outside [abroad].

Even some Christian patients liked the idea of having a "religious" Muslim physician for some of the same reasons cited here. In fact, Dr. Yehia was proud of his large following of devoted Christian patients. As one of these patients stated,

We asked Dr. Yehia many times [about mixing]. He always said, "Don't be afraid. We are not making a lot of these operations—not more than one or two per day." And I think Dr. Abdel-Hamid [Wafik], now we know them very well. We don't want to change. Even if it fails many times, we want to stay with them. We think that they are afraid of God, so this is a very good point.

In general, the tensions that are increasingly pronounced between the minority Coptic and majority Muslim population in Egypt are also played out in the medical realm. There, patients tend to seek physicians of their own religious background and are deeply suspicious that physicians of the "other religion" will not provide them with honest care. Thus, Dr. Yehia's large cohort of devoted Christian patients was quite remarkable. He attributed this overrepresentation of Christians in his practice to the fact that Egyptian Copts are prohibited from divorcing, even if they are infertile. Therefore, those who have the financial means will be compelled to seek IVF in order to have children. Furthermore, at the time of my study, there were no Christian doctors or hospitals offering IVF services in Egypt; thus, infertile Coptic couples were forced to seek out a Muslim doctor. Nonetheless, it is worth repeating that Dr. Yehia's Christian patients were extremely happy with him, as apparent in interviews with five Coptic couples in his clinic, two of whom had produced test-tube babies.

That the ability to trust one's physician on multiple levels matters to both Muslim and Christian patients—and that some IVF doctors achieve trust in part by invoking their religion—is a major theme of the following chapter. Suffice it to say here that moral concerns weigh hard on the hearts and minds of *both* IVF patients and physicians in Egypt, who, in bringing life into the world, place their faith in each other and in God, the ultimate witness.

Conclusion

In the essay "Virgin Births and Sterile Debates: Anthropology and the New Reproductive Technologies," Cris Shore states:

> The lesson from anthropology is that every society has a vested interest in controlling reproduction, and in each, we tend to find dominant institutions—the church, the state, the medical profession, or whatever—competing to monopolize the discourses through which legitimate reproduction is conceptualized.[68]

In this chapter, I have attempted to focus the anthropological lens on the ways in which the reproductive destinies of infertile Egyptian women and men are being constrained—if not directly controlled—by religious forces, which, in the case of the new reproductive technologies, clearly influence the practices of the medical profession. Despite Shore's claim that dominant institutions tend to compete with one another in the control over high-tech reproduction, we find quite a different story in Egypt. There, Egyptian IVF doctors closely follow the Islamic *shari*c*a* as outlined by Al-Azhar religious scholars. Furthermore, their patients, both Muslim and

Christian, rely on them to do so for the many reasons outlined in this chapter. For both physicians and patients, clearly much is at stake here—"not only traditional definitions of family, . . . parenting, kin connection, and inheritance, but the conventional understandings of nature, life, humanity, morality, and the future."[69]

It seems appropriate to conclude this chapter by "globalizing" an argument first made by anthropologist Marilyn Strathern—one that has subsequently been taken up by her many students working on infertility and new reproductive technologies in Western European settings.[70] Strathern has argued that the new technological interventions in reproduction have had a main effect of privileging "biogenetic relatedness" as the ultimate and determinative form of kinship in Euro-America. Basically, because these technologies promise to bring "biological" children to those couples who might not otherwise have them, these technologies powerfully solidify extant cultural notions of what a "natural" family is: that is, one in which children are connected to their biological parents through "blood ties."

Despite anthropologist Susan Kahn's claim that Strathern's argument is inherently Eurocentric—given that it does not seem to fit well with the unique Israeli assisted conception scene, where kinship itself is truly being refashioned by these technologies[71]—I would propose that Strathern's argument about the biologically essentializing potential of these technologies may, in fact, apply to many other global sites. Certainly in the Sunni Muslim world, Strathern's argument takes on perhaps its strongest form. There, the pre-existing Islamic imperatives regarding "pure" lineage, coupled with Islamic prohibitions against adoption, not only privilege but, in fact, *mandate* biological as opposed to social construction of families. It is not surprising, therefore, that infertile Muslims living within this genealogically restrictive environment have rushed to embrace these new reproductive technologies, for, in many cases of intractable infertility, these technologies represent the only hope of creating children of "known relation" to a biological mother and father. In summary, in the Sunni Muslim Middle East including Egypt, biogenetic relatedness—glossed as *nasab*, or blood relations—is an absolute imperative, and the new reproductive technologies have made possible the creation of *nasab* between infertile parents and test-tube children who might otherwise never have existed.

Yet, Strathern and her students, particularly Sarah Franklin, have also pointed to the genealogically "defamiliarizing" potential of these technologies, "whereby familiar legitimations of both specific phenomena, such as reproduction, and the analytical domaining of such phenomena, for example as 'natural' or 'biological', can be challenged."[72] To take this argument to the Middle Eastern Muslim world, these technologies have certainly led to a further entrenchment of deeply held local cultural beliefs about the nature of kinship, family life, and parenthood; on the other hand, they have also fundamentally altered understandings of the ways in which families *can* be made. The effect, in Egypt at least, has been a reinforcement of traditional notions of biological kinship with a simultaneously profound *destabilization* of infertile couples' certainty that "biological children" are, in fact, being created in Egyptian IVF laboratories. As we have seen in this chapter, this acute awareness among Egyptians of the creative possibilities of third-party donation has led to much local angst about and real constraints on the use of IVF, particularly among husbands concerned about biological paternity and sperm mixing. But it has also bolstered a sense of moral superiority on the part of many Egyptians, who, in their tendency to cross-cultural comparison, are convinced that their local moral world is far superior to that which lies outside, and particularly to the West. Indeed, test-tube baby making in Egypt has led to a sort of moral reassessment and re-entrenchment among infertile Egyptians—one that, not surprisingly, has gone hand in hand with what anthropologist Gregory Starrett calls "the Islamic trend" in the country as a whole.[73]

However, I must conclude this chapter with an inherently Eurocentric observation—one made by an American non-Muslim anthropologist who is sympathetic to, but nonetheless coming from outside, the local moral world of my informants. I would like to suggest here that there may, in fact, be a paradoxical down side to the restrictive moral code now in place in Egyptian test-tube baby making. Why? On the one hand, Islam glorifies motherhood and all it entails, insisting that paradise "lies under the feet of mothers" and that children are the "decorations of worldly life."[74] Yet, infertile women in Egypt who attempt to achieve glorious motherhood through resort to new reproductive technologies are quite narrowly limited in their technological options by virtue of a religious doctrine that prohibits any form of ova donation, as well as surrogacy and adoption. Thus, religion in and of itself—and this would include, interestingly, both Islam and Coptic Christianity in Egypt—serves as a fundamental constraint on how families are to be formed and motherhood realized.

In closing, I must reiterate that this view of religion as constraint is *not* one shared by the vast majority of infertile Egyptians, including women, who agree completely with the Islamic prohibitions against all forms of third-party donation, surrogacy, and adoption. In their view, religious prohibitions are a moral good rather than an unfortunate limitation on technological options, keeping infertile Muslims and their doctors on the "straight path" desired by God. Thus, religious morality constitutes a critical dimension of the new reproductive technologies in Egypt, affecting, on a most fundamental level, whether and how test-tube babies are to be made.

CHAPTER 5

Providers

The Movie Star Doctor

I met Dr. Mohamed Yehia, the director of the IVF-ET unit at Nozha International Hospital, on a typically warm, sunny Egyptian morning in late May 1996. Dr. Yehia was the sixth Egyptian IVF provider with whom I had met in the course of one (in)tense week, as I attempted to seek permission to base my anthropological study of IVF in one or more well-established Egyptian IVF centers. Ultimately, Dr. Yehia proved to be the most helpful. Rather than viewing me, as some of the other physician providers did, as an "outsider"—an intruder into the secret world of Egyptian test-tube baby making—Dr. Yehia seemed to regard me as a sympathetic collaborator in getting the word out about the availability of IVF/ICSI in Egypt, particularly in his clinic. Thus, in what appeared to be a mutually beneficial relationship, Dr. Yehia seemed to realize that he could provide me with what I needed, IVF and ICSI patients willing to talk, and in return, I could provide him with publicity of potentially international scope.

Furthermore, when I gave Dr. Yehia copies of my prior books on Egyptian infertility, including one that was "hot off the press" that year,[1] he actually made the effort to promptly read them. My books spurred much future discussion and debate over the state of the infertility treatment scene in Egypt, including issues that were to emerge through my work in his center. Ultimately, over that long and busy summer of 1996, I interviewed Dr. Yehia informally thirteen times, and I concluded our collaboration with a much longer formal, tape-recorded interview that tied up many loose ends regarding my findings. For his part, Dr. Yehia proved to be an eager informant in his own right and an incredibly helpful logistical supporter of my research. He arranged for me to use a private hospital room where I was able to conduct confidential interviews, as confidentiality turned out to be a major issue of concern for many Egyptian IVF patients. And he introduced me to patients like Amira, Mikhail and Georgette, and Dalia and Galal, whose stories have been told in previous chapters precisely because Dr. Yehia encouraged these women and their

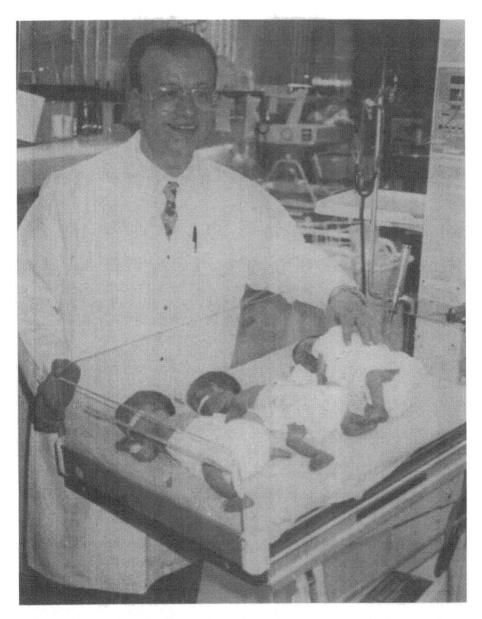

Dr. Mohamed Yehia, clinical director of the Nozha International Hospital IVF unit, with Egypt's first ICSI triplets. (Photo courtesy of Nozha International Hospital)

spouses to share their tales of infertility and test-tube baby making with me. Never did he ask for any of this personal information about his patients in return. Rather, he said he hoped to learn from my study in general terms—not only what patients liked about him and his practice, but also what they did not like—so that he could make improvements in patient care.

Ultimately, over the summer of 1996, as I watched Dr. Yehia rush down the hospital corridors to and from various ultrasound scans, ova retrievals, embryo transfers, patient consultations, and deliveries of test-tube babies, and as I listened to the frank adulation of his many devoted patients, I came to think of Dr. Yehia as the *dynamic* Dr. Yehia, an eager, energetic, highly competent IVF physician with a virtual cultlike following of patients who seemed to deem him more "hero" or "saint" than doctor. Furthermore, his popularity as a charismatic healer of distressed infertile couples had grown relatively quickly and dramatically, and was clearly related to a number of factors in his personal history.

The son of affluent, educated parents, Mohamed Yehia was a movie star before becoming a doctor—and this was a fact that many of his patients found to be both fascinating and titillating. While going to medical school, the young Yehia also studied at Egypt's High Institute of Acting over a period of two years, landing minor to relatively major roles in "about thirteen to fourteen" Egyptian movies. But when the competing demands of acting and medicine became "absolutely difficult," he decided to choose medicine as a more intellectually compelling, long-term career.

Nonetheless, according to Dr. Yehia, his actor's training has been of huge benefit in the establishment of a successful IVF practice. In acting school, he explained, "they teach you how to impersonate the character you'd like to put to other people." He continued,

> They teach you how to speak, when you raise your voice, how to raise it. And I think every doctor should learn that, because it makes life much easier. Because you don't treat every patient the same way. Some patients want you to be authoritative—the doctor. Some patients want you to be more like a friend. And some patients want you to be the father. We were taught these things in the Acting Institute, so that's how I learned it. [But] it will *never* be approved in [Egyptian] medical school. I'm trying to get this into my students now. I just pick two students and get one of them to be the patient, the other the doctor, and see the impression and vice versa. How to act like a patient, how to act like a doctor. But it takes a lot of time, a lot of effort, because it's not systematized here.

When I asked Dr. Yehia whether it would be all right to discuss his prior career as a movie star in the book I hoped to published, he said, "Yes. I have been [back] in Egypt now only five or six years, and I can tell you the things I learned in acting school were of tremendous help in that." Indeed, Dr. Yehia has come back to Egypt after many years "on the hoof" as a transnational physician migrant, moving across Europe and the Middle East in his quest to establish himself as an IVF expert. A full professor of obstetrics and gynecology at Ain Shams University in Cairo by his early forties, Dr. Yehia describes how he expedited his academic career track by traveling abroad for both research and training. With his father's help, he spent two years in France collecting data that would later help him "publish a lot" and achieve the American equivalent of tenure in the Egyptian medical academy. Because of his academic success, he received a fellowship to undertake IVF training in England in the late 1980s. Although he hoped to migrate to England for good, upon returning to Ain Shams, he was asked to replace an Egyptian professor who was taking part in a physician exchange program with a hospital in Jiddah, Saudi Arabia.

What was supposed to be three months in Saudi Arabia turned into a year. Describing this period as "a major turning point in my career," he was able to initiate a successful IVF program in Jiddah, utilizing the talents of additional Egyptian expatriate physicians who continue to operate this clinic. Once the Jiddah program was up and running, Dr. Yehia decided to return (with his Egyptian physician wife and two small children) to Egypt to initiate a similar program in Nozha Hospital.

Like many other small hospitals in Cairo, Nozha is privately owned—in this case, by a group of Ain Shams professors, including Dr. Yehia. In fact, Dr. Yehia is both the director and co-owner of the IVF-ET unit, which is housed almost indistinguishably within the maternity ward of the hospital, but which operates as a separate entity. The other co-owner is Dr. Abdel-Hamid Wafik, a distinguished pathology professor from Al-Azhar University medical school. It is Dr. Wafik who runs the Nozha Hospital IVF laboratory, who "keeps the accounts," and who Dr. Yehia describes as his closest colleague, friend, and "partner for *years*." Although Dr. Yehia is the one with the clinical "reputation"—which he has managed to successfully carry over from Saudi Arabia to Egypt, attracting many Saudi and other Arab Gulf patients along the way—he is the first to admit that his IVF practice would not be successful without the incredible laboratory technical skills of his collaborator "Hamid," who sought his own training in IVF laboratory practice primarily in Australia, but also in England and Germany.

Both Drs. Yehia and Wafik are university professors, which gives them additional credibility with IVF patients who want their procedures performed only by the "biggest professors." Yet, they describe their academic positions in Egyptian medical schools as "part-time jobs," which are not nearly as time-consuming as the private medicine that most Egyptian academic and government physicians practice "on the side." Both Drs. Yehia and Wafik run their IVF clinic in the morning hours—seven days a week, only stopping for medical conferences. And, unlike many other clinics that keep patients waiting so that the doctor can make the "grand entrance like a big movie star," Dr. Yehia (a *real* ex-movie star) and Dr. Wafik have no time for this pretense. Instead, they are sticklers about "timing and organization," insisting to patients still operating on "Egyptian time" that they arrive punctually so that procedures can be conducted to the minute in a tight and efficient schedule. Generally speaking, the two doctors are able to see fifteen patients a morning and still leave the hospital by 1:30 P.M. After stopping off at their university offices and eating the traditional late Egyptian lunch, they then head to their *third* offices located in private clinics they each run in the suburb of Heliopolis.

Dr. Yehia's private clinic is a general ob/gyn practice, which caters primarily to large numbers of infertility patients. Dr. Wafik's private clinic is a pathology laboratory in which his primary patients are men seeking semen analysis (who are often referred there by Dr. Yehia). Very recently, the two doctors have moved into an adjacent clinic complex in which high-tech computer methods and short-circuit television allow them to project visual images of patients' sperm, eggs, and so forth back and forth between offices—right before the patients' eyes. Both doctors are proud of being high-tech mavericks—testing out, sometimes innovating, and then employing the latest, most sophisticated clinical, computer, and cryopreservation technology to improve overall success rates in their IVF practice. Dr. Wafik, for one, was particularly proud of his ability to perform ICSI with immature spermatids retrieved from men's bodies through testicular biopsy. This procedure, he emphasized to me during an informal interview, was the *most advanced* technique in the world, and was being performed successfully in their very own Egyptian center. Furthermore, as noted in the last chapter, theirs is the only IVF practice that provides each patient couple with a videotaped recording of the laboratory fertilization and micromanipulation of the patients' gametes, so that couples may visualize their "future children" as the tiniest embryos.

The technological prowess and highly competent clinical skills of this dynamic duo seem to have paid off on a number of counts. According to Dr. Yehia, their IVF clinic, which was neither the first nor the second in the country, has grown tremendously over a five-year period and is now the busiest year-round. He also believes that their clinic probably has the highest success rates in all of Egypt—rates that he monitors carefully (in order to report to the hospital's board of trustees) and believes that competing clinics should also attempt to track.

Nozha Hospital's success rates, particularly for the newer and more difficult ICSI procedure, are impressive. Drs. Yehia and Wafik were the first to introduce ICSI to Egypt in 1994, leading to the delivery of healthy ICSI triplets who were much heralded by the Egyptian media. Since this initial victory, their ICSI success rates have risen to at least 35 percent per trial—high even by Western standards. Proof of these rates is evident in statistical data that Dr. Yehia collects and was happy to share with me over the course of the summer I spent in his clinic. For example, during one week in June, Dr. Yehia delivered six ICSI babies. During the month of July, there were forty-four ultrasound-confirmed pregnancies out of a cohort of 110 IVF and ICSI patients, with still "one week to go" in terms of confirming additional pregnancies. Initially calling July 1996 an "incredible month," he later modified this to "a really incredible month," adding that "we never got this far before," including with a number of older patients, now pregnant, who might not have been expected to conceive.

The fact that many patients with long-term, seemingly intractable infertility problems *do* get pregnant and deliver test-tube babies under Dr. Yehia's care—and I met many of these ecstatic new parents with their healthy babies over the course of the summer—has made Dr. Yehia's reputation as a "genius" of IVF and ICSI spread like wildfire among infertile patients in Egypt and throughout the Middle East. Dr. Yehia says he has patients from "all over the Middle East," including Sudan, Oman,

Saudi Arabia, Yemen, Kuwait, Syria, Lebanon, Libya, *many* Palestinians from the Gaza Strip, and even one Jewish Israeli couple and two Russians. Like all of his Egyptian patients, these patients always see Dr. Yehia when they arrive at his clinic from abroad. Dr. Yehia is adamantly opposed to the team approach used at some other IVF centers, where a series of junior physicians and other ancillary personnel handle much of the patient care. Rather, Dr. Yehia is a "do-it-yourself-er," who employs only one female assistant to field patient questions and handles all of the direct patient care by himself. He believes that this consistency of care, the "sentimental family feeling" of his IVF practice, and his attempts to establish immediate rapport with patients have been the major factors in his success. As he explained,

> Well, I'm quite sure that patients evaluate you as much as you evaluate the patient. I think patients have far more insight than doctors, because they go doctor-shopping, right, and it's the rapport around you that really makes the difference. I think that this is *very* important, and once you establish this patient-doctor relationship and they have faith in you, you actually get 50 percent of the problems ruled out. So it *is* important to get this thing "sewed down" right away.

This basic insight—that IVF/ICSI patients attempt to evaluate their doctor's character—is the theme of much of this chapter. Some Egyptian IVF doctors are considered brilliant technicians; others pious Muslims; others "handsome" and "gentle" handlers of distressed women patients. But finding an IVF doctor who combines all of these virtues proves difficult for many patients, who end up switching from one clinic to another. That many of them end up on the doorstep of Dr. Yehia's clinic bespeaks the fact that he has passed the "character test" on all of these scores. For many infertile Egyptian couples, he has literally brought to them the only available global technology, ICSI, that can help to solve their infertility problems, but he has done so in a way that appeals to local sensibilities about the way a good Muslim Egyptian IVF doctor should comport himself with his distressed patients. Perhaps most important, he has delivered into the hands of many of these patients the best possible reward of globalization—namely, the precious babies of the tubes, one, two, or three at a time, who are nothing other than "God's gift," brought to them with the "technical assistance" of Drs. Yehia and Wafik.

Private Providers and the NRT "Epidemic"

Dr. Yehia represents the new face of Egyptian reproductive medicine—a technologically savvy, Western-trained subspecialist who has drawn upon his substantial reservoirs of both technical and interpersonal competence to quickly build a highly successful IVF practice catering to Egyptian (and other Middle Eastern) elites. Although Dr. Yehia's personal history as a handsome movie star is certainly unique, he is but one of a number of successful providers of new reproductive technologies in the urban Egyptian setting. By the time I reached Egypt in 1996, there were three well-established centers for IVF and ICSI in greater Cairo, all of which had been established during the preceding five to ten years. In addition, there were two well-established centers in Alexandria, including the public one at the University of Alexandria's Shatby Hospital, the site of my earlier study. But, by 1996, in addition to these, there were at least five to ten (depending upon the source) other start-up centers in Cairo and Alex—small, recently developed operations, usually in private hospitals and often reliant on technical expertise from foreign consultants. For example, according to Dr. Yehia, there were four additional IVF centers being developed in his own Heliopolis neighborhood—one in a physician's privately owned hospital, one in the Egypt Air Hospital, one in the military intelligence hospital, and one in a maternity hospital. Indeed, the years 1995 to 2000 represented a true new reproductive technology boom period in Egypt, with the virtual mushrooming of new assisted reproduction centers throughout metropolitan Cairo and Alexandria. By 1999, the number of IVF centers in the country had more than tripled, bringing the total number to nearly forty centers, more than any other Middle Eastern nation, including Israel with its twenty-four IVF centers.[2]

On the one hand, this rapid global penetration of new reproductive technologies into the local Egyptian landscape at the turn of the twenty-first century provides firm evidence of Egypt's medical "modernity" and its ability to provide "cutting-edge" Western technologies to highly sophisticated consumers in a competitive medical marketplace characterized by ample consumer "choice." On the other hand, as we shall see in this chapter, these rapid developments have not come without a cost. According to Dr. Yehia, who has been informally monitoring the development of IVF centers in Egypt and in the Middle East as a whole, the situation in Egypt by the year 2000 could best be described as "an epidemic of new centers," most of them offering "low-quality service." Quality issues, in his mind, are linked to the lack of any formal mechanism for regulating assisted reproduction in the country, leading to a mercenary environment and the potential for real "damage" (both physical and financial) to those seeking such services. As he put it succinctly in an interview conducted with me in August 1996, "The *worst* thing is competition. Even though it means that IVF services *should* improve, there will always be more failure than success."

Dr. Yehia's concerns about the adverse effects of competition in the private medical sector are echoed in a recent volume, *Private Health Providers in Developing Countries*.[3] In that volume, the editors warn of the four major problems of unfettered reliance on the private health sector in Third World countries, when little empirical evidence exists to suggest that such privatization results in "improved health care" for the population. These problems include (1) adverse forms of competition, whereby providers compete in terms of quality or service intensity, with potential adverse effects on people's health; (2) lack of formal regulation, whereby the government along with professional associations lack information about the activities of private providers and are therefore unable to provide adequate "policing" activities to prevent potential provider abuses; (3) equity issues, whereby private medical services are asymmetrically distributed in favor of elites, with privatization ultimately "hurting the poor," particularly in the absence of health insurance programs; and

(4) the overprivileging of private-sector activity at the expense of the public health care sector, which generally needs improvement in developing countries, as outlined in a recent detailed report by the World Health Organization.[4]

Nonetheless, on a global level, the World Bank and other international organizations have been placing high priority upon increasing the role of private providers in the social sectors, including health care. Their campaign for such reforms began in the late 1980s with the World Bank's publication of *Financing Health Care: An Agenda for Reform,* achieving full support with the publication of a report entitled *Investing in Health: World Development Report 1993.*[5] Even though their recommendations were based upon "a relatively weak information base . . . the message from international financial institutions (IFIs), such as the World Bank, and bilateral donors, such as USAID, was a simple one: reduce the level of government involvement in health care and promote the private sector."[6]

Not coincidentally, the global campaign toward increased privatization has reverberated throughout the Middle East, including Egypt. Although most countries in this region have had government-supported health care systems with guaranteed access for all citizens in place during the postcolonial period (i.e., since the 1950s or 1960s), the region has moved during the 1980s and 1990s toward an increasing public-private mix. Although poor citizens, especially in remote rural areas, still rely on government health clinics for most of their care,[7] those living in urban areas of the Middle East are increasingly relying on private practitioners, who run everything from home-based offices to their own massive hospital complexes. Such privatization is certainly evident in the cities of Egypt, where private doctors' offices, clinics, and hospitals are found from the lowest- to the highest-income neighborhoods. Indeed, Egypt, which formally "opened" to the West during the period of Anwar Sadat's presidency, seems to fit into what analyst Barbara McPake calls a "Pattern 2 country":[8] a country with a large and concentrated population, where the formal private for-profit sector now seems to dominate all types of health provision, and particularly in the secondary and tertiary levels of provision (which would certainly include specialized infertility services), where public-sector performance is weak. However, McPake warns that this pattern of increasing private health care provision is plagued by numerous potential problems, including the neglect of preventive measures, unethical behavior on the part of private-sector providers in recommending "more, and more profitable interventions which are not medically indicated," failure to achieve equitable access for the whole population, and poor technical quality of care. As she concludes, "The preferability of 'health-threatening' private providers over none at all is by no means clear from a public health perspective."[9]

The recent dramatic growth of assisted reproduction centers in Egypt is part and parcel of this recent historical trend toward increasing privatization. That privatization of IVF services has "hurt the poor" has already been demonstrated in Chapter 2. But in this chapter, we shall examine a number of other dimensions of privatization, including both its benefits and its costs. In particular, this chapter focuses on quality of care in Egyptian IVF centers, from the perspectives of both patients and physicians, the latter of whom have much to say about six major systemic problems plaguing the IVF industry as a whole.

On the positive side, some private providers of Western-generated new reproductive technologies in Egypt have been exceptionally competent in providing excellent services to their patients. This competence, furthermore, involves multiple dimensions of technical and interpersonal skill.[10] In this local setting, infertile patients who hope to make a baby of the tubes have very specific ideas about what makes a good IVF doctor, and these ideas are deeply imbued with a very local sensibility that incorporates notions of appropriate communication, trustworthiness, and religiosity. As realized by Dr. Yehia, infertile IVF patients "evaluate their doctor's character," given that they must entrust this person with the creation of their child's life. Thus, physicians such as Dr. Yehia must be able to negotiate multiple and sometimes conflicting roles as both providers of high-tech global technologies and upholders of local religious and cultural traditions.

On the other hand, we will examine what happens when infertile patients encounter an IVF doctor who is less able to negotiate this delicate balancing act. Some IVF providers—who are characterized by their ex-patients as arrogant, paternalistic, and even abusive, either technically or emotionally—constitute yet another arena of constraint on patients' use of new reproductive technologies. Many infertile women can relate horror stories of their poor treatment, both physical and mental, at the hands of IVF physicians—as well as the hosts of nonspecializing gynecologists who see themselves as being in competition with these IVF providers. In other words, many of the problems of Third World private health care provision—including poor quality of services, overreliance on and overpromotion of high-technology interventions, lack of formal regulation and monitoring of clinics, and even unethical behavior—have surfaced in the Egyptian infertility treatment landscape in ways that will be described in this chapter.

Because many Egyptian IVF physicians wittingly or unwittingly "turn off" their patients to treatment, finding a clever and caring physician is considered a stroke of good fortune. We will begin here by examining what physicians in the three most successful IVF practices in Cairo have done to make their patients evaluate them and their services positively. We will listen to what their patients have to say about physician competence and about establishing trust and comfort in the doctor-patient relationship. When this happens, IVF patients typically attach themselves with reverence to their IVF doctor, resulting in the formation of true "cults of personality" around some IVF physicians such as Dr. Yehia, whose IVF center is one of those to be described further in the section that follows.

Private IVF Providers of Egypt

As noted earlier, by the time I arrived in Cairo in 1996 to conduct my study of Egyptian test-tube baby making, there were three well-established IVF centers in the city, all located in elite suburbs on the city's periphery. I worked directly in two of these clinics, one at Nozha Hospital and one at Nile Badrawi Hospital, spending about half of my time in each. Although I did not work directly in the third center, one of its clinical directors gave me permission to interview patients at his private infertility clinic, from which he routinely made referrals to his jointly owned IVF center. Thus, over the course of my study, I was involved directly or indirectly in all three of these IVF clinics, where I learned as much as possible about their organization and approach to the treatment of IVF-seeking patients.

Of these three centers, the oldest and best known is the Egyptian IVF-ET Center located in Maadi, an affluent suburb on the southern edge of Cairo with the largest community of American expatriates. Routinely referred to by other physicians and patients simply as the "Maadi Center," this IVF clinic was the first to open in Egypt—symbolically on March 21, 1986, which was Mother's Day. It was also the first center to create an Egyptian baby of the tubes—the little girl named Heba Mohammed, whose parents have "gone public" since her birth in 1987 to promote the cause of test-tube baby making after their own eighteen-year struggle with infertility.[11]

The clinical co-directors and co-owners of this clinic are Dr. Gamal I. Serour and Dr. Mohammed Aboulghar, both highly distinguished professors of obstetrics and gynecology. Along with their scientific director, Dr. Ragaa Mansour, who runs the center's IVF laboratory, these three represent a well-known triumvirate in test-tube baby making in Egypt and in the Muslim world beyond. They operate a busy center, with a relatively large staff of assistant physicians and laboratory personnel. In addition, their patient population is large—as of 1995, approximately eighty new patients visited the center per week.[12]

However, at the time of my study in 1996, this free-standing unit—the only one not part of a larger hospital complex—was facing considerable space constraints. Indeed, the first day I visited the center, which was tucked away in a small building on a tree-lined street near the massive Maadi Military Hospital, I was truly surprised by the small size of the clinic and the large number of patients, who were squeezed into seats lining the walls of the waiting room. Because of the lack of space, my initial plans to conduct interviews in this IVF center were foiled, for there were no extra rooms in which to conduct confidential interviews. Furthermore, the physicians running this center perceived (correctly, I believe) that few patients would be willing to meet me outside the clinic to talk about this sensitive subject. Although plans were well under way at that time to move the Maadi Center to a larger facility next door, the building of the new structure would not be completed for at least another year.

Thus, instead of working in this center directly, I worked in the evenings at the private infertility clinic of one of the center's co-directors, Dr. Serour. Dr. Serour is the one who initially sponsored my research on IVF in Egypt and who linked me to other IVF centers in Cairo by virtue of his collegial connections. Thus, over the course of my 1996 research, I came to learn more about Dr. Serour, who is highly esteemed by his patients and colleagues. Within Egypt, Dr. Serour is widely known for bringing some of the latest Western infertility treatments to the country, particularly microsurgery for the repair of damaged fallopian tubes and cryopreservation techniques for the storage of excess embryos conceived through laboratory fertilization techniques.[13] As was discussed in the last chapter, Dr. Serour is also known for his religious expertise as the director of Al-Azhar's International Islamic Center for Population Studies and Research. Among his patients he is highly regarded as a very religious doctor, who can therefore be trusted to perform IVF and ICSI techniques according to Islamic mandates. Among his IVF colleagues Dr. Serour is a "doctor-scholar," who has published more than any other single physician about the state of assisted reproduction in Egypt and the "Muslim viewpoint" regarding this practice.

Dr. Serour's medical partner, Dr. Aboulghar, is also considered a "brilliant technician" of IVF by other doctors and patients. Based on his reputation for success, he draws large numbers of patients to the center, including other doctors who are infertile and who trust Dr. Aboulghar to make their test-tube babies for them.[14] The author of the book *There Is Nothing Impossible in Infertility*, described in Chapter 3, Dr. Aboulghar has helped to popularize IVF in Egypt and to bring patients to what they sometimes call the "Aboulghar Center." Although Drs. Serour and Aboulghar have considered splitting several times—so that each might develop his own profitable IVF center—they have made the politically savvy decision to avoid competition with each other as two famous gynecology professors each practicing alone. Instead, they have both committed considerable personal resources to the building of their new, larger facility, where they will certainly continue to draw large numbers of patients from throughout the Middle East and other parts of the Muslim world.

Located less than a mile away in a high-rise hospital tower owned by Hamdy and Hosam Badrawi, two famous physician brothers, is the second successful IVF center in Maadi, Cairo, known as the Nile Badrawi Hospital Center for Medically Assisted Conception. This private hospital-based IVF unit, sharing space with the tenth floor maternity ward overlooking the Nile River, was established by the hospital in the early 1990s and, like the Maadi Center, relies on a team approach. The Nile Badrawi center employs a clinical director, Dr. Salah Zaki; a laboratory director, Dr. Ashraf Hakam; and a number of physician assistants, many of whom also double in the unit's laboratory as embryologists.

In addition, the Nile Badrawi center has a special relationship with a foreign consultant, an Egyptian-born physician named Dr. Hosam Abdulla, who regularly practices IVF/ICSI at Lister Hospital in England, but who travels back and forth between the Nile Badrawi IVF center, sometimes with his entire Lister laboratory team, for the purpose of treating infertile patients in Egypt. Nile Badrawi patients who seek Dr. Abdulla's services directly are charged slightly higher prices. Furthermore, some of the physicians on the Nile Badrawi team have used their own financial resources to seek training in Dr. Abdulla's unit in England. Thus, the Nile Badrawi unit operates on a mutually beneficial "dependency" relationship: Its foreign consultant brings special expertise "directly from the West" to Nile Badrawi's physicians and patients; at the same time, this consultant maintains profitable ties to his home country. For example, at the time of my 1996 study, the Nile Badrawi IVF unit had just initiated an ICSI program, buying an expensive micromanipulator for the purposes of the microscopic injection. Dr. Abdulla and his Lister Hospital team had played major roles in bringing ICSI to Nile Badrawi and were expected to arrive in Egypt in July 1996 in order to carry out ICSI on a large cohort of hopeful patients who were being prepared for the ICSI procedure. Patients who chose to wait for Dr. Abdulla to do their ICSIs were charged significantly higher prices than those who chose to rely on the local Nile Badrawi team.[15]

However, on a regular basis, Dr. Abdulla is not part of the picture at the Nile Badrawi IVF Center, where patients rely instead on the considerable clinical skills of the resident IVF physician, Dr. Salah Zaki, who is the year-round clinical director. Although he is not a "famous professor," Dr. Zaki is a famous gynecologist in Maadi and is highly revered by his grateful patients. "Tall, light, and handsome" by Egyptian standards, Dr. Zaki is often described by his patients as a "great person," who is known for both his devout religiosity (including his reading of the Qur'an over patients on their way to the operating room) and his gentle and kind manner with distressed infertile women. Soft-spoken and self-effacing, Dr. Zaki is known for his tender mercies, such as calling and returning calls of distraught patients, making middle-of-the-night house calls on IVF patients who believe they are in trouble, or taking on occasional charity patients who he knows can never afford to pay for even a single IVF trial. In interviews, many patients described their profound "attachment" and "gratitude" toward Dr. Zaki, and told me that they wanted me to express their appreciation for him in the book I would write. As one woman summed it up,

> From the first day I came here, I saw how perfect the doctors are here, and how nice the hospital is, and I didn't think of going to any other doctor, especially after being with Dr. Salah [Zaki]. He treats me like a baby—in a very gentle way. He makes you feel hope. He gives you this time to ask questions, and, in my case, I *need* to ask questions. He makes me feel comfortable and supported.

This kind of comfort and support are also found at the third IVF center in Cairo, the one run by Dr. Yehia at Nozha Hospital. On the other end of town near the Cairo International Airport, Nozha Hospital is a relatively small, two-story private hospital tucked away on a sandy back street of the affluent Cairo suburb of Heliopolis. The hospital is unobtrusive (and hence difficult for cab drivers to find). And so is its IVF clinic, which is located on the second floor in the midst of a general gynecology and obstetrics ward. As at Nile Badrawi Hospital, patients seated in the large general waiting area could be IVF patients, or they could be there for some other reason, making waiting less obvious and stigmatizing for those seeking IVF or ICSI services. Within this floor of the hospital, Dr. Yehia occupies a number of rooms, including his current consulting office, his former consulting office where I conducted my private interviews, an ultrasound room, and many private hospital rooms where his patients spend time after oocyte retrievals, embryo transfers, and deliveries of test-

tube babies. Furthermore, his partner, Dr. Abdel-Hamid Wafik, operates his laboratory on the same floor, even though he is one of the few physicians at the hospital to
come from a competitive university (i.e., Nozha Hospital is co-owned by Ain Shams
University professors, whereas Dr. Wafik is a professor of pathology at Al-Azhar
University, the religious university, which has helped to develop Nozha's reputation
as a religiously responsive IVF unit).

As with Dr. Salah Zaki, a considerable "cult of personality" has formed around
Dr. Yehia, as suggested in his story at the beginning of this chapter. Considered a "genius doctor" by his adulatory patients, Dr. Yehia is said by them to be "world famous" for bringing ICSI to Egypt, thereby making babies for men with otherwise
hopeless infertility. Among his patient couples—150 of whom had born ICSI babies
by 1996—Dr. Yehia is considered to have exceptional technical skills leading to high
success rates. But he is also appreciated for his honesty—particularly his frankness
with couples whose chances for success are not so good. Described by one patient as
"honest but gentle," Dr. Yehia was admired for his ability to deliver bad news in a
straightforward but sensitive manner. This seemed to be particularly important to
infertile men, for whom infertility is both demoralizing and emasculating. As one
husband with a case of serious mumps-orchitis-related azoospermia described it,

> He was so honest with us, from the first day. He told us, "The chance is very
> little to get [a baby] from you. We are telling you the truth. But you have to
> have hope. We will do our best, but if something doesn't happen, don't be
> upset." He was very straightforward, and I appreciated that. But today, he
> told us, "We never expected this. It's much better than we hoped for!"

The ability to give hope to otherwise hopeless patients—in part by invoking
God's will and mercy—was considered by many to be part of Dr. Yehia's "human
touch." As with Dr. Zaki, Dr. Yehia was described by many patients, both women and
their husbands, as "comforting," "reassuring," and "friendly," delivering his care on a
very "personal basis" and "with a smile." Many patients, furthermore, appreciated
Dr. Yehia's communication skills. Even though he was seen as extremely busy, Dr.
Yehia was considered to be a good listener who took time for questions (which he
usually asked patients to write down in advance of office visits) and who generally
prioritized doctor-patient relations. As one husband in need of ICSI described his
feeling about Dr. Yehia,

> The doctor must be excellent. I can't take the risk and do something like this
> [ICSI] unless the doctor is famous, has experience, has traveled abroad and
> studied. We feel comfort with Dr. Yehia. He is excellent in his way of talking;
> he makes you feel he is a father or a brother. He is gentle and explains every-
> thing.

Similarly, an infertile male physician explained, "Dr. Yehia is world famous to a
lot of doctors. He's the best in his manner and behavior of speaking. He's calm, honest, and self-confident, which is very important. The patient feels his doctor is

strong, the guide to a quick cure." Putting in her two cents' worth, the physician's
wife added, "And he's very handsome!"

Quality of Care: Patients' Perspectives

Clearly, all of these IVF providers have built successful practices based on their technical competence—their proven ability to bring test-tube babies into this world.
However, I would argue that the two clinical directors of the IVF clinics in which I
based my study, Drs. Mohamed Yehia and Salah Zaki, have also achieved a different
kind of competence not taught in Egyptian medical schools, which is therefore not
common among Egyptian doctors but is nonetheless highly appealing to Egyptian
patients—particularly the highly educated elites who seek IVF services. These physicians practice what medical sociologists call "patient-centered medicine,"[16] involving high degrees of "interpersonal competence,"[17] marked by caring, concern, and
compassion.

Medical sociologists who study doctor-patient relationships have identified five
key differences between patient-centeredness and the traditional "biomedical
model" of patient care.[18] First, doctors employing a patient-centered approach
adopt a biopsychosocial perspective—a "willingness to become involved in the full
range of difficulties patients bring to their doctors, and not just their biomedical
problems."[19] Second, such doctors regard the "patient as person," and are concerned
with understanding the individual's experience of illness by attending to the patient's
illness story. Third, doctors who practice patient-centeredness divest themselves of
paternalistic power by sharing power and responsibility in the doctor-patient relationship. As a result, "once passive recipients of medical care, patients are increasingly regarded as active 'consumers' (and potential critics) with the right to certain
standards of service, including the right to full information, to be treated with respect and to be actively involved in decision-making about treatment."[20] Fourth,
doctors employing a patient-centered approach afford far greater priority to the
personal relationship between doctor and patient, centered around the notion of
the "therapeutic alliance." The core features of this alliance include empathy, con-
gruence, and unconditional positive regard, such that a personal bond develops
between doctor and patient, the latter of whom perceives the doctor as caring, sensitive, and sympathetic. Finally, patient-centeredness invokes the notion of "doctor-
as-person." Doctors who are oriented this way approach their clinical practice as
"two-person medicine," whereby the doctor and patient are seen "as influencing
each other all the time and cannot be considered separately." Thus, as summarized
by Mead and Bower:

> Interpersonal aspects of care are key determinants of patient satisfaction. Pa-
> tients report valuing highly such attributes as doctors' "humaneness" (e.g.
> warmth, respect and empathy), being given sufficient information and time,
> being treated as individuals and involved in decision-making and aspects of

the relationship with the doctor such as mutual trust. Increasingly, patient-centredness is regarded as a proxy for the quality of such interpersonal aspects of care.[21]

Although "patient-centeredness" and "interpersonal competence" are academic heuristics that are never used in Egypt, either among doctors or their patients, these medical sociological terms nonetheless seem to summarize the model of care provided by Drs. Yehia and Zaki. What patients seem to appreciate most about these two physicians is their finely honed interpersonal skills, including the attention they pay to each and every patient. Patients spoke eloquently and at length about these two doctors, and the importance of the doctor-patient relationship in general. In doing so, they revealed why a patient-centered approach is deeply appealing to Egyptians seeking IVF or ICSI services. One devoted patient of Dr. Zaki's, who was returning to him to make her second test-tube baby, explained,

> Dr. Salah [Zaki] is a very good person. Even when I had some problems in my pregnancy, and my husband wanted to do the pilgrimage [by himself], Dr. Salah made him comforted, and told him not to worry. He said, "I'll take care of her, even if she needs anything at night, I will come and take her from your house." Once I started with him, I felt I couldn't deal with any other doctor. The most important thing is that the doctor makes you feel comfortable like this.

Another one of Dr. Zaki's patients, who he introduced to me as his "friend," told me,

> It's *very* important to have a good relationship with your doctor. Dr. Salah, he is *everything*. He is so patient, cooperative, kind. You feel like he loves each one of us. And he's *so* religious. Any procedure, he always reads something from the Qur'an. I can call him *any* time, and if I didn't find him, he'll return my calls. Last night, he called at 2 A.M. because I was worried. This is something unusual for the doctors here.

Embedded in these comments about the exceptional qualities of Drs. Yehia and Zaki were critiques about the general "bedside manner" of Egyptian physicians, including other IVF providers practicing in Cairo. One woman whom I interviewed hoped that I would help her convey this message to other Egyptian IVF physicians in the book that I would write:

> The main problem in Egypt is that the doctors are very, very busy. . . . Usually in Egypt, the woman goes to the doctor, and he tells her, "Do this. Do that." Doctors give orders and women follow. The doctors in Egypt could be better. Doctors must give patients more time, *especially* for IVF, because it's something very sensitive. They have to give importance to the *morals* of the woman, too. The woman is coming to have a baby, not just to take medicine! So I would like to tell the doctors of Egypt, "Please give time to the patient."

This complaint about Egyptian doctors neither asking patients questions nor listening to their responses was repeated in many other interviews, including with an infertile man who described the problem this way:

> The typical Egyptian doctor wants only "two words." He doesn't listen and doesn't give you the satisfactory answer. You come out of his clinic saying, "Why did I come to him?" Dr. Yehia has the quality of listening and giving time for his patients to say what they suffer from. He is an excellent doctor who listens and realizes that you may also have psychological reasons for being here.

The fact that both Drs. Yehia and Zaki prioritize doctor-patient communication and are perceived as warm and empathic listeners is clear from these interviews, which reveal the high levels of patient satisfaction and devotion consistently expressed by patients in both IVF centers. Both of these physicians value what they call "the human dimension," a dimension that may be missing from some of the other competitive IVF practices in the city. As I have argued elsewhere,[22] Egyptian biomedicine is characterized by rather blatant "medical paternalism,"[23] marked by asymmetrical doctor-patient relationships, authoritarian communication styles, and lack of informational disclosure. And this style of medicine can be found in at least some Egyptian IVF clinics, according to patients who have visited them. Why might this be the case, especially given clinics' desires to attract paying patients?

In general, Egyptian physicians as a professional group, consisting of individuals drawn mainly from the upper-middle to upper classes, seem to maintain the privileges of elite status through asymmetrical interactions with and social distancing of their patients. Such social distancing is achieved through lack of disclosure of medical information, with physicians controlling what can be asked by patients and revealed to them; brief interactions with patients, often involving brusque commands and "muting" of patients who wish to speak; and use of English-language "medicalese" (including on patients' medical records and prescriptions) to obscure patients' understandings of their own medical conditions.

For their part, Egyptian physicians tend to rationalize their general lack of doctor-patient communication by pointing to their lack of time to provide adequate patient education and counseling; their belief that most patients actually fear explicit questioning and exchange of information and will seek treatment elsewhere if a physician is too communicative, especially about "bad news"; and their belief in the inherent ignorance of patients, especially uneducated, illiterate ones, but even highly educated patients who are not medically trained. In short, most Egyptian physicians believe that a traditional paternalistic model of biomedical care is highly justified; as a result, relatively few have moved toward the egalitarian patient-centered model of medicine being practiced by Drs. Yehia and Zaki.

Further evidence of such medical paternalism can be found in a recent study of Egyptian family planning clinics.[24] Two researchers, one Middle Eastern and one American, collected audio-tapings of thirty-four physicians consulted by 112 contraceptive-seeking women in thirty-one Egyptian family planning clinics. According to their findings, fully two-thirds of physician consultations were "physician-centered" and only one-third of consultations were "client-centered." Client-centered interactions, according to their definition, involved showing solidarity with the client, facilitating client participation, giving information, asking questions, instructing the client, and giving her directions. Women patients in the study who received client-centered care were significantly more likely to comply with the physicians' recommendations and were much more satisfied with the medical encounter.

Given these findings, the authors conclude, "The present study showed that family planning consultations in Egypt are predominantly physician-centered and that client participation was to a large extent passive, mostly serving the doctor's agenda, which is gathering information about the client."[25] They attribute this dominant style of patient care to "the hierarchical nature of the Egyptian society," noting that "traditional acceptance of a passive client role and physician dominance may not be because clients prefer this model of relationship, but because they were not aware of the alternatives. The present study shows that a less authoritarian and less physician-centered style of communication is more effective in achieving desirable client outcomes."[26]

That the patient- or client-centered approach is missing even in Egyptian IVF practices reflects, to some degree, the current state of medical education in Egypt. As noted by Dr. Yehia, few Egyptian physicians have the opportunity to learn this highly teachable approach to care,[27] as doctor-patient relations are not routinely covered in the Egyptian medical school curriculum. There, the recognized model is one of physician-professor "demi-gods," who stand high above their medical students as well as their patients. These kind of asymmetrical physician relations become enacted in the outside world, as Egyptian medical students graduate and enter into their own medical practices. Although there are certainly exceptions to this rule, it is fair to state that many Egyptian physicians, and particularly those of the older generation, remain haughty, aloof, uncommunicative, and even disrespectful of their patients, particularly those of the lower socioeconomic classes.

Although Egyptian patients of all social backgrounds come to expect this kind of treatment in clinical interactions with physicians, many of them have clearly come to resent it, as revealed in the interviews I conducted. Infertile Egyptian patients, especially those of the middle to upper classes, question whether they can truly trust a physician who directly or indirectly demeans them. In short, in the "trust calculations" made by highly educated Egyptian IVF patients,[28] physician authoritarianism no longer denotes physician competence and authority. Instead, measures of interpersonal competence—as opposed to sheer technical competence—factor much more heavily in patients' assessments of physician trustworthiness.

Not surprisingly, numerous studies of doctor-patient interaction conducted in Western locations confirm this Egyptian finding. Of seven categories of physician behavior that have been found to promote trust, five of these are interpersonal, including understanding of patients' individual experiences, caring, communicating clearly and completely, building partnerships, and honesty with respect for the patient.[29] Mechanic and Meyer emphasize that interpersonal competence of this kind is "particularly central to trust," and that "patients are quite skillful at observing interpersonal competence in a detailed fashion, and they have many more ways to describe it."[30]

Although the trust engendered through interpersonal competence in the doctor-patient relationship has been little studied in Egypt,[31] suffice it to say that trust matters—and particularly in the world of test-tube baby making. As revealed in the last chapter, patients care deeply about whether they can count on their IVF physicians to carry out the procedure in a morally acceptable fashion. They also want to feel that their physicians are being sincere with them about success rates, risks of side effects, and future health of offspring. Thus, notions of physician trustworthiness factor prominently in IVF patient discourse about the perceived character and honesty of particular IVF physicians. Patients perceive real differences between "trustworthy" and "untrustworthy" doctors, the latter of whom they consider to be unfortunately common in the country. For example, one infertile man explained how his growing lack of trust in Egyptian infertility physicians had led to costly treatment delays:

> We spent about ten years seeing five or six doctors. Some of them, we don't trust them. Sometimes, we spent all night waiting to see the doctor,[32] and when we saw him, he says something and we don't trust it. I feel bad when we listen to him. So, for some time, about three to four years, when she told me we should go to the doctor, I say, "No," because sometimes they don't tell me the truth. But when she told me we *have* to go see the doctor because our time is running out, I said okay, and I told her it will be the last time.

Egyptian patients seeking IVF services often make negative trust calculations based on three factors: perceived greed of the physician, perceived dishonesty (particularly regarding success rates), and perceived lack of religiosity. With regard to the last factor, patients are constantly seeking cues that a doctor is religiously inclined, given the enormity of the religious concerns described in the last chapter. Some physicians—for example, Dr. Zaki—invoke religion overtly and frequently, by citing religious aphorisms, reading passages from the Qur'an or *hadith,* praying for patients before procedures are conducted, and generally engaging in reassuring "talk of God" (e.g., "it's in God's hands now," "let's leave it to God," "God will bless you," "it will happen if God wants it to"). In fact, the physicians at all three of the top centers in Cairo are considered by their patients to be religious men who "fear God" and face their tasks with the kind of humility and reverence appropriate for a good Muslim. Physicians who do not invoke such religious elements are judged harshly by their patients, both Muslim and Christian, who wondered aloud during interviews with me whether a physician who is not a devout Muslim can be trusted to carry out IVF or ICSI in a morally licit fashion.

Similarly, many patients complained about the mercenary quality of the physicians they had encountered at other Egyptian IVF clinics, and in the world of infertility treatment in general. Because so much medical care in Egypt is now privately run, physicians are seen by patients as being in competition with each other over limited resources. This limited-good mentality makes many physicians greedy, according to patients, who are sometimes made to feel that they are viewed only as "pots of gold" rather than as people. This is as true in IVF clinics as it is in the offices of private gynecologists, who are often loath to refer their patients to IVF centers (even bad-mouthing such centers) in order to keep such patients—and the patients' money—for themselves. In other words, patients perceive that infertility is a "big business" and that doctors who specialize in this malady are often "in it for the money."

In practical terms, it means that at least some nonspecializing gynecologists hold on to infertile patients too long, preventing many of them from seeking IVF services in a timely fashion. In my first meeting with Dr. Yehia, he spoke about this problem.

> The major problem is with the *doctors* here in Egypt, maybe even more than with the patients. The doctors here may not be convinced about IVF, or that their own treatments are nearly obsolete. They say anecdotally, "Well, one of my patients got pregnant with so-and-so." If you tell them that this is just coincidental and that we have new technologies that can increase success to 20 percent, they won't believe you, because it will cause economic privation for them. This is a *big* problem in Egypt, because about one-third of most gynecologists' practices are infertility [patients], and about 50 to 60 percent for andrologists.

A few patients in this study had the good fortune of being "let go" and even referred to an IVF center by a competing gynecologist. As they explained it, occasionally a gynecologist will "give up" on an infertile couple and refer them directly to an IVF center. More commonly, physician referrals come from gynecologists somehow affiliated with an IVF center or the hospital in which it is located. In other cases, referrals come from physicians in the patients' own kinship or social network. For example, some infertile couples in this study had family members, friends, or "friends of friends" who were physicians and had somehow helped them to obtain IVF or ICSI services.

More often than not, however, infertile patients get caught in the middle of the untoward competition between nonspecializing and specializing gynecologists. As a result, the vast majority of patients I interviewed at IVF centers had undergone years' worth of diagnostic procedures and failed treatment attempts, including repeated rounds of hormonal therapy and "useless" surgeries on the part of both husbands and wives. Many patients described the suffering they had endured at the hands of other physicians, some of whose surgical interventions had caused even worse infertility problems. The problem of iatrogenesis—or physician-induced harm—is a major theme of my previous work on Egyptian infertility[33] and is one to which we will return in Chapter 7. Suffice it to say here that many infertile Egyptian women and men feel that they have been exploited by dishonest, unethical, money-seeking gynecologists who have pretended to treat their infertility with

old-fashioned procedures that have been a waste of time at best and a source of irreparable harm at worst. As one woman explained,

> The problem here is, you go to a doctor and he never tells you, "I'm not spe-
> cialized in this." He says, "OK, I'll try," and he makes many problems. They
> don't know what they're doing, but they don't want to say that. First of all,
> they want to help. But they also want to take money. How can he let you go?
> It's a business, and it's a bad habit here.

Many infertile patients also had horror stories about their experiences *within*
Egyptian IVF centers. I spent countless hours talking to patients about what had already happened to them at other IVF clinics, usually at the hands of physicians who
were perceived as being more motivated by financial incentives than by true quality
of patient care. Many patients clearly wanted to talk about their mistreatment, offering lengthy narratives with little prompting on my part. IVF patients generally had
four sets of complaints: dishonest inflation of success rates (a topic to be taken up in
the next chapter); crass demands for money; authoritarian styles of patient care; and
the insensitivity, even cruelty, with which some IVF physicians dispatched poor-
prognosis patients from their clinics. All of these ills can be seen in the case of one
notorious Egyptian IVF physician, who will be referred to here only as Dr. X. Although Dr. X has used media publicity to his advantage to promote the accomplishments of his IVF center, he has clearly developed a negative reputation among at
least some disgruntled IVF patients, who subsequently switched to the clinics in
which I was working. Many of the patients I encountered at both Nozha and Nile
Badrawi hospitals (sixteen to be exact) considered themselves to be survivors of Dr.
X, succeeding neither in making a test-tube baby at his clinic nor in being treated as
human beings in the process. I spent hours listening to IVF patients vent their rage
at Dr. X, who was accused of being "dishonest," "cruel," "using people for money,"
and "inhumane." For example, one woman, now in her early forties, described how
she was coldly dispatched by Dr. X from his clinic after he misdiagnosed her case as
premature menopause:

> I went to a big doctor I heard about on TV—Dr. [X]. Honestly, he destroyed
> me completely psychologically. From the second time I visited him, he told
> me, "You have no hope. You will not have any children." He said very cruel
> words to me, and told me not to go anywhere else because they will deceive
> you. The psychological desperation I felt almost destroyed everything. I be-
> came very depressed for a long time, and I started thinking about leaving my
> house and breaking my marriage. But our faith helped us. Only a month
> after [the Dr. X incident], one of our relatives encouraged us to come here
> [to Nile Badrawi, where she was being successfully treated to stimulate her
> ovaries].

"Cruel" was the strong term used by several patients in this study to describe Dr. X.
For example, one woman, whose physician husband was infertile, told me, "When

my husband went to Dr. [X], he told him, 'You need a miracle to have a baby.' It was *very* cruel. Even though he's a very 'big-name' doctor, what he did was really cruel." Other patients called Dr. X a "merchant" who treated his patients like pieces of "furniture." As one infertile man put it,

> Before we came here, we went to Dr. [X]. I don't know him personally, but once we went through the door [of his clinic], we didn't have a good feeling. And once we met him, he asked for lots of money—LE 9,000 for IVF—right away. We didn't feel very good. He made us kind of nervous. He's very straight—he doesn't even smile, when a little smile will go a long way. He himself, I don't think he cares about his patients. He's like a merchant.

How do patients protest this poor quality of care from Dr. X and others like him? In all of these cases, patients had "voted with their feet" by walking out of Dr. X's clinic in order to seek alternative IVF services. Doctor shopping is a particularly common form of Egyptian medical protest, one that was as common among the lower-class infertile women in my earlier study as it was among the educated elites in my more recent one. In fact, exactly one-third of the women I interviewed at Egyptian IVF centers had doctor-shopped *between* competing IVF centers. Furthermore, prior to their IVF and ICSI attempts, almost all of them had visited numerous physicians—sometimes to seek second opinions, sometimes to begin new lines of treatment when a physician's remedies had failed, and sometimes to escape abusive treatment of the kind described here. One highly educated woman who had made the rounds of the infertility specialists in Cairo and who had gone through her own demoralizing experiences at Dr. X's clinic described this phenomenon as the "circle of doctor-shopping" among infertile Egyptians in need of IVF or ICSI.

Part of the reason why infertile women and men get caught up in this circle is that they would rather switch providers than confront them directly about their practices. The "consumer model" of medicine, which has been described widely in the West[34]—including among the American IVF patients featured in Gay Becker's recent book *The Elusive Embryo*—is not in place in Egypt, where widespread medical paternalism prevails. The consumer model is located on the opposite end of the spectrum from the paternalistic model, and shifts the balance of power toward the patient. In theory at least, the patient autonomously decides which medical intervention should be made, regardless of the physician's opinion and values. The doctors' task "is simply to provide the patient with all relevant information, i.e. the means to exercise control."[35]

In Egypt, medical information is usually controlled by physicians, leaving infertile women and men with little sense of empowerment in the doctor-patient interaction. Furthermore, because deference to medical authority is the cultural norm in Egypt—and is expected by physicians—few Egyptian patients are willing to openly confront their doctors or even to question them directly. Thus, when patients believe that a physician is not acting in their best interests, they generally continue to be polite and respectful in his presence, registering their protest only by failing to reappear at his clinic for later appointments. In other words, in the Egyptian medical encounter, few patients perceive their own role as that of the "assertive consumer," with expectations of and rights to medical information, high-quality care, and recourse to malpractice suits when doctors mistreat them or make mistakes.

However, this may be slowly changing. As noted by Dr. Yehia in an interview in 1996, medical malpractice lawsuits—once unheard of in Egypt—are on the rise in the country, with nearly eighty cases being taken to court in 1995 alone. In fact, by the mid-1990s, the number of new cases of malpractice was increasing so rapidly that the Egyptian Ministry of Health was compelled to create a new ministerial section devoted to this subject. Furthermore, for the first time, Egyptian physicians are being forced to consider purchasing private malpractice insurance, as more and more physicians are being taken to court. Increasingly, Egyptian physicians are being asked to testify as expert witnesses in malpractice cases against their colleagues, and several gynecologists have lost their licenses because of this.

According to Dr. Yehia, the privatization of Egyptian medicine is largely responsible for this surge in malpractice suits. Nowadays, both public and private patients in Egypt are being asked to pay sometimes considerable fees for their medical care under a capitalist system. As a result, they are beginning to demand better quality care and more accountability from physicians. As Dr. Yehia put it, "There was a lot of complacency and passivity when people expected free care from the government. But now, even public hospital patients have to pay small amounts, and so they won't take any kind of bad care."

Although the Egyptian media have "gone wild" in covering cases of medical malpractice, forcing the head of the Egyptian Physicians' Syndicate to calm public anxieties about the state of Egyptian medicine, malpractice suits are, in fact, still relatively uncommon. For one, few Egyptians are in a financial position to pursue a lengthy court trial. In addition, few patients are willing to suffer the perceived indignities that may accompany a lawsuit. The reluctance to engage in malpractice proceedings was clear from my study: Only one of the numerous infertility patients who had been harmed by a physician's treatment had ever seriously considered suing her physician. In the case of the woman who had considered suing, the doctor confessed to making a gross (and irreparable) error during the actual outpatient procedure. However, the patient's comments reveal why she did not pursue a malpractice suit:

> I wanted to sue him, but that will be a scandal, and they will send many doctors to examine me and that will be a problem. He's a professor in a faculty of medicine—very, very famous. But, like most of the doctors I've seen, he has no conscience.

Clearly, even among elite patients with the money to hire lawyers, malpractice suits are not seen as a very viable means of protesting the quality of their care. Instead, some patients are beginning to "talk back" to their physicians, venting their rage directly. Amira, the woman whose story opens this book, was one of a handful of Egyptian women I met who had "told off" an IVF physician, in her case the notorious Dr. X. Telling him that he had treated her like she was "not a human being," she stomped out of his office, promising never to come back—a promise that she kept, despite her dilemma about the remaining frozen embryos stored in his clinic. Similarly, another highly educated, upper-class woman who felt entitled to respect from her IVF physician described her husband's failure to produce a crucial semen sample, and her resultant anger at the cavalier response of the treating physician:

> Unfortunately, I told [the IVF doctor] that my husband has difficulty in making a sample in the clinic, and I asked can we do it at home. He said, "No, it's better at the center and come on Friday [i.e., the Egyptian weekend]; you'll find no one there, and he'll feel free and feel so good." So, the doctor told us at the last minute, "Come on Friday, and he will do it [i.e., masturbation] easily." When he went there, he found many, many, many people. It was crowded even on a Friday. It was in September, so the weather was very hot. And it was a small, small bathroom right beside the nurse's office. And he started sweating and couldn't do it. After that, he was very upset and said, "I hate marriage." My ovaries had started to work, and I took all the expensive medicine, and then there was no use, because he couldn't provide a semen sample. [The doctor] said, "Oh well, you can try next time." I was really angry, and I told him, "You are not a doctor! You are not honest. You're wasting the time and money of people. We are not people from a village, to be told 'Come here. Do this. Do that.'" Really, these doctors are savage—against humanity.

Although not all Egyptian IVF providers are "savages" who care little for "humanity," their interpersonal skills and quality of patient care could generally stand improvement, according to the patients in this study. As suggested by this woman's comments, there is also inordinate time spent waiting at Egyptian IVF clinics—not only by patients in crowded waiting rooms, but also by clinic staff members themselves, who literally sit around chatting (and, among the men, smoking) until the director of the clinic makes his "grand entrance." According to Egyptian IVF patients, such pretenses on the part of physicians are inherently disrespectful, for they ignore the busy professional lives of their patients, most of whom also hold demanding jobs. Thus, few Egyptian IVF patients enjoy being treated as if their own tight schedules do not matter. They cite the lack of "timing and organization" as one of the endemic problems of the current test-tube baby making scene in the country.

Quality of Care: Physicians' Perspectives

What do Egyptian IVF physicians have to say about quality of care? In interviews I conducted with eight physicians in both Nozha and Nile Badrawi IVF centers, I found that most were engaged in an auto-critique of the private IVF industry in

Egypt as a whole. Additionally, some were quite open about how systemic problems, many deriving from uneven processes of globalization, had affected their own clinics. And most were openly critical, perhaps in a competitive way, about how the spate of new start-up IVF centers would affect both the industry and quality of care. For example, the laboratory director at Nile Badrawi's IVF unit, Dr. Ashraf Hakam, told me,

> Most of these [new] centers will be ill-prepared to do IVF and will have very poor results. These centers will be opened by gynecologists specializing in infertility who have the money, but don't have the expertise and won't have the professional incentive to take the time to properly learn IVF procedures. They will rely on outside "experts" coming every so often, so will have problems with volume and flow of patients. I'm asked to "consult" for such centers all the time, but I call them "hit-and-run operations." Even though I think these future centers will proliferate, there will probably continue to be three or four major centers, all privately run.

This kind of subversive critique is common among Egyptian physician elites, who have received subspecialized training (usually in the West) in infertility and new reproductive technologies, and hence are in a position to comment on what they see as the inadequacies of the IVF industry in the country. An indigenous, physician-led critique of this sort was also a major finding of my earlier study at Shatby Hospital, and it resurfaced when I returned to study Egyptian IVF centers in 1996. The IVF physicians I interviewed cited six major industry-wide problems in Egypt, including (1) clinic maldistribution; (2) dependency upon Western experts and materials; (3) costs and shortages of equipment and supplies; (4) problems of local infrastructure; (5) local shortages of qualified staff, especially laboratory personnel; and (6) lack of a nationwide regulatory system to monitor clinic operations and coordinate data collection.

With regard to the first point, IVF clinics are poorly distributed in Egypt. Of the thirty-six clinics in existence by 1999, all of them were located in Egypt's two major cities, both in the north of the country. Although Egypt is home to many relatively large provincial cities in both the northern delta region, as well as along the Nile River to the south, none of these other cities could boast an IVF center by 1999. Because of this maldistribution of services, infertile patients from these cities must seek new reproductive technologies in the congested megacities of Egypt, where travel is difficult and accommodations are expensive. The logistical difficulties frankly prevent many infertile Egyptian couples, particularly those from the countryside, from seeking IVF services at a distance. Those who do, usually because of physician referrals,[36] must literally travel back and forth between rural and urban locales to receive their care.

According to a number of IVF physicians I interviewed, the need for strategically located IVF centers in cities other than Cairo and Alexandria is now pressing—not only to serve the large demand for these services among patients in other parts of the country but also to alleviate the growing, untoward competition between the urban centers. According to knowledgeable physicians, IVF centers in Cairo have begun to compete with each other for patients, supplies, qualified personnel, and the hormonal medications that are in short supply (resulting in patient waiting lists). As more and more patients try their luck at newer start-up centers in Cairo and Alexandria, which may offer lower prices as an alluring incentive, the major centers are beginning to lose patients to clinics without proven track records and less-than-optimal success rates. This siphoning effect, according to those I interviewed, will ultimately hurt everyone, patients and physicians alike, in an overly competitive marketplace.

In an attempt to alleviate some of these distributional problems, a few Cairo-based IVF physicians are attempting to establish centers in some of Egypt's provincial cities. For example, by 1996, Dr. Yehia had been asked to help develop IVF centers in Mansoura, Tanta, and Zagazig, all small cities in the northern delta region. By 2000, the first of these units had opened in Mansoura, approximately 150 kilometers northeast of Cairo. Drs. Yehia and Wafik had personally trained eight gynecologists and four lab technicians. They were confident that this new semi-rural unit, located at Mansoura University's teaching hospital and partially subsidized by the state of Egypt, would be successful as long as it did not succumb to "administrative difficulties," which they considered to be a key factor in clinic viability.

The second major problem facing the private IVF industry in Egypt is its ongoing dependence upon the West—or what some social scientists have referred to as the ongoing "neocolonialism" in health services in the Third World.[37] Although Egypt formally ended its relationship with Britain upon independence in 1952, Egyptian biomedicine was heavily influenced by the British colonial medical system and has carried both the benefits and burdens of that system into the postcolonial period.[38] In the world of test-tube baby making, this neocolonial dependency upon the West is quite evident: New reproductive technologies and medications are exported to Egypt by Western manufacturers, and Egyptian IVF clinics deficient in locally trained personnel literally import European consultants to carry out their work. Yet, this overt reliance on Western technology and highly skilled Western experts is not thought to detract from a clinic's prestige. Quite the contrary! By the mid-1990s, many of the newer centers were engaged in aggressive marketing campaigns, which boasted their direct ties to Western experts, their technology, and know-how. Clearly, the anti-Westernism so apparent in the moral discourse surrounding these technologies has not affected physicians' perceptions that Egyptian patients still want Western technology and expertise—but without the accompanying "moral baggage" of Western IVF practices.

According to Egyptian IVF providers, this direct incursion of the West into the local IVF scene has been both a blessing and a curse. On the one hand, it has allowed some successful centers, such as the one at Nile Badrawi Hospital, to introduce the newest of the new reproductive technologies, such as ICSI. Patients at these centers are grateful beneficiaries of Western expertise and are pleased to think that their own local physicians are receiving technical training from abroad. On the other hand, dependency upon foreign experts clearly has its disadvantages. According to Dr. Wafik of Nozha Hospital, relying on an outside consultant automatically puts local Egyptian staff in a "second-class" position, thereby privileging foreign expertise over the sometimes considerable skills of local doctors. Furthermore, few European consultants reside permanently in Egypt. Instead, they come to the country two to three times a year to handle whatever patients may be available at that time. Significant problems in patient volume and flow may result as infertile Egyptians literally wait for the foreign expert to arrive and compete for care during the congested periods when the expert is in residence. According to those physicians I interviewed, an IVF program can only be clinically sound if it has a certain volume, or flow of patients on a regular basis. The worldwide average is thirty patients per month, or at least one per day. However, in Egypt, many centers have fewer patients than this, particularly as patients wait for foreign consultants to arrive. These problems of low or otherwise irregular flow may ultimately lead to lower-than-average success rates in the country.

Furthermore, if European consultants change their plans for any reason, infertile Egyptian women and men suffer. To take but one example, in the summer of 1996, both patients and staff at Nile Badrawi Hospital were dismayed when Dr. Abdulla, the Egyptian-born foreign consultant to the center, put off his planned summer visit until December, causing considerable angst among those who had been scheduled for ICSI. Many patients were forced to cancel their trials, while some women who had already taken the expensive and risky hormonal medications opted to continue treatment with the less experienced local team. Ultimately, many high hopes were dashed that summer when few pregnancies occurred in the cohort of ICSI patients.

Dependency upon the West also exists at the level of the technologies themselves. Local Egyptian IVF providers must purchase costly equipment and supplies from Western manufacturers (primarily from the United States and Germany) and increasingly from Japan. According to Dr. Ashraf Hakam of Nile Badrawi Hospital, American equipment is bought at considerable expense through the Egyptian branch of the United States Agency for International Development (USAID). However, the Egyptian dealers who distribute this equipment are only concerned with their own profit margins; as a result, they offer very poor follow-up, warranties, or technical support. As Dr. Hakam lamented, "These dealers want to turn a huge and quick profit, with no long-term thinking or even good short-term thinking. This is just another example of the problems of poor management and training in Egypt." Although manufacturers from other countries, such as Eastern Europe, also sell their wares in Egypt, their equipment tends to be unreliable and can cause more trouble than it is worth. Thus, many of the laboratory physicians in the well-established IVF centers must double as techies who can innovate and troubleshoot to keep the laboratory equipment running.

At other centers, especially newer ones without experience, completely unnecessary equipment is sometimes purchased—the costs of which are absorbed over time by patients, who are either subjected to unnecessary technology or charged exorbitant prices in order for physicians to make good on their overhead investments. According to Dr. Hakam, "Doctors at new centers, who have the money but no experience, usually don't really know what equipment they need, and they often drastically misjudge and buy too much equipment because of the poor recommendations of dealers." Similarly, some Egyptian universities have been known to purchase IVF laboratory equipment at the urging of dealers, even though they have no need for this equipment. As Dr. Hakam explained, "The university ends up buying equipment with no real use intended, sometimes in great numbers. The centers like Nile Badrawi that actually need and use this equipment receive poor support from dealers, who are more interested in making larger sales to these other places." That this equipment is costly, and thus a tremendous waste of Egyptian government research funds is revealed in cost estimates provided by both the Maadi and Nozha IVF centers. At the Maadi Center, the doctors estimated the total value of their equipment to be LE 2 million (nearly $600,000) in 1995.[39] At Nozha Hospital, Dr. Yehia estimated the cost of a single, Western-manufactured heating plate to be 10,000 British pounds (LE 50,000). Proclaiming this to be "bloody expensive," Dr. Yehia went on to describe how he and Dr. Wafik "invented" their own piece of equipment at a total cost of LE 4,000, adding that "it worked beautifully!"

Because of these extraordinary equipment expenses, many Egyptian IVF centers lack crucial technology. Shortages of imported technology—"from the most advanced equipment to the most basic of drugs for ovulation induction"[40]—have plagued the Egyptian IVF industry from its inception. The result is a patchwork of partial services. To take but one example, some Egyptian centers offer IVF, but not the newer ICSI, which requires the purchase of an expensive micromanipulator in order to directly inject oocytes under a high-powered microscope. Similarly, some centers lack cryopreservation facilities, preventing infertile couples from storing excess embryos (or frozen sperm) for future use. When cryopreservation freezers are lacking, excess embryos must either be disposed of (and hence wasted) or placed inside a woman's uterus with the ensuing risks of a high-order multiple pregnancy. Yet, as of 1996, cryopreservation was not one of the services routinely offered at most of the IVF centers in the city, including Nile Badrawi Hospital. Although Nile Badrawi IVF unit had purchased a cryopreservation freezer by the time of my 1996 study, the laboratory still lacked containers for embryo storage. As a result, patients there were not being offered cryopreservation services, and all unused embryos were being destroyed.

Furthermore, the operation of such high-tech Western equipment is plagued by local infrastructure problems. For example, in an early publication describing their own experience in bringing new reproductive technologies to the country, the Maadi Center team of Drs. Mansour, Serour, and Aboulghar admitted, "In our initial period, we faced a lot of problems related to local factors in Egypt such as the interrupted power supply, the supply of the highest purity water, the permanent supply of disposables needed."[41]

Such local infrastructure problems, particularly the frequent power outages and the questionable water supply, have not gone away, meaning that IVF centers must take extraordinary measures (e.g., backup generators) to operate on a day-to-day basis. One physician, who was also an IVF patient, lamented, "Our centers in Egypt are not very well prepared to do IVF, space-wise, lab-wise, embryo-transfer-wise. I've seen them taking cells from one room to another room and improvising in various ways. I'm a doctor, and I know this is not right." Her comment points to another endemic problem—namely, the shortage of qualified laboratory personnel with the skills and know-how to carry out IVF and ICSI successfully. As I was told time and time again by both IVF physicians and patients themselves, the success of an IVF center is dependent upon the skills and trustworthiness of those "back in the lab." Yet relatively few such individuals have been trained in Egypt, where laboratory medicine in general and reproductive endocrinology in particular are not considered high-status specialties. Although laboratory physicians at both Nozha and Nile Badrawi hospitals have made efforts to train other physicians in IVF-related laboratory techniques, the laboratory science of IVF is not offered as a subject in Egyptian medical schools, forcing all those who want to learn these techniques to seek training outside the country or to learn by trial and error.

Dr. Hakam, the laboratory director at Nile Badrawi Hospital, explained how he learned to microinject ova for the ICSI procedure by observing his British colleagues, who came to Egypt for a six-day period in 1995 to initiate the ICSI program. As Dr. Hakam described that period,

> They [the Lister Hospital team] were so busy that they worked until midnight every night, and we did not have any time for real training. So I learned by watching them, and then experimenting with extra eggs. It was very time-consuming for me, but I have now reduced the amount of time it takes for me to do the procedure from hours to about ten to fifteen minutes. I would like to reduce this further to five minutes, but it requires a lot of technical skill, and there are nuances and tips that I would like to learn more about, maybe by going to England or the U.S.

Meanwhile, Dr. Hakam is considering starting a training program in Egypt for others to learn ICSI. He told me in a 1996 interview:

> I was contacted yesterday by someone who has the ICSI equipment and would like to "advertise" it for the purposes of training. Personally, I believe it's important to train other Egyptian doctors, especially from the smaller cities, in these embryological techniques, quality control of the lab, and so on. Many centers are lacking good quality control and laboratory skills at this time.

This lack of quality control in IVF laboratories is part and parcel of the larger problem of lack of official government oversight of the Egyptian IVF industry in general. As of this writing, no formal state legislation has been enacted to regulate IVF centers in the country. Each IVF center operates on its own, without official scrutiny of its practices or demands for data or record-keeping. However, according to Dr. Yehia, small steps are beginning to be taken in the right direction. For one, the Egyptian Society of Obstetrics and Gynecology has enacted a code of ethics for IVF centers and is working on a law requiring regulation and oversight of assisted reproduction units in the country. Furthermore, as of 1997, the Egyptian Ministry of Health issued a statement banning foreign laboratory personnel from working in Egypt. This was following a highly publicized case in which a French physician, expelled from his position in France, was invited to an Egyptian IVF center to carry out an experimental form of ICSI that had not been subjected to previous research in animals. In Egypt, he carried out twenty-three of these experimental procedures on local patients—at a total price tag of LE 230,000—without any resulting pregnancies. When the Egyptian Physicians' Syndicate and Ministry of Health learned about this unethical experiment, they immediately banned foreign consultants from working in Egyptian IVF centers until further regulatory guidelines could be worked out.

However, bureaucratic wheels in Egypt move slowly. In particular, national guidelines for the regulation of Egyptian IVF centers have proven difficult to enact. For example, using a grant from a major pharmaceutical firm, Dr. Yehia attempted in the mid-1990s to organize a national data registry of Egyptian IVF centers—of the kind already in place in Latin America.[42] However, his efforts were in vain. Other centers refused to cooperate in the sharing of data—including "simple information," such as the number of patients treated each year. Dr. Yehia believes that this unwillingness of most Egyptian IVF centers to cooperate in this important task of nationwide data collection is a reflection of the poor success rates at most centers, which few IVF directors are willing to admit. Instead, it is likely that most Egyptian IVF centers artificially inflate their success rates in the ways to be described in the following chapter.

Conclusion

In summary, the private provision of new reproductive technology services in Egypt is plagued by endemic problems, ranging from the microsociological disturbances surrounding poor doctor-patient communication to the macrosociological obstacles surrounding national regulation. Although some of these problems, particularly inadequate regulation and clinic oversight, are more global in scope and can be found as well in the West,[43] many of the problems described in this chapter are local in nature, involving long-standing, vexing issues of medical paternalism, urban-rural maldistribution, and particular Egyptian responses to increasing medical privatization.

Furthermore, because of their location on the receiving end of global reproductive technology transfer, Egyptian IVF centers are plagued by problems of feasibility, cost, and shortages of skilled labor and technology that make the very provision of new reproductive technologies in such Third World settings a questionable practice. Indeed, some critics have charged that new reproductive technologies are simply not appropriate for developing countries, where transfer of technology, resources, and expertise is still a "one-way street." Friday Okonofua, the Nigerian professor of obstetrics and gynecology whose essay "The Case Against New Reproductive Technologies in Developing Countries" was first introduced in Chapter 2,[44] has argued vociferously in the *British Journal of Obstetrics and Gynaecology* that new reproductive technologies are less likely to be feasible and successful when carried out under Third World conditions, marked by lack of technical expertise among staff, chronic shortages in supplies, and dependence on operating materials from foreign countries.

But what about Egypt—a country mentioned specifically by Okonofua as one of two African countries (along with Nigeria) to successfully implement IVF? One could argue that Egypt occupies a unique niche on the African continent in terms of global transfer of new reproductive technologies. Located betwixt and between the resource-poor countries of north and sub-Saharan Africa and the petro-rich countries of the Arab Gulf, Egypt has truly been the site of unprecedented new reproductive technology development over the past decade and half. In at least a few established IVF centers—such as the ones featured in this chapter—IVF and ICSI have come to flourish, with the proof of their success revealed in the sweet, wrinkled faces of test-tube babies now being born on a daily basis into the hands of revered IVF physicians.

However, this "Egyptian test-tube baby making miracle" has not come without high costs. The three founders of Egyptian IVF—Drs. Serour, Aboulghar, and Mansour—have written a series of cautionary pieces, warning the Egyptian and international medical communities about the pitfalls of IVF provision in countries such as Egypt.[45] Reminding readers that Egypt is "already an overpopulated third world country,"[46] they argue that IVF is prohibitively expensive for many couples, particularly given the repetition required to achieve pregnancy in most cases. Furthermore, they point to the high cost of establishing IVF centers, which rely heavily on imported technology. The lack of quality control of such centers, moreover, may lead to low rates of success when personnel are not well trained and qualified to perform complicated IVF and ICSI procedures. Finally, they emphasize that some of the techniques that have been used to improve the results of medically assisted conception in the West—specifically third-party donation—"cannot be implemented in the Arab and Islamic world,"[47] for all of the reasons laid out in the last chapter. Thus, according to Drs. Serour, Aboulghar, and Mansour, these factors taken together make "the establishment of any IVF centre in this part of the world a cumbersome task."[48] Ultimately, they urge the Egyptian medical community and policy makers to expend considerable efforts on the primary *prevention* of infertility in Egypt rather than on its *treatment* through new reproductive technologies.

Unfortunately, this day has yet to come in Egypt. The increasing movement toward the private side of the public-private mix has meant lack of attention to preventive services and overreliance on expensive technologies that are proven income generators for competing physicians. Egyptian test-tube baby making, in fact, provides an example par excellence of much that can go wrong when unplanned, unregulated medical privatization takes hold in a resource-poor country such as Egypt. That Egyptian IVF patients realize they are the unfortunate pawns in an aggressive game of private medical competition is revealed in the cynical statement of one patient, who said, "The Egyptian doctors make this IVF now 'for commerce,' because they say that they can make a lot more money from it than from normal deliveries."

The mercenary character of some Egyptian IVF physicians is part of the critique voiced by elite patients, who resent the ways in which such physicians seem more concerned with payment than with patient care. As seen in this chapter, many Egyptian IVF patients have had untoward experiences with IVF providers, whose style of, and commitment to, patient care they question. Preferring a patient-centered model of care—where physicians listen to their patients, giving patients a say in their own treatment—many Egyptian IVF patients eventually gravitate toward physicians such as Drs. Yehia and Zaki, who are committed to practicing this style of medicine. However, as shown in this study and in the recent research on family planning in Egypt, patient-centered medicine is *not* the norm in Egyptian reproductive health circles. Instead, the physician-centered medicine practiced in rural family planning clinics and urban IVF clinics alike is reflective of professionally based social hierarchies that many Egyptian physicians seem all too willing to maintain, even with their most elite patients.

Ultimately, then, the private provision of new reproductive technologies in Egypt is fraught with obstacles and constraints—for the providers themselves, some of whom are quite candid about the need to reform the local IVF industry, but especially for the infertile patients who must rely on their IVF services. As seen in this chapter, finding a compassionate, communicative IVF physician who can be entrusted with one's gametes and embryos is a major ordeal for many would-be users of new reproductive technologies in Egypt. Finding one who is honest about the true efficacy of these technologies is yet another problem—to which we now turn.

CHAPTER **6**

Efficacy

The "Mother of the Tube"

As I have interviewed Egyptian women on the topic of infertility and the use of new reproductive technologies over the years, I have always been grateful for their characteristic candor and willingness to talk about a topic that, in most cases, has rendered much emotional pain and sorrow in their personal lives. Yet, I am also often struck in these interviews by the amount of levity and good humor Egyptians bring to conversation, and life in general, even in the face of serious adversity. In short, most Egyptians are artful jokers and can be downright funny. And thus, despite the seriousness of my topic, many of the IVF/ICSI patients I encountered in Egyptian IVF centers helped to lighten up our discussions of their often painful lives by interspersing their interviews with comic relief.

Such was the case with Huda, a twenty-seven-year-old civil engineer who provided me with one of my most lengthy and enjoyable interviews during the summer of 1996. I met her with my infertile research assistant, Tayseer, at the Nile Badrawi IVF center, where the three of us were introduced by Dr. Salah Zaki. We were a study in contrasts—I, the forty-ish, American anthropologist with my comfortable gauze dress and sandals and my long light brown hair; Huda, young, very pretty, with a Western-style short-sleeved blouse and skirt and her dark hair, fashionably styled and revealed by her (now relatively atypical) lack of head covering; and Tayseer, a more characteristically Egyptian *muhegabba* (veiled woman), whose scarf covered her hair and neck and whose clothing covered all but her hands and feet, despite the blistering temperatures of mid-July. Despite our different "looks" and the fact that I couldn't quite keep up with Huda's rapid-fire Egyptian Arabic (which is why Tayseer was there to help me), the three of us definitely "hit it off" and undertook an interview that was more like a conversation, with questions and answers that were moving back and forth between us. Plus, Huda was simply funny, humor she seemed to have inherited from her father, who was supporting her IVF treatment quest financially and emotionally, in his own paternalistic Egyptian way.

Huda told us that her father liked to call her *Umm Il-Anbuba,* "Mother of the Tube." She told us that he joked about telling his future grandchildren, "You are tubes." He also told Huda that he hoped she would have IVF triplets, so that she would name at least one of them after him. Huda appreciated her father's humor, which she did not view as the least bit insensitive, for it helped her to cope with the difficulties of her situation and raised her hopes that at least her father wanted her to become an Egyptian mother of one or more test-tube babies.

Like several of the other women who participated in this study, Huda recounted a long and painful story of iatrogenesis, or physician-induced harm. When she was only sixteen years old and living in the United Arab Emirates with her labor-migrating parents, she underwent a laparotomy, or abdominal surgery, for a painful ovarian cyst. The Swedish female consultant who performed the surgery removed the ovary with the cyst and, through the surgical procedure itself, caused adhesions around the remaining fallopian tube. In short, this surgery, which Egyptian physicians later deemed questionable and even unwarranted, rendered Huda with irreparable tubal infertility and a missing ovary.

Despite her preexisting infertility problem, Huda married an Egyptian physician, Omar, who accepted the fact that achieving pregnancy with Huda would require extraordinary means, probably resorting to IVF. However, Omar and Huda could not fully anticipate the troubles ahead. Following their marriage, Huda developed a uterine fibroid tumor, which was improperly diagnosed by at least one "big" Egyptian infertility specialist. With the help of Omar, she sought many second opinions about whether or not to undergo an additional surgery to remove the tumor. Ultimately, she arrived at the Nile Badrawi IVF center, where Dr. Salah Zaki counseled her to undertake the surgery in order to remove both the fibroid and the thick adhesions surrounding her only viable ovary and fallopian tube. She explained,

> He told me he won't be able to do IVF now. The fibroid is in a place where the embryo sticks to the uterus. So even if I did IVF and it succeeded, I will continue until the fourth month and then I will have a [spontaneous] abortion. He is a very clever doctor. He's very honest to tell me that. He could say, "I'll do IVF," and then when I have the miscarriage, he won't take responsibility.

Indeed, Huda has "lived" many of the problems of poor quality care described in the last chapter. Having had bad experiences with more than one physician, even as a teenager, Huda has a profound distrust of medical experts, especially those gynecologists who have advised her *not* to undertake IVF. As she explains,

> Psychologically, I need second opinions, because I suffered from doctors' mistakes. When I was told I need IVF, I went to *many* doctors, and I went to one in Muhandiseen [a Cairo suburb]. He said, "Trying to remove adhesions is something useless—not good here in Egypt, or anyplace in the world. And IVF is a kind of gambling." When he told me this, I couldn't see anything "in front of me" [i.e., she was blinded by despair]. He made me feel that the operation won't work, IVF wouldn't work—*very* hopeless that I won't have

children. He said I won't succeed unless I do IVF in Israel. There's a very good hospital there, and I will come back pregnant. But I will *never* go to Israel to do that [nor would most Egyptians, who have a profound distrust of everything Israeli]! He told me this, I believe, to make me unable, in general, to do *anything*.

When I asked Huda why a doctor would be so cruel, she stated simply, "Any doctors who *don't* do IVF try to make [infertile] patients feel very hopeless."

After several months of emotional turmoil, indecision, and consultations with numerous doctors whom Omar helped her to contact, Huda decided to undertake IVF in Nile Badrawi Hospital. She explained, "After consulting many doctors, at last, I decided I *must* do IVF—here in *this* hospital. It's just a feeling. After dealing with Dr. Salah [Zaki], I trusted him more than any other doctor."

Following the removal of her fibroid four months ago, Huda is preparing to undertake her first trial of IVF under Dr. Zaki's care. Although she, like many other patients, is grappling with the high costs of IVF and the problems of finding hormonal medications that are rarely available in Egypt, Huda's major concern involves efficacy—whether or not she will be able to take home a test-tube baby.

Huda's concerns about efficacy are manifold. First, she does not believe that Egypt is very advanced in IVF compared to the West, where the technology was developed. For example, one of the questions she posed to me was whether the 25 percent success rate that she was quoted at Nile Badrawi was the "same in America." She explained her interest in global comparisons:

> Here in Egypt, they are not so advanced to reach that percentage. In England, 1978 was the first one [test-tube baby], but here, it's new in 1991. I wanted to make it outside this country, and I argued with my husband. We decided we would try here two times, and if it doesn't succeed, we will try outside in London. The success rate there reached 50 to 60 percent.[1]

In addition to her concerns about Egypt's position in the global arena, Huda is worried about the lack of regulation of Egyptian IVF centers and what she believes are the resultant attempts by many centers to inflate their success rates.

> The important thing is to have *legal* centers for these things, IVF. Not anyone can do it. When a center says we have a success rate of 15 or 20 percent, this number must be true. And they need to tell me exactly that number [so that I can] know whether I want to try. A *true* percentage, not fabricated. This is very important to me, because when I say that one trial in London equals four trials here [in terms of cost], when I know the *real* success rate, I can decide whether to do it here or in London.
>
> The [Egyptian] Physician Syndicate or the Ministry of Health has to supervise these centers. The Ministry of Health supervises all hospitals in Egypt, but not IVF centers. I need to know the success rates *exactly* for IVF— just like when doing an appendectomy—but not *from* the center itself.

Rather, a neutral party [needs to monitor]. This is not happening in Egypt yet, so every center writes whatever it wants, because no one supervises.

So far, despite her ongoing uncertainty about her *real* chance of success with IVF, Huda remains hopeful—partly because of her acquaintance with another successful IVF patient at the Nile Badrawi center.

I know someone, thirty-five years old, who became pregnant from the first time with IVF, and came back two years after, because she has a boy and wants a sister or brother for him. She gave me hope when she spoke to me, and she said, "I have a baby of the tubes. I have a boy, and he is an IVF baby, and I came to try again."

When I asked Huda how she had met this woman, given the anonymity that most couples seek to maintain, she explained, "I was crying, so she came to comfort me and told me her story. She knew I suffered from the same problem, and would be happy to know someone with the same problem who was 'cured.'"

When I asked whether Huda's and Omar's families knew they were about to embark on IVF, she said that only her mother, father, and sister knew. Although Omar comes from an educated family whose members have actually encouraged Huda to do IVF (since they know she has postoperative tubal infertility), Huda told them, "No, I'll fix the tube, and I'll do it naturally, not by IVF." She continued,

I'll be the only person in the family who did IVF, and it will be strange. It may affect the baby, because it may affect his psychology. If the baby grows up and someone tells jokes, it may affect him. Our traditions here, we have many jokes about IVF. Right now, it's not common yet, something very new. So it's *very* secret, although I see *many, many* patients. Maybe after ten years, it will change. My mother says, "Half the children in Egypt will be 'tubes!'"

More than anything, Huda hopes that two of those "tube" children will become her own.

The (In)efficacy of NRTs

In Huda's story, we find the embodiment of much that is wrong with privately offered reproductive medicine in the Middle East—including the neocolonial reliance on imported European consultants who may have little vested interest in Middle Eastern women such as Huda; unnecessary and iatrogenic surgeries that are a common cause of tubal infertility in the region;[2] nonspecializing physicians who compete for infertile patients such as Huda by dissuading them from trying IVF; IVF physicians who attempt to entice infertile patients such as Huda with grossly inflated claims of success; and the overarching lack of regulation of the private IVF industry, leading to what Huda calls the "scientific dishonesty" of these mostly "commercial" IVF centers. For highly educated Huda, who has relied heavily on a physician spouse to help her navigate this dangerous terrain, seeking second opinions has become a way of life, eventually leading her into a comfort zone at Nile Badrawi Hospital. But, as much as Huda respects Dr. Zaki and his IVF clinic staff, she has already negotiated with her husband to seek IVF services outside the country, where she is convinced that test-tube baby making is probably more "advanced" and more "honest" than in Egypt.

In this chapter, we will interrogate the thorny issue of efficacy—whether test-tube baby making in Egypt is as successful as many IVF providers say it is and how their claims of efficacy affect IVF patients such as Huda. These problems of efficacy, furthermore, must be placed in global context. Even in the best centers in the West, overall success rates for the new reproductive technologies are never more than 40 percent and are usually much lower, in the 20 to 30 percent range.[3] However, in Egypt, these poor odds of success play out in a particular local fashion, which has much to do with the problems of privatization and untoward competition described in the last chapter. In other words, ongoing global problems of IVF efficacy—rather, *in*efficacy—may take specific local forms in Third World sites such as Egypt. There, IVF providers who are entirely unregulated compete for willing clientele by making what might be best characterized as "extraordinary efficacy claims"—claims that unsuspecting patients often take to heart. That the majority of Egyptian IVF and ICSI patients, 70 to 80 percent or more, do *not* become pregnant with these new reproductive technologies is rarely emphasized, creating a climate whereby Egyptian physicians not only "sell hope,"[4] but also sell *false* hope to their otherwise hopeless patients.

But what is the problem with these technologies? Why do they not "cure" more people of their infertility? And why might providers of IVF and ICSI be inclined to overestimate success rates to their clients? In perhaps the best extended discussion of new reproductive technology success rates available in the Western literature, medical writer Judith Steinberg Turiel, in *Beyond Second Opinions: Making Choices About Fertility Treatment*,[5] describes in some detail the prominent factors influencing the success of a new reproductive technology, focusing her description (and critique) primarily on the state of affairs in the United States. Yet, as we shall see in this chapter, many of the ongoing problems found in America are only intensified in Egypt, for reasons having to do with the ways private IVF services are provided there, as well as factors that are culturally unique.

The first major factor affecting new reproductive technology success rates involves the characteristics of patients themselves, particularly the woman's age and the couple's diagnosis. Fertility in women generally declines after the mid-thirties; yet, many women seeking IVF and ICSI in Egyptian as well as Western centers are in their late thirties or older. As described by Turiel, "the age of forty for women using their own eggs [becomes] a rough boundary, beyond which success rates fall to extremely low levels."[6] In Egypt, the biological issues surrounding declining fertility rates at age forty are exacerbated by the social constraints on donor egg technology, meaning that for infertile Egyptian women who are religiously prohibited from accepting a donor egg, age forty marks a key watershed, one that is dreaded among women in IVF centers. Furthermore, for women of any age who undergo IVF or ICSI, the type and number of infertility conditions also has a major impact on success. Male-factor infertility and the diagnosis of multiple infertility problems in the woman, the man, or both "bring lowest rates of success," according to Turiel.[7] Yet, male infertility and complicated cases of so-called multiple-factor infertility are quite common in Egyptian IVF centers and may in fact comprise the majority of cases.

The second major factor affecting IVF success rates involves characteristics of the IVF process, particularly the number of embryos transferred to a woman's body during a treatment cycle. As Turiel notes, "Transferring more embryos . . . increases the pregnancy rate, but it also increases multiple gestations (possibly necessitating selective reduction procedures),[8] pregnancy loss, and obstetric and neonatal complications."[9]

Some Egyptian IVF physicians are willing to "hyperstimulate" a woman's ovaries to ensure that large numbers of eggs are harvested and embryos fertilized. This may lead to ovarian hyperstimulation syndrome (OHSS), a life-threatening condition that occurs when too-high doses of hormonal agents are used to stimulate high-order egg production. Although only a few patients die from this condition, many experience miserable symptoms, to be described in the following chapter. Furthermore, in Egypt, those centers lacking cryopreservation facilities are often too willing to transfer any excess embryos to a woman's body to increase the chance that one or more will implant, thereby boosting the clinic's success rates. Even though multiple-order births are greatly desired among Egyptian IVF patients, for reasons that will be revealed later in the chapter, multiple gestations of twins or more are actually much riskier and are prone to the problems, including pregnancy losses, described by Turiel.

A third issue affecting efficacy has to do with repetition—namely, the need to repeat IVF or ICSI procedures several times before achieving a successful pregnancy. As Turiel explains it,

> Since individual patients often undergo many treatment attempts, which can extend over many years, reports of live deliveries also need to indicate which cycle resulted in this outcome. That is, how many attempts did a woman go through before the success?[10]

A cumulative success rate that incorporates as many as six IVF cycles is "overly optimistic" for a woman who will attempt no more than two treatment cycles—which, in the case of many Egyptian patients, is often all that they can afford. Yet, with fewer attempted cycles in each patient, fewer successful pregnancies will accumulate, giving a clinic a lower cumulative success rate. Clearly, then, Egyptian IVF centers want wealthy patients who are willing to become "repeaters." But the need to repeat is rarely emphasized as Egyptian patients embark on this line of treatment, in order to maintain the false hope that a first trial will be successful.

A fourth factor has to do with the way in which IVF programs present their success rates. Turiel emphasizes that selecting and comparing only one number, such as the percentage of deliveries out of all embryos transferred, "does not provide a valid evaluation of a fertility clinic."[11] As she explains,

> Most success rates now reported by [IVF] programs present the number of live deliveries (i.e., at least one live newborn) as a percentage of the total number of attempts to achieve this goal during one year. This proportion of successful outcomes, however, depends on which step in the ART [advanced reproductive technology] process is used to define the number of "attempts." Some calculations inflate the degree of success because they do not include all of the women who began a treatment. In fact, a crucial dimension underlying measures of success is an "attrition rate." Patients drop out at each stage of an [IVF] cycle for a variety of reasons, physical, financial, and/or the stress of it all.[12]

Virtually all Egyptian IVF centers do the very thing that Turiel decries—presenting one overarching, inflated percentage, which may be written on an informed consent form, but which is then verbally "uplifted" to an even higher percentage by the treating physician. To make matters worse, most Egyptian centers do not offer a percentage based on actual live births—what is usually referred to in the world of IVF as "the take-home baby rate." Instead of reporting the percentage of *deliveries* out of all embryos transferred, Egyptian centers usually report the percentage of resulting *pregnancies,* many of which are not clinically confirmed (by ultrasound) and which may end in pregnancy loss. By calling all "chemical pregnancies" (apparent on an initial pregnancy test) IVF or ICSI successes, Egyptian IVF centers downplay the fact that many of these pregnancies do not progress, failing to deliver the take-home babies who are the only real measure of success for infertile couples desiring a child. Furthermore, Egyptian IVF centers do not base their calculations of success rates on the total number of women who start treatment, but then drop out early on. In other words, Egyptian centers do not report attrition rates, leading to the kind of insidious rate inflation described by Turiel.

Egyptian IVF centers also do not offer a breakdown of success rates by patient age group, a practice that has become standard in the glossy brochures often presented to patients in Western IVF centers. Given the problem with advancing age and efficacy described above, presenting a 35 percent success rate to a thirty-nine-year-old Egyptian woman and her husband is simply misleading. Nonetheless, by presenting single, highly generalized (and usually inflated) percentages, many Egyptian IVF centers make themselves look highly successful, even suggesting to patients that they succeed with nearly half of all their cases. However, as Turiel warns, any IVF clinic that appears to be highly successful based on an overall statistic may, in fact, be treating only the easiest patients—for example, young women with relatively mild problems who have tried to conceive without treatment for only a short time and who stand a relatively good chance of pregnancy with or without treatment. Or, a clinic may select patients "for whom a treatment is most effective"[13]—for example, patients who are younger than thirty-five and whose only fertility problem is blocked fallopian tubes, the problem for which IVF was invented. In other words, clinics that report better success rates may, in fact, be practicing significant patient selection, choosing only the easy subfertile patients and rejecting others, particularly women over forty, patients with previous treatment failures at other centers, or couples with several and sometimes severe problems in both the husband and wife. Such difficult patients are accepted for treatment at some Egyptian IVF centers, including both Nile Badrawi and Nozha Hospital. For example, Amira, whose story opens this volume, was taken on by Dr. Yehia as a forty-year-old patient after several failed trials at Dr. X's clinic for her husband's severe male-factor infertility. Had Amira initially contacted Dr. X in this condition, she would have been rejected by him, for he routinely refuses to perform IVF or ICSI on older patients with the most recalcitrant infertility problems. Indeed, he tells these patients, quite callously, that they are "hopeless" cases who will "bring down" his clinic's rates, which he purports are 40 percent or above.

Finally, success rates are affected by the very quality of care at an IVF center—whether "a program has qualified, experienced personnel and a track record open to public scrutiny."[14] Yet, as Turiel laments, even in the United States,

> Information needed to complete the [IVF] picture has not been systematically gathered and reported. Patients and their doctors could benefit from more numbers, sharper calculations, more insight into the medical complexities that affect an individual's outcome. Even more disturbing than the lack of adequate statistics is the absence of regulation, oversight, internal checks, and public scrutiny—with outcomes that became apparent only years after flagrant medical practices were occurring.[15]

Turiel's critique is seconded by American reproductive endocrinologist Nancy Reame in "Making Babies in the 21st Century: New Strategies, Old Dilemmas." Reame argues that, despite more than twenty years of assisted reproduction in the United States, the industry is neither adequately "self regulating"[16] nor subject to sufficient government oversight. The result is a lack of uniform standards regarding safety and efficacy, as well as lack of protection of infertility patients in terms of informed consent and record-keeping. Drawing upon bioethical standards for the protection of human subjects, Reame ultimately characterizes infertility patients—even privileged "middle-class, college-educated, white infertile couples"—as "vulnerable research subjects" who are "decisionally impaired,"[17] by virtue of false and misleading advertising and marketing and questionable research protocols in at least some IVF centers in the United States.

The Egyptian Game of Inflation

As bad as things may be in the United States—one of the few remaining Western countries without a national policy on assisted reproduction[18]—matters are likely worse in Egypt, where quality of care in IVF clinics is quite variable for the reasons described in the last chapter. That poor quality of care diminishes success rates is something that Egyptian IVF providers themselves acknowledge. But they also realize that most Egyptian IVF providers are engaged in a deceptive "game of inflation," whereby lower-than-expected success rates are massaged, juggled, twisted, reshaped, or simply lied about in order to appear much better to potential patients. The result is a statistical free-for-all, with some (although not all) centers seeming to pull exaggerated success rates "out of a hat," with flagrant disregard for any clinical or statistical reality. This Egyptian game of inflation and sometimes outright deception in the reporting of success rates is clearly a result of the unhealthy competition between centers that generates the felt need to inflate in order to attract patients. However, it is also related, in terms of both cause and effect, to a number of other specific factors, including (1) the lack of an agreed-upon definition in Egyptian IVF centers of what constitutes a successful pregnancy; (2) the attempt to inflate success rates by eliminating all women age forty and older; (3) the introduction of ICSI at some centers, which can significantly lower success rates but is rarely presented as such; (4) the lack of uniform standards for informed consent; (5) the lack of uniform standards for record-keeping, leading to a lacunae of statistical information within centers and within the industry as a whole; and (6) the lack of any form of effective regulation or monitoring of Egyptian centers on a national level.

With regard to the first factor, Egyptian IVF providers have yet to enact a uniform standard for calculating success rates based on an agreed-upon definition of what constitutes a successful pregnancy. According to Dr. Yehia of Nozha Hospital, "there is a big problem in the different definitions of pregnancy used by different centers in Egypt." For example, pregnancy rates can be calculated to reflect pregnancies per total number of IVF or ICSI cycles initiated (including all women who begin treatment, but eventually drop out), or they can be defined using clinical pregnancies per embryo transfer (thereby eliminating all the treatment dropouts). The first definition lowers overall success rates to significantly less than 20 percent, which is why most Egyptian IVF centers prefer to use the latter figure, which is in the 30 percent range, according to Dr. Ashraf Hakam, laboratory director at Nile Badrawi. However, when all of the subsequent pregnancy losses are factored in, the true take-home baby rate is only about 17 percent, according to Dr. Hakam, a low figure that Egyptian centers do not want to advertise. Therefore, patients are routinely quoted the 30 percent figure and are led to believe that nearly one-third of all couples take home a test-tube baby, when, in reality, less than one-fifth do (and probably even less than that in some poorly equipped centers).

Furthermore, a major discrepancy exists between success rates based on "biochemical" versus "ultrasound-confirmed" pregnancies. At Nozha Hospital, Drs. Yehia and Wafik have stopped using the biochemical pregnancy rate as a marker of success because this rate includes many false-positives—women who are not truly pregnant but who appear to be so because of the hormones circulating in their blood following embryo transfer. Hormones administered to women for so-called luteal phase support following embryo transfer can induce what is sometimes called a "borderline" or "chemical" pregnancy, creating false hopes that are then dashed upon further ultrasound investigation. Because these false-positives are so devastating to infertile couples, Dr. Yehia has stopped administering the hormones that cause this confusion between reality and false-positives. His laboratory is also using a very sensitive blood-based pregnancy test designed to reduce the false-positive rate even further. However, such attempts to avoid the confusion between reality and false-positives have not been undertaken in all Egyptian IVF laboratories, according to Dr. Yehia, meaning that many centers inflate their success rates by including the "biochemical pregnancies" (i.e., false-positives) in order to make their rates appear better than they really are.

Furthermore, according to Dr. Yehia, many Egyptian IVF centers routinely reject all patients older than forty from their practices, and those who take them routinely eliminate these patients from the calculations used to generate clinic success rates. By eliminating the least successful older patients, a clinic can avoid "spoiling" its overall figures. To take but one example of how this might work, of the 110 trials of IVF and ICSI initiated and completed at Nozha Hospital during a three-month period in 1996, twenty-nine resulted in ultrasound-confirmed pregnancies, for a "clinical pregnancy per embryo transfer rate" of 26.3 percent. However, three of these patients had spontaneously aborted, bringing the take-home baby rate to 23.6 percent. Of these 110 patients, approximately twenty were age forty and older. As Dr. Yehia explained,

> Maybe the success rate of those less than forty is more like 32 percent. But we don't know, because we don't eliminate all patients over forty from our rates. Most centers do this—removing the older patients from their calculations to make themselves look much more successful. Centers need to be honest about their criteria and the definition of pregnancy they're using. Some centers say, "60 to 70 percent successfully fertilized," which means *nothing* in terms of pregnancy.

Dr. Yehia went on to argue that this problem of overreporting success rates could be solved "if everyone just broke the rates down by age. This is better than eliminating, for example, all women over forty or even over thirty, which will happen here if everyone is competing to achieve the highest [single] success rate."

Additional problems with success rates have emerged since the introduction of ICSI at some Egyptian IVF centers. Prior to ICSI's arrival in Egypt in 1994, virtually all couples affected by male infertility, including many in this study, were routinely treated with multiple rounds of artificial insemination using husbands' sperm (AIH). According to Dr. Hakam at Nile Badrawi Hospital,

> AIH is less successful than either IVF or ICSI, but many Egyptian doctors do AIH, overestimating its success rate. For male-factor infertility, it is not very successful at all,[19] and actually the first line should be ICSI, not AIH. But it is very difficult to convince Egyptian doctors of this. In fact, the only reason AIH is still being used in some Egyptian IVF centers is economic: If ICSI is

too expensive for a couple, sometimes AIH will be used repeatedly in patients with open tubes.

Per Dr. Hakam's remarks, ICSI was designed specifically to overcome the relatively low success rates of both AIH and IVF in cases of serious male-factor infertility. With the introduction of ICSI, patients at Egyptian IVF centers where ICSI is available are now told that ICSI is "much more successful" than either AIH or IVF for the treatment of male infertility. On the one hand, this is true: ICSI has overcome many more cases of male infertility, including severe cases with sperm counts of less than 5 million and motility rates less than 20 percent, than either AIH or IVF alone. On the other hand, ICSI is a variant of IVF and, like IVF, it fails much more often than it succeeds. For example, of the ninety patients who had completed trials of ICSI at Nile Badrawi Hospital as of May 1996, only twenty had become pregnant, for an overall success rate of 23 percent (based on all the women who had undergone ova retrieval, versus 26 percent for all those who had undergone embryo transfer).

Furthermore, according to Dr. Zaki, clinical director at Nile Badrawi, success rates for ICSI will become even lower over time as more and more couples affected by male infertility seek out ICSI services. As he explained,

> The problem we are beginning to see, which results in lower success rates for ICSI, is older-aged women, whose egg quality and numbers are not good. Now that ICSI is available, these women and their husbands want to try, but these women are no longer good candidates based on their age. This can bring success rates down from 35 percent in the best-case scenario to 5 percent in some cases.

At both Nile Badrawi and Nozha Hospitals, couples such as these with a "reproductively elderly" wife are told the truth about the very low chance of success (in the 3 to 10 percent range, depending upon the case). However, such candor is not typical of other IVF centers, where older patients may be given the false impression that ICSI, at last, represents "true hope" for their long-term male infertility problems. Indeed, ICSI is clearly the new "hope technology" of Egypt, one which is presented as the long-awaited solution to male infertility when, in fact, ICSI resolves relatively few of these often intractable cases.

That few ICSI patients realize the extent to which this technology does *not* overcome male infertility is a reflection of the lack of standardized informed consent procedures in Egypt. According to Dr. Yehia, every Egyptian IVF center has an "ethical obligation" to present accurate success rates on written informed consent forms, which patients must read and sign before they embark on treatment. Dr. Yehia was an instrumental participant in a government meeting held in the early 1990s to develop a standard informed consent form for use in Egyptian IVF centers.[20] At Nozha Hospital, as well as Nile Badrawi, this consent form is presented to all patients, who are asked to read and sign it. In the consent form, success rates are clearly stated—25 percent for IVF and 20 percent for ICSI (the latter of which was superimposed over an initial 10 percent figure at Nozha Hospital). According to Dr. Yehia, these written statistics actually underestimate current success rates at his center. But he leaves the 20 to 25 percent figures so as not to create false hopes that can be psychologically devastating to patients. In his view of things, it is better to have realistic patients who are pleasantly surprised by unexpected success than to have overly optimistic patients who are traumatized by unexpected failure.

Unfortunately, Dr. Yehia's approach does not appear to be widely shared in the Egyptian IVF community. Informed consent procedures are not standardized in private Egyptian IVF centers, which unlike public hospitals (where informed consent procedures for all invasive procedures are now required) are beyond the realm of government control. Thus, whether informed consent forms are being uniformly applied, and what success rates are being quoted to patients, remain major questions in Egypt. For their part, IVF physicians at both Nozha and Nile Badrawi hospitals are major advocates for increased government regulation, including the creation of an ethically responsible third-party agency to monitor and ensure the honesty of success rate reporting in the country. However, as noted in the last chapter, the Egyptian government, so far at least, has adopted a laissez-faire approach to the private IVF industry. And few private IVF centers are ready to participate in the formation of a national registry of IVF patients. Yet, only through such a registry can *true* success rates be determined, both within individual centers and for the nation as a whole. Until this day comes in Egypt, and in the Middle East as a whole, the private IVF industry will be plagued by a lack of credible statistics—leading to the kind of *in*credible claims described so far in this chapter. As one infertile Egyptian physician, who happened to be an IVF repeater in my study, lamented,

> When they open a new IVF center here, the doctors do not take enough time to compile statistics, so they don't give exact success rates. I'm a doctor, so I know that if they say "20 percent," I say, "No, I know it will be less than this." There needs to be more honesty in giving success rates. This is what I liked most about England [where she went seeking IVF]. One of the women doctors there said, "You have to have a gambling spirit. Only one out of six attempts is successful, and it's a closed box: You never know which side of the dice will come up." Even though that was distressing for me, it was honest. But here, they're looking at it from an economic point of view. The competition now in Egypt is big, and centers are competing with each other, so they inflate their success rates. The doctors need to have the guts to be more frank with patients. Instead, each time, they give you hope that this is the first and last time you'll have to do it.

Positioning Egypt in the Discourses of Hope

This woman's comment, that Egyptian IVF providers are engaged in the creation of hope, is not surprising, given all that is now known about the ways in which demand for new reproductive technologies has been created among infertile couples in the

West. In a number of compelling ethnographies of the IVF treatment experience in the United States and England,[21] anthropologists and sociologists have characterized the NRTs as "hope technologies,"[22] whereby hope is "commodified" as part of a "marketing tool" by which IVF physicians "sell hope and persistence."[23] However, as noted by Becker in her recent book, *The Elusive Embryo: How Women and Men Approach New Reproductive Technologies*, at least some infertile Americans have come to see themselves as "smart consumers," who view part of their job as questioning the providers who supply the services.[24] This kind of questioning—which is explicitly encouraged by Turiel in *Beyond Second Opinions: Making Choices About Fertility Treatment*—may involve careful scrutiny of success rates between American IVF centers, which usually market their programs with materials focusing on the efficacy of different procedures among various patient age groups.

Clearly, the same process of "selling hope" is at work in Egypt. There, IVF providers, invoking inflated success rates along with God's will, attempt to convince infertile patients that they should try these technologies as their only hope of getting pregnant. However, the kind of fancy marketing tools found in the West are missing in Egypt, where printed patient education materials are still uncommon and relatively few citizens have regular access to computers and the World Wide Web. Furthermore, as seen in the last chapter, relatively few Egyptian IVF patients, even the most highly educated ones, view themselves as assertive consumers who have the right to ask questions and challenge physicians about basic aspects of their treatment, including success rates. Although infertile Egyptians such as Huda may express their discontent by doctor shopping or seeking second opinions, Huda was one of the few IVF patients in my study to explicitly interrogate the success rates quoted to her in Egyptian IVF centers. Although most Egyptian IVF patients do, in fact, worry a great deal about whether IVF or ICSI will ultimately be effective in their own cases, their ardent desires for success, along with religious convictions that success is ultimately in God's hands, seem to make them less critical of inflated efficacy claims than they should be.

Consequently, the critique of rate inflation described here is an *internal* critique among Egyptian IVF providers at well-established centers, who are appalled by what they view as the adverse effects of private competition on actual success rates and the reporting of them. As for patients themselves, I met only three couples who were at all skeptical about the success rates quoted to them; each of these couples (including Huda and Omar) involved at least one physician partner. In other words, Egyptian physicians, who know how private medicine is practiced in their country, may have reason to be skeptical about IVF rate inflation. For patients without such medical expertise, however, few have any knowledge of this endemic local problem.

As we have seen so far in the preceding chapters, infertile Egyptian women and their husbands are more than willing to talk about the many problems they encounter in the land of test-tube baby making. These include, among other things, prohibitive costs, concerns about laboratory mixing of biogenetic substances, and supercilious physicians who mistreat them. But rate inflation, much to my surprise, does not present itself as a major concern. Instead, most of the Egyptian IVF patients I interviewed seemed to adopt a nationalistic stance about the excellence of test-tube baby making in their country, claiming it to be as good as, if not better than, the "most advanced countries of the West."

Have Egyptian IVF patients, then, been sold a "bill of goods" by the private IVF industry? Are they unwitting cultural "dupes," entirely unaware of one of the most serious constraints facing them, namely, the low rates of IVF and ICSI efficacy? Why do they not realize that IVF and ICSI are being oversold in most Egyptian IVF centers as real solutions to the problem of infertility?

In my view, there are two major responses to these questions, one having to do with Egypt's particular position on the regional and global stage, and the other having to do with local Egyptian discourses of hope and reproductive agency. As mentioned in Chapter 2, Egypt maintains a privileged regional position as one of the countries with the most advanced biomedicine in the Middle East. Although Saudi Arabia has achieved rapid and impressive gains in its biomedical health sector, due in part to its extraordinary economic resources, Egypt's biomedical history and reputation are literally thousands of years older than Saudi Arabia's, as well as any other country in the Middle East.[25] Today, Egypt boasts more medical schools (seventeen) and more medical school graduates (five thousand per year) than any other country in the Middle Eastern region,[26] which is why (rightly or wrongly) the estimated 130,000 qualified Egyptian doctors enjoy the reputation of being among the "best-trained" and most "clever" of all Middle Eastern physicians. This is one of the reasons why wealthy Arabs from other Middle Eastern countries often travel to Egypt for their medical care, including IVF.[27] This is also why Egyptian expatriates routinely travel home on annual IVF holidays to place their trust in Egyptian physicians, who are perceived as starting IVF in the region and who are therefore more experienced than physicians elsewhere, including in the petro-rich Arab Gulf. With few exceptions (e.g., Libya, Yemen), IVF centers are now found in most countries in the Middle East. However, Egypt is still regionally regarded by many as the "place to go" for those who truly desire an IVF or ICSI success.

Even on the global stage, Egypt is considered, by most Egyptian IVF patients at least, as now offering IVF services that are as successful as those in Western countries. Although I was questioned about this by a handful of IVF patients (four to be exact, including Huda), most of those patients who had thought to compare Egyptian success rates to those "outside" (i.e., in the West) told me that they were convinced that Egypt's capabilities now equaled, or even surpassed, those of Western centers. As one woman, whose husband was infertile, said,

> Those who have money consider going "outside." In England and France, they do [ICSI] with maybe 90 percent success. But here, because it's newer, the success rates are lower, so people travel because they feel the success rates are higher outside. But now, the [Egyptian] doctors are good [at it], and we have the same success rate.

According to Dr. Yehia, many patients still ask him if they can "improve their chances" by seeking IVF services abroad. His strategy is to tell such patients to go abroad, viewing it as a "win-win situation." He explained, "I have many contacts and colleagues all over the world, so I can direct patients to them. If they get pregnant, they are happy and grateful to me. If they don't, they come back and want to try it with me."

For patients who are less inclined to go abroad but wonder about the comparability of Egyptian and Western success rates, Dr. Yehia can state confidently that "here is the same as there." Nozha Hospital's success rates are, in fact, comparable to the best centers in the West. Each year, Drs. Yehia and Wafik are required by the hospital's board of directors to prove this record of success in a detailed annual report. In fact, part of the reason for Egypt's regional reputation is that the most well-established IVF centers in Egypt, including the Nozha Hospital, Nile Badrawi Hospital, and Maadi IVF Centers, have impressive records of success. In these centers, test-tube babies are being created and born on a daily basis. Ironically, however, the Egyptian IVF centers with the best track records are also the ones least likely to engage in the deceptive inflation strategies described earlier. Thus, they may appear less successful than some newer centers, which are making extraordinary efficacy claims in the 40 to 70 percent range.

Although it can never be known how many new patients are lost by virtue of deceptive marketing strategies from the most to the least efficacious IVF clinics in Cairo, it is clear from interviews that not all infertile Egyptian patients are being duped by deceptive success rate claims. Both Nozha and Nile Badrawi hospitals, which do not participate in egregious inflation, have gained rather than lost patients, who feel they can trust the honest physicians at these centers. When I asked nearly sixty IVF patients at these centers about the "percentage of success" that had been quoted to them, nearly all of them offered figures in the 20 to 35 percent range; in fact, 25 percent was the single figure most frequently cited, clearly reflecting the informed consent form figures. However, strikingly, nearly one-quarter of these patients had been told by their physicians that their "individual percentages of success" were much lower, often in the 5 to 15 percent range. Some of these cases involved older couples with a wife at or older than the age of forty. Others involved men with serious male infertility problems, including azoospermia or lack of mature spermatozoa. Some cases involved both problems of reproductive aging and male infertility and had been deemed hopeless at other IVF centers in the city.

As noted earlier, such low-odds patients are often rejected out of hand at other centers. At both Nile Badrawi and Nozha hospitals, however, patients in this difficult position may be accepted for treatment, but only after being counseled about their extremely low chances of success. One woman described how she and her husband were won over by Dr. Yehia's honesty:

> Maybe it was his frankness that made us feel so comfortable. He told us from
> the very beginning that our percentage of success is very low—something

like 10 percent in our case, because of the age factor (I'm thirty-seven now, but I was thirty-six then) and my husband's count. The question I asked him was, "Is there any chance without [ICSI]? Do we have [a chance] any other way?" He said, "There's *probably* no other chance. Of course, we can't predict. It's in God's hands." Before we went home, I found my husband telling him, "We're willing to go through this process." Even though we had a low chance of success, we decided we were willing to go through both the financial and emotional burden so that we wouldn't regret later that we had something in front of us and we rejected it. We wanted to feel like we tried the most that we could have done. And we prayed—during this period I was praying a lot, actually—and I felt signs from God that he would reward us [which he did with the birth of healthy male and female ICSI twins].

And this brings us back to the issue of hope. The new reproductive technologies—and especially ICSI, which is presented as the only solution, the last resort for these particularly difficult cases—are hope technologies in a society where hope, patience, faith, searching, and reward have significant cultural currency. Indeed, the discourses of hope, which seem to be generated by IVF physicians and their patients wherever these technologies are applied, take a particular cultural form in Egypt, where hope and belief in technology are always tied to God, the ultimate creator. As emphasized by anthropologists working with IVF-seeking couples in Britain and the United States,[28] Western discourses of hope invoke beliefs in "technological progress and scientific authority," but seem to be devoid of the religious references that might still be expected there. In Egypt, on the other hand, infertile couples and even doctors themselves, most of whom are religiously observant Muslims (or Coptic Christians), place their hopes in God, who "rewards" those who have demonstrated their patience and faith during long periods of adversity. Clearly, long-term infertility is widely perceived by Egyptians of all social backgrounds as a special test of faith and patience;[29] thus, the new reproductive technologies, and particularly ICSI, represent a means of passing this test among infertile couples who have patiently waited for years and even decades in some cases. Although the odds of success for these technologies are extremely slim, Egyptian couples with the financial resources are compelled to try them, for as good Muslims, they regard these technologies as gifts from God, who may, at last, reward them for their long suffering.

The importance of searching and trying, of being resourceful actors in the face of adversity, is also a deeply felt religious value on the part of many Muslim patients, who believe that God wants them to attempt to solve their own human problems in an agentive fashion. As shown in my previous book *Quest for Conception,* poor infertile Egyptian women who cannot afford new reproductive technologies are nonetheless tireless reproductive actors, who believe that they are religiously mandated to "search for children" as long as they are able. Among the elites at Egyptian IVF centers, this theme of reproductive agency in the face of adversity clearly resurfaces, as do themes of hope in the face of hopelessness and faith in God, who rewards the "patient patient." Thus, discourses of hope and reproductive agency take particular cultural forms, highlighting the ways in which global hope technologies are accommodated and even valorized as "technologies of God" in local cultural landscapes such as Egypt. For religiously oriented Egyptians, the very existence of ICSI in their country provides concrete evidence of the way in which God "gives hope" to those who are hopeless, thereby reinforcing local beliefs about the importance of maintaining hope, being patient, keeping faith, and trying to achieve God's will through resort to the newest technologies. As one woman who become pregnant with twins on her third trial of ICSI told me,

> I thank my God. Anything he has to make for me, I'll be thankful. I'm satisfied. [Reciting a Qur'anic passage]: "God gives to whom he wants boys, and to whom he wants girls, and makes others infertile." God may make someone infertile forever. But, for us, medicine has progressed, so we had hope. For example, before, we didn't hear about the microscopic injection, so we had stopped doing anything and we were satisfied and decided to live without children forever. The doctors before the microscopic injection said, "No." But when there was hope, we tried. The first time, we tried and it failed, so there was hope on the second try. But on the third time, I felt it will fail because it failed two times before. So I was very much expecting that it will fail. *El-hamdu-lillah!* [Praise be to God! She became pregnant.]

Similarly, a severely infertile man, who was waiting for the results of his wife's first trial of ICSI, explained,

> The doctors are placing their faith in God, too. Even my doctor friend said, "You have to keep trying. Don't lose faith. If not from the first time, then try a second and a third." Even in normal cases, pregnancy doesn't come from the first month. Don't lose faith, and *insha Allah* [God willing], it will happen.

As seen in these individuals' comments, both IVF patients and their doctors invoke their beliefs in God to explain a series of otherwise inexplicable phenomena, including why some people are infertile while others are not, why new medical discoveries such as ICSI are suddenly made, why some trials of IVF or ICSI succeed while others fail, and, ultimately, why some couples have children while others are destined to remain forever childless. Although most Egyptian couples emphasize that they accept their fate, whatever God has "written" for them, most still hope and pray that they will be among the successful ones who overcome their infertility—in this case, through final resort to the newest technologies. Furthermore, although most infertile Egyptian couples emphasize that they will be satisfied with whatever God gives them, they nonetheless have two specific desires: first, the desire for a successful pregnancy on the first trial of IVF or ICSI, and second, the desire for a first-time pregnancy with twins or even triplets.

With regard to the first desire, many infertile Egyptian couples want "quick results" to avoid the inevitable financial, physical, and emotional strains entailed in the failure of repeated IVF/ICSI cycles. Some of the couples undertaking their first trial know it will be their last, usually by virtue of absolute financial barriers. But others see their major obstacle as a "race against time," particularly for wives approaching the dreaded age of forty, when success rates begin their precipitous decline. Thus, those who are about to embark on their first trial of IVF pray for immediate success, or what they call a "100 percent success rate" on their first trial. Yet, given the low efficacy rates of all forms of new reproductive technologies, first-time success is relatively uncommon in Egypt, as it is elsewhere around the globe. This lack of first-time success, according to both infertile Egyptian women and their physicians, is experienced as one of the most difficult, disappointing, and depressing aspects of test-tube baby making—the "shock" for which no one in this situation is really prepared. This is especially true given the multiple other constraints on IVF utilization, particularly the fact that many women cannot afford to undertake more than one trial for financial or other reasons. Whereas women in Western sites seem to accept the fact that multiple repetitions of IVF are necessary—and therefore become quickly socialized into what Franklin has called the "treadmill effect," or the engulfing "way of life" associated with serial IVF failures[30]—Egyptian women do not experience these technologies as inevitable, as ones that they are "compelled to try" over and over by virtue of what Sandelowski has called the "never-enough quality" of new reproductive technologies.[31] The particularly American adage, "If at first you don't succeed, then try, try again," simply does not play out in the world of Egyptian test-tube baby making as it has been shown to in the West.

In fact, when I asked women in my study about whether they would consider repetition, I received a wide range of responses, which were not necessarily predicated on a woman's position in the treatment process. Some women in this study had yet to complete an IVF/ICSI cycle, others had completed but failed one or more cycles, and still others had succeeded in making one or more test-tube babies. But within each of these categories, responses were varied. Although all those I interviewed endorsed the importance of trying at least once, many of them had, by choice or necessity, put firm limits on the numbers of trials they would ultimately undertake. Some women insisted that once was enough, whether or not they were able to produce children, and that they planned to leave their cases "up to God" from that point on. Others viewed the number of repetitions strategically, calculating how much money, how many annual vacations, or how many years of age they had left ahead of them—and how many trials this would ultimately buy them. Some women who had borne a test-tube baby or test-tube twins said they would never repeat the procedure again, while others had already begun the process of planning for the next trial. A few women said they would repeat as many times as necessary to produce two children. Indeed, family size concerns were a major consideration for many, as we shall see.

But the kind of "never enough" approach to these technologies demonstrated by many Western women and their physicians was much less clear in Egypt. Only seven women of the nearly forty I questioned told me that they were prepared to repeat "as many times as necessary" to achieve their reproductive goals. Not surprisingly, all of these women were financially well endowed, viewing money as no object in their way to repetition. Their comments on repetition were often striking, emphatic, and even desperate in tone. They used phrases such as "until the last hope in my blood," "as long as I am alive," "until the end of the world," "over and over," and even "addiction" (not a common term in Egypt, where alcohol and drug abuse are relatively rare). However, these women—some of whom were engaged in multiple repetitions, while others had yet to go through this process—were *not* representative of the women in this study. Most women I interviewed realized that repetition of IVF or ICSI cycles might be necessary, but they viewed their own ability and desire to become repeaters as quite limited in scope. In short, the purported inevitability of these technologies and their treadmill effect are simply not experienced as such by infertile women in resource-poor countries such as Egypt, where individuals pay dearly, economically and otherwise, for their right to access these exclusive technologies.

Because many Egyptian women cannot afford multiple repetitions, they ardently desire pregnancy on the first trial, with twins or more. For infertile Egyptian women and their husbands, one of the most exciting prospects of the new reproductive technologies is their largesse—their proven ability to deliver multiple infants at one time. From a biomedical standpoint, high-order multiple gestations are considered by many infertility experts, including Egyptian ones, to be among the greatest risks of the new reproductive technologies.[32] Dr. Yehia explained how, in Egypt, high-order multiple gestations of triplets or more are clinically very problematic, given the requirements of extra monitoring and obstetrical and neonatal care. In cases of twins and triplets, he monitors these high-risk pregnancies himself, but admits that they cause "headaches" for him because they require extra prenatal attention.

In his practice, he sends all women with *more* than three viable fetuses for "selective reduction" procedures. Selective reduction is a form of therapeutic abortion of one or more fetuses in multiple-gestation pregnancies, where the high number of fetuses poses a threat to the mother's health, to the health of the fetuses themselves, or to the ultimate viability of the pregnancy. This procedure, which, according to Dr. Yehia is technically simple, involves inserting an instrument into the embryonic heart. However, because the procedure amounts to abortion of precious test-tube babies, some Egyptian IVF physicians find it emotionally difficult to carry out. Dr. Yehia, for one, refers all of his selective reduction cases to colleagues. As for the women themselves, the procedure may be emotionally harrowing, although not usually physically painful (as it is done under general anesthesia). Women who undergo it are, in effect, aborting some of their ardently desired test-tube babies, and then must live with the worry about whether the remaining fetuses (usually twins or triplets) will survive. In my study, I encountered only one woman who had undergone selective reduction, bringing her number of viable fetuses from five to two. She went through the procedure without her husband's knowledge, for she feared he would tell his family, resulting in a "big story" with rumors and gossip. Despite the emotionally torturous decision to go through with the reduction, she had told only her own twin sister about what she had done. Relieved by the confidentiality of our interview, she unburdened this painful dilemma to me, including her feelings that she had somehow lied to her husband. He was now thrilled that his wife was having twins, and she, too, was praying that the twins would be born healthy.

From the perspective of most infertile Egyptian couples, having twins is one of their greatest desires. With twins, triplets, or even more, an infertile couple can "complete" the family and "finish quickly," leaving the world of test-tube baby making behind them. Mention of *tauwum*, or twins, therefore, inspired animated discussion, particularly among women in my study. When they heard me say the word "twins," most women, almost reflexively, voiced immediate responses of *yarait* (I wish), *insha Allah* (God willing), or among those fortunate enough to be pregnant with twins, *mash Allah* (thank God) and *el-hamdu-lillah* (praise be to God). Most Egyptian women have had personal exposures to sets of twins or triplets, in part because multiple births are becoming more common in Egypt as a result of the widespread (over)use of Clomid and other fertility drugs (given by physicians to women who are probably not truly infertile). Through such exposure to twins, a handful of women in this study, seven to be exact, were more realistic about what birthing and raising multiple children entailed; most of these women claimed that they did not truly desire IVF or ICSI multiples, based on the medical complications and parenting difficulties they had already observed. For the rest, however, twins were seen as a blessing, a great "gift from God," and a source of immeasurable joy. Reflecting this general sentiment, one woman described her ardent desire for twins as follows:

> I hope from God that I have twin girls. I hope. I *adore* girls . . . and I *want* twins. Last time, they put four embryos [inside her uterus]. I was thinking with my husband, "If four are going to succeed, what will we do?" But I *want* the four. He said, "I'm going to leave home until after they become one year old, and then I'll return!" But I don't mind. Anything from God. In IVF, if I had twins, I don't want *anything* else. I always tell God, I don't want *anything* . . . I don't want anything more. I want the babies only.

In Egypt, having no children at all is clearly a social onus, necessitating the kind of treatment seeking described among women and men in this book. But for many couples, having only one child is also socially unacceptable. Egypt is decidedly *not* a "one-child-only" country. Although long-term family planning campaigns introduced in the 1960s have brought the total fertility rate down to 3.5 per woman,[33] most Egyptian couples want at least two children, with two children being the ideal family size according to most urban, educated couples.[34] Thus, having only one child, and especially an only daughter,[35] is considered deviant and strange. Furthermore, parents fear that an only child will be left an "orphan" after their deaths, lacking the kind of family support that only siblings can provide. Thus, most Egyptian couples want to give their first child a sibling, which, for those who are fertile, usually happens relatively quickly after the first child is born.

Infertile Egyptians, on the other hand, often remark that they will be "satisfied with only one." But, learning through ultrasound visualization that more than one embryo has "taken hold" is a source of unremitting pleasure for the lucky few who become Egyptian parents of *multiple* test-tube babies. One woman, who had just given birth to male and female ICSI twins, described the exaltation she, her husband, and her family members felt when they received the initial news of a twin pregnancy:

> When Dr. Yehia saw the ultrasound, he said, "More than one." I said, "How many?" And he said, "Twins." My husband was with me. We were *very* happy, really very happy. Twins are a lot of work and effort, but they're a blessing from God. If I had had only one baby, a "one-time shot," I would not have tried again. I would have been satisfied. But I've always liked two kids, because I don't like having a lonely child. When we told our families later, we broke the news to our parents and sisters, everyone was crying—my husband, our parents—screaming and crying and ululating. It was a big celebration.

Realities of Success and Failure

And this brings us to the question of success: How often do Egyptian women get to celebrate the birth of their test-tube babies? How many of them are rewarded for their patience and long-suffering? Or, to return to the question first posed by Huda, what is the ratio of failure to success?

In this study at Egyptian IVF centers, I asked women about their reproductive histories, including the number of times they had been pregnant and the number of times they had tried either IVF or ICSI. Of the sixty-six women in my study, more than half (thirty-eight women) had never been pregnant, although most had been trying to get pregnant for many years and were now in the process of undergoing either IVF or ICSI. Eleven women were experiencing so-called secondary infertility, or the inability to conceive following a previous pregnancy (although only three of these women had living children). Only seventeen women in my study, or 26 percent, had achieved IVF or ICSI successes, including ten who were currently pregnant (five of these with twins) and seven who had given birth to IVF or ICSI children (including three sets of twins). These seventeen successes, eight of them on the first attempt, emerged out of seventy-seven total IVF or ICSI trials, for an overall ultrasound-confirmed pregnancy success rate of 22 percent. But the take-home baby rate—that is, the number of IVF or ICSI pregnancies that had resulted in actual live births by the end of my study—was considerably less, seven out of seventy-seven trials, or 9 percent. If all ten pregnancies among the women in my study ultimately led to live births, then the take-home baby rate would be closer to 20 percent.

Clearly then, test-tube baby making in the best IVF centers of Egypt is a low-odds proposition, similar to the reality in the very best centers in the West. With the proliferation of many new, "low-quality" IVF centers in Egypt, the percentage of success at other Egyptian clinics is likely to be even lower, reflecting the kind of technical difficulties described at length in the last chapter. Despite the inflated claims of success that many of these centers are making, infertile Egyptian women and their husbands, for their part, remain reflective about the realities of a medical technology that, despite its hype, brings no guarantee of success. Several Egyptian women I interviewed told me that they tried to buffer themselves psychologically by keeping their expectations low, predicting each time that they would *not* succeed in order to recover more quickly from what was likely to be a failed trial. Others used "gambling metaphors," which are also commonly employed by IVF patients in the West,[36] to explain the low probabilities and loss of large amounts of money associated with this form of treatment. As one of the most Westernized women in my study, who traveled widely and wore chic Western-style clothing, philosophized,

> It's just like playing roulette, which is the most risky and least controllable form of gambling. Sometimes I get shocked when I come [to Nozha Hospital] and find people here covering their faces and bodies [i.e., Islamic "fundamentalist" women], because it says in the Qur'an, "If God wants people to be fertile, God gives children and money," or something like this. I'm sorry, because it's not good to quote the Qur'an if I'm not doing it accurately. So, these people, they consider the God part very important. How come they try something that is not guaranteed? So it's a game, and even *they* are in it! But I believe in this game. You *can* have control; you have a role. You can get the best of your ovaries and everything, by the "psychological" way. Even though the worst kind of gambling is roulette, with the dealer just putting cards on the table, some people can estimate numbers. So, if you want to play this game, you need to support yourself psychologically just to know what's "after zero," to know what to do if you fail.

This woman, as well as nearly half of the others in my study, had in fact experienced the devastation of prior IVF and ICSI failures. At the time of my interviews, nineteen women in my study were on their second trials; but fourteen others were "multiple repeaters," who, like the philosopher Amira, had undergone two, three, four, or even more failed trials. Women who had tried and failed at IVF or ICSI, and particularly those who had failed many times, described the "disaster," "depression," "desperation," "frustration," and "shock" they felt upon receiving negative pregnancy test results. Most of these women were working in high-powered jobs at the time; yet, knowledge of an IVF or ICSI failure typically immobilized them, making their work and life in general seem meaningless. One wealthy architect described the psychological devastation of her second failed trial in these terms:

> The second time was worse than the first, because, after doing IVF, I was always "willing" it to be better and waiting for the result. I tried to get back into my work. But I was at the office when my husband called and told me the result was negative for the second time. He had called the hospital to find out. We had many meetings that day, and it was just terrible for me. I had to wait until 9 until my last meeting ended. Then I went to my mother's house, and was very upset. It was even harder on my mother; she was also crying. Psychologically, it is really difficult. I didn't feel like going back to work, and my

husband said, "You were working too much. Maybe [it didn't work] because you are always very tired."

The husband of another woman, who was currently in the midst of her fourth ICSI trial, described the tension around their home, where they worked as business partners:

> It's very hard. I cannot speak with her while she's waiting for the pregnancy results. She quarrels every day. When she starts to make the operation, it's very high tension. She's nervous and thinking all the time, "I don't want to be failed again!" But what can you do? I *am* caring about the success, but when I tell her, it makes her feel high tension, so it's better if I make her feel I'm not caring to decrease her high tension. But, believe me, we've done the pregnancy test three times now, and it's always a "black night." She feels *very* bad for two to three days, and after that, it continues until we start a new cycle.

Multiple repeaters like these women, as well as women who have undergone multiple cancellations due to lack of successful fertilization of their eggs, literally embody the failures of these new reproductive technologies, a fact that is also depressing for the laboratory staff and clinicians who treat them. Dr. Yehia, describing a thirty-five-year-old woman who had undertaken multiple trials of IVF, including with frozen embryos, remarked, "She asked me once, 'Are you getting tired of us?' I told her, 'No,' but, honestly, this is depressing for us. We, the doctors, need the psychiatrist!"

Another woman, now on her fourth trial, described her own and her doctor's reaction to her third failed trial:

> I came here on the day of embryo transfer, but Dr. Salah [Zaki] didn't want to talk to me immediately. It was supposed to be "my day." There were seven patients—six went inside and me, no. So he took me aside and said, "Please don't be upset. I'm going to explain it to you . . . but your percentage of success will be less than the others." I was desperate. But, you know something? It's all from God. [She started crying.] Yes, this keeps me trying, my hope in God.

Not surprisingly, given the religious implications of this treatment in Egypt, women who are multiple repeaters routinely couch their acceptance of failure in religious terms, explaining how God ultimately decides if and when a trial of ICSI or IVF is going to be successful. Many women told me that their hope and belief in God kept them coming back, even after the emotionally painful deflation surrounding a failed trial. In a few cases, doctors tried to boost these women's spirits by attempting to connect them with other women who had finally succeeded in becoming pregnant after many trials. For, in each clinic I studied, physicians were proud of these cases, the difficult ones who had tried and tried again, and were ultimately rewarded for their persistence.

One woman—who underwent three laparoscopies,[37] one complicated tubal microsurgery, and five failed trials of IVF, before finally depleting her financial and emotional reserves—described her disbelief when she learned that she was pregnant at last, in a miraculous conception that occurred without the assistance of either IVF or ICSI:

> I went through IVF five times . . . because I was told, "You have no hope to achieve pregnancy except through IVF." But I eventually decided to stop meeting any doctors. I was physically and emotionally tired, and I sold all my gold bracelets to pay for the last trial. So since January 1995, I stopped, because while I was doing IVF, it was one month of rest and one month of a trial. It was *very* stressful, so I decided to stop everything. One year later, by God's will, I became pregnant with twins. I didn't know I was pregnant with twins. I was on a diet. I was going to start a new life. So, I got gastric upset, and I thought this was from the diet. For the first time in my life, I forgot the date of my last menstrual period! Finally, I got some home kits for making pregnancy tests. The first time, when it was positive, I said, "No, there is a 50 percent error rate." I didn't believe it. The second time, I said, "50 percent error." The third time, I asked for the test to be brought from abroad by one of my friends, and it was positive. Then, I did a hormonal analysis at a lab. You cannot believe that day I did the lab test! I didn't hear the results for several hours. My friend was with me, and each of us thought the result is negative and the lady doesn't want to call. But my friend called, and the lady said, "Tell her *mabruk* [congratulations]! She's pregnant." She hung up out of shock, and had to call back to apologize for her rudeness. We both started crying and got hysterical, and my friend's little son said, "Why are you crying?" That was on November 18, and I started to pray, "God, keep it, keep it, keep it." After one month, on a routine ultrasound, the doctor said "Twins." And I was almost shocked. Since then, I've hardly gone out in a car. My husband tells me, "Don't move. Don't carry. Don't answer the telephone." The most important thing is: You have to start all of this with the belief that if God wants, you're going to achieve this sooner or later [which she did in the birth of healthy identical twin sons, Hassan and Hussein].

Conclusion

In Egypt, this woman's remarkable story of an unassisted conception following years of intractable tubal infertility and numerous failed IVF cycles is regarded as proof of God's will and His otherworldly control over the success (and failure) of human procreation. As seen in this chapter, infertile Egyptian couples place their faith in God to reward them with an IVF or ICSI success. This profound belief in God's role in the production of efficacy is perhaps the major reason why infertile Egyptians are much more sanguine than they should be about the *worldly* role of local Egyptian IVF clinics in producing, measuring, and accurately reporting success for the benefit of their hopeful clientele.

Although infertile Egyptians contemplating the use of new reproductive technologies consider the lack of guaranteed success to be one of their greatest obstacles, many of them do not fully realize that problems of efficacy are, in fact, a fundamental and monumental arena of constraint. Success rates for these technologies are not good anywhere in the world. But they may be particularly bad in Third World locations such as Egypt, where conditions in most IVF clinics are suboptimal, leading to success rates that are negligible or at least much lower than the already low average. The problem is: Few clinics are willing to admit this, for if they did, they would jeopardize the generation and maintenance of hope among the local clientele upon whose financial resources they depend. Thus, as seen in Egypt, most IVF clinics—and particularly the ones that can least afford to brag about their successes—are engaged in a deceptive game of inflation, in which rates are subtly inflated and even wildly exaggerated to outlandish levels by some practitioners. The few well-established centers with demonstrated and respectable records of success find themselves caught in the middle of this success rate competition; if they refuse to participate, the cost may be the loss of many patients. Not surprisingly, then, the most vocal critique of success rate inflation comes from within the physician corps of these better centers, which are actively seeking government oversight and monitoring in order to establish some neutrality and honesty in the success rate battles that are currently plaguing the local IVF industry in the country.

Although most Egyptian IVF patients are oblivious to this industry infighting, they realize that low success rates are, indeed, a "big problem" with these technologies, and they worry and fret over whether their own expensive trials will ultimately be successful. As seen in this chapter, some trials succeed, while most do not. But for the many repeaters, who try and fail, and then try and fail again, the price of inefficacy is high, taking its toll on their pocketbooks, psyches, and bodies in the ways to be described next.

CHAPTER 7

Embodiment

The Movie Star Patient

Upon arriving at Nozha Hospital one Saturday morning in early August 1996, I spotted a beautiful, statuesque woman, with long, dyed-blonde hair, dressed glamorously (and very atypically) in a sleeveless blouse and a colorful sarong-type skirt and sandals. Given her beauty, her slim but voluptuous figure, her natural olive tan, and her high-fashion Western clothing, she looked like she belonged either on a Paris runway or in the streets of Hollywood, but not in an Egyptian IVF center on a hot and dusty Cairo morning.

As I would soon discover, this was Nadine, Dr. Mohamed Yehia's fellow "movie star" patient—who he very much wanted me to interview, despite cautioning me that she was *not* representative of Egyptian women. He was right. In a lengthy and multifaceted interview in the hospital, delivered in rapid, impeccable English, and in later visits to her home and introductions to her sisters, I learned that there was nothing ordinary at all about Nadine. Although she was born and raised in Egypt, Nadine seemed much less Egyptian than the hundreds of other women I have come to know over two decades of experience in the country. With what seemed to me like one foot in the West, Nadine was much more reflective than most Egyptians, including other elites in this study, about what she deemed to be the shortcomings of Egyptian society, particularly in the areas of gender relations, class differences, and the practices of Egyptian biomedicine. She was the *only* patient I met who was openly critical of her experience at Nozha Hospital. My sense was that Nadine, as an Egyptian celebrity, had come to expect only the very best and was unwilling to accept the passive and deferential role that most Egyptians, even elites, assume in the biomedical realm. As a movie star patient of a movie star doctor, Nadine saw herself as Dr. Yehia's social equal—who could easily challenge him, assert her own authority and demands, and complain about perceived injustices in a way that would be highly unusual for an Egyptian patient who was not a celebrity. Thus, in a series of interviews I conducted with her, Nadine launched into a lengthy and circuitous laundry list of complaints—which, when all was said and done, was more like a tirade—about what she called the "game" of Egyptian test-tube baby making. And, as we shall see in her comments that follow, much of her critique revolved around troubling issues of embodiment.

Nadine had experienced considerable discomfort over a series of bodily changes resulting from her preparations for ICSI, and she was dissatisfied with both the lack of forewarning and the insufficient level of information and sympathy she received from Dr. Yehia and the Nozha clinic staff. Although many other women in this study reported troubling treatment side effects, often making sense of them through traditional Egyptian idioms of somatic distress, Nadine seemed more acutely aware of her own body and what might best be described as "the embodiment of risk" inherent in the use of new reproductive technologies.

Once I had heard Nadine's entire story, I realized that Nadine's acute bodily sensitivity might be due to the fact that, over the course of two disastrous marriages, her body had "been through a lot." Furthermore, her story reveals, more than many others, the degree to which infertile Egyptian *husbands* suffer from both the humiliation of their reproductively faulty bodies *and* the treatment protocols for male infertility, which are inherently emasculating and ineffective.

As her story goes, Nadine, now thirty-eight, had been married before to an Egyptian doctor, a first marriage that she could only describe as bad. Like Amira, whose story opens this book, Nadine had not contracepted in this marriage and became pregnant "many times, like a rabbit." Although initially she did not report these pregnancies to me, she later, in the comfort of her home, told me that she had been pregnant sixteen times in rapid succession and had undergone fifteen abortions. She did not make clear to me why she had chosen to keep one pregnancy, but she was clearly disturbed by the fact that this pregnancy, too, ended badly. At twenty-four weeks of gestation, she lost the baby, a little boy, either because of a uterine fibroid tumor (of which she later became aware) or because of "nerves." Indeed, Nadine seemed to blame herself for the miscarriage, stating, "I think it was because I was a little nervous. He [her first husband] caused my nervousness. That's why I lost the child. I told him, 'I lost the child, and now I will lose you.'"

Nadine and her first husband divorced and, after a tumultuous two-year courtship with a wealthy Egyptian contractor named Fuad (who lied to her about his involvement with another woman), she married him—a marriage that also seems to be in crisis. The problems in Nadine's and Fuad's marriage are multiple. First, Fuad is a serious alcohol abuser, which is *not* common in a Muslim country where relatively few Egyptians regularly drink alcohol, particularly hard liquor. According to Nadine, Fuad's whiskey drinking starts on Thursday night (the beginning of the weekend) and ends two days later in a horrible hangover with vomiting and headaches. His binge drinking has led to mild cirrhosis of the liver, for which he is under a doctor's care, and sexual dysfunction, which is a problem for his wife who is trying to get pregnant. At her home during dinner, I also observed Nadine drinking several glasses of wine (highly unusual for either men or women, but particularly women in Egypt), and her sister later reported to me that Nadine, herself, has a drinking problem (which may doom a child to fetal alcohol syndrome if she *does* conceive by ICSI).

The second problem in their marriage is that Fuad is infertile, a condition that he has attempted to hide from everyone, including his family and, initially at least, Nadine. As she explained,

> We had been married five years, and I didn't know something is wrong with him. He didn't tell me before marriage [that] he can't have children. But I found a file in the closet. Every month, I see his anger in his face. He's acting like *I'm* "the cause." So I went to a lot of doctors. Every one said I'm okay, and they said, "Bring your husband." He had been married for eleven years, and he told me he left her because *she* couldn't have a baby. She's the cause. Of course, this was not the truth. He knew for sixteen years from the file he has. 1981 was his first semen analysis. He went to Switzerland to find a solution. The reason was a disease. Dr. Mohamed [Yehia] knows; you should ask him. It was a sexually transmitted disease, I believe so, "epididymitis." The quantity of sperms was zero [due to infectious scarring and blockage of his seminal ducts].
>
> I forgive him for doing this [i.e., hiding his infertility problem from her]. I understand the Egyptian man. They believe this is very related to their sexuality. They need education, even for young people. This is something else— to be sexual is different than to make a baby! In Arabic, he'll say, "*Ana mish ragil*"—I'm not a man. This is a very sensitive subject.
>
> But I told him, "If we have a future together, you *have* to get treated." The newspapers and magazines say it's easy to treat this—there's been a kind of publicity lately. Of course, it took him about three months, and he went to the wrong doctor. He went to a kidney dialysis doctor, because he's a relative. He will not go to just "any doctor." He feels shy. So [the doctor] gave him Pergonal—like what we [women] take for IVF—and Clomid [another fertility drug]. Suddenly, [his sperm count is] 6 million! I asked [the doctor] if I could now do IVF in Switzerland [where her husband had once lived]. He said, "Better to do it in Cairo, because there are lots of good doctors. I'll get you the address of one."

However, Fuad's "shyness" over his male infertility problem made him very reluctant to try IVF in Egypt. When Nadine finally convinced him to go with her to the recommended Egyptian IVF center, the results were disastrous. First, the clinic receptionist called Fuad by his wife's name, "Madame Nadine," making him very angry. The second insult to Fuad's masculinity occurred when a "lady doctor" at the IVF center told him, "You are *very* weak. You should go to see a doctor specialized in this. I can't help you." As Nadine explained,

> She damaged everything I'd done. He said, "How can a lady tell a man this?"
> It took another two years of thinking to convince him to try again. We were

in Sharm El-Sheik [a resort on the Red Sea], and I saw a newspaper article: "Dr. Mohamed [Yehia] took a sample from the testis and got triplets." I gave him the newspaper, and said, "He's a good doctor." You see, it's much easier for him [to see Dr. Yehia] because he's a man and he can talk to him directly.

Eventually, Fuad was convinced to visit Dr. Yehia at Nozha Hospital, where he and Nadine are now on their second trial of ICSI. Although Fuad, at last, is complying with treatment, Nadine is not at all happy about her treatment experience so far. In a lengthy and somewhat circuitous critique, she explained,

> They don't take you as a case, these kind of people making IVF. They need to make psychological treatment available—somebody to talk to, to give you confidence that you can do it.[1] In my case, I had a pregnancy test, and it was "borderline."[2] And of course, they didn't tell me what "borderline" meant. I'm not a doctor! I found blood, and I was in a bad way. If I'm "borderline," advise me at least to sleep or relax! After I "lost" [what she perceives to be her ICSI pregnancy], I asked Dr. Yehia. He said, "Borderline means the hormones of pregnancy are there, and there is a curve like this [motioning with her hands]. And you should be up here, but you were down there." So what can I do? I have to try again.

Unfortunately for Nadine, Dr. Yehia canceled her second trial of ICSI when she produced only three ova. Although this was sound medical advice, Nadine returned to the clinic, insisting to Dr. Yehia that she continue with her trial. Her anger and frustration over her cancellation came through clearly in her interview. She stated, "First, I may be wasting my money, but not wasting time. Second, we don't know why or how we will get pregnant. Abeer [Dr. Yehia's female assistant] is telling me 'If God wills' all the time. So if God wants, I *will* be pregnant!" She continued,

> Another problem—they don't feel how much you're suffering from the medicines and the exams. I need to rest after egg collection, because after they take the ova out, I feel pain and sick. Only two days later, embryo transfer! How come, when you are sick, they make you do this? You're not prepared! They could freeze the embryos and put them back in [you] after a month, when you're not sick any longer. Don't tell me that when they open the cervix [for ova retrieval and embryo transfer], it isn't hard on the body. Me, myself, inside myself, I feel my uterus is not normal as before—the muscles are not normal. But they open it two times within forty-eight hours. This is hard on the body. I believe so! I'm not a doctor, but I believe so.

In addition to her complaints about the bodily invasive aspects of these technologies, Nadine is also extremely concerned about the hormonal medications that she and Fuad are both required to take. Prior to her ICSI trials, Nadine had great difficulty finding the necessary medications. Ultimately, she ended up spending LE 4,000 (nearly $1,200) for the drugs alone on the first trial of ICSI and LE 3,000 (nearly $900) on the second trial—inflated amounts that she believes allows pharmaceutical companies to make huge profits off desperate patients.

Speaking about one of these medications, Superfact, a medication that controls the timing of oocyte development and is used by patients as a nasal spray, Nadine commented, "There is a warning on the package, 'If you had depression before, you shouldn't take.' No doctor here ever asked me if I've been through depression or not." When I asked Nadine if she had, she said "yes," and told me that she had been under the care of a psychiatrist, who almost caused her to become addicted to sleeping pills. Nadine continued,

Before the medicines, all my hormone tests were normal. I was a normal person. But when I take these medicines, these hormones cause a "not normal body." Hormones—they make you feel excited all the time. At the same time, very depressed. You want to cry with no reason. You're shouting, getting fat, feeling stores of fat under your skin. Your tummy is getting heavy. You feel the feeling of being pregnant at the same time. You feel the excess hormone coming out with your urine. And I didn't even take that much hormones! Last time, I gained weight—seven kilos or more. I just watched this time and decided to diet, not let myself eat that much, because the last time, it was very difficult to lose the weight. I was working out for a whole month. It's very difficult to lose weight as you get older.

When I probed further about her weight concerns and whether they were related to her screen image as an actress, she denied this connection, saying "This is important to *me*—not just me, my whole family, including my two sisters. We are concerned with being slim." She added, "And you look, under your eyes, your hair, your skin, it becomes very greasy from the hormones."

Furthermore, like most Egyptians, Nadine and her concerned family members are worried about the long-term consequences of hormonal use.

Hormones make people panic. They're not good to take when you are young. People are scared of future side effects. At least it is their right to know what changes [to expect], the warning signs of hormones, so that I can sign on my paper, "Yes, I know." But I took hormones, *then* I signed [the informed consent]! I don't blame the doctor, because I was a dummy not to ask.

Although Nadine is unhappy about her IVF experience so far, she describes herself as "in the game" with no easy way out.

I was in such a hurry—happy to find myself being accepted [as a patient]. And now I'm "in the game." I'm doing it again, because I don't want to feel I failed. Not only me—everybody feels this, I believe. If the cause is from the man, if you go through IVF and it doesn't succeed, then the *woman* feels now *she* is the one who failed. And people don't want to be failures. So they try again, and again, and again.

I'm not a fool. I understand what I'm doing. This is the name of the game. They [the doctors] know they will get you for another time if you fail. It's almost like an addiction. I felt this word exactly. I felt, "Am I getting addicted?" when I refused cancellation [of her ICSI trial]. So this is why I refused cancellation, because maybe I'm caring too much, trying to give hope—trying to give my husband a chance to get out of his problem.

Embodying the Patriarchal Bargain

Neither Nadine nor her pointed critique are characteristic for an Egyptian woman. Nonetheless, her story exemplifies many of the themes of embodied suffering that are common in the world of Egyptian test-tube baby making. Almost every woman who arrives at an Egyptian IVF center brings with her a tortured "body history," usually as a result of years of relentless treatment seeking. In Nadine's case, she manifests a rather unique body history, involving numerous unwanted pregnancies and abortions, a stillbirth of a desired child, a fibroid tumor in her uterus, and a history of "nervousness" and depression, causing a close call with sleeping pill addiction. But, in some ways, Nadine is like other childless Egyptian women, who, having undergone "*so* many procedures and experiments," lament how these physical insults have taken a toll on their bodies. In Nadine's case, her reproductive history haunts her, now that she is a woman in her late thirties who is desperately seeking a child partly to stabilize her tumultuous marriage.

Like other Egyptian women in childless marriages, Nadine has also assumed the responsibility for the infertility, initiating repeated physician visits, even though she has been told (and has proven) that she is not infertile. Like Nadine, half of all childless Egyptian women have infertile husbands, and they are often forced to coerce reluctant, sometimes truculent men into treatment settings where their male infertility is revealed. Because male infertility is a particularly emasculating condition, Nadine says she understands why her Fuad, like most Egyptian men, wants to hide his problem, even from his wife. But, as suggested by her story, Fuad's problem becomes Nadine's problem, in two important ways. First, although Nadine has proven her biological fertility, she is nonetheless considered *socially* infertile because she has been visibly unable to achieve a pregnancy with her husband of five years. Second, because severe male infertility is an essentially incurable condition, the only hope for men such as Fuad, whose sperm count is very poor, is ICSI. But, as a variant of IVF, ICSI is a treatment focusing almost exclusively upon *women's bodies.* Thus, if Nadine wants to have a child with Fuad, she must put her otherwise healthy body "on the line" again—by accepting treatment with powerful hormonal medications that create bodily discomfort and long-term health risks, by submitting to the bodily invasive procedures required in any cycle of IVF or ICSI, and by suffering the emotional consequences of canceled cycles, the unbearable waiting period following embryo transfer, and the borderline pregnancy results that are usually an indication of failure. Although many Egyptian women suffer the physical and emotional embodiment of these risky technologies in silence, Nadine is not so complacent, and she enjoins both her Egyptian physician and her American anthropologist interlocutor to appreciate the extent of her suffering.

It is to this physical and mental suffering—the ways in which new reproductive technologies are experienced by and through the psyche and the soma—that this chapter is dedicated. Here, I want to forward three main arguments, as revealed in part in Nadine's story and in the ethnography that follows. First, the new reproductive technologies to overcome infertility embody a fundamental gender inequality, in that these techniques are carried out on women's bodies even when the bodily pathology is located in the male. This insight is not new; in fact, it has been forwarded by a number of Western feminist theorists, particularly through the work of Irma van der Ploeg[3] and Judith Lorber.[4] Lorber has questioned why it is that women so often consent to new reproductive technologies in cases of male infertility. Comparing IVF (then the only form of technology used for male infertility prior to ICSI) to kidney donation, she questions whether women's acquiescence to these reproductive technologies constitutes an altruistic gift, especially "a gift of love," or something that is much less voluntary. Drawing upon the work of Middle Eastern feminist theorist Deniz Kandiyoti,[5] Lorber argues that a woman who consents to the new reproductive technologies in order to overcome her husband's reproductive pathology is, in fact, making a "patriarchal bargain"—"resolving a situation in which she has limited options in the best way she can."[6] Thus, according to Lorber, IVF use among healthy wives of infertile men is "not a true choice, given the cultural pressures for women to become mothers."[7]

Certainly, women of all social classes in pronatalist Egypt experience inexorable pressures to become mothers, which is what sets them on their treatment quests.[8] Egyptian women who find themselves in the unenviable position of being childless (whether by virtue of their own or their husbands' reproductively faulty bodies) are by necessity compelled to become artful patriarchal bargainers, which, in the case of Nadine, involves cajoling a truculent husband into treatment with ICSI. In Egypt at least, the feminist argument that women are coerced by patriarchy to undertake physically taxing treatments is true, as seen in the case of Nadine. As reflected in her narrative, she believes that she is giving her husband (and herself) "a chance to get out of his problem" by the only available means.

However, for many other Egyptian women in happier marriages, accepting the physical risks of new reproductive technologies is less a patriarchal bargain than an act of connubial love and commitment, particularly among women who are deeply in love with their husbands and have long ago made peace with their childlessness and their husbands' role in it. As I would argue here, most infertile Egyptian marriages are characterized by a powerful commitment—by what anthropologist Suad Joseph has called "patriarchal connectivity"[9]—which manifests itself conjugally in the form of intense bonds of love, protectiveness, and emotional intimacy. That this deeply felt conjugal love may also enter into the willingness of at least some otherwise healthy fertile women to be "treated" for their husband's infertility is an aspect of gender relations that, in my view, has been much less privileged in the Western feminist literature, probably for ideological reasons. I would argue, however, that *both* patriarchy and conjugal love are at play in Egyptian marriages. In the case of Nadine, the conjugal love is, unfortunately, much less present than the patriarchal pressure to have children with a subfertile man. But, as noted earlier, Nadine's case is probably *not* representative of most childless marriages in Egypt, where conjugal love is prominent and commitments are strong, *particularly* if the infertility stems from the husband.

The second main argument of this chapter involves another modification of the Western feminist position on the gendered embodiment of new reproductive technologies, this time having to do with the question of whose body suffers most. In her provocative essay "Hermaphrodite Patients: In Vitro Fertilization and the Transformation of Male Infertility," Irma van der Ploeg argues that the biomedical deployment of new reproductive technologies assumes the very "permeability" of bodily boundaries in ways that are highly gender specific.[10] Whereas women's bodies are regarded as "particularly permeable," men's bodies, "by contrast, seem to remain relatively stable and untouched, even when . . . male pathologies are at issue."[11] In order to sustain this feminist argument, van der Ploeg and other feminist writers (including myself)[12] have downplayed men's contribution to infertility treatment seeking, regarding a man's role in the process as relatively minor and consisting only of "time-sensitive, masturbatory ejaculation of his 'weak' semen into a plastic cup."[13] However, this underprivileging of men's role in the infertility treatment process now seems to me to be wrong—an idea that is ideologically driven in order to make an important feminist point, but which also ignores the lived realities of many infertile men's lives. As this chapter will show, infertile Egyptian men's bodies are also heavily "doctored," to use Mike Lloyd's provocative term,[14] in ways that can only be revealed through talking to men and hearing their own pain and suffering. In Egypt, infertile men such as Fuad are subjected to the same "nasty" medications as their wives, and many of them undergo a variety of agonizing genital operations in the pursuit of fertility. Especially since the advent of ICSI, where sperm are being removed from men's bodies through testicular biopsies and aspirations, the feminist adage that infertile men's bodies are somehow untouched by these technologies is both dated and untrue. As we will see here, infertile men seeking new reproductive technologies suffer, both somatically and psychically, in ways that have been barely reported in the literature.[15]

The third main argument of this chapter is about the local specificity of bodily conceptions, complaints, concerns, and lived experiences. Human beings live in their bodies in particular places, at particular historical moments, with particular culturally informed ideas about what makes them healthy and what ails them. As shown by Pierre Bourdieu,[16] who was among the first to develop notions of culturally regnant forms of embodiment, bodily "hexis"—the very living *in* one's body— takes specific, culturally imbued forms among the Algerian peasants with whom he worked; these forms of bodily practice involved the subtlest nuances of posture, gesture, gait, and even gaze, all of which have powerful meanings within the rural Algerian setting in which he observed them. Similarly, Evelyn Early's insightful work on illness narratives among poor *baladi* (traditional) women in Cairo shows that cultural "logics of well-being," as well as idioms of distress, have a particular local flavor, in both their substance and the form in which they are conveyed.[17]

As was shown already in Chapter 3, local, culturally embedded notions of human reproductive bodies in general, and infertile bodies in particular, are highly culturally specific. Thus, the new reproductive technologies may not so easily transfer to new cultural sites where they profoundly disrupt indigenous knowledge systems. In this chapter, we will further explore the cultural variability in perceptions of bodily risk and vulnerability. How are the physical risks associated with these technologies perceived by infertile Egyptians who are contemplating the impact of these technologies on their own bodies? Or, put another way, how are local Egyptian articulations of IVF and ICSI risk embedded within local ethnophysiologies and idioms of distress?

As I will argue here, local perceptions of risk—of how new reproductive technologies act adversely upon the body—are quite different from the standard medical discourse on this subject. For one, Egyptians themselves do not deploy the language of "risk," in the epidemiological sense of that term. Perhaps because epidemiology (as a basic public health discipline) is in an inchoate stage of development in Egypt,[18] Egyptians are not confronted with daily messages about the many risks to their health and thus do not seem to view themselves as living in a threatening "risk society."[19] Whereas some authors have suggested that Westerners now live in "cultures of fear,"[20] where the media have helped to promote an obsessive focus on health, safety, and survival leading, in turn, to many anxious and self-destructive individual behaviors and social effects,[21] this sort of preoccupation with health and safety risks is much less evident in Egypt. To take but a few examples, seatbelts are never worn; children do not ride in car-seats; condoms are rarely used, and not for the practice of safe sex; most men smoke; fitness fanaticism has yet to take hold, even among elites;[22] and, hence, urbanites are increasingly overweight, diabetic, and hypertensive.[23] Instead, in this predominantly Muslim setting, concepts of pervasive health risk are supplanted by notions of *rizq,* or beliefs in God's grace and sustenance of every individual who he brings onto this earth. For most Egyptian Muslims—and probably Middle Easterners in general—proof of God's generous sustenance is manifest in the very lifestyles (e.g., smoking, heavy meat consumption, lack of physical activity) that are now seen in the West as health-demoting and dangerous.

This does not mean, however, that Egyptians do not perceive dangers to their health and well-being, and this is especially true of those who are confronted, head on, with significant health problems such as infertility. In Egyptian IVF centers, I learned of the many health-related fears and worries confronting Egyptians who, by virtue of their failure to conceive, were either contemplating or had actually undertaken IVF or ICSI. Couching their concerns in the language of emotion, infertile women and men talked about what aspects of the new reproductive technologies "frightened" them, made them "upset," or were suspected of posing "dangers" to their bodies and those of their test-tube babies. Although some individuals had only one or two major concerns, many women in Egyptian IVF centers, and sometimes their husbands, could reel off lists of fears surrounding the embodied dimensions of IVF and ICSI that made them anxious and worried. Thus, like infertile couples everywhere, Egyptian women and their husbands are forced to consider issues of safety, both immediate and long-term, as well as individual somatic and psychic vulnerabilities to the debilitating aspects of such procedures.

However, I would go on to argue that the very embodiment of new reproductive technologies is experienced by Egyptian women and their husbands in culturally specific ways—ways that often magnify the psychic costs of this type of treatment and that in some cases may prevent Egyptian couples from going forward with IVF or ICSI. The highly educated, well-informed couples who decide to use these technologies often have deep concerns about the embodiment of a potentially dangerous and "experimental" line of therapy that is perceived to "weaken" them in various ways. These concerns, furthermore, are exacerbated by real structural tensions having to do with the lack of local access to the pharmaceuticals necessary to carry out these medical procedures.

Thus, to summarize, the physical risks of the new reproductive technologies are not necessarily experienced nor perceived in the same way around the globe. The embodiment of risk is a particularly localized phenomenon, one that is dependent upon local understandings and even "local biologies" that shape the embodied experience of medical technologies at particular local sites. As Margaret Lock has shown in her provocative work on menopause in Japan,[24] the very experience of the reproductive body may, in fact, be mediated by a host of local factors, including cultural ideologies of how one *should* experience reproductive processes; exogenous environmental factors such as diets rich in phyto-estrogens (in Japan) or ambient air filled with spermatotoxic lead (in Egypt); and endogenous biological factors, such as hormonal variations affected by body mass index. Together, such factors may generate unique "local biologies" that have profound implications for both bodily experience and bodily risk at various local sites.[25] The very local nature of lived risk thus throws into question what might best be described as the "standard medical discourse" on risk,[26] which generally highlights two basic problems with the new reproductive technologies: the occasional severe reactions to fertility drugs experienced by some women (particularly hyperstimulation syndrome, which can be life-threatening) and the problems of "too much success" associated with multiple births. As we will see, these are *not* the physical risks that most concern infertile Egyptian IVF patients. Their worries revolve around the more mundane, day-to-day, adverse reactions, both physical and emotional, that are associated with the treatment process. The quotidian experiences of treatment, such as the bloating, weight gain, and moodiness described by Nadine, may be common to women everywhere,[27] but they are experienced and made meaningful in particular ways in Egypt, as will be seen in this chapter.

Furthermore, as suggested by Nadine, physicians may not give credence to the daily suffering of women undergoing IVF or ICSI treatment cycles. That physicians themselves may seriously underestimate the physical risks of IVF and its attendant drug therapies is an argument that has been powerfully forwarded by feminists in the West. For example, in "Hormonal Cocktails: Women as Test-Sites for Fertility Drugs," Renate Klein and Robyn Rowland charge that IVF scientists and practitioners completely underestimate the degree to which women suffer from the side effects of fertility drugs and fail to inform women of the possible harm to their health.[28] In their view, women are being used as "living laboratories"—as "living test-sites" for experimental and potentially life-threatening fertility drugs.[29] They call the practice of IVF, with its attendant hormonal therapies, "medical abuse of women that takes place under the guise of 'doing good.'"[30] Accordingly, this "failed and dangerous technology" should be banned, in their view, to make way for a "child-free existence" that is a "true life option."[31]

Klein and Rowland's call to "stop all the nonsense," more than a decade after its publication, seems in retrospect both naïve and ethnocentric. The global expansion of IVF and the development of even more powerful hormonal agents has been kept apace by the very fact that "child-free living" is neither an "option" nor a genuine desire for most people living around the world. In reality, there will probably always be a global demand for these technologies on the part of millions of infertile women and infertile men, as long as they live in pronatalist, child-centric societies. Thus, they will continue to submit willingly to the new reproductive technology "experiment," thereby embodying the patriarchal bargains and risks of these technologies in the ways to be described now for Egypt.

Body Histories

It is important to begin by acknowledging that few Egyptian women and men who end up at Egyptian IVF centers come to these facilities as "treatment virgins." Part of the reason that they are ready to put their bodies on the line is that they have already been "medically deflowered," as it were, through numerous genitally invasive, often painful diagnostic procedures and failed treatment attempts. For most Egyptian couples, IVF and ICSI represent the end of the line in a long history of medical interventions. When Egyptian IVF patients are asked what brings them to an IVF center, their stories typically begin many years in the past, with a detailed recounting of the diagnoses, the various treatments, the frustrations, and even the iatrogenic horrors that eventually impelled them toward their last hope in this new technology.

When I first began interviewing poor infertile Egyptian women in the late 1980s, I was often struck by how little they knew about their own diagnoses, even though most of them had submitted to years of inefficacious and even iatrogenic biomedical therapies.[32] However, when I returned in 1996 to study elite women in IVF centers, I was equally struck by how much they *did* know about their own cases. Of the sixty-six women in the study, all of them had undergone a battery of diagnostic tests, including, most commonly, assays of their serum hormonal profiles; hysterosalpingography (HSG), in which a pelvic x-ray is taken after dye is injected into the upper genital tract; and diagnostic laparoscopy, the surgical procedure designed to visualize the condition of the ovaries, fallopian tubes, and uterus. Each of these procedures, and particularly HSG, is accompanied by pain and discomfort. Yet, some women, including many healthy fertile ones, had undergone such diagnostic procedures repeatedly over the course of many years. Similarly, most husbands of women in this study had undergone repeated semen analyses, with semen collected through the regular means (i.e., ejaculation). However, some men, especially those with no sperm in the ejaculate (azoospermia), had submitted repeatedly to more invasive diagnostic procedures, mainly testicular biopsies.

As a result of these diagnostic interventions, all of the couples in this study knew the underlying pathology of their infertility condition, according to the biomedical model. Nearly half of the women in this study, 47 percent to be exact, suffered from some form of female infertility—primarily tubal infertility, which was present among more than one-quarter of the women. However, ovarian-factor infertility, characterized by recalcitrant anovulation, accounted for 14 percent of cases. A few women, seven to be exact, had specific conditions such as endometriosis or uterine fibroid tumors that were thought to be impeding their fertility. However, in 11 percent of the cases in this study, no specific infertility factor could be found, resulting in the diagnosis of "unexplained infertility."[33]

The most striking diagnostic finding, however, was the considerable presence of male infertility among couples in my study. Exactly 75 percent of these couples were plagued by a single infertility factor, and in most cases it was male infertility. A full 71 percent of the husbands suffered from male infertility, and in 47 percent of all cases, or nearly half of the couples in my study, male infertility was the sole cause of the childlessness. This high percentage of male infertility cases, in the 70–75 percent range, has become representative for most Egyptian IVF centers offering ICSI. Not only are they handling new cases of male infertility, but they are also seeing the backlog of old cases that could not be resolved by any other means.

According to the biomedical model, the causes of such male infertility cases are manifold. They can include (1) low total volume of the ejaculate; (2) irregularities in the pH of the seminal fluid; (3) hyperviscosity of the seminal fluid or presence of pus (from infection) in the seminal fluid (so-called *pyospermia*, a problem in parts of the world where sexually transmitted diseases go untreated); (4) low sperm count (*oligospermia*); (5) poor sperm motility (*asthenospermia*); (6) abnormal sperm morphology (*teratospermia*), involving sperm with deformed heads and tails (including microcephalic heads, double heads, coiled tails, or multiple tails); (7) a complete absence of sperm (*azoospermia*) because of (a) defects in the hypothalamo-pituitary axis causing maturational arrest, (b) a varicose vein in the scrotum (*varicocele*), which has raised the temperature of the testes, or (c) various obstructive conditions of the ejaculatory seminal ducts in the male genitals due to congenital abnormalities (e.g., no vas deferens) or acquired testicular damage (e.g., following infections such as mumps or epididymitis or following an iatrogenic varicocele surgery); (8) autoantibody formation against one's own sperm, as well as the presence of male-derived protein complexes on the surface of the sperm that may act as antigens, inducing an immune response from the female partner leading to premature destruction of the sperm cell within the female reproductive tract; and (9) defects in the proteins of the acrosome that reduce the sperm's ability to tunnel through the zona pellucida of the ovum and engage in fertilization.[34] Although some of these types of infertility can be easily diagnosed—including the most common forms of oligospermia (low count), asthenospermia (poor motility), teratospermia (sperm deformities), and azoospermia (absence of sperm in semen)—the underlying pathogenesis of most causes of male infertility remains "idiopathic," or unknown.[35] Thus, the reasons why so many men in Egypt and elsewhere—in fact, more than half of all cases of infertility worldwide—are infertile remains elusive.

I heard much speculation in Egyptian IVF centers, including on the part of physicians, about why increasing numbers of Egyptian men seem to be infertile. In a lengthy discussion with Dr. Ashraf Hakam, the IVF laboratory director at Nile Badrawi Hospital, he told me that, over the past two years, semen sample quality of men presenting to their clinic seemed to be "deteriorating" below levels that were once considered acceptable for IVF (i.e., counts of 3–5 million, 20 percent motility). This, he believed, could only be due to two factors. First, centers such as Nile Badrawi that offer ICSI might be attracting the worst, most intractable cases of male infertility, including the backlog of long-term cases that have failed other treatments. Or, alternatively, the decline in semen quality being observed in Egypt could simply be part of a much wider global pattern of decreasing semen quality—a controversial issue in the world of infertility studies, which has being called, rather playfully, the "big drop" theory.[36] Although the most recent meta-analysis suggests "no consensus that sperm counts are declining on a worldwide basis,"[37] the very notion that male sperm counts may be declining globally has led to speculation (as well as some research) on a variety of causal risk factors, including environmental pollutants, particularly xenobiotics such as DDT;[38] occupational exposures to arsenic, lead and other heavy metals, solvents, pesticides, and industrial chemicals used in workplaces;[39] ambient lead pollution, which has become a major problem in urban areas of the Middle East;[40] exposure to high heat or heat-generating clothing (the so-called jockey-short hypothesis);[41] and various "lifestyle" factors, including smoking and caffeine consumption, both of which are epidemic among Middle Eastern males, including Egyptian men.[42]

For their part, Egyptian men and their wives wonder aloud about why they suffer from this condition—what, exactly, has happened to make the sperm "weak." Factors that were mentioned to me during interviews included smoking, cousin marriage and other hereditary factors, heat, diet (especially hormonal additives in food), pollution, and stress. For example, a pharmacy professor, reflecting on her husband's severe infertility, commented,

> Really, I don't know [why he's infertile.] Maybe it's pollution, something having to do with stress. He's a pharmacist. He's working in a corporation

and has a high-stress job. But there's always stress, and it's difficult to change [one's] lifestyle. He was a smoker, but not heavy. He stopped completely six years ago.

Smoking was the single causal factor cited most frequently by women and their husbands. Cigarette smoking has been shown to diminish fertility in both women and men, and especially if both a husband and wife are smokers.[43] Although relatively few Egyptian women smoke, many Egyptian men are heavy smokers, smoking between one and three packs a day (of unfiltered cigarettes with high nicotine levels). Smoking has been "targeted" by Egyptian public health authorities as well as Islamic leaders, who have declared smoking to be against the tenets of Islam because it harms oneself and those around them.[44] Nonetheless, many Egyptian men (including some Egyptian physicians) are addicted smokers. Thus, infertile smokers often find smoking cessation difficult, even when they are told that smoking may decrease their sperm quality. One infertile man, whose brother was also infertile, blamed their mutual infertility problem on their father's smoking, a smoking habit that both he and his brother had inherited:

My brother did ICSI, because he had the same problem. The main problem is from our father. When our mother was pregnant with both of us, our father was smoking. We know that smoking "goes into" the baby and makes a problem for both me and my brother. [A doctor] told us that smoking decreases sperm, and I smoke two packs of Marlboros a day. I've been smoking for twenty-one years, since ten years of age, and my brother, too. One time, I tried to stop, but I only went about a week without cigarettes.

In addition to such lifestyle factors, some Egyptian men suffer from other health conditions that are clearly related to their infertility. These include diabetes, a highly prevalent chronic disease in Egypt,[45] which is related to a problem called "retrograde ejaculation" leading to azoospermia;[46] and a high incidence of inflammatory lesions of the testes, due to mumps orchitis, sexually transmitted epididymitis, schistosomiasis (a common parasitic infection in rural Egypt), and other infectious diseases that are significant etiological factors for male infertility in Africa (as opposed to the developed world).[47] For example, Dr. Abdel-Hamid Wafik, IVF laboratory director at Nozha Hospital, told me that mumps orchitis, one of the adverse effects of mumps in adults who were never vaccinated, leads to male infertility in 14 percent of cases. Among these, approximately 10 percent will have "extensive damage to the testicles." Thus, he and Dr. Yehia were "very excited" to have achieved a successful ICSI fertilization in one couple in my study affected by orchitis-related male infertility, when "we were not even sure what we were getting out during testicular biopsy."

Indeed, many of the cases of male infertility in my study could be characterized as severe, involving multiple sperm problems or complete azoospermia. I asked women in my study, and sometimes their husbands if they were present, to describe the details of male infertility diagnoses to me. Among thirty-six couples able to do so, seven of the husbands suffered from a single cause (usually low count), whereas seventeen suffered from more than one factor (usually low count and poor motility). Oligospermia and asthenospermia are defined as a total sperm count of less than 20 million per milliliter ejaculate and less than 50 percent motility, respectively.[48] Yet, many men in this study suffered from what they, themselves, often described as "very weak sperm." Indeed, the sperm counts of men in this study were extremely low—for example, 9,000, 50,000, 70,000, 1 million, 3 million, or 6 million, when 20 million is already considered a "low count." Furthermore, motility rates often ranged in the 20–40 percent range, and husbands used terms such as "sluggish," "very weak," "not active at all," or "very bad movement," to describe their poor motility scores.

In twelve cases, or 18 percent of all the couples in my study, the diagnosis was azoospermia, or the absence of sperm in the ejaculate. Some of these cases involved so-called obstructive azoospermia, caused by a blockage in the epididymis (the male duct system between the testicle and penis where sperm mature and move out during ejaculation). In these cases, an operation called microsurgical epididymal sperm aspiration (MESA) can be performed to literally extract sperm from the epididymis prior to ICSI. In the worst cases of azoospermia, accompanied by so-called maturational arrest, no mature sperm are being produced at all, for reasons that are unclear. According to Dr. Hakam, approximately 15 percent of cases of male infertility involve this form of azoospermia, which may be variable, or "coming and going" in some men. Patients such as these may require testicular sperm extraction (TESE), an operation in which multiple testicular biopsies are performed to locate areas of spermatid (immature sperm) production. Such testicular "needle-work" for the purposes of ICSI sperm(atid) retrieval is "very painful for the patient," according to Dr. Hakam, and can even lead to an iatrogenic condition of obstructive epididymitis. Thus, even though ICSI with TESE is the most advanced treatment for male infertility, it entails considerable suffering for male patients, such as the fifteen husbands in this study (23 percent) who had undergone this procedure or were being scheduled for it.

And this brings us back to the question, posed in the last section, of who suffers more. In this study, it was not clear to me that women had endured the most suffering. The typical infertile husband in this study had undergone years of continuous hormonal therapies and invasive testicular procedures. Regarding hormonal therapy, most Egyptian men (like infertile men elsewhere) are treated with hormones—hormones that may cause somatic "feminization," including hot flashes; gynecomastia, or the development of breasts; and storage of fat deposits in "feminine" sites (hips, buttocks). Yet, hormones rarely cause significant improvement in men's sperm parameters, which may, in fact, diminish during periods of treatment. Such medical therapy for male infertility has been sharply criticized in a number of recent Western studies; in fact, one of these critics, commenting in *The New England Journal of Medicine,* stated pointedly that "the compounds used for such therapy fall into two broad categories: those whose use is irrational and clearly not effective and those that are unproved."[49]

In Egypt, andrologists do an active trade in prescribing such hormonal medications, and few Egyptian men who are infertile are able to bypass this form of therapy. Thus, husbands in my study, some of whom showed the tell-tale signs of long-term hormonal therapy in their pudgy, pear-shaped bodies, often described to me the "years of useless medicines" to which they had been subjected. Many wives of such men described their husbands' suffering, including the inevitable weight gain and the frustration of therapies that did little to improve their low sperm counts. One woman, reflecting on her ten-year marriage to a hopelessly infertile man, began their story as follows:

> We went to many doctors, starting maybe six months after marriage. My husband went to doctors also, and he discovered that he was the cause. "Sporadic azoospermia." He took *a lot* of medicine—oh yes! Humagon, Prophassi, Pergonal, vitamins. Sometimes there were sperm, and sometimes not. His sperm analyses—for example, once there were 20 million, then they disappeared. Another time, 6 million. Now, there are no sperm at all. From the beginning of marriage, he has had this problem. And, of course, the doctors said, "Hopeless case. Don't think about this [having children]." At first, we were very sad, and I thought about divorce many times. But I couldn't. He was a friend in college, and we were in love. I love him. At first, I was sad, then I said, "God's will," and I accepted it.

Other husbands had undergone both hormonal therapy and genital surgeries, most commonly varicocelectomies. Varicoceles are varicose-type dilations of the scrotal veins that drain the testes, and they occur in about 15 percent of men. If left untreated, they lead to a progressive decline in semen quality, causing male infertility.[50] Among husbands in my study, 17 percent had undergone a varicocelectomy to correct a varicocele. Some had undergone this surgery twice, due to failure of a previous repair or a recurrence of the varicocele. In at least one case, the surgery itself caused the iatrogenic outcome of obstructive azoospermia. Yet, despite the high prevalence of varicocelectomies in this study, recent medical evidence suggests that varicocelectomies are not medically indicated for most cases of male infertility, as they do not succeed in improving fertility outcomes.[51]

In summary, then, the agonizing and emasculating body histories of male infertility patients coming to Egyptian IVF centers would make most healthy men cringe. Some men are stoic in the face of such medical interventions, while others, such as Fuad, make every effort to avoid them. Thus, the very anticipation of what lies ahead may make some men think twice about undergoing ICSI, especially when it involves a painful, invasive genital procedure. One terrified husband, who was about to undergo testicular biopsy at Nile Badrawi Hospital so that his healthy wife's eggs could be microinjected with his weak sperm, literally fled the operating room before the procedure. Although Dr. Salah Zaki kindly interpreted this as a "phobic response," the patient's wife admitted that her husband, "the type of guy who's scared of blood," had caused a kind of "scandal" in the IVF unit when he bolted off the table.

For some men such as this one, the embodiment of physical pain is a most fundamental arena of constraint on the use of the new reproductive technologies, acting as a kind of "physical barrier" to access. Throughout the years that I have studied infertility in Egypt, I have heard many stories about men refusing to go through with the treatments—be they hormonal medications, varicocelectomies, artificial inseminations, or IVF and ICSI—because of the physical indignities and suffering that they fully anticipate. At least some infertile men, such as Fuad, are not brave in the face of physical (and emotional) adversity; yet, their refusal to be treated creates incredible frustration for their wives, who must either accept the situation or cajole their husbands into treatment. Such opposition among infertile men is especially upsetting for those wives who have assumed the burden of infertility treatment, even though they are not infertile. This gender inequity is acknowledged by some Egyptian wives of infertile men, including Nadine, who commented on the unfairness of being treated by ICSI for Fuad's infertility:

> Here, they're working *not* with the man, [but] with the woman. Everywhere, not just here. . . . My husband gets more nervous when the time gets close, and he starts acting crazy. He doesn't want to feel a failure again. But the woman is the one who needs kindness, support, loving care. But they can't get it at this time from their husbands, because they're more worried than their wives! This is because there's lot of uncertainty.

Similarly, the woman whose husband literally jumped off the operating table explained,

> Always, people think the problem [of infertility] starts with the woman. I started with [a well-known doctor] in his clinic, and he said I had better come to meet with Dr. Salah Zaki. So I came to this hospital and did everything here—all the nonsense—the laparoscopy, the x-ray with dye. Only after this did they shift to him [her husband]. But now they're "playing" with me again. My husband, he never comes with me, or he comes only at the last moment. But I started insisting that he become involved. Now, he's involved, but only after I told him he's irresponsible. He knows he's going to have to have a biopsy, and that's the scandal. I tell him, "That's the only thing that you're going to be doing." And Dr. Salah tried to convince him, "You're going to be on the same floor, with your wife." But he's scared, even though he wants kids.

This kind of fear of medical procedures is also found among Egyptian women as they contemplate their impending treatment. But, in the fifteen years that I have studied infertility in Egypt, I have rarely heard of a woman who refused to undergo treatment because of the embodied risks. Quite the contrary! What has often struck me most is the amount of embodied suffering, including profound vaginal and pelvic pain, which infertile Egyptian women seem to endure in their "search for children." For poor women who are unable to access the new reproductive technologies, they are usually subjected to an array of outdated, inefficacious, and even iatrogenic treatments that often lead to a great deal of physical pain and suffering. Such "treatments" include tubal insufflation, in which carbon dioxide is pumped into the upper genital tract to purportedly "blow open" blocked fallopian tubes; dilatation and curettage, in which the lining of the uterus is "scraped off" to supposedly "clean out" the womb; and cervical electrocautery, in which a heated instrument is used to "burn off" supposedly eroded sections of the cervix. Such nonsensical and harmful therapies, which are performed by many physicians primarily to make money, are described at length in *Quest for Conception*. Suffice it to say here that poor infertile Egyptian women undergo such therapies repeatedly, often commenting stoically on the pain and other complications produced by such procedures.

While few of the elite women I encountered at Egyptian IVF centers had undergone such bitter experiences with these old-fashioned remedies,[52] many of them had undertaken numerous, failed treatment attempts, some of which were truly iatrogenic. Like Huda, whose story was recounted in the last chapter, four other women in my study had come to Egyptian IVF centers after having undergone pelvic surgeries, either on their fallopian tubes or ovaries, which led to absolute tubal blockage. Hearing them recount their stories of iatrogenesis was, in and of itself, painful, particularly as many of them had been later told by physicians that these unnecessary surgeries were the cause of their tubal infertility. Other women who had avoided the surgery experience nonetheless felt their bodies had been subjected to what they sometimes called "years of suffering," comprised of "*so* many procedures," "experiments," and "useless medicines." In fact, if there is one feature that typifies the body histories of childless (although not necessarily infertile) women in Egypt, it is the medicine-taking, particularly of hormones, and the unhappiness that such "drugging" of their bodies entails.

The Unhappiness of Hormones

Taking hormones is an almost inevitable part of women's lived experience of biomedical infertility treatment, in Egypt as in other parts of the world. With IVF and ICSI, this hormonal treatment often intensifies, as efforts are made to induce "superovulation," or the production of numerous ova during a single treatment cycle. As explained by Turiel in *Beyond Second Opinions*:

> For assisted reproduction, the aim is to replace a woman's ongoing monthly interplay of hormones with a hyperstimulated, superovulating cycle. In this cycle, numerous eggs can mature, and the time of ovulation can be more accurately predicted and controlled. . . . Most women undergoing controlled ovarian hyperstimulation receive daily or twice-daily injections of hormones to mature several eggs, each within an enlarged fluid-filled sac (the egg follicle); in some women the ovary responds to hormonal stimulation with maturation of one or two eggs, in others as many as thirty or forty. To monitor

this process, women must also receive ultrasound scans of ovaries and have blood drawn to test hormone levels. Immediate side effects of the drugs—which may include headaches, backaches, breast tenderness, bloating, nausea, insomnia, increased vaginal discharge—are generally considered a tolerable if unpleasant burden of fertility treatment.[53]

As captured by Turiel in her concise description of the hormonal treatment regimen, the drug taking associated with the new reproductive technologies engenders an intense experience, involving a daily onslaught of injections, blood draws, and ultrasound scans. Furthermore, most women suffer side effects, but these are too often downplayed by IVF scientists and practitioners as a minor burden of treatment. For women themselves, however, having one's body hormonally hyperstimulated may engender a different kind of response, one in which the physical tolls of this kind of therapy are deemed serious, warranting caution and concern. Furthermore, for those who actually experience the side effects of treatment, the adverse reactions produced by these medications are made sense of, given meaning, within ethno-physiological belief systems that are locally situated. Thus, an American woman's bloating may be interpreted by her as a simple fluid retention, while in Egypt, it is considered a serious sign of the generalized "weakness" produced by hormones of all kinds. In short, drugs, their mechanisms of action, and the adverse reactions they produce have no inherent universal meaning. Instead, they are always interpreted within local, cultural logics of health and illness that throw into question the unfettered global transfer of Western-produced pharmaceuticals into non-Western sites, where their consumption may be locally resisted.

In this study, virtually every woman had been prescribed some sort of hormonal medication(s) in the past, and most of them were in the process of being medicated again as they embarked on IVF or ICSI therapy. I asked each woman to describe as specifically as possible the drugs she was currently taking. I was usually impressed with the exacting nature of the responses, including the names of all medications, the numbers of boxes purchased during a cycle, the number of daily injections and administrations, the unit cost of the drug per box or per injection, and how these drugs fit into the total regime of IVF or ICSI therapy. Most women (61 percent) were taking either two or three medications, staggered over the treatment cycle. However, a small number (9 percent) were taking four or five medications during a single cycle.

The most commonly used hormonal agents were a pair of drugs, usually given consecutively, called Superfact and Pergonal. Superfact, or buserelin acetate, manufactured by the German pharmaceutical company Hoechst AG, is a gonadotropin-releasing hormone (GnRH) agonist that shuts down the body's natural process of ovulation so that superovulation can be artificially achieved according to an exact timetable. Superfact is given as a nasal spray every four hours around the clock during the first days of the IVF treatment cycle, in preparation for later Pergonal administration. Pergonal, manufactured by the former-Italian, now-Swiss company

Serono, and distributed through its Egyptian subsidiary, is human menopausal go-nadotropin (hMG). This powerful fertility drug combines two hormones, luteiniz-ing hormone (LH) and follicle-stimulating hormone (FSH), which stimulate the ovaries to mature several eggs during one treatment cycle. Pergonal, and a similar brand called Humagon (manufactured by the Dutch company Organon), are given by injection; usually this requires an individual other than the patient (e.g., either a neighborhood pharmacist or a husband or mother who is taught how to give injec-tions) to become involved in daily administration. Once these drugs have been administered, a third hormone called human chorionic gonadotropin (hCG), man-ufactured and marketed in Egypt under the brand names Pregnyl (Nile Pharmaceu-tical Company, under license of Organon) or Prophassi (Serono), is given to some women as a single injection to trigger ovulation at a specific time. However, because residual levels of this drug can result in false-positive pregnancy tests, some Egyp-tian IVF centers, such as Nozha Hospital, have stopped prescribing hCG. Instead, at Nozha, women often receive another hormone, a vaginal suppository of progester-one called Cyclogest, which is designed to offer luteal phase support in the days fol-lowing ovulation (when progesterone is necessary to prepare the uterine lining for implantation of a fertilized egg). Some couples are also required to take a prophylac-tic course of Vibromycin, an antibiotic, to ensure that no shared genital infections impede the treatment cycle.

Thus, when all is said and done, most women undergo a complicated drug-taking regimen, consisting of the "three S's"—shots, sprays, and suppositories—most of which require constant refrigeration (in a country with frequent power out-ages) and extreme vigilance for correct administration. It is no wonder that many women, such as Nadine, worry about whether they have taken these drugs properly, and often feel defeated when mistakes are accidentally made, resulting in a "poor re-sponse" (i.e., failure of more than one or two eggs to mature). Describing the diffi-culties of drug taking, one woman who became pregnant with ICSI twins on her first trial commented:

> You can't imagine what it's like having to take the medication on time. Each is at a certain time. Daily, at a certain time, I would have to get shots at the pharmacy near my house. And every day, the nasal spray, I had to wake up very early in the morning to take [it], and then take it at work two times a day. This was hard to go through, and hard for my husband to watch.

Although most women who take these hormones complain of the pain (with in-jections) and inconvenience, their two biggest worries regarding hormones have to do with the side effects and drug availability. With regard to the first issue, hormonal fertility drugs are associated with a series of uncomfortable side effects, which rela-tively few women seem to escape. In Nadine's account, she was highly aware of a range of adverse reactions in her own body, ranging from increased greasiness of her skin and hair to significant weight gain and abdominal bloating to moodiness, agi-tation, and depression. In my study, Nadine was not alone in the reporting of such side effects. Although some women commented, stoically, that the side effects were temporary and bearable, most emphasized the suffering they had endured as a result of hormonal medications.

By far the most common complaint was weight gain, which ranged from small amounts of three to four kilograms (six to eight pounds) to massive weight gains of thirty to forty-five kilograms (sixty-six to ninety-nine pounds) in several women who had been on long-term hormonal therapy. Some couples, who had both been on hormones throughout their marriages, had gained significant amounts of weight together, as described by one woman:

> One problem for my husband has been the weight gain. After he takes hor-mones, he became fat. And me! I became very fat after taking hormones—15 kilograms [33 pounds]. And I was very thin before marriage. And my hus-band, he was 60 to 65 kilos [132–143 pounds], and now he's 80 [176 pounds].

Acccording to Dr. Yehia, such significant weight gains are probably not related to hormones alone. Rather, he opined, "People who don't get pregnant are usually de-pressed, and they start to eat more. And they don't exercise because they think they might be pregnant. And this cumulatively is going to put on a tremendous amount of weight."

One woman, who was becoming obese, attributed her weight gain to the depres-sion surrounding two previous ICSI failures:

> I was thinner than this before these operations, but the hormones made me gain more. So, I went on a diet and lost fifteen kilos. It was a "hard" diet. My husband said I shouldn't do it, but I took it very seriously. After the opera-tion [which failed], I gained some more. Going through that made me gain weight, because I said, "No use." It was depressing, and I would eat more. Whenever I'm depressed, I eat more. Some do just the opposite. But with me, it's chocolate and ice cream.

In addition to weight gain, other common side effects included the pregnancy-like symptoms of abdominal cramping and bloating, nausea and vomiting, and profound tiredness and lethargy. In some women, these were accompanied by cog-nitive/psychic symptoms of headache, dizziness, extreme nervousness bordering on panic, and depression. Taken together, such symptoms suggest to Egyptian women that hormones are "powerful" drugs that "weaken" the body.[54] "Weakness" is a com-mon cultural illness idiom in Egypt,[55] one that is viewed both as a general condition of ill health and as a problem localized to specific parts of the body (e.g., "weak heart," "weak lungs," "weak blood"). The idiom of weakness is rife in popular Egyp-tian reproductive imagery, and it is given further support by Egyptian gynecologists, who tend to use the adjective "weak" to describe reproductive processes to layper-sons. Thus, *mibayid da'if,* or "weak ovaries," is a term used by both Egyptian physi-cians and patients to describe ovarian problems, particularly anovulation. And such weakness is often translated into more condemnatory terms by patients themselves, who refer to their own ovaries as "tired" or "lazy" and in need of "activation."

The hormonal medications that women are given before an IVF or ICSI cycle are generally viewed as "strengtheners," capable of stimulating ovarian function even in the weakest ovaries. However, the paradoxical problem with these agents is that they may overcome weakness in one set of organs, the ovaries, only to produce a more generalized body weakness apparent in the noticeable list of side effects that they produce. Indeed, in the minds of Egyptian women, IVF hormones belong in the same category as contraceptive hormones, including oral contraceptives, Depo-Provera injections, and Norplant, all of which are widely available in Egypt. Although their mechanisms of action and desired effects are different, all reproductively re-lated hormonal agents are viewed as powerful drugs, which, over time, produce a generalized condition of weakness. Thus, women taking hormonal fertility drugs over extended periods generally report feeling "sick and weak," and they worry about whether such ill effects will be temporary, lasting, or even permanent. One woman, recounting her own bad brush with a particular fertility drug, worried out loud,

> I thought about doing IVF or ICSI before this, but every time I saw doctors, they said, "There's no need for it. Let's start a new treatment." And they gave me a lot of hormones, such as Clomid, Pergonal, and Parlodel. [Parlodel] lessens the progesterone in the blood, which causes milk production, which may [in turn] stop pregnancy from happening. But I don't have milk; only when you press my breast, a little water which is yellow comes out. They gave me a lot of Parlodel for about a year and a half, and its side effects were very strong. It caused nausea and diarrhea. I felt like I'm going to die. But, thanks to God, I was "saved," and I recovered. But my weight increased from sixty-four to eighty-eight [kilograms]. I became fat and no matter what diet I have, I can't decrease my weight. This is because every doctor I go to gives me hormones, although my ovulation is normal and the period is regular.

That hormones occasionally produce deadly side effects, including feelings of imminent death among women so affected, is well known in the world of test-tube baby making. Some hormones, especially Pergonal when used alone or in combina-tion with other drugs, can cause a severe, potentially life-threatening adverse reac-tion called ovarian hyperstimulation syndrome (OHSS). During OHSS, too many eggs mature simultaneously, causing enlargement of the ovaries. In the most severe cases, the ovaries rupture, accompanied by abdominal bleeding and liver, kidney, and/or lung failure.[56] Women experiencing the tell-tale signs of OHSS, particularly extreme bloating, must be hospitalized immediately and carefully monitored. In in-experienced hands, a common problem in Middle Eastern IVF clinics, some women may die. Three women in this study had experienced OHSS at other IVF centers in the region, but had lived to tell their stories to me at Nozha Hospital. One of them, an Egyptian physician working with her infertile Egyptian physician husband in Saudi Arabia, described the hyperstimulation she developed when being prescribed pre-ICSI medications in Saudi Arabia "by phone and fax" because she lived 2½ hours by plane from the IVF center:

The IVF physicians convinced us that they could do stimulation by phone—with phone and fax. They should have advised us to make ultrasounds, but [instead] they said, "Just give her the injections, and then you come." At fourteen injections, I was already overstimulated, but not severely. But they gave us twenty-six injections—with no ultrasound, by phone [with her husband administering the injections]. By the time I got to Jiddah, they saw I was overstimulated, and they continued to give six more injections. I developed hyperstimulation, very severe, an intensive care case. The distention was severe. I can't breathe, cough, sneeze, laugh. I was completely bedridden for three days, and I couldn't sleep on my back. One week, I was *totally* in bed, in a very bad condition. After one week, I started to recover a bit. But after all this, there was no pregnancy. I think all the embryos died because of overstimulation. Because the embryos were good, but the high level of estradiol made toxicity.

Her husband added, "One of my colleagues, a gynecologist, came and looked after her. We know bed rest is the treatment. But it was very dangerous, and I was scared."

Responding to my question about the (in) experience of the treating Saudi physicians, the woman added,

They have experience, but they have too many patients. There are only one or two IVF centers in all of Saudi Arabia,[57] and they're too overcrowded. They can't think about each patient. It's just routine work. They care only about the technical aspects. They want only ova and sperm, and they don't care about you as a human being.

Although nearly dying from the immediate effects of hormonal hyperstimulation is a relatively uncommon experience, most Egyptian women who take hormones wonder whether they will succumb to life-threatening diseases later on. Such concerns are especially pronounced for women who have undergone repeated cycles of ovulation induction before IVF or ICSI. Yet, even newcomers to hormones, such as Nadine, may be extremely concerned about long-term health risks. Their fears are, in fact, justified. Studies published in the West since 1993 suggest that fertility drugs may increase women's risk of ovarian cancer, a particularly deadly form of malignancy.[58] In all my years in Egypt, I have rarely heard women use the dreaded "C" word directly—referring to it instead as "*the* disease," in an effort to keep this unmentionable killer away. But, among the Egyptian IVF patients I interviewed, allusions to "serious diseases" hinted at their concern. When I asked women what worried them, fear of hormones and their long-term health effects emerged as a prevalent theme. As one woman related,

I worry most about the hormones. I've gained a lot of weight—thirty kilos from the hormones. Hormones make you retain water. I've been taking them since 1990, and I can't lose this weight. That part doesn't bother me,[59] but I heard hormones are not "healthy." All women who have made IVF took so many hormones, and we don't know what diseases might occur.

At the same time that women worry about the health risks of hormones, they realize that they must take them if they are to complete an IVF or ICSI trial. And this brings us to the second major concern: the unavailability of such hormones in local Egyptian pharmacies, which are located on nearly every city block.

It is important to begin by saying that Egypt is one of the relatively few Third World countries (along with India, Cuba, Argentina, Brazil, Mexico, and Sudan) that has an indigenous pharmaceutical manufacturing industry, producing a considerable share (e.g., 85 percent by 1974) of all the drugs consumed locally.[60] Egypt's pharmaceutical industry began during World War II, when two local drug companies were created.[61] By 1973, as a result of the protection afforded it under policies implemented by President Gamal Abdel Nasser, the Egyptian drug industry claimed an 88.2 percent share of the market and accounted for considerable export revenue.[62] However, by 1975, under President Anwar Sadat's *infitah*, or "open-door" economic liberalization policies, the private importation of drugs was legalized. These policies resulted in a steady rise in imported drugs, which were marketed in Egypt by transnational drug companies.[63]

These large transnational corporations (TNCs) constitute a "formidable force" in the global pharmaceutical industry.[64] As noted by Masuma Mamdani in the introduction to *Drugs Policy in Developing Countries*,

> Over the past four decades, world pharmaceutical sales have been increasingly concentrated in the hands of a small number of companies, about 25, which accounted for about 60 per cent of total production. Almost 70 percent of world production of pharmaceutical products took place in only five developed market economy countries: Britain, France, Switzerland, Germany and the USA.[65]

> There has been virtually no transfer of relevant technology by these companies to the countries of the developing world. In fact, by using the power that control over technology brings, they have eliminated many potential competitors and prevented indigenous pharmaceutical industries from developing to meet the real needs of the people of the Third World.[66]

Given this history, it is not surprising that the world of fertility drugs is now dominated by a handful of Western pharmaceutical manufacturers that market and distribute their products globally. Unfortunately, nations on the receiving end of this global fertility drug transfer are subject to a variety of woes created by the neocolonial dependency on these Western-based TNCs. These problems include global fluctuations in the drug supply pipeline, resultant local shortages of critical hormonal agents, high prices for these imported medications, and the formation of black market drug rings designed to get these *legal* drugs to desperate consumers. Thus, ever since the late 1980s, when IVF was first introduced in Egypt and I went

there to carry out my initial research, important hormonal agents were in short supply, leading to sometimes futile searches on the part of desperate infertile couples.[67]
Returning after a seven-year hiatus, I was surprised to discover that the drug supply
problem had not been alleviated, and instead, seemed to have been aggravated by
the tremendous growth in the local IVF industry. In fact, some Egyptian IVF physicians, such as Dr. Abdel-Hamid Wafik of Nozha Hospital, argued that drug shortages
might serve as a kind of absolute barrier on the growth of the local IVF industry, if
consumers were unable to purchase the necessary medications.

The most blatant example of this drug supply problem revolves around the hormone called human menopausal gonadotropin (hMG), sold under the brand names
Pergonal and Humagon. When I went to Egypt in 1996, local supplies of hMG were
running out as the Western manufacturers phased out hMG to make way for a new,
superior (and three times more expensive) genetically engineered version of "recombinant FSH." Although the shortages of hMG were reported to be global, affecting infertile patients in the West (including the United States) as well as the rest of the
world, the local shortages of hMG were felt keenly in Egypt during the summer of
1996, the busiest time of year for local IVF practices. IVF clinic directors, such as Drs.
Yehia and Zaki, were lamenting the local shortages of both Pergonal and Humagon.
Such shortages were seriously impeding their ability to go forward with IVF or ICSI
in patients who were unable to locate the medications. Dr. Yehia's strategy was to purchase these drugs himself—"from wherever I can get them"—and supply them directly to his patients. Before the shortage, he was able to supply all of his IVF patients
with full doses of Pergonal or Humagon. But once the global phase-out of hMG
began, his supplies began to dwindle, and he had to implement new strategies. At
first, he started a waiting list, which grew longer and longer, delaying treatment for
some couples up to four months. Worried about patient flow and volume, he then
decided to do away with the waiting list, taking couples on a first-come, first-serve
basis. He offered to provide each couple with half of the required medication if they
could obtain the other half on their own. He also reduced the amount of hMG prescribed to most patients. But, for repeaters—ones who had been through panicked
hMG searches during previous trials—he often took pity on them and provided the
entire amount. In his view, none of these strategies seemed very fair, and he personally hoped that the TNCs artificially creating these shortages (in order to launch an
even more expensive product) would be brought to their knees. He remarked,

> Because of the increasing number of patients coming, we're selling much
> more than we used to be selling, so we don't have any left over. The drug sup-
> ply problem is just going to increase. Everyone is going to be getting less
> hMG until the new "rec FSH" is going to be the "standard" and take over and
> that's it. *Unless, unless*—and this might happen—there are two to three com-
> panies in Korea, China, and Japan, and they're introducing their hMG on the
> market. And if this is going to become available, this is going to force the al-
> ready established companies to "keep in line," or they will be out of business.

So what we have is a very limited supply of hMG right now, but if they manage to get onto the market, this is going to make some competition to keep the "old" hMG on the market as well.

For their part, Egyptian IVF patients, the ones ultimately most affected by these kinds of TNC machinations, were clearly in a panic about the local lack of hMG when I arrived on the scene in May 1996. Many considered this their biggest problem, the major arena of constraint facing them. The frustration, anxiety, and despair of infertile couples trying to find hMG were palpable in their lengthy odes on this subject. For example, one woman described her despair as she drove from one pharmacy to the next, only to be turned away at each one:

> When Dr. Yehia said, "Get Humagon," I drove two hundred kilometers in my car, from pharmacy to pharmacy. In one hospital in Heliopolis, there is a pharmacy. The pharmacist is a woman. I said, "I want Humagon," and she said, "To whom?," and I said, "Dr. Mohamed Yehia," and she said, "Oh, he is my friend, but I don't have [any Humagon]." Then I thought, "No, I will never have a baby." But I called [the Maadi IVF Center], and someone there was coming from Saudi Arabia with two packs of Humagon. He wanted to sell them to Dr. Ragaa [Mansour, the laboratory director], but he didn't have the bill so she wouldn't accept this. But she told him that if anyone asks for it, she would give them his number. So I told her, "I'll take it," even though it was about LE 200 [$57] more than the normal price.

What was truly striking was the resourcefulness with which many couples had managed to find the necessary medications—through resort to the black market, "connections" in the pharmaceutical industry, and even bribery. For example, one woman described the last-ditch efforts of her parents' neighbor, who embarked on a veritable crusade to find her the drugs that she needed to "make a baby,"

> I was supposed to start taking Pergonal on Monday, and I looked at many pharmacies or called those far away. It is not in Nile Badrawi or other big hospitals now. This is a *huge* problem now for me, because I have an appointment to do IVF, and Pergonal is not very available in Egypt. But my parents' neighbor is very friendly. He went on Sunday [the day before her appointment] to Tenth of Ramadan City, near Ismailia, which is very far, and he paid LE 1,080 [$309] for three boxes, and at 1 A.M., he got it from a place there and brought it back so that I could start on Monday morning. They sell it on the black market for LE 500 to 800 [$143–229] a box. And there is another kind of medicine with the same effect, Humagon, for LE 900 [$257]. He bought it for me for the fixed price, but he had to pay *baksheesh* ["tips," or bribes].

As revealed in these anxiety-ridden accounts, Egyptian IVF patients must demonstrate considerable ingenuity to locate hMG in this hMG-barren landscape. Several women commented that obtaining hMG, a perfectly legal drug, was more difficult than buying heroin on the streets of Cairo, and they resented the fact that they had to resort to a black-market underworld charging extortionist prices in order to obtain a drug to make a baby. In reality, these high-end, imported fertility drugs have never been widely available in Egypt and have often been limited to particular specialty pharmacies dealing in imported medicines (which are usually purchased by Egyptian pharmacy owners on drug-buying trips to Europe). Yet, as seen in these accounts, by the summer of 1996, even the well-known specialty pharmacies were out of hMG. So were the big hospital pharmacies in Cairo, often known for their superior stocks of medication. Many IVF-seeking couples, who as elites owned cars, had scoured the pharmacies of Cairo, Alexandria, and even the provincial cities in an attempt to find the medication. Those with even remote connections in the local pharmacy world used them, enlisting the support of relatives, friends, and "friends of friends" who happened to be pharmacists or employees in the pharmaceutical industry.

But perhaps the most interesting phenomenon engendered by the local hMG crisis was the transnational "suitcase trade" in hMG,[68] which constituted a prominent local response to the problem. By 1996, patients in Egyptian IVF clinics were relying heavily on their international contacts, including family and friends living abroad, working in the airline industry (e.g., as "air hostesses"), or traveling abroad for business, pilgrimage, or pleasure, to obtain and then personally carry the drugs back to Egypt in special refrigerated handbags. For example, one woman recounted how she eventually got her hMG from her brother, who scoured the pharmacies of Jiddah, Saudi Arabia, while visiting the country on a religious pilgrimage:

> We looked at different pharmacies [in Egypt], and finally we got Humagon from Saudi Arabia. My brother was going to Saudi Arabia for a vacation to do the *hajj* [religious pilgrimage]. So I asked him to bring the Humagon for me. He became so tired trying to find this huge quantity. I asked him for sixty injections, and he could find only fifty-five, even though he had to search all over Jiddah. But I've looked in Cairo, and my niece is a pharmacist, and she was looking, too. She finally found me Pergonal, but it was very expensive—a single injection cost LE 50 [$14]. Since I need sixty [injections], this would be LE 3,000 [$857]. And the Humagon from Saudi Arabia was the same price!

As revealed in this woman's statement, most Egyptian patients sought these drugs in the Arab Gulf countries, where approximately 3 million Egyptians currently live and many more travel for religious purposes. For those Egyptians working as labor migrants in the Gulf but planning their IVF or ICSI trials back home, they were usually instructed by Egyptian physicians to purchase (and refrigerate) the hMG in the host country before returning to Egypt for the treatment cycle. In some of these cases, excess drugs brought over were then sold either directly or vis-à-vis IVF physicians to other needy patients in Egyptian IVF clinics. As one infertile man, who was deeply religious and was returning with his wife from Abu Dhabi to undertake ICSI, explained,

> The medicines themselves were more than LE 2,000 [$570]. We brought the Humagon from Abu Dhabi, and it's very expensive there—LE 4,000 [$1,143,

for a full course]. They said it is not available in Egypt; it is very difficult to get. So we brought it from there, and we brought extra. We thought we need six [boxes], but we used only four. So we have two left, and we'll sell them at the same price, or we'll give them away to someone who cannot afford them.

As suggested by this man's remarks, these drugs are expensive and therefore are not easily afforded by the average Egyptian. In fact, hMG and the other fertility hormones have actually been significantly *less* expensive in Egypt than in other Middle Eastern and Western countries. This is because Western pharmaceutical manufacturers practice "tiered pricing" in the Third World, in order to sell their drugs at prices the local markets will bear. Because most Egyptian patients cannot afford Pergonal and Humagon at the prices charged in Europe, the United States, or even the neighboring petro-rich Gulf States, the manufacturers have, at least in the past, lowered the price in Egypt so that their drugs can be marketed there. However, with the phase-out of hMG, prices in Egypt began to soar, such that a single injection of Pergonal could go for as much as LE 100 ($29) on the black market, a cost that even most Egyptian IVF physicians considered outrageous.

Nadine, in her typical acerbic fashion, condemned the international pharmaceutical industry for making infertile Egyptians suffer over the lack of available hormones and their exorbitant prices.

Pergonal, Humagon, you can't find them anywhere now except in [IVF] centers. They care for infertile men with Pergonal, and even men here can't find Pergonal! The doctors are making money [off these drugs], but I believe it's not the doctors creating these problems. It's the people producing this medicine, who bring it to the doctors rather than to the pharmacies, because they know they will make more money. The drug reps will take, for example, LE 100. Something needs to be done to get control over these prices. If they were selling drugs illegally, it would be cheaper!

The suitcase and black-market trades in a very legal fertility drug and the high prices desperate Egyptian IVF patients were willing to pay for that drug are emblematic of the very unevenness of globalization and the ways in which receiving nations and consumers in those nations must pay dearly to access globalizing technologies, including pharmaceutical technologies. But what happens when Egyptian IVF patients do manage to bypass this hurdle? What occurs after they "take their meds" and embark on IVF or ICSI? What other forms of embodiment does test-tube baby making engender? As we'll see now, in Egypt, the next steps typically involve worrying, waiting, and bedding down.

Worrying, Waiting, and Bedding Down

It would not be an exaggeration to say that, in Egypt, women undergoing IVF or ICSI move "from meds to beds." Once the hormones are taken during the first fifteen days of the treatment cycle, the next fifteen days involve a long, and in its own way even more tortured, process of waiting and worrying, usually from the privacy of the bedroom.

Before describing the importance of the bed as an Egyptian cultural site, it is important to emphasize that Egyptian women who succeed with their medications and are adequately superovulated proceed through the next two stages with relative aplomb. These two stages are at the very heart of IVF and ICSI, but, perhaps because they generate relatively little embodied suffering, women typically have little to say about them. The first stage, called "oocyte pickup," involves retrieval, or "harvesting," of multiple ova from the woman's superovulating ovaries. In Egypt, as in most other sites, oocyte pickup is always performed *bil-bing*—by general anesthesia—because it takes approximately one-half hour to perform and causes painful cramping, whether it is performed surgically (through incisions in the abdomen) or transvaginally (through probes inserted into the vagina). A few women in this study experienced postretrieval pain and cramping, but they reported it as mild and relatively short-lived.

The next stage, occurring usually within forty-eight hours of oocyte pickup, is called "embryo transfer" (ET), where the fertilized embryos are transferred back to the uterus, usually through the vagina.[69] Embryo transfer may or may not require surgery and general anesthesia, depending upon the exact type of procedure that is performed. Those women who have the procedure performed transvaginally are sometimes awake and aware (although local anesthesia may be used), and most report that the procedure is quick and painless, entailing little if any embodied suffering.

Nadine was, therefore, highly unusual in her bitter complaints about being "opened twice" within forty-eight hours for the purposes of ova retrieval and embryo transfer. Most Egyptian women I met had relatively little to say about these stages, although a few did mention their initial fear. Most women were happy to be given anesthesia, which may have served to dull the pain and any bitter memories of the experiences. When I was introduced by Dr. Yehia or one of his staff members to women in their hospital rooms following ET, I was often struck by how happy, animated, and hopeful they (and their husbands) appeared. Most wanted to show me their "reports," their detailed discharge summary sheets. These reports fueled what might best be described as beautiful "egg-and-embryo stories"—women's sometimes jubilant and often detailed accounts of egg size, quality, number, and fertilizability, accompanied by discussions of how many embryos had just been transferred into their wombs. From their hospital beds, some women wondered out loud how many of these "pretty embryos"—two, three, four, or even more[70]—might become their future test-tube babies.

It is only when women move from the hospital bed to their beds at home that the worry begins. As described to me by numerous women who had been through this stage, a tormented, fifteen-day waiting period typically sets in, as women take to bed during this second half of the treatment cycle. Why? Basing their immobilization on cultural notions of reproductive ethnophysiology, women hope that by remaining still and inactive, the embryos will "stick" or "hang" (i.e., implant) and will not "fall down" (resulting in what they view as a very early spontaneous abortion of a pregnancy). Women maintain this belief even though Egyptian IVF doctors usually inform patients that movement and activity have little to do with the success of implantation and that bed rest beyond the day of embryo transfer is, therefore, unnecessary. Yet, even highly educated women who have been encouraged to "live normally" and to "relax and clear your mind" rarely heed their physicians' advice. Instead, they literally bed down for a two-week period, interrupted only by trips to the bathroom or kitchen.

Those days spent in bed are rarely restful for women, who tend to brood excessively about whether the IVF or ICSI trial has been successful. Many women, reflecting on their experiences, regard this as the most difficult part of the IVF treatment cycle. Worrying about all that could go wrong, many women described themselves as "incredibly nervous" and unable to relax during this period—even joking that this is the part of the cycle that should require anesthesia to "put them to sleep"! Thus, waiting, worrying, and bedding down are the typical psychosomatic triad for Egyptian women who have passed through the critical stage of embryo transfer. One woman, who eventually learned that she was pregnant, described the waiting period as torment:

> These fifteen days are *very, very* difficult. Waiting! Waiting! Every so often, I go to the bathroom, and I pull down my underpants to see if there is blood, and to tell myself, "Please don't cry" if there is. I stay in bed all the time, and, at night, I feel insomnia, and I ask myself, "Oh, will it be or not?" I'm dreaming. "Oh, the operation failed, and I lost my baby." Many times, I wake up and I can't sleep, and then, *el-hamdu-lillah* [she found out she was pregnant].

Although this woman was one of the lucky ones, women who learn of a failed trial through an early pregnancy test or the tell-tale signs of menstruation generally experience the emotional devastation in relative isolation, for reasons that will be made clearer in Chapter 9. Suffice it so say here that it often takes women months to muster sufficient courage to repeat the procedure, assuming financial resources are available. The lucky few who *do* become pregnant through IVF or ICSI may spend the rest of their pregnancy on bed rest, sometimes reflecting doctors' orders, but also following widely held Egyptian injunctions about avoiding pregnancy loss through overexertion. In a society in which most individuals still spend their lives in bodily-taxing forms of manual labor and domestic work, it is not surprising that physical overexertion is seen as the source of many forms of ill health, including pregnancy loss. Thus, Western warnings about the need for dietary monitoring and exercise during pregnancy are rarely heeded in Egypt. Rather, the opposite injunctions, to move as little as possible and to eat rich foods and gain weight in order to take care of oneself and one's baby, are much more likely to be followed, even among women who, by Western standards, are already mildly to moderately obese. In other words, pregnancy, especially if achieved through new reproductive technologies, engenders a clearly non-Western form of bodily "discipline,"[71] marked by self-enforced, and socially reinforced, inactivity, immobilization, and inertia. More than anything, Egyptian women who have succeeded in conceiving through IVF or ICSI fear losing their precious baby of the tubes through physical activity that could have been avoided. And so, to the extent that they can, they (and their husbands) pamper their bodies through prolonged bed rest.[72] As one woman, reflecting on her ICSI pregnancy, which led to the cesarean birth of a healthy daughter, recalled,

> Until the last day before giving birth, I didn't come out of the house. The doctors told me *complete rest* for nine months. Psychologically, it was very difficult. I was worried through the whole pregnancy. *Always* I couldn't sleep; it was too difficult to sleep, so I was getting maybe two hours the whole day. Anything, any little thing I feel, I start weeping, "Maybe something happened inside." After the third month, they made a cervical circlage, to make sure [there would be] no miscarriage. If, for a day, I didn't feel the baby's movement for a day, I'd become sick with worry. Sometimes I tried to get the baby to move; I'd wake her up, and when I felt the movement, I would feel comfortable again. . . . I'll never forget this experience. It's something I can never repeat.

As reflected in this woman's account, most women who become pregnant by IVF or ICSI, and especially with multiple fetuses, undergo yet another surgical procedure called "cervical circlage," designed to "tie" or "tighten" the cervix to prevent cervical incompetency and premature labor. As the end of the pregnancy draws near, virtually all of these women undergo their final surgery in the form of a scheduled cesarean section. During the course of my study, I never met, nor heard of, any Egyptian mother of a test-tube baby who had *not* given birth by cesarean. When I asked Egyptian IVF physicians why this was so, I was told that these babies are more "precious" than other infants; therefore, physicians must exercise additional "control" over the birth process, thereby avoiding the possible negative outcomes that can occur during a normal vaginal delivery. According to Dr. Yehia, in the world of test-tube baby making, such cesareans are justified, because most IVF and ICSI patients are "high risk"—first-time mothers over the age of thirty-five, pregnant with multiples, and suffering from various infertility-related reproductive problems. Whereas the cesarean section rate in general maternity hospitals in Egypt is only 12 percent—which, as Dr. Yehia noted, is much lower than the 25 percent or more found in the United States—private hospitals such as Nozha have a much higher cesarean rate, usually in the 30 percent range, due to the many "special-needs" patients being seen there. At Nozha Hospital, many of these women are infertility patients, whose "extra-special babies" are delivered into the hands of Dr. Yehia himself.

But what about the husbands, who are normally absent from these deliveries in a society where "husband-coached childbirth" has yet to take hold? Do they have their own set of worries and concerns about becoming Egyptian fathers of test-tube babies? The answer is an emphatic "yes"! While their physical suffering ends once their weak sperm are successfully retrieved, men's psychic suffering may, in fact, intensify once pregnancy is achieved. Although this may seem counterintuitive, given the profound sense of happiness and relief that might be expected, infertile Egyptian men worry considerably about the health of babies borne of weak sperm.

As I discovered through my conversations with a number of Egyptian husbands, men who have lived for years with knowledge that their sperm are weak are concerned about the biological transmission of "weakness" to their children. As with "weak ovaries," "weakness" is the cultural idiom by which most male infertility problems are glossed, and it seems that many infertile Egyptian men take this idiom to heart, feeling that they are somehow weak, defective, abnormal, and even unworthy as biological progenitors. Many men coming to Egyptian IVF centers are openly concerned about whether they will "pass their weakness" on to their children, and this is especially pronounced among men with immature sperm or spermatic deformities, who wonder if their children will suffer from congenital malformations. For example, one azoospermic man admitted to me that he was "very worried about the 'shape' of the baby": "I had to have a 'sample' of spermatids taken from the testicles. So I'm worried that maybe the baby won't be normal. Dr. Yehia said, 'Don't worry. Many babies have been born and are normal. It's okay.' But I'm still worried, of course." Another infertile man said that he asked Dr. Yehia,

> "These babies from IVF, if they grow and marry, will it be normal for them to have children?" Because they started IVF in 1980, and no one yet got married or has children. What will happen in the next generation? Are they weak, normal, strong, healthy, with the ability to have children? I think it's a normal pregnancy, but it's not normal when they inject the sperm. Sometimes they say it's not a normal baby, it's abnormal, a mongoloid. The baby will suffer and we will suffer, too, because here in Egypt, there are no facilities for these babies like in the United States or Europe.

As reflected in this man's statement, fears of abnormalities were clearly present among many of the men in this study, particularly those with severe male infertility cases. Yet, many infertile couples told me that they would rather have a disabled child than no child at all, and at least some infertile couples with heritable genetic disorders were going forward with ICSI in Dr. Yehia's clinic following genetic counseling.

On the final day of my study in 1996, I asked Dr. Yehia about this, for I had come to recognize the prevailing fear among infertile Egyptian men that their "weak sperm" might beget a physically deformed or mentally disabled child. Dr. Yehia, the founder of ICSI in Egypt, replied,

> I'm speaking about that on TV, I think, in a couple of days. And I think it will be in the newspapers in a couple of days, because it's now a major issue. Now we are having something like 150 babies—150 babies and all of them are normal. These are from microinjection, from very weak sperm or sperm from the testis. So now that we are having a huge number of babies, and they are all all right, I can say this in public. Although there are studies abroad, from Belgium, that look very promising—that say [these children] are al-

right—I think now *we* can say it. So, I'm starting to "attack" this point now, because it's very important.

However, looking to the future, Dr. Yehia continued,

The babies all look normal, but we are honestly not sure what will happen when these children reach puberty. Will they be infertile or have other problems? This is "tampering with nature," because nature somehow meant for these individuals [who do not produce mature spermatozoa] to be completely sterile. I mean, there is no known reason for such spermatogenic arrest, and though, in mice, in animal models, the offspring seem normal, translating this to humans is problematic. For example, there's something called "ciliac disease," where all the cilia in the body, including the tail of the sperm, are completely immobilized. This causes serious lung problems, and it's hereditary. But we just delivered the male baby of a couple where the husband has this problem and would never have had children without ICSI. This is "nature's way" of getting rid of this problem by preventing reproduction. But the couple, who we informed of this, chose to go ahead. So, there are still many implications of this, and it's too soon to see the results of this in the next generation.

Indeed, as made clear in the recent volume *Infertility in the Modern World: Present and Future Prospects*,[73] the infertility produced by a number of genetic disorders, in both males and females, can now be overcome through the use of ICSI and donor oocytes. However, as noted by the authors, "there may be a high risk of transmission to progeny following fertilization via ICSI, which has caused concerns on dysgenic grounds."[74] In other words, the "tampering with nature" mentioned by Dr. Yehia suggests a fundamental ethical debate about whether individuals have the right to use technology if it will effectively reproduce their own genetic diseases in their offspring. In Egypt at least, the felt need to produce a child, including one with a debilitating disease or a physical or mental disability, may cause couples to forge ahead with ICSI, effectively throwing such caution to the wind.[75]

In my own study, ten babies were born, half to men with "very weak" sperm, and all appeared to be healthy and normal at birth.[76] But the concerns of their fathers, and most of the other infertile men in this study, about the hereditary passage of their weakness was telling. In Egypt, the limitations imposed by reproductive biology, as played out in semen profiles marked by inactive, immature, deformed, and deficient sperm, plague men both before and after the conception of their ICSI offspring. This may be one of the reasons why some men, such as Fuad, are extremely resistant to being treated for their infertility, for the children they produce may literally make visible to the world their father's biological inadequacy. Although the Egyptian IVF physicians who perform ICSI reassure most men that their fears are unfounded, they themselves wonder about the implications of "tampering with nature," thereby alluding to the ways in which biology itself constitutes a fundamental arena of constraint on the act of test-tube baby making.

Conclusion

In their essay "Suffering and Its Professional Transformation: Toward an Ethnography of Interpersonal Experience," Arthur and Joan Kleinman define suffering as "a universal aspect of human experience in which individuals and groups have to undergo or bear certain forms of burdens, troubles and serious wounds to the body and the spirit."[77] Clearly, in Egypt, test-tube baby making bespeaks this world of embodied suffering, with somatic and spiritual "wounds" occurring at multiple sites. In the case of Fuad and Nadine, there were wounds to the male ego, which were ultimately suffered, physically through ICSI, by a profoundly unhappy and emotionally burdened wife. Writing to me three years later, Dr. Yehia noted that Nadine "never made it to egg collection due to bad response," forcing me to wonder whether the deep wounds riving Nadine and Fuad's tumultuous marriage could ever be fully healed.

In that same letter of August 31, 1999, Dr. Yehia wrote of other troubling developments in the world of Egyptian test-tube baby making. Speaking of the drug shortages that were another source of suffering for Egyptian IVF consumers in 1996, he said,

> There is no problem regarding the medications now, as they are being manufactured in Egypt by two pharmaceutical companies. This, however, is not going to last for a long time. The new form of medication which is genetically engineered is already on the market, and due to the globalization of the market now, and the feasibility of ordering medication by the Internet, it was decided by the drug companies to have worldwide uniform pricing. This, in effect, will increase the prices in the Third World, as there is preferential pricing for poor countries now.

As revealed in this succinct statement, the alleviation of one fundamental arena of constraint in Egypt, namely, the local drug shortages that impeded couples' access to IVF and ICSI technologies, led to another, namely, exorbitantly priced recombinant FSH manufactured by two powerful multinational TNCs (Organon and Serono). If a global pricing structure for essential hormones is not adjusted downward for resource-poor Third World countries such as Egypt, then these medications will be out of reach for many Egyptian consumers. As noted by anthropologist Robert Rubinstein in his essay "'Breaking the Bureaucracy': Drug Registration and Neocolonial Relations in Egypt," such ill effects are an example of the ongoing neocolonial dependency of nations such as Egypt upon Western-based pharmaceutical companies, which reap "huge financial rewards . . . from their activities in lesser developed countries."[78]

Ultimately, then, the globalization of the Western-based pharmaceutical technologies that are necessary to sustain the global IVF industry has brought with it new dilemmas and dystopias in a rapidly evolving, high-tech, cyber-connected world. What creative, resilient, or resistant local responses will emerge to counter this new dilemma are unclear. But certainly the Egyptian drug crisis highlights the ways in which powerful structural impediments, this time enforced by the global pharmaceutical industry, serve to restrict the reproductive agency of Third World actors, who *need* these drugs in order to become parents.

Yet, as also shown in this chapter, taking these drugs is viewed as a "necessary evil," the source of much unhappiness, *for men as well as for women.* If there is one argument that I would like to reiterate as I conclude this chapter, it is that men's embodied experiences of infertility treatment in general, and new reproductive technologies in particular, have been seriously underprivileged and even erased by infertility scholars, feminist critics of these technologies, and those of us who "walk in between."[79] Although it is absolutely essential to acknowledge the patriarchal bargains that women make as they embark on ICSI to facilitate their husbands' damaged fertility, it is also important to realize that the gendered suffering, both psychic and somatic, that accompanies the new reproductive technologies is not the exclusive domain of women. Men suffer, too, sometimes alone, but often *with and for* the wives they love and who love them in return. And it is to these gender dynamics, and their implications for marriage and family life, that we now turn.

CHAPTER **8**

Gender

The Man Who Replaced His Wife

Shahira is the twenty-five-year-old wife of Moustafa, a well-to-do, forty-three-year-old lawyer whose father was once a powerful politician. In addition to his legal practice, Moustafa rents a villa to a foreign embassy and owns a business center (office supplies and copying), which Shahira runs for him. Shahira is Moustafa's second wife, married to him now for ten months. Prior to this, Moustafa was married for seventeen years to Hala, a woman now in her forties whom he divorced two years ago as a result of their childlessness.

Early in his first marriage, Moustafa was told by physicians that he suffered from severe male-factor infertility, involving low sperm count and poor motility. He underwent repeated courses of hormonal therapy, none of which improved his semen profile. Ultimately, he and Hala underwent several cycles of artificial insemination using concentrates of his sperm, as well as five cycles of IVF, three times in Germany and twice in Egypt. Each trial was unsuccessful.

According to the physicians at Nozha Hospital who undertook one of the failed trials in Moustafa's home country, it was obvious to them that Moustafa and Hala's marriage was deteriorating during the course of therapy—a deterioration they implied had something to do with Hala's "very strong personality." Shahira seemed to agree:

> Here in Egypt, if a man knows he doesn't get his wife pregnant, he's always upset. And if you're pushing him all the time, and he's the reason for the problem, he feels like giving up [on the marriage], because there are no children to keep in the house. In my husband's case, he preferred to divorce her because their relationship became bad. They had different attitudes and behaviors, and in this case, the major reason for the divorce was that he knows he's the reason for no pregnancy. He's very kind, and she's very nervous and always asking too many questions. So my husband asked for divorce because their marriage became bad.

Although Hala has not remarried, Moustafa remarried in little over a year. He chose Shahira, a Christian woman approximately half his age, after knowing her for five months. Moustafa was less interested in Shahira's pedigree (a college degree in tourism from prestigious American University in Cairo, with fluency in both French and English) and in her religious background (a Muslim man is allowed to marry a Christian woman) than in her youth, potential fecundity, acceptance of his infertility problem, and willingness to try additional treatments with him. He told her, "I want to marry you, but you are a young lady, and I'm sure you want a baby." Shahira told him that, to the contrary, she needed a "father figure" and felt that Moustafa could be "both a husband and a father" to her. This was because her own father works in the United Arab Emirates, and she has not seen him in several years. Her mother died when Shahira was ten, and she has lived alone with her younger brother and sister and two servants since their father emigrated in the early 1990s. As Shahira explains it,

> If I married a young man, he will ask first about himself. He wants to live with his wife alone. But my husband sees my case [i.e., she is like the "mother" to her younger siblings], and he accepts my case. But I accept his case [i.e., infertility]. He's feeling for me—I can't separate from them [her siblings]—and he loves this in me. Because he says, "If you care for your sister and brother, you will care for me."
>
> I took my decision in two months, without love before marriage, but with my mind. But love has grown—100 percent I love him. A very important thing in marriage is understanding, feeling secure. That's more important than love. He's kind and when I'm sick, he'll sit beside me and ask how I'm feeling. When I married him, I accepted 100 percent that I will not have children, and I wouldn't push him. But since I knew his case before marriage, I told him I'd be willing to try [IVF] more than once because he's very kind. I was afraid, but I'll try.

A few months into their marriage, Shahira went to a gynecologist in Maadi, the elite Cairo suburb where two of the major IVF centers are located. The physician told her, "You are young and you haven't anything wrong, but the lab report of your husband is very bad." She asked the physician about IVF, and he said, "No way, because your husband is a *very* bad case." Moustafa, meanwhile, underwent five months of drug therapy. His andrologist told him, "Your wife is very young. ICSI *may* be successful, because she's young and has no problem. You can try. Don't hesitate. You should use any time you have."

At that point, Moustafa decided to take Shahira to see Dr. Mohamed Yehia at one of the two Egyptian IVF clinics where he had also taken his first wife. Dr. Yehia confirmed that because Shahira was young, with no known reproductive impairments, their chances of conceiving with ICSI were greater than in Moustafa's previous IVF attempts with Hala. Moustafa was delighted that Shahira and he were candidates for

ICSI, but Shahira's reaction was different. "I'm very afraid of *any* operation," she said. "I was *so* afraid, and I was not thinking it was going to be successful. But Dr. Yehia told me, 'Don't be afraid. It's easy. A small operation. It will be successful.'"

Shahira suffered uncomfortable side effects from the medications used to stimulate ovulation. Her gastric ulcer symptoms were exacerbated, and she felt abdominal cramping and pain at various points in the treatment. "It's too difficult doing this ICSI," she complained. "*I* take all these injections, *I* come to the hospital every day, *I* prepare for the operation, *I* see the anesthesia, the doctors. It's frightening. My husband—they just take the semen from him."

Once the ICSI procedure was completed, Shahira was still unconvinced of its efficacy. Thus, when she was scheduled for a blood test to determine her pregnancy status, she refused to be tested—despite continuous urging from her husband and siblings. Indeed, she was so intransigent that Moustafa finally called the laboratory and had a doctor sent to their home to draw the sample. The next day, Moustafa and Shahira went to the laboratory, where the physician told them: "Congratulations. I wanted to tell you personally." Repeated pregnancy tests, along with three ultrasounds, confirmed that Shahira was pregnant—with twins in separate amniotic sacs.

Although Moustafa has begun to tell people that his new wife is pregnant with twins, he refuses to reveal anything about his history of infertility or about this miraculous ICSI conception. He lets people believe, albeit indirectly, that his childless first marriage was somehow the fault of Hala and her advancing age. Shahira explained, "Here in Egypt, if the man is infertile, it is very, very, very bad for him psychologically. So, after I became pregnant, [Moustafa] tells them, 'It's normal. She got pregnant easily because she's young.'"

Although Shahira and Moustafa are keeping their ICSI conception secret from their friends and his family, Shahira's brother and sister, to whom she is exceptionally close, know the truth of the twins' conception. "I told my brother and sister because they're in my home, and I'm always tired after having two operations. So they have to know."

Furthermore, now that Shahira is pregnant with twins, she is expected to undergo cervical circlage, an operation to close her cervix and thereby prevent early delivery. For her part, Shahira is relatively concerned about the potential difficulties associated with a twin pregnancy and the routine cesarean childbirth expected with test-tube babies and especially multiples. She is also concerned about the demands of taking care of two infants simultaneously. If, "God willing," all goes well with the pregnancy and childbirth, Shahira says she won't do ICSI again. "Once is enough. One operation, one delivery. It's too difficult and too frightening."

Ultimately, Shahira hopes that the birth of his ICSI twins will make Moustafa stop smoking three packs of cigarettes a day, which may be implicated in his male infertility problem. She also hopes that at least one of the infants will be a girl, although Moustafa hopes for a son that he can name Ahmed. For his part, Moustafa looks at Shahira's expanding belly every day and says, "Now I can't believe I will have children. I will believe it if I touch my son or daughter by myself." In truth, "replacing" his first wife now all seems worth it to Moustafa, and he looks forward to the day when he truly becomes an Egyptian father of test-tube twins.

Infertility: His and Hers

The story of Moustafa and his two wives can be read in many ways.[1] On the one hand, it may be seen as a tale of callous patriarchy, in which a Middle Eastern man forgoes his marital vows in order to prove his paternity with a younger woman. On the other hand, it can be read as a tale of gendered suffering, in which *both* Moustafa and his first wife are victims of a cultural system in which hegemonic masculinities and femininities are instantiated through fertility. Viewed from a different perspective, Moustafa's story could be read as a modernist narrative, in which ICSI promises technological salvation to a hopelessly infertile man, who thereby reestablishes his masculinity through the achievement of fatherhood. Yet, this story could be also be read much more ambivalently as a cautionary tale, in which new reproductive technologies take their toll on marriages and on the gender identities and status of reproductively aging women who cannot be helped by these new technologies even if their husbands can.

What is clear from this story, and from the stories of other Egyptian couples told in this book, is that infertility and its treatment through IVF and ICSI give rise to "gender responses" on the part of women and men, responses that may be both gender- and culture-specific.[2] Clearly, the biological problem of male infertility described here is experienced differently by each of the actors in this story. Moustafa becomes so demoralized that he decides to cast off his first wife Hala, whose reaction to "his problem" becomes an unacceptable reminder to him of his diminished masculinity. Hala, who stands by Moustafa for seventeen years and undergoes five IVF trials with him, is subtly blamed for the emasculation of Moustafa—by Moustafa himself, by the doctors who attempt to treat them, and by the second wife who willingly takes her place. Yet, since Hala is no longer in the picture, we do not hear her side of the story. Instead, we hear the views of Hala's physicians and Moustafa's new wife, both of whom implicate Hala's strong, nagging personality in the demise of her marriage. In short, Hala is seen as bringing divorce upon herself in her relentless pursuit to understand and overcome the male infertility that has become her problem as well. Clearly, her divorce at a time when she is no longer highly fertile does not bode well for her own future happiness or gender identity, in a society in which virtually all women achieve adult personhood through marriage and motherhood. Finally, there is the youthful Shahira, the main interlocutor of this story, who is willing to marry an older, infertile, divorced man in order to achieve the semblance of a normal Egyptian family, which would include a male patriarch who is present and involved in the lives of junior family members. Yet, in order to obtain the father figure she feels she needs, Shahira makes a "patriarchal bargain"[3]—

agreeing before marriage to pursue high-tech infertility treatments with her hus-band-to-be in order to guarantee his future fatherhood. Although youth is on Shahira's side, she experiences ICSI as an unpleasant and nerve-wracking process, one she hopes never to repeat if her ICSI twins are born healthy and survive.

As is clear in this story, infertility strikes many blows in Egypt—to individual women and men and to the marriages they attempt to sustain through what often become years of relentless treatment seeking. As a threat to gender identities, infer-tility compromises both femininities and masculinities in a society where mother-hood and fatherhood are simply expected of all married persons and where the expressed desire for children is strong on the part of both women and men. In addi-tion, infertility affects the quality of married life, but in ways that may be highly gen-der- and culture-specific. When issues of responsibility, blame, and guilt come to the fore, the dynamics of marriage are forever altered, particularly in Muslim societies such as Egypt, where barrenness is seen as one of the justifiable grounds for divorce. Furthermore, the treatment seeking often required to overcome infertility may so-lidify some marriages, while other marriages are torn apart by the blame, resent-ment, and very rigors of the therapeutic process. With the recent advent of ICSI, conjugal dynamics are further complicated in places like Egypt, where infertile Muslim men must decide whether preserving one's marriage or remarrying in the pursuit of paternity is the more worthy goal. In short, infertility is a gender- and marriage-threatening condition, which may be complicated by the option of new reproductive technologies.

As I will argue in this chapter, gender dynamics within marriage are, in and of themselves, among the most fundamental arenas of constraint surrounding test-tube baby making in Egypt. In Egypt, infertility is a condition that implicates two people, a wife and a husband, in a society where virtually all procreation occurs within the confines of marriage. Yet, given that the notion of the "couple" is not at all well defined in Egypt,[4] the tension that may develop between marital partners who do not stand united may complicate treatment seeking in a variety of ways. Most commonly, some men may refuse to acknowledge their own infertility or may refuse to seek treatment with their infertile wives, leading to cajolements and frustrations that are hard for women to bear. Furthermore, infertility in a man may elicit a wife's sympathy and protectiveness, but in at least some cases, it may lead women to as-sume marital power and authority in ways that are deeply threatening to men in a male-dominant society. In other words, gender shapes the experience of infertility and its treatment for men and women differently, leading to what some infertility researchers have called "infertility: his and hers."[5]

Furthermore, the implications of the use of new reproductive technologies and the success of marriage, particularly in non-Western sites where marriage and child-bearing go hand in hand, are poorly understood. As we shall see, the option of IVF and ICSI for elites in Egypt may, in and of itself, create marital turmoil. Not only are infertile men such as Moustafa forced to choose between first and second wives with differing levels of fecundity, but psychologically wounded infertile couples are forced to confront the many arenas of constraint inherent in the IVF/ICSI treatment-seeking process. If worrying about the infertility problem itself weren't enough, Egyptian couples seeking new reproductive technologies must contend with treatment costs, physical risks, religious concerns, supercilious physicians, low success rates, drug shortages, and the many other woes that have been described so far in this book. Such tangible stressors may take their toll on marriages in ways that have heretofore been little described in the literature, even in Western sites where infertile couples have been more thoroughly studied.[6]

Ironically perhaps, Western feminist scholars, who have exposed many of the negative implications of new reproductive technologies for women's lives,[7] have remained relatively silent on the matter of marriage. The now voluminous feminist literature on IVF has criticized the objectification of women's bodies in the assisted reproduction process by male "technopatriarchs" who control the medical encounter, as well as the substantial medical risks to women for a procedure with relatively poor success rates. Perhaps most important, Western feminist scholars have criticized the essentializing potential of IVF, which by its very nature promotes the hegemonic, patriarchal presupposition that biological motherhood is imperative to women's lives and well-being as members of society.

These criticisms are apt, but they have often remained at the discursive, even polemical level. In much of the Western feminist literature on IVF, little attention has been paid to the empirical reality of infertile women's lives *as lived with their husbands.* On the ground, in the everyday interactions between husbands and wives, IVF and the newer ICSI may be experienced positively or negatively, with hope or despondency, on the part of men and women, who although married to one another, may respond to these technologies quite differently. From the perspective of gender, IVF and ICSI have the potential to produce positive outcomes, by helping to salvage damaged gender identities in both men and women and by bringing spouses closer together through the mutual commitment to the treatment process.[8] On the negative side, IVF and ICSI have the potential to create highly gendered disjunctures within marriage, as husbands' and wives' interests in pursuing these technologies diverge in dramatic ways. As we will see in this chapter, in resource-poor societies such as Egypt, where the costs of IVF/ICSI are high on many levels, these technologies may serve to strain marital commitments among couples already troubled by the lack of a child in a society where having children is socially mandatory for *both* men and women.

In this chapter, we will explore the implications of test-tube baby making for gender, marriage, and family life in Egypt. To begin, we will examine the implications of infertility for Egyptian notions of femininity and masculinity in an attempt to understand the gender context in which new reproductive technologies are deployed. However, the bulk of this chapter will be devoted to the intimate politics of marriage. Although many Egyptian marriages are in fact fortified by infertility and the IVF treatment experience, others are damaged beyond repair—an untoward outcome that has been little studied, despite its increasing prevalence in the age of ICSI.

Femininities, Masculinities, and Child Desire

Egyptians often like to think of themselves as the most child-loving people on earth. Every time I have lived in Egypt, I have been struck by the tremendous amount of desire for children expressed by married couples and by the affection heaped upon children by both men and women. Despite gradually declining birth rates in the country since Western-backed population control efforts began in the 1960s,[9] Egypt remains a patently pronatalist country, as reflected in a total fertility rate of 3.5 and a population of 70 million, making Egypt the largest country in the Middle East and the fifteenth largest in the world.[10]

In Egypt, no adult, male or female, admits to not wanting children. This is as true among the highly educated, career-oriented, upper class as it is among the poor women who were the focus of my earlier research. In fact, when I returned to Egypt in 1996 to conduct my study of elites in IVF centers, I would soon discover that pronatalist sentiments cross class boundaries. Women and sometimes their husbands expressed their ardent desires for children, sometimes specifying their ideal number and sex of offspring. I was told time and time again how Egyptians "love children," with men professing this love as much as women. For example, one infertile man, a wealthy merchant, told me,

> I love kids *very, very* much. All of my sisters have lots of kids, three, two, two. . . . My littlest sister lives in Tanta. Last night, she was with us with her two babies, one four years, and the other a year and two months. They come running to me when they see me. I and [my wife] love babies very much. Maybe this is because God didn't give us babies, [so] we love them more. But, my [infertile] brother, too, when he sees kids, he's very happy.

When I asked him how many children he wanted, his first response was the Egyptian formulaic one: "Whatever God gives." But he immediately continued, "Maybe after that operation [ICSI], my sperm will increase. Maybe I don't need the operation after that, and if it doesn't increase, I will make another ICSI after one or two years—until I have eleven children! I love to play football [i.e., soccer], so I want to make a team!"

Other Egyptian elites sometimes expressed their desires for "many children," although normative responses were in the range of two to three. As noted in Chapter 6, the strong desire among IVF- and ICSI-seeking couples for twins or triplets reflects the common desire to complete the family in a single technological attempt. Furthermore, the common desire for twins is usually accompanied by the desire for a child of each sex, the names of which couples such as Shahira and Moustafa have often chosen beforehand. However, as seen in the case of Shahira, daughter preference was apparent among many women in this study, and sometimes among their husbands as well. Despite historical patterns of son preference in the Middle Eastern region as a whole,[11] desires for a "gender-balanced" family of only two to three children have clearly taken hold in urban areas of Egypt, among the middle and upper classes, as well as among the poor families who were the subject of my earlier research.[12]

Although most elite women such as Shahira expressed satisfaction in their careers, their marriages, and their other accomplishments (e.g., hobbies), they nonetheless felt that their lives were "incomplete" without the experience of motherhood. Most women expressed a strong personal longing for children, sometimes adding that they would give up their careers in order to become a mother. For example, one highly educated, Egyptian professional woman told me, "I have a *beautiful, beautiful* house, my [wealthy] mother's taste. I have my car, my job, my husband. And if something goes wrong, I have my mother's money. I don't want anything more. I want the baby only."

Another woman described how she planned to give up her career in order to "educate" a child:

> To have a child, I believe it's [a woman's] nature, to feel she's a woman. . . . I would love to have children because I know now it's about time. I can give up anything, including my career, to be a mother—not only to be a mother, but to raise a child in the right way, to educate it. I believe it's every woman's aim to have a child. Even little girls play with dolls; it's their nature.

As revealed in this last comment, most women in Egypt, including elite women, deem motherhood to be a "natural" part of their lives, linked to feminine drives and desires that emerge at a very early age. Religiously supported beliefs in an innate "maternal instinct" are strong in Egypt among all social classes, and this instinct is said to make women naturally desirous of and loving toward children. Thus, women who are "missing motherhood" by virtue of infertility are deemed "incomplete" as feminine subjects and adult human beings, since they are unable to express the instinctual desires for children that, in effect, complete their gendered personhood. This maternal instinct, furthermore, is believed to be much stronger than men's paternal instinct, making the tragedy and gendered suffering of infertility potentially much worse for women. Indeed, Egyptian women at IVF centers used terms such as "desperation," "depression," "exhaustion," "sensitivity," and "nervousness" to describe the effects of infertility on their wounded psyches. One woman used the phrase "destroyed by infertility," while another described herself as "living in hell," even though her husband was the infertile partner. In short, Egyptian women may suffer the psychosocial consequences of infertility quite acutely. Even for elite women in this study—who do not necessarily look to their children as a form of social security or as a way to fill their empty hours at home—the psychosocial toll of infertility is felt most acutely in the realm of gender identity, given that to be a "real woman" in Egypt one must have children. Such feminine imperatives are as pronounced among highly educated career women as they are among illiterate housewives in Egypt. No matter one's social class, infertility, even if caused by a husband, is nothing short of an identity disaster for women, with childless women reminded in everyday interactions that they have failed to become pregnant.[13]

Yet, even though infertility poses an acute crisis for femininities in Egypt, this does not mean that Egyptian masculinities are unscathed by childlessness. Although the relationship between male fertility and masculinity has been poorly studied in Egypt and elsewhere in the Middle East, emerging research suggests that men in this region of the world deem paternity an important achievement and a major source of their masculine identities. "Intimate selving" in Middle Eastern families involves expectations of so-called patriarchal connectivity,[14] whereby men assume patriarchal power in the family not only with advancing age and authority, but also through the explicit production of offspring, whom they love and nurture, but also dominate and control. Thus, in this region of the world, which "with some truth, is still regarded as one of the seats of patriarchy,"[15] men who do not become family patriarchs through physical and social reproduction may be deemed "weak" and ineffective[16] and may be encouraged to take additional wives in order to prove their masculine virility to family members and friends.

Accordingly, proving one's manhood is a competitive affair in the Middle East. As seen in two recent volumes devoted in part or in total to Middle Eastern masculinities,[17] R. W. Connell's concept of "hegemonic masculinities," or the notion of hierarchy and competition *within* masculine social relations, is particularly apt for this region of the world. As Connell argues,

> We must also recognize the *relations* between different kinds of masculinity: relations of alliance, dominance and subordination. These relationships are constructed through practices that exclude and include, that intimidate, exploit, and so on. There is a gender politics within masculinity.[18]

For many Middle Eastern scholars, Connell has opened up the possibility for examining both hegemonic and *subordinate* masculinities, including "the ways in which certain categories of men may experience stigmatization and marginalization."[19]

Most of the ethnographic literature to date has examined the ways in which Middle Eastern men are subordinated by economic impoverishment[20] or by the hierarchical and often humiliating relationships within all-male institutions such as the military.[21] Yet, a repeating theme in the small but growing literature on Middle Eastern masculinities is one of homosocial competition between men in the realms of virility (qua potency) and fertility, which are typically conflated.[22] According to Lahoucine Ouzgane, an expert on contemporary Arabic literature, virility emerges as the "essence of Arab masculinity" in the novels of some of the region's most eminent writers, with men in these stories both distinguishing themselves, and being distinguished from other men, through the fathering of children, and especially sons.[23] If this is, in fact, the case, as the emerging scholarship from this region suggests, then the experience of male infertility for a Middle Eastern man can only be "imagined"[24] as an extremely threatening and emasculating condition, particularly in a world where the performance of hegemonic masculinities is homosocially competitive.

Indeed, my own research in Egypt on male infertility and masculinity strongly suggests the following scenario:[25] Male infertility is a profoundly emasculating and demoralizing condition for Egyptian men such as Moustafa. For one, infertility negatively implicates male sexuality, despite the fact that there is usually no association between infertility and impotency. In addition, infertility threatens the achievement of paternity in an area of the world where men work very hard to sustain their public images as powerful, virile patriarchs.

The clues that infertility acts upon both virility and fertility, engendering a sort of "double emasculation," are manifold. Some men refuse to face up to their infertility by avoiding diagnostic semen analyses, bribing laboratory technicians for inflated reports, or failing to show up at physicians' offices once diagnoses are made. Furthermore, most Egyptian men such as Moustafa do not admit openly to the problem, keeping it secret from their own family members, their in-laws, their co-workers, their male peers, and sometimes even their wives. Consequently, women tend to shoulder the blame for childlessness, wittingly or unwittingly. Those who know their husbands are infertile sometimes excuse their husbands' behavior through empathetic acknowledgment of the negative social repercussions this condition evokes. Many of them attempt to "protect" their husbands from the perceived "embarrassment" and "humiliation" of male infertility by keeping the condition secret, thereby assuming the blame for infertility themselves. One woman explained her protectiveness in this way:

> All these years, I've been telling my relatives and friends that I'm doing the treatment, and not him, because I don't like [for] him to be embarrassed. *I* can carry on and take the responsibility for the infertility. But, in Egypt, for males, this is embarrassing in front of their families. Not for all males, but for most.

Interestingly, when I interviewed one couple together, the husband expressed his amazement at his wife's willingness to "cover" for him, "Once I told someone, 'I'm the cause,' and I was amazed to see [my wife's] reaction. She cried, and she said, 'Why? You can say I am the cause.'"

That women participate, often willingly, in the cover-up of their husbands' infertility makes sense in the context of a patriarchal gender system where public knowledge of an infertile man's subordinated masculinity could have major implications for his relative social status—even in the eyes of his male relatives. As one woman put it succinctly, "The 'Eastern' male will not want to speak about it [male infertility], because it affects his manhood." However, I would argue that women's protection of their infertile husbands, as well as their willingness to undergo multiple invasive therapies with them, also stems from the love and "conjugal connectivity," which, perhaps ironically, may actually be bolstered by male infertility. To understand how male infertility may fortify marriage in Egypt, as well as how it may disrupt conjugal commitments, it is important to examine the institution of marriage itself in Egypt and to ask how the newest new reproductive technology, ICSI, threatens to change it.

Conjugal Connectivity

It is important to begin by stating that, in Egypt, marriage is a highly valued and normatively upheld institution. Islam extols the virtues of marriage, regarding it as

Sunna, or the way of the prophet Muhammad, and as the "completion of half of the religion" (with worship and service to God completing the remaining half). Among Egyptian Copts, marriage is so highly valued that men and women, once married, are forbidden to divorce. In addition, among Egyptians of all denominations, marriage is regarded as a "protection" for both a woman and a man, especially against the desire for illicit sexuality and procreation, both of which must occur with the confines of marriage. Remaining single, especially to experiment with multiple sexual partners, is socially penalized for both men and women; thus, permanent bachelors and spinsters are rarely found in Egypt. Furthermore, cohabitation between unmarried adults of the opposite sex, a historically recent pattern in the West, is unheard of among Egyptians of any social class or educational background. Given this propensity and pressure to marry, Egyptians are, like Middle Easterners in general, among the "most married" people in the world.[26] They take the call to marriage quite seriously, with most adults marrying at least once in a lifetime. As noted by Diane Singerman and Barbara Ibrahim,

> Marriage is an event infused with multiple meanings in the lives of Egyptians. It is a civil contract between two families with legally binding conditions on both parties. Marriage is a means for consolidation of social status, and in a conservative society, it also provides the only approved access for young men and women to sexual and reproductive partners. In the Arab world in general, and in Egypt in particular, marriage is considered a "social pinnacle and major turning point in the lives of both men and women," heralding the transition to full-fledged adulthood.[27]

Given the high cultural value placed on marriage, it is perhaps surprising that the notion of the married "couple" is not well developed in Egypt; in fact, a word for the human couple does not exist in either classical or Egyptian colloquial Arabic. In Egyptian cultural terms, marriage is for the purposes of procreation and family building. Thus, marriages are typically arranged or at least semi-arranged through family intercession, even among elites. Love is expected to emerge *after* marriage through the intense experience surrounding the birth and parenting of children. As a result, few Egyptian newlyweds postpone marital procreation through the use of contraceptives, and most hope to achieve parenthood within the first conjugal year.

Given this cultural backdrop, it is not surprising that marriages in Egypt are deemed inherently fragile and unstable until the birth of children is achieved. The absence of a culturally constructed notion of the couple is particularly problematic in infertile marriages, because in social structural terms, a husband and wife without children do not constitute a socially recognized, definable unit within Egyptian society. For their part, infertile husbands and wives realize that they are not "taken seriously" by other Egyptians, and they are usually also under intense family pressure, especially on the part of husbands' relatives, to realize their procreative potential.

Yet, despite all this, infertile marriages in Egypt are often quite successful, and are even more successful in many cases than fertile marriages with children. Why? A number of factors seem to be at work. For one, more and more marriages in Egypt, even among the urban and rural poor, seem to be evolving toward a "companion-ate" ideal, whereby marital partners look to each other for love, emotional intimacy, and companionship.[28] Despite the historical absence of the couple, scholars of Egypt have found historical precedents for companionate marriage in the country,[29] a pat-tern that appears to be intensifying over time. According to anthropologist Lila Abu-Lughod, even though the companionate marriage is probably a Western import—brought to Egypt during an early twentieth-century period of Western and Egyptian feminist reform—it is nonetheless endorsed today by both liberal secularists and Is-lamists in the country, the latter of whom are "framing an ideal of companionate marriage in Islamic terms."[30]

Given these multiple affirmations of companionship in marriage, even poor Egyptian couples today desire love, romance, intimacy, and friendship within mar-riage, an ideal to that which many of them aspire and are, in fact, able to achieve in their own marriages.[31] I would argue that the patriarchal connectivity that bonds Egyptian (and other Middle Eastern) family members together in intensely en-meshed relationships of loving commitment also carries over into the marital realm, where husbands and wives look to each other for demonstrations of love and sup-port in times of adversity.

Desires to be conjugally connected to one's marital partner are important in the context of marital infertility. Although some relationships, such as that of Moustafa and Hala, are torn asunder by infertility, the majority, it seems, experience an even more intense connection as a result of the childlessness. Why? On the one hand, couples without children come to know each other better and to appreciate each other for their virtues apart from parenting. Although parenting, in and of itself, may be very joyous and rewarding for couples everywhere, children are also a major responsibility for a husband and wife, who may focus more on the children than on each other. As I have argued in *Infertility and Patriarchy* but must reiterate here, feel-ings of conjugal connectivity may be *more likely* to emerge in the absence of chil-dren. Infertile couples are not distracted from their marital relationship by children. Infertile couples do not have to worry over childhood sicknesses and troubles in school. Infertile couples are not required to feed and economically support children in a country where most citizens face serious economic constraints. And infertile couples do not feel the diminished marital intimacy that comes from exhaustion and little ones in the bedroom. In short, children do not come between infertile partners, who instead look to each other for love, affection, and support. The actual improvements in marital intimacy that may occur among infertile couples who are "in this together" have also been reported in the United States, a society where com-panionate marriages are a widely held ideal.[32] However, the fact that such marital fortification may occur elsewhere, including in highly patriarchal societies such as Egypt, is an underappreciated reality that is only beginning to be reported from other parts of the world.[33]

In Egypt, not all men and women are able to connect with their infertile partners in this way, but I would venture the guess that most do. In both of my studies of infertility in Egypt, the vast majority of couples had achieved long-term, relatively stable marriages, and they openly professed their feelings of love and enduring marital commitment. In my first study of poor urban Egyptians, such marital success was not what I expected; it was, perhaps, one of the most important and surprising findings in *Infertility and Patriarchy*. In my second study of Egyptian elites, such love and acceptance was manifest in the sheer length of infertile marriages. To wit, 20 percent of couples in my 1996 study had been married less than five years; 45 percent had been married six to ten years; 22 percent had been married eleven to fifteen years; 11 percent had been married sixteen to twenty years; and 3 percent had been married over twenty years, with the longest marriage lasting twenty-eight years. Overall, the average length of marriage was nine and a half years, or nearly a decade.

Many women, including those who were themselves infertile and those with infertile husbands, told me that they had strong marriages to loving husbands. They considered their husbands to be their friends, whom they would never leave over infertility and whom they believed would never leave them either. One woman with a severely infertile husband told me,

> All of our life, we don't talk about this [infertility]. I love him very much. He's a very kind and nice man. Not just with me—with his family, my family, his friends. Children love him. I can't change all of this for children. Children won't make us better than this. You know, when I was young, I prayed and when my head was on the earth, I asked "God, give me a husband who believes in God, is a good Muslim, very kind, not nervous, and is steady," and he [her husband] is the first one I got to know after this asking, and so I agreed [to marriage.] My mother had many reasons to say, "Think! There are many different men." But I said, "No, I asked God, and He gave me this [one], and if I refuse, He will punish me." And it was a very good decision. I never regretted marrying my husband.

Another woman described how her infertile husband gave her the choice to leave him:

> I can never leave him. He is *gamil* [beautiful]—not in his face, that's not important. More important is the man who respects the woman. He told me, "You have the freedom, the choice," when he came back home from the doctor the first time. He said, "You are free to do whatever you like." But I told him, "If God will give me children, it will be from you."

This response was just as common among men with infertile wives. One woman described how she had encouraged her husband to divorce her:

> My husband *never* asks me to have a baby. So I asked him to divorce me and remarry, and he said, "It's all from God. If I divorce you, I may remarry and not have any. I love you so much—to take another woman to have a baby, no way!" For him, it's all from God. He never pushes me at all, to do IVF. *I* am

the one who wants babies! But, of course, he will become so glad to have babies, but it's all God's *rizq* [sustenance]. We can't force Him to give.

As seen in all of these statements, many women felt grateful to have religiously observant husbands who believe in God's will regarding procreative outcomes. Religiosity on the part of a husband is considered by many women to be one of the major guarantees of marital success and happiness. In addition, infertile women in successful marriages often thank God for husbands who are *asil*, or of "good character," and who can be relied upon to be kind, responsible, and steady marital partners. Furthermore, when infertile marriages are successful, they often are accompanied by explicit vows of marital commitment. As apparent in interviews with both women and men, infertile spouses sometimes offer to "free" the fertile partner through divorce and remarriage, only to be told that such a course of action will never be pursued. Such expressions of conjugal loyalty in the face of potential liberation appear to be quite common in Egypt, from the poorest to the most elite couples. In short, the overwhelming response among Egyptian couples who are faced with infertility and the possibility of permanent childlessness is a re-avowal of marital commitment and a forging of deeper love, affection, and intimacy.

I would argue that this response is particularly likely when male infertility is the acknowledged cause of a couple's childlessness. Why? For one, knowledge of their secret failing often serves to make infertile men more solicitous of their wives, largely because of the guilt that they feel over depriving their wives of children. Because of the gratitude and attentiveness of their infertile husbands, wives are often extremely satisfied in their marriages, despite the absence of children. As shown here, many women who find themselves in this situation are exceedingly protective of their husbands and of their husbands' secret, and they may pretend that the problem stems from them. This wifely willingness to accept the social blame is often quite impressive to their husbands, serving to further cement the marital relationship. Moreover, Egyptian women are socialized to be nurturant, compassionate caregivers and, if given the opportunity, they will play this role with their infertile husbands. When a man's infertility condition is intractable, some men take pity on their wives and encourage them to seek a divorce or offer to initiate a divorce in order to free them from the childless union. However, unlike men, who are known to leave their infertile wives over childlessness, very few wives of infertile husbands choose this route. Instead, they are often relieved and happily secure in their marriages to infertile men, and they are often *more* loving toward their husbands out of sympathy for their condition and the physical suffering that many men endure during treatment. In short, male infertility, ironically enough, may have a particularly salutary effect on Egyptian marriages, once peace is made with the diagnosis on the part of both partners.

Having said this, it is important to point out that such rosy connubial scenarios are never guaranteed. In both of my Egyptian infertility studies, some couples were experiencing significant marital duress, and, in at least a few cases, divorces had taken place or were about to ensue. In addition to Moustafa, two other infertile husbands in this study had already divorced previous wives. I met these men as they were about to embark upon ICSI with much younger "replacement" wives. Further-more, several women in my study who were themselves infertile knew that their marriages were unstable, for their husbands had become cold, distant, and openly angry about the excessive time and expenses surrounding treatment. In the case of my research assistant, who was told in the summer of 1996 that she would never be able to have children due to post-chemotherapy ovarian failure, her husband of nearly ten years cold-heartedly divorced her in September of that same year—mak-ing her seriously question what kind of lie she had been living for nearly a decade.

In addition, several wives of infertile men in this study, including Nadine, the movie star, were seriously considering whether they should divorce their husbands. Although male infertility is considered a significant ground for female-initiated di-vorce according to contemporary Islamic legal opinion in Egypt, a woman's initia-tion of divorce remains highly stigmatized. Thus, few Egyptian women consider this option unless their marriages are truly unbearable. However, for a handful of elite women in my study, being married to an infertile man had made them seriously consider whether they wished to remain with husbands who were unlikely to pro-vide them with children. In other words, for both men and women in Egypt, infertil-ity may provoke a crisis of commitment in which husbands and wives face difficult decisions regarding the future of their marriages. With the introduction of ICSI in Egypt, such crises of commitment are on the rise, for reasons to be explored now.

Marriage and Divorce in the Age of ICSI

In a conversation with Dr. Mohamed Yehia, the physician in charge of Moustafa and Shahira's case, we turned to the topic of marriage. Dr. Yehia quickly admitted that he tried "not to get involved" in his patients' marriages, as he had neither the time nor inclination to "open this topic" with them. Nonetheless, he told me that the clinical encounter with infertile couples was often quite telling. He said he could usually as-sess within minutes whether a marriage was in serious trouble. As he explained,

> Most of what we see now are male infertility cases, since ICSI came into being. The situation with male infertility has changed very much in the last few years. Now, it is absolutely known in all cases if there is a male factor, and this shifts the "balance of power" in the marriage in favor of the wife. She has two choices—to divorce him or to stay with him. Most choose to stay, but they may wield power over their husbands, because even when others "out-side" the marriage pester the wife and blame her, "inside" she knows that it is her husband. And this gives her some sense of relief and control.
>
> In fact, when it comes to blaming, I believe that women can be even cru-eler than men, but this might be an overreaction to all the blame they have received "outside" over the years. Some women, once they get to me, they are only too happy to say [to their husbands], "Ah-ha, the blame is on you after all!" Within about two minutes of meeting these couples, I can know exactly

who is to blame by the way they interact in front of me, and I try to neutralize this "blame game" that goes on. However, what I'm seeing now with ICSI patients is that men with male-factor infertility try to shift the blame back onto their wives. "Okay, my sperm fertilized the egg, and the reason you're not pregnant is that *your* womb failed to accept the embryo! So there must be something wrong with *you!*" I try to neutralize this by pointing out the *joint* nature of the whole process, but in some couples this doesn't work.

As suggested by Dr. Yehia, from the perspective of gender and marriage, ICSI has significantly complicated Egyptian gender politics and conjugal dynamics. Why? On the one hand, ICSI is a truly remarkable new "hope technology" for men—one that, according to my male informants, had given them "new hope," when all other "doors of hope" had been closed to them.[34] As a variant of IVF, ICSI allows men with seemingly intractable infertility problems to produce a child through a kind of "forced fertilization" with their own defective sperm. If successful, such a technology has the potential to effectively remasculinize these very emasculated men, especially in an Islamic cultural context where adoption, donor insemination, and resultant social fatherhood are strictly prohibited. However, ICSI also has the simultaneous potential to defeminize women, given that egg donation and surrogacy are also strictly prohibited in Egypt. As a variant of IVF, ICSI is highly reliant on the viability of a woman's ova. If a woman's ova do not respond to hormonal stimulation or fail to be fertilized through ICSI microscopic injection, then ICSI cannot succeed. In other words, ICSI is only as good as the function of a woman's reproductive body. Yet, as shown in Chapter 6, reproductive response in women begins to decrease dramatically with advancing age.

In fact, as demonstrated graphically in a recent, rather alarmist *Newsweek* cover story, "The Truth About Fertility: Why More Doctors Are Warning That Science Can't Beat the Biological Clock,"[35] fertility begins to decline in women by age thirty. By age forty, the decline is steep due to a still unknown combination of factors; these include lower quantity and quality of ova, which are more susceptible to genetic errors that can compromise the success of fertilization, as well as less hospitable uterine conditions as women reach the end of their reproductive life spans. Age forty, therefore, marks a key watershed, after which the statistical decline in fertility is quite precipitous. For this reason, women age forty and older may be turned away from IVF centers in the West, as well as in Egypt.[36] Yet, in Egypt, many couples only reach IVF centers at a time when they are already middle-aged. In fact, Egyptian IVF centers today are flooded with a backlog of older couples, now in their late thirties, forties, and even fifties, who have suffered from years of intractable male infertility and are now hoping to try ICSI, even though their chances of success are quite slim.

Unfortunately, ICSI has not created a revolution of hope for middle-aged women in these marriages. Many of these wives, who have stood by their infertile husbands for years, even decades in some cases, have grown too old to produce viable ova for the ICSI procedure. Because of the Sunni Islamic restrictions on ova donation, couples with a reproductively elderly wife face four difficult options: (1) to remain together permanently without children; (2) to foster an orphan, which, as we have seen in Chapter 4, is a frankly unpopular option in the context of Islamically prescribed adoption restrictions; (3) to partake in a polygynous union with a younger, more fertile co-wife, which is unacceptable to most Egyptian women today; or (4) to divorce outright so that the husband can remarry a younger woman. According to the IVF doctors who treat these middle-aged couples, more and more highly educated, upper-class Egyptian men are choosing the last option—believing that their own reproductive destinies may lie with younger "replacement" wives, who are allowed under Islam's personal status laws governing divorce and remarriage.

To take but one example, during the summer of 1996, the physicians at Nozha Hospital related a story to me about an extremely affluent but severely infertile Egyptian man whose first wife had undergone eight failed IVF trials at Nozha Hospital. When ICSI was introduced at Nozha Hospital in 1994, the aging wife was by this time a poor candidate for ICSI. Upon learning of ICSI, the husband promptly replaced his first wife with a younger one, who became pregnant with ICSI triplets on her first try. The doctors, who had recently verified the pregnancy by ultrasound, were heartened by the conception of triplets from the sperm of a severely infertile man. Yet, they lamented the circumstances of the first wife, whom they had come to know well as a result of her many IVF trials. They told me that they wished they could give one of the triplets to the first wife, out of sympathy for her plight. But, as one of them remarked in a moment of black humor, "She would probably kill it!" In short, the doctors themselves were clearly troubled by the potential marital consequences of ICSI, whereby some heartless men might decide to cast off their once-fertile wives of many years.

In fact, doctors themselves are placed in a fundamental predicament: namely, to go forward with a costly procedure in a middle-aged couple with little chance of success or to level with the couple by telling them that the wife's advanced reproductive age no longer makes *her* a good candidate for the procedure. As they realize, the cost of their honesty may be the breakup of long-term marriages, as husbands decide to try their reproductive luck with younger, potentially more fecund women. Among the doctors with whom I spoke in 1996, there was no consensus on the best course of action. Dr. Yehia, for one, believed in an "honest" approach. As he explained,

> We are doctors, and we have to say the truth, all right? We can't deprive the father from his chance, because we are faced with this same situation in women. Sometimes we have a young woman who is totally free [of infertility problems] and a husband who's having spermatids [immature sperm] only, and you have to tell the couple what are the real chances for her and for him. So, it's not fair to say "You don't have a chance." You have to say, "The wife is all right," and it's up to her to take the decision [to divorce] or not. In other words, the situation might be in the reverse, okay? So, why wouldn't you say the truth to the man, just because he's been married for fifteen years? I don't think this is fair. And actually, *actually*, they might fight for another reason and get divorced. You *never* know. You never know. But I can't really twist the

facts just because there *might* be social consequences. I always believe that you are a doctor. Your message or your duty is to help patients as much as you can, and you can't do that by hiding facts. Because *if* he knows ten years from now that he would have been able to [re]marry and have a child, then you have deprived him of his right. So I'm not here to make a social judgment. I'm here to help patients.

Dr. Salah Zaki, director of the IVF unit at Nile Badrawi Hospital, did not advocate this approach. Instead, he justified a "compassionate" approach:

It is not fair for a woman who has been married to an infertile man for twenty years, and who has suffered all the comments, to all of a sudden be divorced, or to even be faced by a co-wife now that ICSI is available. We are trying to make people happy by doing this—not unhappy! So I don't even mention the age factor when I consult with patients. And I don't tell them that their success rates would be higher if the woman were younger. Ashraf [Hakam, the laboratory director at Nile Badrawi] disagrees with me on this. But since I am the head of the unit, this is what we do. Because if I mention any of this, some husbands will definitely divorce or marry a second woman, and they'll use the excuse, "This was the doctor's orders." So I don't want to give them the chance of even thinking about it.

Although I told Dr. Zaki at the time of our interview that I agreed with his approach, I wonder, in retrospect, how successful it can be in a cultural context where news of scientific achievements travels quickly. As shown in Chapter 3, the Egyptian media have been a forceful presence in the world of test-tube baby making, letting the Egyptian public know about each new scientific innovation. Among the highly educated, literate patients who make up the clientele of Egyptian IVF centers, I suspect that most will quickly discover—be it from a doctor, other patients, the newspaper, or television—that a woman's age *does* matter in the realm of ICSI.

Indeed, by 1996, only two years after the introduction of ICSI to the country, most of the women in my study lamented their advancing ages and recognized this age factor as one of the most basic biological limitations on the success of both ICSI and IVF. This nervous discourse on aging was a striking feature of women's interviews, as they worried about their biological time-clocks running out in the era of ICSI. One forty-five-year-old woman, a patient who was being "compassionately" treated by Dr. Salah Zaki, lamented,

I've done IVF now six times, but there's no fertilization and no embryo development because the oocytes are not good quality, or sometimes they're not collected after induction. Psychologically, from the whole procedure, one after another, I feel psychologically desperate. I wish I had started earlier, so that my eggs will be more. I believe I should have been told to start earlier. I went to very good and famous doctors to give me the right directions, and still this didn't lead me to the right treatment. And now, my age can't be made up.

Just as infertile men worried about their sperm counts, aging women worried about their "egg counts" and the implications of "low counts" for IVF and ICSI. As one woman pined,

> The eggs they took out of me were few—only four, and only three fertilized. One was 100 percent, and the other two were so-so. With the *huge* amount of treatment, I have to give a huge amount of eggs. Some women have eleven to twelve eggs, but I had only a few. These treatments are supposed to give a large number of eggs, but, in my case, I'm forty years old, which is why there were so few.

That women are nervous about their advancing age is clear, especially as several of these women had been turned away on the basis of age from other IVF centers in Egypt and abroad. During the period of my study, I noted that both Nile Badrawi and Nozha Hospitals accepted women patients over the age of forty. However, Dr. Yehia said he advised most of these patients not to go forward with IVF or ICSI, based on the low percentage of success. His laboratory partner, Dr. Wafik, disagreed with him, believing that every woman should be given the right to try. As Dr. Yehia opined, "I weigh the success rates against the expense and the patients' feelings when they fail. I have to deal with the patients. All [Dr. Wafik] sees are the eggs."

Interestingly, none of the doctors who participated in my study, and only two of the women I interviewed, raised the issue of abnormalities in the offspring of older women. The two women who mentioned this concern had spent considerable time in England. There, physicians they had consulted had refused to do IVF, using the risk of Down syndrome as one of their justifications. One of these women, now a patient at Nile Badrawi, told me,

> I know without [Dr. Zaki] explaining to me. But I asked him this time if there is any risk for abnormalities in the child. He said, "There are tests we can do at the sixteenth week." This is the only thing that makes me a little worried—the risk of an abnormality in the child. This is the first time I asked Dr. Salah about abnormalities, and he said that if there is any problem, they will need to make an abortion.

Although therapeutic abortions are legal in Egypt (while other forms are not),[37] they are rarely practiced. Similarly, prenatal testing of any kind, and particularly the invasive forms of amniocentesis and chorionic villus sampling, are rarely carried out in Egypt. According to Dr. Yehia, such forms of testing can be performed at various specialty hospitals in Cairo; however, few Egyptian gynecologists condone such invasive interventions in an otherwise healthy, God-given pregnancy. Instead, pregnant women in urban areas may nowadays undergo numerous prenatal ultrasounds, by which fetal anomalies may be detected. However, the screening for anomalies, which has become such a routine part of maternity care in the United States,[38] is simply not part of the obstetric landscape in Egypt, a society that otherwise condones the use of high-tech obstetric and gynecological interventions.

The fact that highly educated, literate women in Egyptian IVF centers do *not* make the connection between Down syndrome and advancing maternal age, and thus do *not* desire prenatal testing, is quite telling. To me, this means that the "age-anomaly" connection has yet to be made in their minds; otherwise, they might worry about it and ask to be tested. Having said this, it is also important to point out that Egyptians, in general, display a greater degree of tolerance toward disability and difference than do most Westerners; thus, disabled people, like the frail elderly, are generally well cared for by family members in the home. In my studies of both poor and elite women in Egypt, I was told many times that it would be better to have a disabled child than to have no child at all. Thus, I would suspect that an "age-anomaly" connection, if made, will never decrease the desire among aging Egyptian women for IVF and ICSI offspring, even if a child who is mentally or physically "weak" is the product of this new technology.

Furthermore, just as most childless women in Egypt would rather be the mother of a disabled test-tube baby than to have no baby at all, most childless women would rather be the wife of an infertile man than to be a stigmatized divorcee. However, in the age of ICSI, remaining married to an infertile man is no longer a guarantee. With the advent of this newest new reproductive technology, the masculine hopes and technological dreams of at least some infertile men may lie elsewhere with younger replacement wives. Thus, the spread of this global technology to the local Egyptian cultural landscape has come at a potentially very high cost to *women,* for whom "aging out" of this newest technology may come as a cruel blow to their gender identities and to their marriages.

This is not to say that the use of ICSI in Egypt will inevitably lead to an exponential increase in male-initiated divorces. As of yet, there is no systematic evidence to prove such a trend. Quite likely, infertile men who cast off their aging wives will remain in the minority, with most men choosing to remain married. Why? One reason is that divorce is considered a difficult and serious affair in Egypt, both socially and economically. It is not a matter to be taken lightly, given the huge financial investments most families make in marrying off their children. As shown by Diane Singerman and Barbara Ibrahim in their essay "The Cost of Marriage in Egypt: A Hidden Variable in the New Arab Demography," in urban areas of Egypt, the average marriage costs are now LE 24,969 ($7,365), or almost six times GNP per capita.[39] In total, Egyptians spend over LE 13 billion annually on the costs of getting married, "a figure which dwarfs the figure for total economic aid to Egypt from the United States."[40] On an individual level, this high investment in marriage typically involves a major intergenerational transfer of wealth, larger in many cases than the inheritance following a parental death. It also has numerous secondary consequences, including male labor migration, second jobs for men, deployment of women to the labor force, and new "substitutes" for marriage, including once-stigmatized marriages of younger men to older (financially stable) women, as well as *urfi,* or customary, common-law marriages that are either secretive or unregistered.[41]

From the standpoint of couples who discover that they are infertile, the significant financial commitments that have been made in their marriages may serve to keep them together. For just as marriage is costly, so is divorce—making even hopelessly infertile couples think twice before they consider this option. Perhaps because divorce is so difficult in Egypt, the state has issued a new standard form of the marriage contract, put out by the Ministry of Justice in June 2000, which involves various "check-off options" that can be chosen by both bride and groom.[42] One of the provisions of this contract is that both parties must declare that they have no "serious diseases," including those that may impede their fertility.[43] Accordingly, the new provision has led to "more pre-marital testing of women and men for HIV, sterility, etc."[44]

On the one hand, this new marriage contract has the potential to curb the pain of childless marriages, particularly for women, who can find out well in advance that a potential groom is infertile or suffering from a sterilizing STD. On the other hand, premarital testing of this sort may lead to the stigmatizing rejection of many Egyptians, both men and women, as potential marriage partners. Particularly for infertile men, whose infertility problems are often diagnostically detectable but therapeutically intractable, this new legislation may come as a very mixed blessing.

In addition, women who find themselves married to an infertile man may now divorce them more easily as a result of the new marriage contract. Previously, a Muslim woman in Egypt did not have access to divorce without proving through a court that her husband had wronged her, including by preventing her from childbearing. However, with the new marriage contract, a woman may check off an option allowing her to maintain the right to divorce without showing cause (i.e., known locally as keeping the right to divorce "in the bride's hand").[45] Whether more and more Egyptian women will, in fact, seek out divorces, including from their infertile husbands, is not yet clear.

Judging from my own research over two decades, these cases of female-initiated divorce in the context of male infertility may remain relatively rare for two reasons. First, female initiation of a divorce, even for just cause, may remain stigmatized—a sign of "bad faith" in a wife, particularly in one who considers herself to be religious and accepting of God's will. Second, divorce simply does not make sense when a woman truly loves her marital partner, even if he is infertile. As was shown in this chapter, conjugal love is often a prominent feature of childless marriages. Thus, the fact that most infertile marriages, both rich and poor, do *not* break up in Egypt is a reflection of two phenomena: the many social and economic disincentives to divorce operating in Egyptian society *and* the conjugal connections among most childless couples, who experience deep bonds of love and commitment.

Conclusion

Thus, even in the age of ICSI, most childless Egyptian marriages will probably go on, with or without the birth of a test-tube baby. The fact that infertile Egyptian marriages are often deeply connected is supportive of Western research on this subject. In *Healing the Infertile Family: Strengthening Your Relationship in the Search for*

Parenthood, medical anthropologist Gay Becker shows how many infertile American couples, despite initial periods of "identity crisis" and feelings of failure, eventually "work together" to achieve resolution, be it through use of technologies, the pursuit of adoption, or acceptance of childlessness. In the process, many relationships become strengthened, much in keeping with my Egyptian findings. Similarly, medical sociologist Larry Greil, in *Not Yet Pregnant: Infertile Couples in Contemporary America,* shows how initial periods of "marital tension" often resolve as couples are "pulled together" through the experience of confronting crisis. However, Greil and his colleagues also note the fundamental ways in which gender shapes the experience of infertility in American society:

> For the wives, infertility presented itself as an intolerable, identity-threatening situation, and they were willing to do whatever it took to get out. The husbands saw infertility as an unfortunate event that was to be put in perspective and then ignored. For the wives, the basic problem was the inability to have children and to be a mother, and the solution was treatment. For the husbands, the problem was that their wives were unhappy and that home life wasn't as enjoyable as it used to be; the solution was to achieve stability *either* by pursuing treatment to a successful solution *or* by terminating treatment and moving on to other things.[46]

According to Greil and his colleagues, such "his and her" responses to infertility may stem from the fact that "[t]he expectation to be a father is not as important a part of male identity as the expectation to be a mother is of female identity. . . . [Thus] few husbands spoke in terms that would lead us to believe they experienced infertility as a role failure."[47]

Such gender responses to infertility, I would argue, are not culturally invariant. Although American men may experience infertility as a transient disappointment—as something to be "ignored" or solved by "moving on to other things"—Middle Eastern men, including Egyptian men, are unlikely to respond to marital infertility in this way. Instead, under the particular patriarchal cultural systems in place in most Middle Eastern countries, hegemonic masculinities essentially demand proof of male virility (qua potency) and male fertility (qua paternity). Hence, infertility, especially that stemming from a husband, performs a sort of "double emasculation," as it strips a man of both his masculinity *and* his patriarchal power. Given that male infertility is nothing short of an identity disaster for men in this region of the world, it is likely to engender alternate gender responses not found in the American setting.

As shown in this chapter, Egyptian men's response to this identity crisis can take many forms. It may lead to profound denial, avoidance of all forms of diagnosis and treatment, and overt or covert wife-blaming. It may lead to acceptance of childlessness as a manifestation of God's will and resultant fortification of the marital relationship. It may lead to relentless treatment quests, including resort to new reproductive technologies. And, in the age of ICSI, it may lead men to "move onto other things"—in this case, to younger fecund wives.

Clearly, then, ICSI is a very mixed blessing in Egypt, given the restrictions on all forms of third-party donation. On the one hand, ICSI represents a revolution in the treatment of infertile Egyptian men, who *need* a child to "prove their manhood." On the other hand, ICSI may be a catastrophe for aging wives, who also *need* a child to satisfy their "maternal instinct" and to save their marriages. Whereas ICSI may facilitate male fertility in a society where virility/fertility are the essence of hegemonic masculinity, it may do so at the expense of women, including the once healthy fertile ones, whose increasing age has worked against them. In short, ICSI has introduced a sad new twist to Egyptian gender and marital politics—one that was probably not anticipated when this technology was introduced in Belgium in the early 1990s and then spread around the globe.

In short, in the age of ICSI, such gender responses may serve as a profound arena of constraint in terms of *who* ultimately benefits from these technologies. Whereas severely infertile Egyptian men such as Moustafa have reaped the fruits of globalization in the form of their ICSI offspring, their "old" wives may pay a heavy price for a technology explicitly designed to promote biological paternity in the severely infertile male. Thus, reproductive technologies themselves are highly gendered, acting upon preexisting local gender systems in ways that may be both surprising and unanticipated. In the local Egyptian cultural setting, the technology that has brought high hopes to infertile men has also brought profound disruption and despair to the lives of some women. Thus, ICSI is both blessing and curse, the salvation of masculinity for some and the destruction of femininity for others. In neither case is this technology neutral, nor can it ever be.

CHAPTER 9

Stigma

The Woman with the Secrets

Maisa, now thirty-nine, and her husband, Ahmed, forty-six, have been married but involuntarily childless for seventeen years. During that period of time, their "search for children" has led them down paths of pain, suffering, sorrow—as well as stigma, secrecy, and surgical malpractice—as reported to me by Maisa one early afternoon in the Nile Badrawi IVF clinic.

Maisa now suffers from blocked fallopian tubes, following an unnecessary and iatrogenic operation on her ovaries called a "wedge-resection." Maisa recalls, "Eleven months after marriage, I did a small operation. There was a cyst and adhesions on my ovaries. They didn't try to remove them; I took cortisone injections in the uterus." But when this medically useless therapy failed to make Maisa pregnant, she underwent a "big operation," in which they "opened above the fallopians." This wedge-resection—an invasive surgery that is deemed ineffective and even dangerous by most Western infertility specialists—"was a big mistake," Maisa explained. "[Afterward] many famous doctors told me I shouldn't have done this operation above the tubes, because it closed them. And they told me it is not necessary to remove this [cyst]." When I asked Maisa why the physician would have undertaken such a harmful surgery, she stated, "He has no conscience. [The other doctors] told me he has no conscience and he did it wrong, and they can give me a letter for the [Egyptian] Physician's Syndicate to complain, because he shouldn't have done what he did."

While a hysterosalpingogram (x-ray with dye of the uterus and fallopian tubes) prior to the operation showed that Maisa's fallopian tubes were "very okay," all x-rays and diagnostic laparoscopies undertaken since that time sixteen years ago have shown that both her tubes are now permanently obstructed. Ahmed, for his part, has both poor sperm count and motility, as well as evidence of a prostate infection. He, too, underwent his own share of surgical misery—namely, two unnecessary varicocelectomies (one on the right testicle in 1984, and one on the left in 1992), which, not surprisingly, were unsuccessful in improving his semen profile.

In 1989, Maisa and Ahmed visited the first and what was then the only Egyptian IVF center to inquire about making a test-tube baby. But, as Maisa explained, Ahmed flatly refused to become a patient at the clinic once he heard how IVF was performed. "He was afraid that there may be mixing of sperm," she said. "From the religious side, he didn't want to make IVF, because at any stage, with the steps they're taking [outside of the body], there may be mistakes and mixing."

However, Maisa was remarkably fortunate when one of her physician relatives became involved in the opening of a second IVF Center in Cairo's Nile Badrawi Hospital. Because he was her relative, she felt very confident in him.

> It's very important to trust your doctor. For us, because he's my relative, I know that he's very religious. We see here that everything is done very perfectly and accurately. The tubes for the samples, the names are written on them and there is no chance for mistakes.

Furthermore, Maisa's pharmacist brother proved to Ahmed that IVF is *hallal,* or religiously permitted, by finding him the necessary *fatwas* from Cairo's religious university Al-Azhar, as well as from a *fatwa*-issuing center in Saudi Arabia.

However, Maisa's "enlightened" pharmacist brother and her physician cousin are the *only* members of her family who know that Maisa and Ahmed are undertaking ICSI. On his side, no one knows. Like the vast majority of couples in Egyptian IVF centers, Maisa and Ahmed fear the stigmatization and *kalam* (gossip) that would ensue if they revealed their status as IVF/ICSI patients. Thus, they feel the need to remain secretive, hiding this information from even their closest family members.

> On the subject of IVF, from the beginning, it was a secret—in my family and his family. This is between me and my husband *only.* But, when [Ahmed] objected to making IVF, I had to involve my brother. He is a pharmacist, and he convinced him.

Fortunately for Maisa, she succeeded in becoming pregnant with ICSI during her second treatment cycle. When she learned that she was pregnant, she and Ahmed decided, at first, to reveal the pregnancy only to her mother and sisters. Then, after a month and a half as they began to feel more confident about the success of this much-cherished first pregnancy, they began to tell others that she was pregnant—although *never* did they reveal the test-tube nature of the conception.

Still, Maisa worried that her good news, pregnancy after so many years of childlessness, might be the subject of another infertile woman's envy, and so she was careful about disclosing her pregnancy. Despite her caution, Maisa believes that she *was* envied by another infertile woman, because soon after they began sharing their happiness with the world, she began bleeding. Ultrasound scans of her uterus at the end of her first trimester showed that the fetus had stopped growing, and she ultimately lost her one and only pregnancy after seventeen years of intractable infertility. This she could only describe as a "very bad, terrible shock."

As she now prepares for her third ICSI trial, Maisa vows that she will tell *no one* this time if and when she becomes pregnant. Instead, she will suffer through ICSI and the potential difficulties of an ensuing ICSI pregnancy in silence. Yet, her need for psychological support is clear. She describes the process of test-tube baby making as "*very, very, very* difficult," adding that from the moment she began treatment until the time her first pregnancy ended, she was "very nervous; I can't express it, I was crying and nervous, and prayed all day to God so that he'll be generous with me." This time, she joked with the doctors that she wished there was a way of undergoing the ICSI procedure "by remote control" in order to ease her suffering.

Thus, Maisa's story bears witness to the ongoing stigma, secrecy, and profound human suffering accompanying the use of the newest new reproductive technology in Egypt, a society that has yet to come to terms with the test-tube baby making in its midst. Although infertile Egyptian couples such as Maisa and Ahmed may be forced to choose these rapidly globalizing new reproductive technologies as their only hope of overcoming stigmatizing childlessness, this "choice" comes at great personal costs to patients themselves, whose secret participation in a high-stakes game of high-tech baby making bespeaks the moral opprobrium and social disapproval still attached to this technology.

The "Top Secret" Stigma

Why do IVF-seeking infertile couples such as Maisa and Ahmed feel the need for privacy, even absolute secrecy in some cases? As I will argue here, IVF in Egypt performs a kind of "double stigmatization," whereby the very treatment designed to overcome an already stigmatizing health condition leads to an additional layer of stigma, secrecy, and suffering. Or, to use the words of the medical sociologist Arthur Greil,[1] the already "secret stigma" of infertility, and especially male infertility, is intensified into a "top secret stigma" by virtue of participation in the morally ambivalent, even disreputable world of test-tube baby making. To understand the dual stigmatization of infertility *and* the new technologies to overcome it, we must begin by interrogating the nature of stigma itself and how it inheres in both the social condition of childlessness and the utilization of new reproductive technologies in Egyptian society.

What is stigma? Sociologist Erving Goffman attempted to describe it in his seminal work *Stigma: Notes on the Management of Spoiled Identity*. According to Goffman, a stigma is

> an attribute that makes [her] different from others in the category of persons available for [her] to be, and of a less desirable kind—in the extreme, a person who is quite thoroughly bad, or dangerous, or weak. [She] is thus reduced in our minds from a whole and usual person to a tainted, discounted one. Such an attribute is a stigma, especially when its discrediting effect is very extensive.[2]

Even in the United States, where adult identity is less tied to parenthood than in other pronatalist societies around the world, the stigma of infertility has been described in some detail by a number of ethnographic researchers. For example, in their study of twenty-five infertile women in south Florida, anthropologists Linda Whiteford and Lois Gonzalez describe the "lived experience of infertility [as] one of stigmatization, isolation and alienation."[3] American women who are infertile "feel as though they have broken some accepted, if unspoken, cultural rule and they pay for it by being classified as 'other.' . . . Women who have children, they say, are understood and accepted; women without children are neither."[4] Similarly, in Arthur Greil's study of twenty-two infertile couples in upstate New York,[5] he describes the "secret stigma" of infertility for American women, who may appear normal but for whom infertility becomes an agonizing "master status." In Greil's study, such stigmatization, involving feelings of spoiled identity and unsatisfactory interactions with others due to stigma and fertile people's "insensitivity," is experienced more intensely by women than by men. However, other studies in the United States have also demonstrated the profound stigmatization of male infertility, both in terms of public attitudes toward this condition,[6] as well as in the stigma felt by American men who are deemed infertile. For example, in an article provocatively titled "The End of the Line: Infertile Men's Experiences of Being Unable to Produce a Child," Russell Webb and Judith Daniluk note that men's sense of personal inadequacy constituted a major theme during interviews about their infertility. According to the authors, "The participants used words and phrases like *failure, useless, a dud, inadequate, not a real man, garbage, loser,* and *defective* in reference to their self-perceptions as infertile men—men who were unable to 'give their wife a child.'"[7]

In Egypt, such feelings of spoiled identity among both men and women of all social classes are an almost inevitable part of the infertility experience. Infertile women describe themselves, and are described by others, as "missing" motherhood, and are even called *Umm Il-Ghayyib,* "Mother of the Missing One," as a reminder of their infertile status.[8] Similarly, infertile men often deem themselves to be "weak" and ineffective and may be deemed less masculine by others if their infertility becomes known. However, in Egypt, there is a crucial gender difference between what Scambler has called "felt" versus "enacted" stigma.[9] Felt stigma involves the internalization of the societal evaluation of their condition on the part of the stigmatized, and their resultant sense that they have failed to live up to the standards of normality. In Egypt, both men and women who are infertile feel their stigma in this way, although infertile women, who lack the visible signs of pregnancy, certainly experience these feelings more intensely.

However, enacted stigma, or the stigma that stems from intentional discrimination against the stigmatized, is experienced almost exclusively by women in Egypt. Although infertile men may *feel* diminished and emasculated, they are rarely *discriminated against* by other Egyptians. Why? First and most important, infertile men are typically able to keep their infertility a secret, through their own denial and dissimulation, as well as through the active collusion of wives who, as seen in the last chapter, protect their infertile husbands by accepting the blame for the infertility. Thus, in Egypt, few men publicly reveal their reproductive failing, and most allow their wives to assume the blame, in either a direct or de facto fashion.

Second, infertile men rarely feel under marital threat; that is, they do not live in fear that their wives will become frustrated over their infertility and divorce them. As seen in the last chapter, women married to infertile men rarely seek divorce, given the legal and financial difficulties as well as social prohibitions against female initiation of a marital break-up. Furthermore, in-laws of an infertile man are often sympathetic if they know of his condition, and encourage their daughter to stay with her husband and seek treatment. Thus, when men are infertile, families typically do not interfere, either because male infertility has been kept secret from them or because they do not want to be party to a stigmatizing, female-initiated divorce.

Finally, men who are infertile are rarely reminded or taunted by others about their diminished manhood, since such comments would be deemed profoundly insulting and insensitive. Although men may be unkind to each other in other ways, they rarely "attack" each other directly on this point. According to Egyptian women, fertility and fatherhood are simply seen as less central to a man's adult identity, since virtually all men have other outlets, including work, male peer groups, religious affiliations, sports, games, hobbies, and patronage at favorite cafes. Stay-at-home fathers are rare, and are there by necessity rather than by choice (e.g., because of unemployment or medical disability). In short, Egyptian men are simply freer from the kind of "fertility scrutiny" that is part and parcel of every Egyptian woman's life, especially after she marries and is expected to become pregnant.

As a result, even if an Egyptian man is hopelessly infertile, it is usually his fertile wife who is "reminded" of her childlessness by other women. Childless Egyptian women may be powerfully discriminated against by fertile others—particularly female in-laws, who are on the "lookout" for pregnancy and who may pressure a childless daughter-in-law to seek treatment. In addition, women in the community may be extremely unkind to infertile women; they may "remind" infertile women, in both subtle and direct ways, of their difference. Perhaps most cruelly, they may attempt to hide their children from the infertile, even pulling youngsters off the street as an infertile woman passes by. Such hiding is justified by cultural concerns surrounding *hasad,* or envy—the belief that an infertile woman is uncontrollably envious and may therefore cast the "evil eye," causing childhood illness or even death. As shown in Maisa's story, beliefs in infertile women's uncontrollable envy are found among all social classes and are even internalized by infertile women themselves, who sometimes attempt to avoid situations and celebrations where children are present. Not only do they realize that their presence may make others profoundly uncomfortable, but they also wish to avoid undue blame if a misfortune should occur. These fears that infertile women "spoil" other women's pregnancies or cause children to fall ill may lead, in fact, to community ostracism, including infertile women's self-imposed retreat from community life. As one upper-middle-class woman described her situation,

If a woman has children, I say, "Very good, lovely." But I can tell that the mother is very afraid of *hasad.* Sometimes I feel this. I myself may not like her children very much, but I know that a mother wants compliments, to make her happy. But, with me, I feel the reverse—"Oh, her eyes!" What can I do? So I decided to just stay away.

Among the educated elites whom I met in Egyptian IVF centers, such enacted stigma in the form of frank social discrimination against infertile women is often less pronounced than among women from the lower social classes. Nonetheless, as seen here and in Maisa's case, stigma, both felt and enacted, persists to some degree even among elites, making infertile women and their husbands seem different from and less than others within their social milieus. As one infertile woman, herself a highly educated tour guide, explained,

> Some Egyptians, because you can't have a baby, have a very, very bad idea about you. People look to you and say, "Ma'alish" or "haram."[10] You are different. And it's a shame, even if it's from [both] you and your husband, all the time people ask you [the woman] "Why not? I have a good doctor." They're asking you all the time about why you're not pregnant.

How do infertile Egyptian elites attempt to resist this stigmatization? Many couples in my study described how they attempted to shield themselves from interference and negative scrutiny by invoking their rights to privacy in a culture where privacy is not inherently valued. I was told many times by both women and men that infertility is a "private" or "personal" matter, which does not need to be shared with others, even the closest family members and friends. Thus, to avoid the kind of pestering and interference described by the infertile tour guide, many couples in this study told me how they politely dissembled, often telling others, "Both of us are all right, and this is up to God." Such responses, they noted, were often effective in stopping further prying.

That infertile Egyptian elites are able to "shut down" invasions of privacy in this manner is quite remarkable, given that Egyptians are known for their high levels of involvement in each others' lives. Yet, highly educated Egyptian elites now exist in a social milieu characterized by separate residences apart from family and snooping neighbors, in which they are sensitive to each others' right to privacy, including the desire to establish and maintain private lives that are relatively free from family or community interference. Although their childlessness is highly visible in a society where voluntary childlessness, or even waiting after marriage to conceive, is socially unacceptable, Egyptian elites are able to make their infertility problems much less visible by remaining secretive. Although friends and family may know that they are "visiting doctors" or "taking medicines," few infertile couples in this social class readily reveal the details of their infertility problems or their treatment quests, even to their closest family members and friends. By doing so, elite infertile Egyptian couples attempt to destigmatize themselves by shrouding their own infertility in mystery, keeping the details of their childlessness and its treatment from public view. Infertility thus becomes a "secret stigma"[11]—still stigmatized by virtue of the obvious childlessness, but purposely mystified by those suffering from this affliction.

When an infertile Egyptian couple walks through the door of an IVF center, however, the nature of their stigmatization changes. The use of IVF or its variant ICSI powerfully intensifies the stigmatization of infertility, placing a "double stigma" upon the IVF-seeking Egyptian couple. In fact, in Egypt, IVF is so deeply discrediting to those who must use it that it effectively forces couples like Maisa and Ahmed to "go underground" in order to hide their treatment attempts from others. Such clandestine behavior reflects the magnitude of the stigmatization of IVF, in a world where this "top secret stigma" is surrounded by shame, paranoia, fear, dishonesty, and elaborate cover-ups.

That IVF treatment-seeking *itself* may represent a powerful source of stigma has yet to be reported from other cultures. On the contrary, in other non-Western places such as China, IVF may be highly touted by its users as an emblem of "modernity" and as a route to the creation of morally and physically "superior" babies.[12] That use of IVF may actually represent a source of *pride* in other cultural settings bespeaks the very heterogeneity of local responses to this globalizing technology and the need to interrogate the introduction of IVF and its variants in disparate global sites.

In Egypt, however, IVF engenders shame in a society where ʿayb, or shame, devolves upon those who have done something morally questionable. It is important to point out that infertility itself is not inherently shameful, as it is a nonvolitional status over which the infertile individual has little control. Although infertility may affect a person's *karama*—namely, their "pride" or "dignity"—infertile individuals have "done nothing wrong" to bring this unfortunate status upon themselves. When infertile Egyptians seek IVF, however, they open themselves up to accusations of shame and dishonor in a society where honor itself is highly valorized. Indeed, the stigmatization surrounding IVF is intimately tied to the shame inherent in the very real possibility of morally illicit third-party donation.

The fact that IVF in Egypt is now morally loaded with stigma and shame has led to some interesting and paradoxical results. On the one hand, Egypt has literally led the Arab world in the introduction and implementation of new reproductive technologies, both medically and religiously speaking. Yet, ironically, test-tube baby making in Egypt remains invisible to a large degree. Although most Egyptians realize that IVF centers are present in their own country, few have ever seen a test-tube baby or met a couple who has admitted to conceiving one. For most Egyptians who have no personal experience with infertility, IVF remains surreal—the stuff of fast-breaking news reports or phantasmic, made-for-TV mini-series.

For those who *do* have experience with infertility, however, the often reluctant resort to IVF or ICSI is kept strictly under wraps. Discourses of secrecy—and the actual instantiation of secrecy through practices designed to ensure it—are, in fact, one of the most striking features of Egyptian test-tube baby making today. On the level of discourse, IVF-seeking Egyptian couples are adamant about the need for secrecy and have numerous rationales for why they invoke it in their own lives. Perhaps the most powerful rationale, and the one cited most frequently by couples themselves, has to do with the troubling moral issues described in Chapter 4—namely, infertile couples' acute awareness that most Egyptians view IVF as a morally questionable, even repugnant technology. Ongoing public uncertainty over the moral legitimacy of this practice has put it beyond the pale of social acceptability. The effect has been both frustrating and devastating for infertile couples. Although they realize that they are doing "nothing wrong" according to the dictates of their religion, they cannot admit that they are participating in IVF or ICSI trials for fear of becoming morally disreputable and even ostracized within their own communities. As one woman, who had gone directly to Al-Azhar to convince herself of the religious permissibility of IVF, explained,

> From one generation to another, people will eventually change their mind about this kind of treatment. But, now, it's a new subject, and it leads to misunderstanding. Knowing that there may be a mixture of sperm or eggs makes people very worried. So this gives them bad ideas about this kind of treatment.

Given the moral opprobrium attached to IVF in Egypt, infertile IVF-seekers hope to avoid others' *kalam,* or gossip. As most Egyptians will readily admit, Egyptians are great gossipers, who enjoy the chance to become involved in other people's business and to provide social and moral commentary. Many infertile IVF-seekers consider the revelation of test-tube baby making to be extraordinary fodder for gossip and moral scrutiny, and they fear becoming a "big story" within their families and communities. As one woman explained, "Maybe one of my colleagues will think it's not through the 'right way'—maybe it's not from the wife or the husband. It's likely that people will say that. And here in Egypt, women talk and talk and talk. It *must* become a story!"

The desire to avoid untoward gossip is also tied to another desire: namely, the desire not to be viewed as a pathetic and desperate infertile person. As I was told several times, no one in Egypt likes to be thought of as sick or pitiful—or, as one man put it, "Everyone wants to believe he is in 'good shape.'" This is probably why those with grave illnesses (e.g., cancer) deny that they are sick, or are never even told so by their Egyptian physicians. Infertility is considered a serious, if not life-threatening, health condition; among those who are sympathetic, it may evoke feelings of pity. However, if an infertile woman were to admit that she had used IVF, she would be considered by others to be truly desperate. As one woman commented, "I don't want people to feel sorry for me, and say '*Miskina*' [i.e., 'You poor, miserable woman']! There is a lot of 'talk' here in Egypt. Here, we have 60 million, all [of them] having babies! So people like me can become the subject of gossip."

It is also believed by many infertile IVF-seekers that revealing an IVF trial will cause those who care about them to "worry and wait." This was one of the major reasons why many infertile couples had not told family members about their IVF or ICSI trials. One woman, who had told only her closest physician friend, described her decision as follows: "My husband, and my friend and I, we're the 'Three Musketeers!' No one knows except us. Because if you tell people, then they get worried and come. It's the Egyptian way. If we told our families, everyone would be worried, and they would spend every second phoning."

Similarly, some women and their husbands were concerned that if they tried IVF or ICSI, but failed to achieve a pregnancy, their family and friends would also experience the profound disappointment that comes with a failed trial. Many women did not want to put their family members, and particularly their aging parents, through this, and so chose not to reveal their IVF or ICSI attempts until after a pregnancy was well established. However, as seen in Maisa's case, even established IVF or ICSI pregnancies sometimes result in miscarriage, causing a profound shock and disappointment for the couple and their family members. For this reason, many couples who do succeed wait for several months to disclose the news of a pregnancy, given the belief that widespread knowledge may "ruin one's success." One husband explained it in this way,

> In general, before you do it, it must be confidential. And then if it succeeds, then you can tell people. So, this time [i.e., this IVF trial], it's just me and her. Not even in her family, because her mother is very worried about her. If it works, we'll tell them, but not now, so that no one is waiting and worrying and disappointed if it doesn't work.

This belief about carefully guarding one's plans and successes is clearly related to cultural notions of envy. For example, according to Maisa, the reason she miscarried her ICSI pregnancy was that she had disclosed it to too many people, thereby eliciting the envy of another infertile woman. Ironically enough, infertile women, who know that they are considered envious by others, are nonetheless extremely concerned about not attracting the envy of other infertile women. Thus, they worry and fret about envy, given that they come into contact with so many other infertile women during the course an IVF or ICSI trial.

This fear of others' envy was a major source of discussion during interviews, and it was a topic that caught me off guard, as I was not expecting to find such prominent beliefs in the power of *hasad* among my mostly upper-middle-class and upper-class infertile informants. Yet, elite patients in Egyptian IVF clinics revealed the importance of this belief in contemporary Egypt, as well as the justification it receives within the Islamic scriptures. Most women in this study were loath to tell others about their IVF or ICSI pregnancies for fear of attracting envy. Thus, only one woman planned to reveal the ICSI nature of her conception if she did become pregnant—in this case, to protect her pregnancy from the ill effects of *hasad* by disclosing the details of her suffering to other potentially envious infertile women. As she explained,

> I didn't tell anybody so far. It's better. We said we have to keep it secret. But if it succeeds, they'll know. When they know I'm pregnant, I'll tell them I did ICSI. "It's very expensive! Listen! I did many trials, spent a lot of money, my platelets were low. Really! This is the truth. I'm not exaggerating." I'll tell them this to prevent the evil eye, because envy is in the Qur'an. Our prophet said, "If you want your things to succeed, don't talk about them. Keep for yourself." The eye is very sharp!

That an infertile woman might feel envious over another infertile woman's coveted pregnancy—effectively pitting one infertile woman against another out of jealousy—is one of the sad consequences of infertility the world over, according to Dr. Mohamed Yehia. As he opined,

> Hasad is everywhere. I think it's all over the world. Infertile patients are a very "closed circle." And these circles, once you go out of them, you really don't want to be in them again. So maybe you speak about your experiences after delivery, but not during, because it's *very* personal and *very* stigmatized, and it's the same way everywhere.

Whether fears of envy are, in fact, everywhere, as Dr. Yehia argues, is an open question; this issue has yet to be reported in the growing social science literature on global infertility.[13] However, it is clear that in Egypt, fears of envy, immorality, and the many other rationales for secrecy described here keep the vast majority of infertile Egyptian couples from revealing their test-tube baby making trials, tribulations, and even successes to the world beyond the clinic walls. The result is that IVF is hidden from public view in Egypt.

Furthermore, Egyptian IVF patients behave in secretive ways that are sometimes perplexing and aggravating to the doctors who treat them. To take but a few examples, when I first met with the three founding members of the Egyptian IVF-ET Center, the oldest IVF clinic in Cairo, I was told immediately that IVF "is still very sensitive" in Egypt. When a journalist from the monthly English-language news magazine *Egypt Today* initially tried to interview patients in this clinic, she could find no one willing to talk "on the record" or to have a photograph taken.[14] Eventually, the story was published, but most of the interviews and photographs featured Egyptian IVF providers rather than patients themselves. In fact, in this clinic, the bulletin board designed to showcase the photographs of IVF babies was filled with photos of staff members' children, given that few formerly infertile couples wanted their own identities or that of their IVF offspring to be revealed. Similarly, when one of the center's directors had the idea to have a party for all of the IVF babies created there, only about 20 percent of the families contacted actually participated. He also explained how most of the clinic's patients removed the name of the center from their prescriptions and other treatment records; being linked to an IVF clinic was simply too shameful for patients when they submitted their prescriptions to pharmacists or used treatment records to be excused from work.

Across town at Nozha Hospital, Dr. Yehia also lamented the fact that about 25 percent of his patients were "lost to follow-up," never returning after an IVF or ICSI trial, even for a pregnancy test. He suspected that as many as one quarter of these cases involved successful pregnancies. But, he added, "This will never be known, and it serves to decrease the success rate of the center." When I asked Dr. Yehia why patients who became pregnant would not reveal their happy news to him, he explained,

> These patients are the ones who, if they get pregnant, just want to "forget about the whole experience." And they're also the ones who desire secrecy,

which I believe is a "cultural issue" not found in the States. For example, I had one patient who did not return after the cycle until three months later, when she was pregnant with a threatened abortion. I asked her, "Why didn't you come back, or even phone me to tell me you were pregnant?" She admitted she'd been to a number of other gynecologists for bleeding during the pregnancy, but she did not admit to them that it was through ICSI. Now she is "sticking" to me and doing fine.

This kind of thing makes me very angry, because it is at least common courtesy to make a phone call and say you're pregnant, even if you never return to the center. These patients who never return but do have babies may, two or three years down the road, tell others to go to the center, after they've had a period of "denial." For example, the person who referred a Kuwaiti couple to me was one lost to follow-up. But she, in fact, had twins that I didn't know about.

That patients who are successful with IVF sometimes refer other infertile couples to the same IVF clinic is a phenomenon that is increasing, according to Dr. Yehia. However, at the time of my final interview with him in August 1996, he speculated that as many as 90 percent of those couples coming to his center never disclosed their participation in test-tube baby making to any others, beyond perhaps a small, intimate circle of family and friends. Indeed, Dr. Yehia described a few cases in which he was instructed by infertile siblings, both being treated at his clinic, *not* to reveal their attendance there to the other sibling. This made for some dizzying attempts on the part of clinic staff to keep both siblings from being scheduled for procedures at the same time.

Dilemmas of Disclosure

The perceived need for secrecy on the part of Egyptian IVF patients leads to what might best be described as "dilemmas of disclosure." "To tell or not to tell" is the main question, and beyond that, to tell *whom* and under what circumstances. In the growing literature on new reproductive technologies in the West, disclosure dilemmas have attracted recent attention.[15] However, in the West, these dilemmas seem to revolve exclusively around the use of donor gametes, and whether friends, family, and the children themselves should be privy to couples' decisions to use donor insemination (DI) in particular. As shown most powerfully through the ethnographic work of Gay Becker and her colleagues,[16] many Americans are still extremely uncomfortable with the social and moral implications of DI, despite its use as a treatment for male infertility for nearly half a century. As a result, disclosure of DI on the part of an infertile couple is potentially very stigmatizing, with far-reaching implications for the welfare of the DI child. Ultimately, couples in the United States who have used DI are forced to make difficult decisions about honesty versus secrecy, and they are often ambivalent and uncertain that they have made the right decision.[17]

In Egypt, where all forms of third-party donation are strictly prohibited, disclosure dilemmas are nonetheless tied indirectly to the issue of donation. Despite the fact that third-party donation is presumably not practiced in Egypt, the Egyptian public believes that donation occurs—either intentionally by unscrupulous physicians and their desperate patients or through careless accidents that happen in IVF laboratories. This belief in the likelihood of donation taking place on Egyptian soil has, in effect, tainted the reputation of this technology and those who would seek to use it.

For their part, Egyptian IVF patients know this, and they often refer to the widespread misunderstandings of this technology on the part of the Egyptian public. Although Egyptian IVF patients often lament the "mentality" of the Egyptian masses regarding IVF, they nonetheless are usually unwilling to be publicly associated with this morally disreputable technology. Thus, most Egyptian couples make assiduous efforts to avoid the potentially damaging effects of public knowledge by limiting their actual disclosures to a trusted few.

But who, exactly, can one trust? This was the question I was interested in exploring with the IVF patients in my study, when I asked whether and to whom they had disclosed IVF and ICSI treatment decisions. Of the fifty-three women questioned, six (11 percent) had told neither friends nor family members, choosing along with their husbands to keep this information "between themselves." One woman, who had a three-year-old IVF child and was returning to Nile Badrawi to begin a new treatment cycle, explained her decision not to disclose in this way:

> It's between me and my husband only. From the first time, I refused to tell anyone—from the first moment. This is because of me, not my husband. It was my desire to keep it secret. Even when I did the operation, and I stayed in the hospital for one week, they didn't even know. I told my mother we were on vacation. I don't like anyone to see me when I'm tired. And this must be very confidential, between me and my husband. When I was pregnant, I didn't tell anyone until after three months. My mother insisted she must be the first to know. But I thought I would have some problems in the first three months, and I didn't want her to worry. Until now, no one knows I used IVF. I'm very sensitive of these things, and I think it must be confidential.

Another couple, both doctors, described their decision not to tell anyone about their ICSI treatment seeking,

> He: We haven't told our families. Still, some people in the community don't know what is this. They think some mistakes may happen.
> She: We are doctors, so we're broadminded. It's easy for us to understand. You could tell your friends if they were doctors, but your family, no. Maybe they can't understand.
> He: We will say, "With the help of doctors," but not what kind of treatment. The old mind is not like the young mind. And, besides, it will make no difference. This is our problem, and we can deal with this, and that's all.

She: So, in the near future, we're not planning to tell anything to anybody. Maybe this will change in ten to twenty years. *Maybe...*

He: Now, I don't feel I can tell about my problem or my wife's, because this is something personal, of course. It should stay between the husband and the wife. "Once it goes out, more problems come." Here in Egypt, even if it's not related to this IVF, *any problem* about infertility, and the families make more problems.

Nondisclosers such as these represented a minority of couples in my study. The majority of those questioned (forty-seven women, or 89 percent) could be described as "limited disclosers," who, like Maisa and Ahmed, had decided to tell at least one family member that they were attempting to make a test-tube baby. In eight of these cases (17 percent), the only family member to be informed was the wife's mother, and usually it was the wife's decision to tell her. That women's mothers are often included as the sole confidante is not at all surprising. In Egypt, many women describe their mothers as their "best friends," and women often call their daughters their "sweethearts" and "darlings," who share with them lifelong relationships of love, intimacy, and reciprocal assistance. Furthermore, the feelings of closeness between women and their mothers often extend to other members of a wife's natal family. This is reflected in the fact that, of the forty-four women in this study who had decided to disclose to a limited number of family members, exactly half of them had disclosed *only* to members of their own families, keeping this information secret from their husbands' families. This discrepancy between disclosure to wives' versus husbands' families was quite pronounced; presumably, it reflects not only women's emotional connectivity to their families of origin, but also men's sensitivity over revelation of male infertility, even to their own family members. In other words, whereas most women in this study sought emotional comfort by disclosing their treatment attempts to mothers, sometimes fathers, and occasionally sisters and brothers, at least half of the men in this study did not feel that their own family members could be trusted to react appropriately to the sensitive information regarding male infertility and attempts to overcome it through ICSI.

For infertile men then, the decision to undertake ICSI is a lonely one, not to be shared even within the family. In fact, for all the infertile couples in this study who chose either nondisclosure or limited disclosure of their IVF and ICSI treatment seeking, the very momentous decision to go forward with this form of infertility therapy was made in a strikingly autonomous fashion, rarely entailing active engagement on the part of family members and friends. That IVF and ICSI decision making is done alone, "between the couple," is completely atypical in Egypt. As noted by medical anthropologist Sandra Lane in her discussion of medical ethics in Egypt,

[T]he concept of autonomy derives from the notion of the sovereignty of the individual. In Egypt... however, individual wants and desires are often subordinated to the family and social group. In particular, during illness, the sick person rarely makes decisions for himself or herself regarding treatment. Rather, the family decides if and when to consult a doctor or other practitioner.[18]

In the world of test-tube baby making, however, most decisions to disclose to family members come after the fact—that is, after the couple has already decided to embark on this line of therapy. Many of the couples in my study were already in the midst of IVF or ICSI cycles when they decided to tell family members, and it was often because of their need to explain their daily comings and goings. In several cases, couples had decided to disclose this information only because they needed tangible help, in the form of economic assistance, help with obtaining pharmaceuticals, lodging during a treatment cycle (especially true of those who were returning to Egypt from jobs in the Arab Gulf), or advice from physicians in the family on various aspects of their care. Furthermore, several couples in this study said they worried that if something life-threatening should happen to them "during the operation," at least one or two family members should be fully informed.

In some cases, couples decided to tell their family members about IVF or ICSI only after a pregnancy had been achieved. One man, who told his family members about his wife's ICSI pregnancy only after several failed trials, described how his brother had wanted to help them during the period in which they were secretly attempting ICSI without the family's knowledge:

> Our families told us many times that we should "make a trial" [of IVF]. They didn't know that we did many trials before that. For myself, I promised I would say something *only* when she got pregnant. . . . My brother had offered to help take care of my wife. When he asked me why I don't do anything, I told him because I'm very busy with my work. And he offered to help me, to pay any money. He has time free to take care of my wife, and to take her to any place. He's an engineer, too. But he said, "If you need any money, I am ready to pay, or to take her anywhere in Egypt, or if you need to go outside." I told him that I will try. Of course, *all* my family are very happy now [that she is pregnant]. They say, "*Alf mabruk*" [a thousand congratulations], and they are ready to do anything.

Just as this man had decided not to disclose to his family members, few couples in this study had chosen to tell friends, colleagues, or acquaintances about their IVF or ICSI attempts. In only three cases had women shared this information with a friend, and in all three cases, it was because these friends were doctors who could help them. When I asked women in my study whether they had told or would tell others outside the family about IVF or ICSI if it succeeded, only ten women (31 percent) said "yes"; the other twenty-two (69 percent) said "no." Most of the women who said they would tell others their stories hoped that they could help another infertile woman "find the same solution" to her suffering. As one woman explained,

> If I have a friend who suffers from the same problem, I'll tell her. I have friends who are married for ten years or twelve years and don't have chil-

dren. If God gave us, I'll tell them and bring them here. Since it was something good for us, we have to tell others and make them aware of such a thing. Because we feel deprived and we know how others suffer. That's why we'll tell others if God gave us, because we are a guidance for them. When she asks me, "What did you do? Which doctor did you go to?," I'll tell her.

According to Dr. Yehia, patients such as this are the "best publicity" for IVF centers such as his. When I once asked him how infertile couples, especially those coming from the Arab Gulf, found out about his clinic, he told me, "I think a lot of it is word of mouth from other patients who've had a good experience. I saw a Kuwaiti couple yesterday who just came for an opinion. I asked how they knew about the place, and they said it was through the teacher of their relative's son. A lot of different people were involved in this chain of information."

Indeed, ten of the women in this study had been referred to either Nozha Hospital or Nile Badrawi Hospital by infertile friends who had had a good experience in these clinics. In almost all of these cases, women felt it was their duty to tell other friends and acquaintances in a society where friends, families, and colleagues generally help each other during times of crisis. As one of these women explained, "I'd be ready to help them and tell them anything. Usually here, in our culture, we consult with friends, relatives, and colleagues. People don't just act on our own; we try to get others' opinions, especially if others are more experienced."

Having said this, it is important to reiterate that the majority of the women in this study planned to maintain their secrecy, even if they were successful in making a baby of the tubes. In fact, only one woman in this study had actually told other people about the test-tube origins of her fourteen-month-old twin daughters, explaining her decision to disclose in this way:

I'm very proud of my daughters. I'm not shy. I myself tell anybody they are test-tube babies. But people sometimes couldn't believe this. "Oh my God, they look so similar to you!" One looks exactly like my husband, and one like me. I am *very* pleased that they look identical to us, so that will prove that we are the father and mother, contrary to what others believe. Everyone in both our families knows that we did IVF. But my husband doesn't want them [the twins] to know they're test-tube babies. I don't know exactly why. I'm very happy, but he's afraid. He tells me, "Try to forget that you did it this way." Because when they grow up, someone will offend them as "babies of the tubes."

In fact, many of the couples in this study worried about the future stigmatization of their children, who, if their means of conception were generally known, might be ridiculed for their test-tube origins or even questioned about their status as potential "bastards." Two women in this study opined that if they divulged this information to their offspring, their children might develop "psychological complexes," a consequence that they ardently wished to avoid through keeping the secret conception from the children themselves. As one of these women argued,

I will *not* tell my baby he is from ICSI when he grows up. I wouldn't like at all to tell him, that I and my husband had to do something which is not the "natural pregnancy way." It might affect his psychology. He might think he's different from his friends. The children around might give him a psychological complex. Because I don't think it will become more "open" in Egypt. I think ICSI will remain very secretive.

Similarly, among the seven women (20 percent) who remained undecided about such future disclosure, they worried about the psychological consequences of revealing this unusual form of conception to the children themselves. Many women in this study felt they *should* tell their children about IVF, but only when they had become mature adults who could handle the psychological implications of their IVF and ICSI conceptions.

Of the twenty-six women (74 percent) questioned who said that they would choose disclosure over secrecy, they cited a number of interesting reasons, all with deep cultural significance. The most important reason for eventual disclosure put forward by women in this study had to do with the inherent value of a test-tube child and the significant debt that it owed its parents for its difficult conception. Many women said that they wanted to be able to apprise their adult children of the "miracle" of their birth, so that their children would never take the meaning of their own lives for granted. But, even more important, they wanted to remind their children of the suffering—physical, emotional, and financial—that their parents had endured in order to have them. Women and their husbands frequently joked that their own baby would be the most "expensive in the world!" And they admitted that this information could be used down the road to make adult children feel indebted to their parents. For the reproductively aging couples who present to Egyptian IVF centers, such sentiments are not surprising; not only do these older couples hope to avoid future intergenerational conflicts, but they also *need* to ensure the abiding loyalty of their (only) test-tube child in a society where the vast majority of elderly parents are cared for by their adult children in their old age.

Furthermore, many of these older women suspected that they might only be able to have one test-tube baby and that this would eventually require explanation. In a society where one-child families are nonnormative, only children are pitied as potential "orphans" who lack family support if and when their parents die. Thus, Egyptian parents of all social backgrounds worry about the fate of an only child and are often determined to have a second child in order to give the first a sibling. Several of the women I met in Egyptian IVF centers already had one or even two test-tube children, but were putting themselves through IVF or ICSI again, "only for the sake" of their existing children. One woman, who was ardently hoping to give her three-year-old test-tube son a sibling, was nonetheless adamant about her nondisclosure decision:

No, I won't tell him. Why? Why? I think it's *not* good behavior. Why should I make him feel that I was very tired to get him? And he's *very* sensitive. If he hears me talk with his father, and say, "I have a headache," or "I'm very tired," he cries. And even if he was not like that, there's no use to tell him. I will not make him feel guilty. I will not blame him for what I went through.

Unlike this woman, most women hoped to tie their children to them by making them feel, if not guilty, then at least grateful for the ways in which their mothers had sacrificed to have them. But they also planned to indulge their children, making them feel extraordinarily precious. In fact, most of the women in this study used the term "precious" to describe their IVF and ICSI offspring. And, as wealthy elites, they sometimes described the elaborate ways in which they intended to "pamper" or "spoil" their test-tube children. As one woman remarked,

> My friends and my relatives tell me, "We don't know, if you have a baby, we'll have to wash our hands and put the baby in an incubator just to touch it! You made us so desperate!" I hope from God that I have twin girls, I hope. I adore girls, and they will be precious, precious children. I will treat them *so* preciously. My mother travels a lot abroad, and I think I'm going to bring everything for these children from London. They will be so clean, so chic. Everything so perfect.

Apprising a test-tube child of its worth, through both lavish attention and moments of actual disclosure in later life, seemed to be extremely important to most of the women in this study. However, disclosing to a child its test-tube origins for the sake of honesty—the reason most often invoked by disclosing parents in studies of DI in the United States[19]—was rarely mentioned by Egyptian women in this study, suggesting that honesty is not a highly valorized cultural universal. Indeed, as we have seen in this chapter, infertile IVF-seekers in Egypt have good reasons not to be honest with their children about test-tube conceptions, given the overriding social and psychological stigma of IVF in Egyptian society. Not surprisingly, then, only one woman in this study raised the issue of honesty, saying that she did not like lies, that she hoped to raise her own child to be honest, and that she, therefore, could not sustain a hypocritical position by lying to her own child about his or her test-tube origins. She added that, if the child found out about his unusual conception from another source, "maybe he will hate us, so we have to tell him."

Many of the women who believed that they should tell their adult children about IVF or ICSI hoped that attitudes toward test-tube baby making in Egypt would eventually improve. They predicted, optimistically, that the "next generation" of Egyptians might view test-tube baby making as something "normal" and "natural." If so, then disclosure of IVF or ICSI would no longer have potentially devastating effects on IVF children, including even untoward effects on their future marriageability. Furthermore, generational changes in IVF acceptance might mean that future Egyptian mothers of test-tube babies would no longer have to suffer in silence, stoically bearing the burden of infertility and its high-tech treatment with little social or psychological support.

The Stigma of Support

Which brings us to the issue of support—or rather, to the *lack* of support that is a striking feature of Egyptian women's and men's IVF and ICSI narratives. As seen in the story of Maisa, her psychological suffering was profound, yet she sought no professional help during her ICSI trials to ease her nervous tension. Instead, she prayed and joked with her busy doctors about her desire for a "remote-control" form of ICSI, in which she, the patient, could remove herself, psychically and somatically, from the ICSI experience.

As I will argue here, Maisa's emotional isolation at a time of heightened psychological distress is a consequence of two major factors: first, the pervasive secrecy surrounding test-tube baby making, which militates against the formation of patient support groups; and second, the stigmatization of psychological support itself in a society where mental illness and all forms of professional psychotherapy to overcome it are also profoundly stigmatized and stigmatizing.

With regard to the first factor, the climate of secrecy surrounding IVF in Egypt has clearly affected the establishment of both professional and patient-led support groups, which are now a common feature of the Western infertility landscape. National associations designed to empower infertile persons—in part through the establishment of local, voluntary, patient-led self-help groups—exist today in the United States (since 1974), the United Kingdom (since 1976), the Netherlands (since 1985), Canada (since 1987), Australia (since 1987), France (since 1988), New Zealand (since 1989), Denmark (since 1990), Iceland (since 1990), Switzerland (since 1992), Germany (since 1995), and Italy (since 1995).[20] As noted by social psychologist Frank van Balen, "These kinds of associations are of enormous influence on the well-being of infertile people, and they can serve to counter negative associations and public images of the childless."[21] In the United States, for example, RESOLVE, the first infertility association of this kind, has played a powerful role in organizing voluntary, patient-led, self-help groups at the local level, as well as providing many other functions, including monitoring of the medical profession and pharmaceutical industry.[22]

In Egypt, however, the notion of "patient empowerment" through organized support groups has yet to take hold, for infertility patients as well as for those with other serious health conditions. In fact, numerous factors militate against the formation of patient support groups for infertile couples undergoing IVF or ICSI. First, as seen in this chapter, infertility and IVF treatment seeking are both deemed deeply personal and sensitive matters, not to be shared with others, especially not strangers. When I asked infertile women and their husbands whether they would participate in an IVF patient support group, the answer was almost always "no." Few couples said they would be willing to share such an "embarrassing," "sensitive" matter with complete strangers, thereby opening themselves to a form of public humiliation. Such concerns over embarrassment were of particular importance to men, who simply could not see themselves telling other people, even other infertile men,

about their own male infertility problems. Many women also considered public revelation of their infertility problems to be deeply humiliating, as described by one
woman,

> I will feel more comfortable when the advice comes from a doctor and not
> from another patient. I'm the kind of person who doesn't want to speak
> about these things. I'll feel very embarrassed, because this is something very
> sensitive. I feel that from life. I mean, I know many people suffering from in-
> fertility, but everyone has different reasons and they don't say why. So I don't
> think these groups are going to work.

In addition, in the climate of secrecy pervading the world of test-tube baby making, Egyptian women worried about the lack of anonymity in patient support
groups. Given their perceived needs for confidentiality, they argued that they might
become exposed in a support group, thereby ruining their efforts to hide their treatment attempts. Joining a support group was deemed tantamount to "going public"
with one's IVF or ICSI treatment seeking in a cultural setting where gossip is rampant and virtually all patients are concerned about maintaining anonymity. That
support groups are diametrically opposed to secrecy was explained to me by one
woman as follows: "I refuse this [a support group] because I may know someone or
someone knows me, and someone may spread my secrets. I know I keep secrets, but
some others, I don't know. It may happen by chance that someone knows me and
makes it known. And so I'm afraid of this."

In addition, many women feared that patient support groups would exacerbate
rather than alleviate their own suffering. Some women feared that hearing other
women's sad stories would make them want to cry or become more depressed. Furthermore, women in the beginning stages of IVF and ICSI feared that they would
encounter other women whose treatment successes or failures would only make
them more anxious—in effect, "destroying their hope." As one woman, who had
tried IVF in the United States, explained,

> The doctors in the U.S. said, "Don't ask any other patient, because every
> woman has her own case." If another woman talks to you, and she has ten
> eggs and I have only two, it may make me desperate. And it's the same thing
> here. Women don't like to talk to each other. I tried talking to one once, but
> she didn't answer. It would be nice to go through this together—to have
> friends, to be supportive together, it's nice. You have a curiosity to know
> about their cases. But here, no one answers, because it only causes more
> stress.

Furthermore, as much as infertile women worry about their own emotional responses to other women's IVF successes and failures, they also worry about not
hurting others' feelings. Although successful IVF patients want to hide their pregnancies from the effects of *hasad,* they are also acutely aware of not demoralizing

other less fortunate nonpregnant infertile women. Revealing their own pregnancy success in the context of a support group is deemed very hurtful to others—and something to be avoided out of politeness and common decency. On the other hand, infertile women who are repeatedly unsuccessful at IVF or ICSI fear that disclosure of their multiple failures may have a profoundly demoralizing effect on other hopeful patients. Thus, they deem the sharing of their own sad stories in the context of a support group to be an inherently antisocial act.

Finally, Egyptian women in IVF centers argue that patient support groups simply are not an Egyptian tradition. Those who have traveled to the United States and Europe have seen television shows in which men and women go before an interviewer or a live audience to reveal their darkest secrets. Yet, such public airing of one's "dirty laundry" is considered mortifying to most Egyptians, who consider public revelation of personal problems undignified and even shameful.

Given these various cultural prohibitions against the public disclosure of private problems, formal patient support groups are unlikely to succeed in contemporary Egypt. As soon as I raised this possibility in interviews with Egyptian women, they clicked their tongues or waved their fingers to signal their negative responses. Yet, most of them also admitted to me that going through IVF or ICSI was a lonely process, and they often wished they knew at least one other person who was enduring the same treatment process simultaneously. Only two women in this study had undergone IVF or ICSI with an infertile friend, and in both cases, they believed that they had benefited tremendously from sharing the experience with another woman. Three other women had made friends during the course of an IVF or ICSI trial with another patient, and they described the comfort of knowing others who were "going through the same thing." However, these women were exceptions to the rule; in most Egyptian IVF clinics, patients rarely speak with one another, even though they realize that they are surrounded by other infertile women who are also seeking IVF or ICSI treatment.

At both Nile Badrawi and Nozha hospitals, the physician directors of the IVF clinics had taken small steps to promote what might best be described as "patient solidarity." At Nile Badrawi, Dr. Salah Zaki was a firm supporter of the notion of "patient cohorts," or small groups of six to eight women who were purposely scheduled to go through IVF or ICSI together. According to Dr. Zaki, "women need the support of others," and when placed in intentional cohorts, they "talk to each other in the reception [area], and when they go through their retrievals and transfers at the same time." In one case, a cohort of six women became so friendly with one another during the course of treatment that one member of the group housed the other out-of-towners during the three-day period from egg retrieval to embryo transfer.

At Nozha Hospital, Dr. Yehia had adopted another strategy—what might be best described as an informal telephone hotline. At the time of my 1996 study, Dr. Yehia had recruited about twenty patient volunteers, who had agreed to speak with new patients on the telephone, or even meet with them once telephone contact had been made. According to Dr. Yehia, this was an indirect method of engendering patient support, but one that seemed to be working relatively well.

The only woman in my study who had made a call to the patient hotline had extremely positive things to say about it. As she noted,

> IVF is very confidential here in Egypt, but not in this hospital. They've formed a kind of support group, which is very good, because, of course, you need to hear from people. When you start this "experiment," you want to find someone to encourage you, to say, "I tried this, don't try that." Like a club to call people and relate your problem to them. Fortunately, there is a club here—"Friends" something—on the telephone, or you can meet, and it helps. This is a very good idea, because people can relate their trial to you, and you won't be so afraid. Because I didn't know anybody when I was going through ICSI. It was lonely, and I was thinking about, "Am I doing the right thing?" But I can't talk about this to friends or neighbors, because they're not going through it. So it was encouraging to meet other patients.

Both Drs. Yehia and Zaki said that they created these informal mechanisms in part to reduce their own workloads. As they explained, without other avenues for patient support, IVF patients expect their doctors to serve this role, which is simply impossible given IVF doctors' busy schedules. Granted, both Drs. Yehia and Zaki were highly revered by patients for their supportive bedside manners and their proven ability to receive and answer patients' questions. Thus, when I asked patients whom they turned to for support, the most common answer was either "Dr. Yehia" or "Dr. Zaki," depending upon which clinic the patient was attending. However, both of these doctors were adamant that they could not, single-handedly, meet all of their patients' emotional needs; thus, they had instigated patient support efforts as a means of redirecting emotional energy *within* the patient population itself.

Furthermore, both Drs. Yehia and Zaki believed in the role of professional psychological counseling as part of the IVF treatment experience. Both of them had trained in the West, where psychological counseling is often a prerequisite to embarking on IVF and where IVF patients, once enrolled, often receive a battery of psychological tests.[23] Yet, when both of these physicians had tried to mandate psychological screening of potential IVF couples, patients were resistant. For example, in the early days of Nile Badrawi's IVF clinic, Dr. Zaki recruited one of Cairo's most eminent psychotherapists to consult with each couple prior to an IVF trial. However, according to Dr. Zaki, psychological screening "didn't work," for reasons that were not entirely clear to him. Patients failed to set their appointments or complained that they could not get an immediate appointment with the psychotherapist; in general, they used the excuse of timing to argue against seeking psychological services.

Similarly, at Nozha Hospital, Dr. Yehia had initially thought about including a psychiatrist as part of the IVF unit. However, when he began asking patients to see a psychiatrist, they flatly refused. Ultimately, he gave up on the idea, concluding that "you cannot make this mandatory in Egypt." Nonetheless, he continued to believe that many IVF patients could benefit from professional psychological intervention and support.

Why are psychological services so anathema to Egyptian IVF patients? As one patient put it bluntly, "People here don't believe in psychiatry, because people who go to them [psychiatrists] must be crazy! So they don't believe in their own need for this." As reflected quite accurately in this woman's statement, psychotherapy in and of itself is highly stigmatized in Egypt, given its association with severe mental illness. Because psychiatrists and psychologists in Egypt generally deal with worst-case scenarios—for example, schizophrenics who require institutionalization in mental hospitals—the Egyptian public has clearly associated mental health professionals with "craziness," and they are therefore loath to use their services. Even highly educated elites shun psychotherapists, which is why only one woman in my study (Nadine, the very atypical Egyptian movie star) admitted to me that she had once been under a psychiatrist's care. One other woman in my study, who happened to be a physician, argued quite vociferously that Egyptian IVF centers *needed* psychotherapists. She believed that there was a tremendous, unmet need for psychological services among infertile IVF patients. However, she lamented that routine psychotherapy as part of the IVF/ICSI treatment process will probably "never happen" in Egypt, given the "bad reputation" of psychotherapy in contemporary Egyptian society. It is probably fair to say that the constraints on the use of psychotherapy by infertile Egyptian patients are probably *more* pronounced than the constraints on IVF itself—an indication of the severe degree of stigmatization and marginalization of mental health services in the country.[24]

Conclusion

In summary, the world of test-tube baby making in Egypt is fraught with layer upon layer of stigma. First, infertility itself is a profoundly stigmatizing health condition. In Egypt, it spoils the identities of both men and women in ways that are deeply felt. Moreover, among women, it strains social relationships vis-à-vis the outright discrimination against infertile women, who are stigmatized by fertile others for their purportedly uncontrollable *hasad*, or envy.

Second, infertile couples who choose to seek IVF services are doubly stigmatized by their association with a morally questionable technology—one associated in Egyptians' minds with illicit sex, illegitimate offspring, and enduring sin. Hence, infertile IVF seekers feel compelled to enact elaborate cover-ups to protect not only their own moral reputations but also those of their test-tube babies, whose chances for future happiness depend upon top secrecy surrounding their shameful test-tube origins.

Finally, the stigma of IVF is complicated by the stigma of psychological support. To wit, in Egypt, infertile IVF seekers are essentially unable to access potentially beneficial psychological services because of the stigma that inheres to psychotherapy itself. Thus, an infertile woman who dares to seek therapy must do so in silence. If not, she risks being labeled *magnuna*, or "crazy," the sole condition that psychotherapists are popularly believed to treat.

Given the sheer weight of these stigmata, it is not at all surprising that stigma itself serves as one of the most powerful and enduring constraints on the use of the new reproductive technologies in Egypt. Undoubtedly, among some infertile Egyptian couples, the social and psychological risks of undertaking IVF or ICSI are simply too great, and instead of being guilty by association, they prefer never to try a technology that, if revealed, permanently stigmatizes them and their future offspring.

Thus, "choosing" IVF or ICSI involves crossing a major psychological and social hurdle. For those moral pioneers who decide to cross the threshold into the brave new world of test-tube baby making, their leaps of faith are made in relative silence. Few Egyptian couples reveal their treatment attempts to others, and hence test-tube babies are fashioned in secrecy, behind the walls of IVF clinics, where clandestine meetings take place between IVF physicians and their cautious patients. That this high level of secrecy may not be healthy for already stressed IVF patients is a reality that doctors themselves understand. But they also acknowledge that secrecy in Egypt is an important local "cultural issue," and hence they collude with their patients to ensure the privacy and anonymity that now characterizes the Egyptian IVF treatment scene.

The final question, of course, is whether this stigma and secrecy will eventually dissipate over time, as this new technology becomes socially normalized. For their part, Egyptian IVF patients remain hopeful. Many of them spoke to me of a future day, perhaps ten to twenty years down the road, when IVF and ICSI will be viewed as "natural," "normal" ways to make a baby. Women hoped that continual media exposure will play a part in naturalizing IVF, effectively converting it from a "strange" and "suspicious" technology to a powerful emblem of Egyptian modernity, an example of the "progress of science" for which all Egyptians should be proud. That the media have served to naturalize IVF in other places—for example, in both India and China, where newspapers and television now herald the actual identities of test-tube baby "miracles"[25]—suggests that Egypt may eventually follow suit.

However, I would argue that the naturalization of new reproductive technologies is never an inevitability, particularly when these technologies are morally overdetermined, as they are in Egypt. As noted by anthropologists Margaret Lock and Patricia Kaufert, "'nature' often continues to serve . . . as a moral touchstone," such that "people can be chastised if their behavior does not conform to what is understood as 'natural.'"[26] In Egypt, making a baby "in a test tube" is not a natural act, according to the moral majority. For this reason, the infertile minority continue to fear the chastisement and moral disregard that public disclosure of their test-tube baby making may arouse. As suggested by the case of DI in the West, their concern may be warranted. DI, the oldest of the new reproductive technologies, is still the source of much negative public opinion in the United States after nearly fifty years of use as a treatment for male infertility. As with IVF in Egypt, many American parents today choose *not* to disclose their use of DI to family, friends, or the children themselves, thereby "anticipat[ing] the negative judgments of others and sug-gest[ing] that they are wary of subjecting themselves and their children to public scrutiny and judgment."[27]

If, as we enter the new millennium, DI is still as highly stigmatized in the secular United States as it was nearly fifty years ago, then it provides us with a strong cautionary tale. Depending upon the local moral worlds in which these technologies are both produced and received, new reproductive technologies may or may not be naturalized, or effectively legitimated within a society as inherently beneficial tools of "progress, and of the betterment of humanity in general."[28] In Egypt, the dominant view of these technologies has so far been resistant to such facile Western narratives of technological progress. Indeed, after more than a decade of test-tube baby making in the country, Egyptians' views of the new reproductive technologies can be characterized as deeply ambivalent, even hostile. The net result is the ongoing stigmatization of the very technology—in fact, the *only* technology—that promises to overcome the stigmatization of infertility among many couples. Thus, for intractably infertile Egyptian women such as Maisa, becoming an Egyptian mother of a test-tube baby comes at an incredibly high cost—morally, medically, materially, psychologically, and socially speaking—in a society that has yet to come to terms with the test-tube baby making in its midst.

CHAPTER 10

Conclusion

Reprise: Stories of Suffering

This book began with the story of Amira, a wealthy Egyptian woman who tried many times, but failed to become a mother of a test-tube baby. With each additional chapter, other morally charged tales of suffering were told: of Georgette and Mikhail, the Coptic merchants who had already spent "half a used Mercedes" on their many unsuccessful IVF attempts; of Mabruka, from the oasis of Fayoum, whose uneducated, recalcitrant husband refused IVF out of multiple misunderstandings; of Dalia and Galal, whose moral misgivings about IVF in America led them back to Dr. Mohamed Yehia's clinic in Cairo, where they eventually conceived a test-tube child; of Huda, who questioned if she would be successful in making a test-tube baby after suffering the infectious complications of an unnecessary ovarian surgery; of Nadine, the disgruntled movie star who was angry at both her IVF physician and her infertile, alcoholic husband for their failures to assuage her many anxieties and fears; of Moustafa, the infertile man who got fed up with his long-suffering first wife and eventually replaced her with Shahira, the mother of his ICSI twins; and of Maisa, who believes she lost her cherished test-tube pregnancy because of the uncontrollable envy of another desperate, infertile woman. With the exception of Mabruka, all were relatively affluent, professional elites who had access to "the many things that money can buy" in Egypt. However, what all of them were missing is that which is perhaps most priceless in Egyptian culture—children, who are believed by Egyptians, both Muslim and Christian alike, to be "gifts from God" and the ultimate "decorations of worldly life."

This book has attempted to render visible the suffering of infertile Egyptians, on a mental, physical, social, and spiritual level. For, when all is said and done, infertility is about profound human suffering. It is about the aches in the heart that can never be healed until a desired baby is born and about the incredible risks, worries, and fears that test-tube baby making engenders for infertile couples, especially in resource-poor, Third World societies such as Egypt.

By opening a window into this secretive world, this ethnographic account makes clear that suffering is not the exclusive province of the Third World poor. I, like most other anthropologists working in non-Western settings, have felt a special commitment to the poor and disenfranchised, which is why my two previous ethnographies have focused exclusively on the lives of infertile women from the most economically disadvantaged segments of Egyptian society.[1] The ethnographic literature, including from the Middle East,[2] is now replete with studies of the downtrodden, and the ways in which these subaltern subjects may attempt to resist their social and economic marginalization.

As part of this ethnographic commitment to the subaltern, there has also been, at times, a concomitant vilification of Third World elites, who may use their privileged class positions for the furtherance of neocolonial aims and who may thus be rendered ethnographically as corrupt and heartless oppressors. Such a rendering is apparent, for example, in Nancy Scheper-Hughes's otherwise poignant ethnography, *Death Without Weeping: The Violence of Everyday Life in Brazil*, which depicts the misery of a destitute *favela* community. According to Scheper-Hughes, the "bad faith" economy there drives abjectly impoverished *favela* men and women into often exploitative and demeaning dependency relationships with middle- and upper-class townspeople, who are characterized in the ethnography as a profoundly class conscious but mostly uncaring "power elite."[3]

What I have discovered through my own comparative ethnographic incursions into the world of Egyptian infertility over the course of two decades is that such characterizations may be patently unfair. Not only do they underestimate the humanity that may be found *within* Third World elite populations, but they also overlook the human suffering that can occur at *both* ends of the class spectrum in a society such as Egypt, where social, economic, and political conditions are often "dis-ease"-producing for rich and poor alike.[4] Thus, I have come away from my studies of infertility in Egypt with profound sympathy for *both* constituencies: the poor infertile women of my first study, who will never get a chance to make a much-desired test-tube baby and who will therefore remain physically barren and socially marginalized, and also the mostly elite women and men of my second study, who as members of a patently patriarchal, pronatalist society, are plunged by necessity into the secretive, risky world of test-tube baby making. This ethnographic account clearly demonstrates that infertility-related suffering affects every social class in the Third World. Ultimately, when all is said and done, I am left wondering who among them suffers more—the poor who are barred access to these technologies, or the elites who have such access but must endure these technologies with little hope of success?

Suffering and endurance are clearly the main themes of elite infertile Egyptians' narratives as they enter into the brave new world of test-tube baby making. When I encountered women and their husbands in Egyptian IVF centers, they usually reeled off long lists of concerns, worries, fears, and apprehensions reflecting the many arenas of constraint that they faced as IVF patients. Summing up her suffering in the religious idiom that is a common feature of infertile people's discourse in Egypt, one woman explained to me,

> What makes me feel patient is that I have a belief that any pains humans suffer will make up for the sins that humans have committed. There is a saying of the Prophet, "Anyone who is loved by God, his pain and suffering will increase." That is what makes me patient; I believe there will be a reward at the end.

However, worldly rewards in the form of a *tifl l-anabib*, a precious baby of the tubes, are never guaranteed. As shown in this ethnography, infertile Egyptians, including the most elite members of Egyptian society, are confronted with overwhelming arenas of constraint—structural, ideological, social relational, practical, and even biological in nature—that seriously impinge upon their ability to "choose" these new reproductive technologies and to use them effectively.

Arenas of Constraint, Limits of Agency

This book has attempted to elucidate, theoretically and ethnographically, the eight major arenas of constraint facing would-be users of new reproductive technologies in an "overpopulated," "developing" society, but one that has nonetheless led the Muslim Middle East in its new reproductive technology revolution. Egypt has indeed achieved one form of medical modernity through its implementation of these high-tech methods of baby making; however, this reproductive revolution has not come without high costs at the local level. This book has attempted to elucidate the constraints on test-tube baby making in the local Egyptian context. Such constraints include class-based barriers to new reproductive technology access, which effectively exclude most poor and even middle-class infertile women and men from trying IVF or ICSI, even though they are often aware and highly desirous of these technologies; problems of knowledge and scientific literacy among the Egyptian masses, leading to widespread misunderstandings and media-fueled moral misgivings about the ways in which test-tube babies are conceived; religious prohibitions on third-party donation, which disallow the use of donor sperm, eggs, embryos, and surrogate uteruses and which create profound moral anxieties about the potential for "mixing" and "mistakes" to be made in Egyptian IVF laboratories; problems of social and technical competence among Egyptian IVF providers, whose private IVF clinics face endemic, industrywide problems that have yet to be solved by a nationwide regulatory system; ongoing problems of efficacy, or the low success rates of IVF and ICSI that are nonetheless artificially inflated in Egypt to create false hopes among (paying) infertile patients; local perceptions of new reproductive technology risks and their physical embodiment, not only among the Egyptian women faced with local shortages of the powerful hormones they must take prior to an IVF or

ICSI trial, but also among the infertile men who fear for the well-being of the test-tube babies produced from their "weak" sperm; the gender effects of these technologies, particularly ICSI, which has fueled a local crisis of marital commitment among infertile middle-age men, who are beginning to cast off their reproductively elderly wives in the pursuit of conception with younger, fecund women; and the ongoing stigma of IVF itself, which has led to a socially invisible, "underground" world of test-tube baby making, where Egyptian patients feel forced to maintain their anonymity through a cult of secrecy, silence, and dissimulation.

In enumerating these major constraints on the local practice of IVF and ICSI in Egypt, my intention has been to reveal the tortuous "medical and emotional road of trials"[5] on which the Egyptian infertile, including infertile elites, journey in search of a *tifl l-anabib*, a cherished baby of the tubes. At the end of this journey, the only conclusion that can be reached is that new reproductive technologies are *not* a panacea for infertility—a true "miracle cure" for this condition wherever it occurs. Indeed, the new reproductive technologies are not a "cure" at all, as they can do nothing to resolve or reverse infertility conditions, although they can sometimes manage to bypass them through a growing set of ingenious mechanisms.

In Western media discourses surrounding these technologies, it is this scientific ingenuity—the remarkable technological advancements that are being continuously produced in Western reproductive laboratories—that leads to the sometimes exultant, self-congratulatory statements of Western reproductive scientists. For example, in the recent PBS special "18 Ways to Make a Baby," which aired in 2001 on both *Front Line* and *Nova,* one reproductive scientist crowed, "We can do anything we want with these embryos," a statement that was used subsequently to advertise the television special to potential viewers. Similarly, a recent *Newsweek* article, "Infertility: A Guy Thing," broadcast the "good news" that "most common male problems can be fixed."[6] Even the more cautious scholarly volume, *Infertility in the Modern World: Present and Future Prospects,* opened with a sanguine chapter by British IVF physicians called "Reproductive Possibilities for Infertile Couples: Present and Future."[7] The chapter began with this irresponsibly optimistic statement: "Infertility affects at least 14% of the reproductive population worldwide. Modern technology can provide genetically related offspring to 80% of couples seeking treatment, and pregnancy to a further 10–15% using donated gametes."[8]

Statements such as these ignore the profound obstacles and constraints that prevent the majority of infertile couples from taking home a test-tube baby. As seen in the many fruitless stories of women and men in this book, test-tube baby making is a low-odds proposition, failing 70 to 80 percent of the time, even in the best centers of the West. In the Third World, where serious structural factors impinge upon the operation of IVF centers, failure rates are likely to be much higher, making the establishment of such centers a controversial proposition.[9] It is dangerous, therefore, to romanticize these new reproductive technologies as a form of technological salvation.

Similarly, it is irresponsible to romanticize the reproductive "choices" of those who would attempt to use these technologies. Those of us who work in the anthropology of reproduction have frankly been on the "lookout" for women's agency in the use of reproductive technologies of all kinds. Eschewing stances that would make women appear passive and powerless in the realm of reproductive decision making, we have often represented our subjects, including desperate and destitute infertile Egyptian women,[10] as savvy reproductive actors who make pragmatic, agentive choices about their reproductive lives. As noted by the editors of *Living and Working with the New Medical Technologies: Intersections of Inquiry,*

> Whereas earlier theorizing about relationships of power, hierarchies and re-pression tended to constitute those on whom power was enacted as passive recipients, in recent years an emphasis on individual agency—including a range of responses to new technologies, from a wholehearted embrace of them, to a pragmatic acceptance or rejection, to an ironical distancing—has replaced the former picture of a technological manipulation of subjects.[11]

In our concerns over the dynamics of power, however, we may have highlighted individual agency at the expense of constraint, effectively ignoring the many nega-tive forces that impinge upon successful reproduction for both women and men around the world. Only some of these negative forces are structural, which is why we need to move beyond the prosaic dualism of "structure versus agency." As shown in this ethnography, structural factors rooted in economic power differentials are only one of a host of constraints on the lives of infertile women and men in Egypt. In the realm of test-tube baby making, infertile Egyptians are forced to deal with con-straints on their reproductive agency that are also ideological, moral, social rela-tional, practical, and even bodily in nature. Thus, the finding of multiple arenas of constraint in my research facilitates a much-needed reconceptualization of theories of agency.

Preventing Infertile Bodies in the New Millennium

As noted by Cambrosio, Young, and Lock, the material body itself is "another site of agency"; thus, "medical practice cannot be conceived independently of the material body of the patients."[12] Agreeing with these authors that the body itself can never be ignored in science and technology scholarship, I would like to ask here: What might be done to spare the infertile bodies of Egyptian men and women the pain and mis-ery so excruciatingly detailed in Chapter 7 of this book? Clearly, biomedicine itself is not the answer, for little can be done to treat infertility once it strikes. Rather, as noted by a number of biomedical infertility specialists themselves,[13] more must be done in the new millennium, at both the global and local public health levels, to pre-vent the many preventable forms of infertility from occurring in the first place. Only then will the global demand for expensive, imported, but low-odds new reproduc-tive technologies be ameliorated.

For many years now, the World Health Organization has promoted the idea that "infection is the cause" of Africa's infertility belt.[14] In Egypt, located slightly to the north of that belt, RTIs are clearly responsible for the significant rates of female tubal infertility in the country.[15] Unfortunately, once the damage is done by an RTI to a woman's reproductive tract, her only solution is usually IVF, the technology designed explicitly to bypass the need for healthy fallopian tubes. Clearly for women in Egypt—but also for women throughout Africa and the rest of the developing world—serious attention must be paid to the prevention of RTIs.[16]

In the Muslim Middle East, effective prevention of RTIs requires overcoming the embarrassment, shame, and denial that still keeps the highest-ranking public health officials, as well as the gynecological community, from acknowledging the presence of sexually transmitted diseases, including HIV/AIDS, in their "religiously conservative" countries.[17] In Egypt, the state's new "check-off" marriage contract may, paradoxically, have this effect, by forcing men to be premaritally tested for both sexually transmitted diseases and other male reproductive dysfunctions. Educating the public about the sterilizing potential of RTIs, including those caused by STDs but also by postpartum infections, postabortive infections, and iatrogenic medical practices in both the "traditional" and "modern" realms, must be made one of the top priorities of the global reproductive health initiative, including in Egypt, where this initiative was launched at the International Conference on Population and Development held in Cairo in 1994.[18] Through a serious, concerted global effort to prevent sterilizing RTIs, much of the pain and suffering that *is* women's quotidian experience of living with infertility and enduring IVF could simply be avoided in the new millennium.

Unfortunately, not all infertility *can* be prevented through well-meaning public health efforts. This is especially true of male infertility, which contributes to more than half of all cases of infertility, but has so far has eluded etiological understanding.[19] As this book has shown, male infertility has been a well-kept secret in Egypt and in many other parts of the world, where women continue to be blamed for reproductive failures.[20] With the recent emergence of ICSI, male infertility is beginning to be appreciated as an important men's reproductive health issue in its own right,[21] including in Egypt, where infertile men are literally flocking to IVF centers.

Because of its untoward effects on masculinity and its potential solution through new reproductive technologies, male infertility represents the great uncharted territory of the new millennium—the likely "wave of the future" in infertility research. As an infertility scholar, I will be devoting the next phase of my own career to male infertility in the Middle East, through a comparative study in three disparate sites.[22] By investigating infertile Middle Eastern men's responses to ICSI— with all of the questions this technology poses for masculinity, marriage, medical treatment-seeking, and morality in the Middle East—I hope to contribute to new scholarly "genealogies" within the anthropology of reproduction,[23] where the absence of men is now recognized as a glaring omission.[24]

As seen in this book, men are also important reproductive actors, who deserve a serious and ethnographically nuanced role in the exciting social theory that is emerging in this area.[25] By focusing the anthropological lens on infertile *male* bodies cross culturally, much can be learned about the meanings of fatherhood, paternity, and patriarchy; about the social construction of both hegemonic and subordinate forms of masculinity; about the social reproduction of kinship systems and family life; and about men's experiences of biopower and processes of medicalization.[26] Because men's responses to biotechnologies of reproduction are also quite poorly understood, their uses of and resistances to technologies such as ICSI therefore represent excellent topics for future medical anthropological investigations.[27]

Local Moral Worlds of Adoption

Turning the reproductive spotlight on men may also reveal a great deal about men's reactions to social fatherhood, and particularly men's potential misgivings about adoption, which, as shown in this book, is extremely problematic in Muslim Middle Eastern countries such as Egypt. Even in the United States, men appear to be very ambivalent about social fatherhood, as recently revealed in Gay Becker's fascinating anthropological accounts of American donor insemination.[28] Yet, in places like Egypt, we know relatively little about what biological paternity actually means to men, and therefore why adoption (qua permanent legal fostering) is rarely pursued as an option to overcome male infertility. Because ICSI is a relatively ineffective technology, many infertile Egyptian men will never achieve their desires to become fathers of test-tube babies. Yet, most of these men will also never set foot in an Egyptian orphanage.

By the early 1980s, there were already 176 Egyptian orphanages, caring for approximately seven thousand children.[29] It has truly pained me over the years to see the many beautiful children, both infants and older boys and girls, lingering in Egyptian orphanages, where their futures, including their future marriageability, are unclear,[30] even if they are generally well taken care of within these facilities. This is especially true of children with "African" features, who are rarely fostered by lighter-skinned Egyptian couples because of the lingering racism described in Chapter 4. In Egyptian orphanages today, many of the older children who remain there are dark-skinned, and they usually live in the orphanages until they "come of age" and can find either employment or marriage. The director of one Cairo orphanage described to me how she takes all of the dark-skinned adolescent girls to an "African Cultural Festival" held each year in an affluent suburb of Cairo. There, she hopes that some of these girls will be spotted by African men who are interested in marriage. In my own case, my husband and I attempted to become the permanent legal guardians of a dark-skinned girl (whose biological parents must have been from sub-Saharan Africa) from an Alexandrian orphanage, where she was being raised by kindly caretakers. Unfortunately, we found the restrictions on fostering, especially for non-Muslim foreigners, overwhelming, and we gave up on our attempt to bring her to the United States. To my knowledge, she remains there in the orphanage to this day, where she is now a teenager.

In my view and in that of other scholars,[31] Egypt needs to bring its considerable media resources to bear on the plight of orphans, breaking down some of the social barriers that make their permanent fostering so anathema to the majority of Egyptians, including the infertile. As noted by anthropologist Andrea Rugh,

> In the first instance the children themselves find themselves in the contradictory cross fire of sanctions that rigidly protect the sanctity of the family against the possibly disruptive force of extramarital relations, but which in the process prevent the children from these unions (or ones suspected of being from them) from enjoying the normal family life that is being so drastically protected.
>
> Families provide needs that cannot be substituted for simply by food, clothing, education, and supervision, as the authorities have discovered. There are additional indefinable qualitative aspects of family care that include among others emotional support, exchange of services, social status, mutual material help, and a sense of belonging, that institutions have difficulty in providing. Public efforts to solve these problems have gone full circle at present and are back to emphasizing foster families as the closest equivalent to true families.[32]

Clearly, social resistance to adoption (qua permanent fostering) in Egyptian society reflects in part the moral stances against illegitimacy, which are the same stances that prevent Egyptians from adopting donor technologies in IVF and ICSI. Illegitimate children, whether they issue from extramarital relations or from donor techniques, face an uncertain future in Egyptian society because they are deemed to be the product of *zina*, one of the great sins in Islam. Yet, independent of moral considerations, the local rejection of adoption also bespeaks the powerful desires—which are buoyed in a lineage- and inheritance-oriented Islamic country—of Egyptian men and women to reproduce themselves in both biological and social terms. Within such a moral-social environment, it is not at all surprising that infertile Egyptians "need no encouragement," as one of my infertile informants put it, to try new reproductive technologies, for only these technologies hold out the promise of biological perpetuity, which alone is acceptable to them.

To deny infertile Egyptian couples the opportunity to biologically reproduce themselves simply by virtue of their geographic location in the global hierarchy of rich and poor nations seems, in my view, to be patently unfair and even bespeaks a kind of neo-Malthusian rationing of reproductive rights.[33] Given local Egyptian schema concerning adoption, which may be particularly difficult to unseat, there clearly is a role, albeit a limited one, to be played by these technologies. This limited role applies not only in Egypt, but also in other parts of the Third World where tubal and male forms of infertility take extraordinary tolls on human reproduction and well-being. Thus, I strongly disagree with those feminist scholars who "just say no" to new reproductive technologies,[34] especially when I have seen how the birth of a test-tube baby can relieve years of unbearable pain and suffering for infertile Egyptian couples living in a patriarchal, pronatalist society.[35]

The Local in the Global

As the new reproductive technologies become further entrenched in the urban Egyptian landscape, and additional forms of global reproductive technology become available in this setting, it is important to interrogate the new local dilemmas that are likely to arise in response to this variant of globalization. The pace of change evident in the production of new reproductive technologies themselves[36]—and the rapidity of their globalization and penetration into far reaches of the Third World— is indeed striking. By 1992, for example, at least forty-five IVF centers were operating in twelve Latin American countries, where they had initiated a total of 4,144 IVF cycles.[37] However, the Catholic Church, "which is very powerful in Latin America,"[38] had greatly influenced the growth of the IVF industry. For example, Argentina, Colombia, Brazil, and Chile had all made attempts by 1992 to legislate upon the appropriate uses of these technologies. Among the sixteen different bills introduced in Argentina's Congress,

> Legal arguments are focused on the beginning of human life (or human beings); the amount of oocytes to be inseminated and the embryos to be transferred; human embryo cryopreservation and the use of third persons' gametes; performance in married persons or just couples or singles or lesbians; [and] conditions on the widow's insemination with her husband's semen or its rejection. What seems to have no approval at all is the possibility of surrogacy and research on embryos, as well as manipulation techniques that could in any way cause damage to the embryo without constituting therapeutic research.[39]

Clearly, in Latin America as elsewhere around the globe, the globalization of new reproductive technologies is certain to engender much that is new, including new social imaginaries, new forms of cultural production, new utopias, as well as new dystopias, new forms of local resistance, new arenas of constraint. As one science and technology studies scholar, David Hess, rightly observes, "Anthropology brings to these discussions a reminder that the cultural construction of science is a global phenomenon, and that the ongoing dialogue of technoculture often takes its most interesting turns in areas of the world outside the developed West."[40] In this light, charting the globalization of new reproductive technologies around the world in the new millennium seems a particularly worthy endeavor. The examination of these Western reproductive technologies in non-Western societies offers a heuristic case study of local-global intersections and elucidates the importance of interrogating what is "local" in an increasingly "global" world.

Those of us in anthropology seem particularly well positioned for this task of investigating "how globalizing processes exist in the context of, and must come to terms with, the realities of particular societies, with their accumulated—that is to say historical—cultures and ways of life."[41] This book has attempted to answer this question in the local context of Egypt, that is, by examining how new reproductive technologies have been received in this Middle Eastern Muslim society and how they have variously served to influence local social and cultural life. Sadly, despite nearly a decade and a half of Egyptian experience with new reproductive technologies, the futures of most infertile women and men there remain uncertain, and their chances of taking home a test-tube baby are slim. However, those lucky few who do become mothers and fathers in Egyptian IVF clinics are only too happy to be living in a society where the global has become the local, and the great gifts of globalization are literally the test-tube babies they bear.

Appendix

Fatwa

This Appendix includes the complete text of the first *fatwa*, or religious opinion, on medically assisted reproduction, first delivered on March 23, 1980, by His Excellency Gad El Hak Ali Gad El Hak, the former Grand Shaikh of Egypt's Al-Azhar University, the oldest center of religious learning in the Muslim Middle East. This initial *fatwa*, parts of which are posted in some Egyptian IVF clinics, has proven to be authoritative and enduring, even though it was issued at least six years before IVF and the other new reproductive technologies became available in Egypt and eventually other parts of the Middle East. Since that time, other highly regarded *shaikhs*—at Al-Azhar, the Dar Il-Iftah (*fatwa*-issuing religious center) in Saudi Arabia, and throughout the Sunni Muslim Middle East—have essentially agreed with all the main points of this initial religious opinion on the subject of medically assisted conception among Muslims. Perhaps the key point of this text is the prohibition against any form of third-party donation, either of biogenetic substances or wombs (as in surrogacy), outside of the marital union.

For their part, Egyptian IVF clinics strictly adhere to the limitations placed on assisted conception, as outlined in this *fatwa*, for reasons made abundantly clear in the full text of this opinion provided here. As for the vast majority of Egyptian patients, complying with the provisions of this *fatwa* is one of their main concerns when they contemplate undergoing any of the new reproductive technologies to overcome infertility.

The complete text of the *fatwa*—translated into English under the auspices of the Ford Foundation in Cairo and provided to me by medical anthropologist and former Ford Foundation Program Officer Sandra Lane—follows.

Introduction

Lineage and relationship[s] of marriage are graces of Allah to mankind, highly appreciated, and they are [the] basis of judgment.

It is He who has created man from water, then He has established relationships of lineage and marriage, for thy Lord has power over all things.
(*Furqan*, or the Criterion 59)

Therefore, origin preservation is a most essential objective of Islamic law.
   In this concern, Scholar Elghazali stated:

Allah's goal is to prevent harm and cause welfare; however, human beings are
to gain their benefit upon accomplishment of objectives. The benefit is to
observe targets of Islamic law, which are five: to preserve beings' religion,
themselves, [their] minds, descendants and money. Hence, any act implying
preservation of these five fundamentals is a benefit, and, on the contrary, any
act which jeopardizes them is then a harm.

Therefore, Allah permitted marriage and prohibited fornication to preserve the
origins.

And among His signs is this, that He created for you mates from among
yourselves, that ye may dwell in tranquility with them, and he has put love
and mercy between your (hearts); verily, in that are signs for those who reflect. (*Rum*, or The Roman Empire 21)

Nor come nigh to adultery: For it is a shameful (deed), and an evil, opening
the road (to other evils). (Esraa, or Children of Israel 32)

A legitimate child will grow and be raised by his parents in the best manner they
can afford, while an illegitimate one is a shame for the mother and her people, ne-
glected in the community and will then turn into a disease.
   Islamic scholars discussed illegitimate children in books of Islamic law, [and]
explained that they are human beings who deserve to be brought up properly and
taken care of so as to stimulate what is best in them and avoid their evilness.

And if any one saved a life, it would be as if he saved the life of the whole
people. (*Maida*, or The Table 31)

As for proper origin[s], Islam is highly concerned and hence it was coded in a
way to call for marriage and guarantee stability of the family. Generally, Islam organized people's life in an appropriate pattern with justice and equity.
   There are [a] few rules set by Islam to ensure appropriateness of origin which
will be represented in the following:
   Adultery is forbidden.
   A compulsory period during which a divorcee should not remarry (*iddat*) (to
ensure she is not already pregnant, which confuses father's identification).
   Adoption is forbidden (by Qur'anic definition) for purposes of origin protection and family rights' preservation.

Nor has He made your adopted sons your sons. Such is (only) your mouths.
But God Tells (you) the truth, and He shows the (right) way. Call them by

(the names of) their fathers: that is more just in the sight of God. But if ye know not their fathers' (names, call them) your brothers in faith, or your *maulas*. (*Ahsab*, or The Confederates 4, 5)

In this, Islam is not to approve [of one] who has no origin, or force him on others. Islam, [which] organized relations of a man and woman, emphasized that it should be in [the] form of proper marriage, so as to protect origins and respect a sperm from which a child is created.

Now let man but think from what he is created! He is created from a drop emitted from between the backbone and the ribs. (Tariq, or The Night Visitant 5, 6, 7) Verily, we created man from a drop of mingled sperm. (*Dahr*, or Time; *Insan*, or Man 2)

However, a sperm is not to acquire shape until it is introduced into a woman's womb ready to receive it, and that could be through a sexual body contact (intercourse). The child then will be called after his father, [if] the aspect of marriage is present. However, there are cases where a man's sperm could be introduced to a woman's womb through means other than body contact.

Islamic scholars elaborated in their books on this issue, and mentioned several examples where a woman was able to get and introduce a husband's or a master's sperm into her womb, which consequently will require a waiting period (*iddat*) before she remarries and creates a lineage.

In light of the above mentioned, we will discuss several issues in the following:

Marriage's noble objective is reproduction, so as to preserve mankind; moreover, body contact among husband and wife is based on natural desire.

Thus, body contact (intercourse) is the basic and only means allowing a sperm to reach the proper location as per Allah's will.

If pregnancy could not occur through normal body contact (intercourse) due to some illness, it is then permissible to impregnate a woman by her husband's sperm through medical assistance (provided they are undoubtedly her husband's and not [that of] any other man or animal). A waiting period is then necessary and lineage is proved based on the previously mentioned examples.

If the husband is impotent, it is unlawful to have a stranger donate sperm. This consequently will confuse origins; furthermore, the method implies adultery which is strictly unlawful by [both the] Qur'an and Sunna (what has been taken from Prophet Muhammed, peace be upon him).

If a woman's ovum to be impregnated by a man's sperm (not the husband), then the sperm donor's wife acts as surrogate, it is then considered adultery (confuses origins) as well as unlawful.

However, even though it is the husband's sperm which is not to acquire shape unless by Allah's permission upon unity with the wife's ovum, and since this aspect is not present in the case discussed, the wife then is not the husband's tilth as she should be as Allah says: "Your wives as a tilth unto you" (*Baqara*, or The Heifer 222). A woman shall not be pregnant unless through a normal legal intercourse with her husband or by introducing his sperm into her womb to acquire shape as Allah says: "He makes you, in the wombs of your mothers, in stages one after another, in three veils of darkness" (*Zumaror*, or The Crowds).

Hence, in the case discussed, the ovum is not the wife's, which implies unlawful adultery.

In Vitro Fertilization

[If] a wife's ovum is impregnated by her husband's sperm outside the womb in a tube, then implanted back to the womb with no doubts or confusion about sperm donor (human or animal) due to medical requirements [such] as illness of the husband or wife which might affect their relation.

However, if a trustworthy physician recommends in vitro fertilization and shall be responsible for its appropriateness, then it is permissible and obligatory as a treatment for a woman who has pregnancy impediments. Furthermore, Prophet Muhammed, peace be upon him, mentioned the necessity to seek remedy for any disease, and sterility is a disease that might be curable; therefore to seek lawful treatment is then permissible.

If the case was full surrogacy, in which an animal's womb will be used temporarily to bear and allow an impregnated ovum [to] go partially through stages of growth which are mentioned in the Qur'an:

> Then we placed him as (a drop of) sperm in a place of rest, firmly fixed, then we made the sperm into a clot of congealed blood, then of that clot we made a lump [fetus], then we made out of that lump bones and clothed the bones with flesh, then we developed out of it another creature. So blessed be God, the best to create! (*Muminun*, or The Believers 13, 14)

It will definitely acquire characteristics of the bearing animal according to genetics factors which were previously proven by the Qur'an. "Should he not know he that created?" (*Mulk*, or The Dominion 14). Our Prophet, peace be upon him, instructed us to choose the best woman as a wife for the sake of our children and to avoid beautiful women who grew up in a corrupted environment for genetic purposes as well as [for] ensuring a healthy atmosphere to bring up children.

The above mentioned clarifies even more how an animal's surrogacy is to affect the born creature, who will not be of a human nature. Therefore, a person who uses this method is to ruin Allah's creation. Allah says: "So fear God as much as ye can" (*Tagabun*, or The Mutual Loss and Gain 16).

According to Islamic law, one of the fundamentals is to prioritize harm prevention, then well being provision.

We conclude that this method of medically assisted reproduction [animal surrogacy] is an absolute cause of evil, therefore unlawful.

As for the father who accepts one of the previously mentioned unlawful means of medically assisted reproduction, he is to be considered one who lost his dignity.

Any child who is begotten through one of the stated cases is illegitimate, [if] it is certain that the sperm donor is not the father (adultery). Accordingly, the child is a foundling and is to be called after his mother.

Concerning the position of a physician who undertakes one of the unlawful cases, Islam allowed lawful treatment and the physician being the means to do so according to his experience. He is then responsible in case of negligence or seeking an unlawful (by Islam) method. Therefore, a physician responsible for medically assisted reproduction should study the method thoroughly [so] that it should not be unlawful, or else he will be sinning, for whatever led to an unlawful act is consequently unlawful. [Both the] Qur'an and Sunna indicated a very important principle, which is to cause harm prevention. "Revile not ye those whom they call upon besides God, lest they out of spite revile God in their ignorance" (*Anam*, or The Cattle 108). The principles are very clear as per the aforementioned verse; it calls not to curse polytheist Gods in order not to allow them to take it as a cause and curse Allah. Prophet Muhammed, peace be upon him, said:

"May Allah damn alcohol, [a] person who drinks it, who offers it, who sells it, who buys it, who squeezes it, who carries it, and whom it is carried for."

That proves one should not even assist in an unlawful act. Another example is that Islam forbids a man to study a woman's beauty or be alone with a woman, since that could be an atmosphere that causes adultery.

We herein conclude that based on the above mentioned verses of the Qur'an, definitions of the *Sunna* and examples, a physician who conducts a medically assisted reproduction in an unlawful form is at fault and his earning is bad.

A physician should only offer lawful treatment to a husband and wife wishing to have a legitimate child and establish a family.

Furthermore, it is emphasized that medically assisted reproduction is only lawful among a husband and a wife, but to use such experiments so as to improve [the] race is absolutely unlawful. Instead of establishing a sperm bank taken from [the] best selection of men, then use it to impregnate also well-selected women, Islam instructed [us] to choose the best of either husband or wife in all aspects (health, ethics, mind, and so forth). It set lawful criteria to keep a strong and healthy human generation.

Finally, a human being is not to be taken as a means of experiment[ation], for Allah put him in a respecting position.

"Oh ye who believe, give your response to God and his Apostle, when he calleth you to that which will give you life, and know that God cometh in between a man and his heart, and that it is he to whom ye shall (all) be gathered and fear tumult or oppression, which affecteth not in particular (only) those of you who do wrong: And know that God is strict in punishment." (*Anfal*, or The Spoils of War 24, 25)

Notes

Chapter 1: Introduction

1. See Becker, *The Elusive Embryo*; Franklin, *Embodied Progress*; Greil, *Not Yet Pregnant*; and Sandelowski, *With Child in Mind.*
2. See Ahmed and Donnan, "Islam in the Age of Postmodernity"; and Eickelman and Piscatori, *Muslim Travellers.*
3. "Reproductive tourism" is not an indigenous Egyptian term, but one that is now used to describe the global movements of infertile couples as they seek treatment in other parts of the world.
4. See Population Reference Bureau, 2001, "World Population Data Sheet."
5. See Stycos et al., *Community Development and Family Planning*; and Gadalla, *Is There Hope?*
6. See World Health Organization, *Reproductive Health Research*; and Cliquet and Thienpont, *Population and Development.*
7. See Egyptian Fertility Care Society, *Community-Based Study of the Prevalence of Infertility and Its Etiological Factors in Egypt.*
8. See Inhorn, *Quest for Conception*; and Sonbol, *The Creation of a Medical Profession in Egypt, 1800–1922.*
9. As of 1996, when this study was conducted, Dr. Mohamed Yehia, director of the IVF unit at Nozha International Hospital, was keeping an informal registry of all of the IVF units in the Muslim Middle East. Calling it a "small world," in which most of the IVF personnel were acquainted and had even trained with one another, Dr. Yehia noted the following number of IVF units in the following countries: (1) one in Bahrain; (2) two in Dubai (United Arab Emirates); (3) five in Jordan; (4) two in Lebanon; (5) one in Morocco; (6) two in Oman; (7) one in Qatar; (8) at least ten in Saudi Arabia; and (9) one in Syria. Thus, Egypt and Saudi Arabia each had the largest numbers of centers. However, the largest regional concentration was clearly in the Arab Gulf states—which is not surprising, given their petrowealth.
10. See Kahn, *Reproducing Jews.*
11. At the time of our 1996 study, one U.S. dollar equaled 3.4 Egyptian pounds ($1 = LE 3.4).
12. Parts of this section can also be found in Inhorn, "Global Infertility and the Globalization of New Reproductive Technologies."
13. See Sciarra, "Infertility," p. 155.
14. See Rowe and Farley, "Prevention and Management of Infertility."
15. See Sciarra, "Infertility"; and Reproductive Health Outlook, "Infertility."
16. See Serour, "Bioethics in Reproductive Health."
17. See Cates, Farley, and Rowe, "Worldwide Patterns of Infertility"; Ericksen and Brunette, "Patterns and Predictors of Infertility Among African Women"; Larsen, "Sterility in Sub-Saharan Africa" and "Primary and Secondary Infertility in Sub-Saharan Africa"; Leonard, "Problematizing Fertility"; and World Health Organization, "Infections, Pregnancies, and Infertility."
18. See Cates, Farley, and Rowe, "Worldwide Patterns of Infertility"; and World Health Organization, "Infections, Pregnancies, and Infertility."
19. See Boerma and Mgalla, *Women and Infertility in Sub-Saharan Africa.*
20. See Sciarra, "Infertility."
21. Ibid.
22. See Cates, Farley, and Rowe, "Worldwide Patterns of Infertility"; and Larsen, "Primary and Secondary Infertility in Sub-Saharan Africa."
23. See Egyptian Fertility Care Society, *Community-Based Study of the Prevalence of Infertility and Its Etiological Factors in Egypt.*
24. See Inhorn and Buss, "Infertility, Infection, and Iatrogenesis in Egypt"; and Serour, El Ghar, and Mansour, "Infertility."
25. See Serour, El Ghar, and Mansour, "Infertility."
26. See Inhorn and Buss, "Infertility, Infection, and Iatrogenesis in Egypt."
27. See Inhorn and Buss, "Ethnography, Epidemiology, and Infertility in Egypt."
28. See Irvine, "Epidemiology and Aetiology of Male Infertility"; and World Health Organization, "Infections, Pregnancies, and Infertility."
29. See Howards, "Treatment of Male Infertility"; and Irvine, "Epidemiology and Aetiology of Male Infertility."
30. See Bell and Thomas, "Effects of Lead on Mammalian Reproduction"; and Shahara et al., "Environmental Toxicants and Female Reproduction."
31. See Daniels, "Between Fathers and Fetuses."
32. See Curtis, Savitz, and Arbuckle, "Effects of Cigarette Smoking, Caffeine Consumption, and Alcohol Intake on Fecundability."
33. See Yeboah, Wadhwani, and Wilson, "Etiological Factors of Male Infertility in Africa."
34. See van Balen and Inhorn, "Introduction."
35. See Devroey et al., "Do We Treat the Male or His Gamete?"; Howards, "Treatment of Male Infertility"; and Kamischke and Nieschlag, "Conventional Treat-

ments of Male Infertility in the Age of Evidence-Based Andrology."

36. See Fishel, Dowell, and Thornton, "Reproductive Possibilities for Infertile Couples: Present and Future."

37. See Feldman-Savelsberg, *Plundered Kitchens, Empty Wombs* and "Is Infertility an Unrecognized Public Health and Population Problem?"

38. See Bharadwaj, *Conceptions* and "Conception Politics"; and Widge, *Beyond Natural Conception.*

39. See Handwerker, "The Politics of Making Modern Babies in China."

40. See Sciarra, "Infertility"; and van Balen and Gerrits, "Quality of Infertility Care in Poor-Resource Areas and the Introduction of New Reproductive Technologies."

41. See Inhorn, *Quest for Conception,* p. 23.

42. See van Balen and Inhorn, "Introduction."

43. See Okonofua, "The Case Against New Reproductive Technologies in Developing Countries."

44. See Khattab, Younis, and Zurayk, *Women, Reproduction and Health in Rural Egypt.*

45. See Boerma and Urassa, "Associations Between Female Infertility, HIV and Sexual Behaviour in Rural Tanzania"; Favot et al., "HIV Infection and Sexual Behavior Among Women with Infertility in Tanzania"; Samucidine et al., "Infertile Women in Developing Countries at Potentially High Risk of HIV Transmission."

46. See Van Balen and Inhorn, "Introduction."

47. See Van Balen and Trimbos-Kemper, "Involuntary Childless Couples."

48. See Browner and Sargent, "Anthropology and Studies of Human Reproduction"; and Inhorn, *Infertility and Patriarchy.*

49. See Inhorn, *Infertility and Patriarchy,* especially Chapter 6 on "Child Desire."

50. See Fernea, *Children in the Muslim Middle East.*

51. See Inhorn, *Infertility and Patriarchy;* and Feldman-Savelsberg, *Plundered Kitchens, Empty Wombs.*

52. See Kleinman, Das, and Lock, *Social Suffering.*

53. See Inhorn and van Balen, *Infertility Around the Globe;* and Boerma and Mgalla, *Women and Infertility in Sub-Saharan Africa.*

54. See Sciarra, "Infertility," pp. 155–156.

55. See Inhorn and Van Balen, *Infertility Around the Globe;* and Van Balen and Gerrits, "Quality of Infertility Care in Resource-Poor Areas and the Introduction of New Reproductive Technologies."

56. See Handwerker, "The Hen That Can't Lay an Egg ('*Bu Xia Dan de Mu Ji*')" and "The Politics of Making Modern Babies in China."

57. See Riessman, "Stigma and Everyday Resistance Practices" and "Positioning Gender Identity in Narratives of Infertility."

58. See Upton, "'Infertility Makes You Invisible.'"

59. See Gerrits, "Infertility and Matrilineality."

60. See Liamputtong, "A Barren Body."

61. See Hatem, "The Enduring Alliance of Nationalism and Patriarchy in Muslim Personal Status Laws" and "The Politics of Sexuality and Gender in Segregated Patriarchal Systems"; Joseph, "Connectivity and Patriarchy Among Urban Working-Class Arab Families in Lebanon" and "Brother/Sister Relationships"; and Kandiyoti, "Islam and Patriarchy" and "Bargaining with Patriarchy."

62. See Abu-Lughod, "The Marriage of Feminism and Islamism in Egypt."

63. See Sonbol, "Adoption in Islamic Society"; and Serour, "Medically Assisted Conception" and "Bioethics in Reproductive Health."

64. See Sonbol, "Adoption in Islamic Society"; and Rugh, "Orphanages in Egypt."

65. See Inhorn, *Infertility and Patriarchy,* Chapter 4, for an in-depth discussion of cultural biases against adoption in Egypt.

66. See Bharadwaj, "Why Adoption Is Not an Option in India."

67. See Gerrits, "Studying Infertility and STDs Among the Macua in Montepuez, Mozambique"; Nwagfor, "Childlessness in Cameroon"; and Savage, "Artificial Donor Insemination in Yaounde."

68. See Jenkins, "Childlessness, Adoption, and *Milagros de Dios* in Costa Rica."

69. Ibid.

70. See Janzen, *The Quest for Therapy in Lower Zaire.*

71. See Van Balen and Gerrits, "Quality of Infertility Care in Resource-Poor Areas and the Introduction of New Reproductive Technologies."

72. See Okonofua, "The Case Against the New Reproductive Technologies in Developing Countries."

73. See Inhorn, *Quest for Conception.*

74. Dr. Mohamed Yehia, personal communication.

75. See Van Balen and Gerrits, "Quality of Infertility Care in Resource-Poor Areas and the Introduction of New Reproductive Technologies," p. 217.

76. See Sonbol, *The Creation of a Medical Profession in Egypt, 1800–1922.*

77. See Mogobe, "Traditional Therapies for Infertility in Botswana"; Sundby, "Infertility in the Gambia"; and Van Balen and Gerrits, "Quality of Care in Resource-Poor Areas and the Introduction of New Reproductive Technologies."

78. See Van Balen and Gerrits, "Quality of Care in Resource-Poor Areas and the Introduction of New Reproductive Technologies," p. 216.

79. See Okonofua, "The Case Against New Reproductive Technologies in Developing Countries"; Rowe, "Clinical Aspects of Infertility and the Role of Health Care Services"; and Sundby, "Infertility and Health Care in Countries with Less Resources."

80. See Inhorn, *Quest for Conception.*

81. Although Sarah Franklin has attempted to deconstruct the discourse of "desperateness" that is so often used to characterize infertile women who are seeking treatment, her critique is inherently Eurocentric. In Egypt and other Third World societies where much more is at stake for infertile women, "desperate" is a term that infertile women often apply to their own lives as they describe their emotional responses to therapy-seeking. See Franklin, "Deconstructing 'Desperateness.'"

82. See Handwerker, "The Politics of Making Modern Babies in China."

83. See Bharadwaj, "Conception Politics."

84. See Nicholson and Nicholson, "Assisted Reproduction in Latin America."

85. See Appadurai, *Modernity at Large,* p. 34.

86. Ibid.; see also Hannerz, *Transnational Connections.*

87. See Freeman, *High Tech and High Heels in the Global Economy.*

88. Ahmed and Donnan, "Islam in the Age of Post-modernity," p. 3.
89. Ibid.
90. See Ginsburg and Rapp, *Conceiving the New World Order*; Lock and Kaufert, *Pragmatic Women and Body Politics*; and Whiteford and Manderson, *Global Health Policy, Local Realities*.
91. See Lock and Kaufert, "Introduction," p. 1.
92. Ibid.
93. Ibid., p. 2.
94. See Colen, "'Like a Mother to Them.'"
95. See Ginsburg and Rapp, "Introduction."
96. Ibid., p. 1.
97. See Mohanty, Russo, and Torres, *Third World Women and the Politics of Feminism*.
98. See Freeman, *High Tech and High Heels in the Global Economy*.
99. See Kleinman, "Local Worlds of Suffering" and *Writing at the Margin*.
100. See, for example, Fishel, Dowell, and Thornton, "Reproductive Possibilities for Infertile Couples."
101. See Thompson, "Fertile Ground," for an excellent recent review of the now voluminous feminist literature on new reproductive technologies.
102. See Scheper-Hughes, *Death Without Weeping*, p. 552.
103. See Lock and Kaufert, "Introduction."
104. See Abu-Lughod, "The Romance of Resistance," for a discussion of the ways in which anthropologists have "romanticized" resistance. I borrow this term from her.
105. See Lock and Kaufert, "Introduction," p. 12.
106. For recent examples of this literature, see Becker, *The Elusive Embryo*; Cussins, "Ontological Choreography"; Greil, "Infertile Bodies"; Riessman, "Positioning Gender Identity in Narratives of Infertility."
107. See Cussins, "Ontological Choreography," p. 580.
108. See Fishel, Dowell, and Thornton, "Reproductive Possibilities for Infertile Couples."
109. The importance of listening to narratives of illness and suffering is now well acknowledged in both medical anthropology and sociology. See Kleinman, *The Illness Narratives*; Mattingly, *Healing Dramas and Clinical Plots*; Mattingly and Garro, *Narrative and the Cultural Construction of Illness and Healing*; and Riessman, *Narrative Analysis*.
110. See Frank, *The Wounded Storyteller*.
111. See Kleinman and Kleinman, "Suffering and Its Professional Transformation."
112. See Kleinman, *Writing at the Margin*, p. 45.
113. See Patton, *Birth Marks*, p. 101.
114. See Becker, "Deciding Whether to Tell Children About Donor Insemination"; Kahn, *Reproducing Jews*; Lock, "Perfecting Society"; and Rapp, *Testing Women, Testing the Fetus*.
115. See Lock, "Perfecting Society," p. 234.
116. See Greil, *Not Yet Pregnant*; and Sandelowski, *With Child in Mind*.
117. See Franklin, *Embodied Progress*.
118. See Greil et al., "Why Me?"
119. See Becker, *The Elusive Embryo*.
120. The Public Broadcasting Service recently featured a documentary on the new reproductive technologies called "18 Ways to Make a Baby." It aired for the first time on October 9, 2001.
121. See Nicholson and Nicholson, "Assisted Reproduction in Latin America," for an account of the ways in which new reproductive technologies, including donor techniques, are being widely applied throughout Central and South America, despite the clear prohibition on such practices by the Catholic Church.
122. See Ahmed and Donnan, "Islam in the Age of Post-modernity."
123. By 1995, when the English-language news magazine *Egypt Today* published its first report on IVF, Heba Mohammed's parents had come forward to describe the birth of their daughter after many years of infertility. Heba, at age eight, is pictured in the magazine with her parents. See Stephens, "Fertile Ground."
124. See *Quest for Conception*, Chapter 11.
125. Mansoura University in the northeastern Nile Delta region of Egypt now runs a partially state-subsidized IVF clinic.
126. The greater metropolitan area of Cairo, which includes Giza, home of the Egyptian pyramids, has close to 20 million inhabitants.
127. Because my study in Egyptian IVF centers touched on sensitive religious issues, I was required by the Fulbright Office in Cairo to have a theological supervisor for my study. Dr. Osman turned out to be a delightful and supportive advisor on my study and also an important informant.
128. In fact, many of these women also spoke fluent French or German.
129. In helping me to recruit patients into my study, Dr. Mohamed Yehia was always on the "lookout" for English speakers, especially in the early stage of my study when I was less certain of my Arabic skills. However, by the end, I had interviewed equal numbers of Arabic and English speakers in his clinic.
130. In eight cases, mothers were also present with their daughters, especially following deliveries when they were assisting in childcare. However, none of the mothers participated directly in the interviews, although they occasionally listened to our conversations.
131. In addition, while living in Atlanta following my fieldwork, I became friendly with an infertile Egyptian couple who undertook one trial of IVF in the United States. Although they had earlier inquired about making a test-tube baby in Egypt, they were not convinced that IVF would be "successful" there. Thus, they preferred to try their luck in America, despite the much higher cost. Although their single IVF attempt failed, they proceeded to conceive naturally within the same year, and the wife gave birth to a healthy son in the year 2000. Although they have now returned to Egypt, they helped to confirm many of the findings of my study, particularly regarding Egyptians' perceptions of the relative efficacy of IVF in Egypt versus the West.
132. See Bharadwaj, *Conceptions*.
133. See Kahn, *Reproducing Jews*; and Rapp, *Testing Women, Testing the Fetus*.
134. Alternately, ICSI is known as *hu'an maghari*, or "microscopic injections."
135. See Rapp, "Moral Pioneers."

Chapter 2: Class

1. See Kitzinger and Willmott, "'The Thief of Woman-hood.'"
2. $1 = LE 3.4.
3. For an extended discussion of this term, see the "Introduction" and Chapter 5 in Ginsburg and Rapp, *Conceiving the New World Order*.
4. For a discussion of the exclusion of low-income women and women of color from the use of new reproductive technologies in the United States, see Nsiah-Jefferson and Hall, "Reproductive Technology." For a discussion of the exclusion of African-American women from public discourse about infertility and new reproductive technologies, given a number of racist, sexist assumptions about African-American women's "hyperfertility," see Ceballo, "The Only Black Woman Walking the Face of the Earth Who Cannot Have a Baby."
5. See Okonofua, "The Case Against New Reproductive Technologies in Developing Countries," p. 957.
6. Ibid., p. 961.
7. Ibid., p. 961.
8. See Kahn, *Reproducing Jews*, for an extended discussion of the subsidized nature of reproductive medicine in Israel.
9. For an extended discussion of the problematics of class analysis in the Middle East, See Bill, "Class Analysis and the Dialectics of Modernization in the Middle East."
10. Ibid. See also Moghadam, *Modernizing Women*.
11. See Ibrahim, "Social Mobility and Income Distribution in Egypt."
12. See Datt, Jolliffe, and Sharma, "A Profile of Poverty in Egypt," as reported in Singerman and Ibrahim, "The Cost of Marriage in Egypt."
13. See Haddad and Akhter, "Poverty Dynamics in Egypt," as reported in Singerman and Ibrahim, "The Cost of Marriage in Egypt."
14. See Adams, "Evaluating the Process of Development in Egypt, 1980–97."
15. See Nagi, *Poverty in Egypt*.
16. See Assaad and Rouchdy, "Poverty and Poverty Alleviation Strategies in Egypt," as reported in Singerman and Ibrahim, "The Costs of Marriage in Egypt."
17. See Singerman and Ibrahim, "The Costs of Marriage in Egypt."
18. See Kandela, "Oversupply of Doctors Fuels Egypt's Health-Care Crisis."
19. For a discussion of "Islamic economics," including prohibitions against the taking of interest on loans, see Fluehr-Lobban, *Islamic Society in Practice*.
20. For a discussion of the "eugenic logics" of IVF, see Steinberg, "A Most Selective Practice."
21. For penetrating analyses of early population control efforts in Egypt, see Gadalla, *Is There Hope?*; and Stycos et al., *Community Development and Family Planning*.
22. Population Reference Bureau, 1999, "World Population Data Sheet."
23. For descriptions of Egyptian labor migration and population movement within the Middle East, see La-Towsky, "Egyptian Labor Abroad"; and Omran and Roudi, "The Middle East Population Puzzle."
24. See Rubinstein, "'Breaking the Bureaucracy.'"
25. Ibid., p. 1488.
26. Ibrahim, "Social Mobility and Income Distribution in Egypt."
27. For a discussion of some of the differences in infertile women's lives in the Western and non-Western worlds, See Van Balen and Inhorn, "Introduction," in *Infertility Around the Globe*.
28. See Bouhdiba, *Sexuality in Islam*.
29. For a fascinating discussion of medical migrations of Yemenis throughout the Middle East and beyond, see Kangas, "Therapeutic Itineraries in a Global World" and *The Lure of Technology*.
30. See Collins et al., "An Estimate of the Cost of in Vitro Fertilization Services in the United States in 1995."
31. See King and Meyer, "The Politics of Reproductive Benefits."
32. Fifteen women in this study did not provide information on the costs of IVF/ICSI treatment, either because they had not undergone these procedures or because we did not cover the topic during the interview. In general, when asked about financial details, informants were quite forthcoming and were not embarrassed to discuss their finances with me.
33. For an extended discussion of "child desire" among the infertile Egyptian poor, see Inhorn, *Infertility and Patriarchy*.

Chapter 3: Knowledge

1. See Nader, "Introduction: Anthropological Inquiry into Boundaries, Power, and Knowledge," p. 3.
2. See Birke and Whitworth, "Seeking Knowledge: Women, Science, and Islam," p. 157.
3. See Nader, "Introduction," p. 11.
4. In *Embodied Progress*, Sarah Franklin examines the history of Western anthropological stances toward kinship, which have often assumed that the Western "facts of life" (i.e., the model of duogenetic inheritance from both parents) are self-evident and universal.
5. See, for example, Crapanzano, *The Hamadsha*; Delaney, *The Seed and the Soil*; Good, "Of Blood and Babies"; and Greenwood, "III(a) Perceiving Systems."
6. See Martin, "The Egg and the Sperm."
7. In Reproducing Jews, Kahn argues that Jews are "matrilineal monogeneticists" because of their view of single-source procreation deriving from the mother. For Jews, being born of a Jewish mother confers Jewish personhood and identity. Kahn calls the monogenetic theory of procreation "one of the most compelling kinship myths indigenous to the [Middle Eastern] region," p. 211.
8. Cited in Claeson et al., "Scientific Literacy," p. 101.
9. Ibid.
10. Ibid., p. 102.
11. Ibid., p. 114.
12. See Harding, *Whose Science? Whose Knowledge?*
13. See Birke and Whitworth, "Seeking Knowledge," p. 148.
14. See Condit, "Hegemony in a Mass-Mediated Society."
15. See Armbrust, *Mass Culture and Modernism in Egypt*, p. 7.
16. Ibid., p. 3.
17. See Birke and Whitworth, "Seeking Knowledge," p. 149.
18. See Reame, "Making Babies in the 21st Century."

19. See Delaney, *The Seed and the Soil.*
20. See Crapanzano, *The Hamadsha*; Delaney, *The Seed and the Soil*; Good, "Of Blood and Babies"; Greenwood, "III(a) Perceiving Systems"; and Kahn, *Reproducing Jews.*
21. See Eickelman, *The Middle East*, for a thorough discussion of patrilineal kinship systems in the Middle East. See Inhorn, *Infertility and Patriarchy*, for a discussion of the implications of patrilineality in the lives of infertile women in Egypt.
22. For a detailed history of monogenetic procreation theories in Egypt, see Inhorn, *Quest for Conception.*
23. See Laqueur, *Making Sex*, for a detailed discussion of preformation and other competing procreative models in European history.
24. Of the four historical medical traditions present in Egypt (pharaonic, Greek, prophetic, European biomedicine), only the Islamically based prophetic tradition, based on the Qur'an and the teachings of the Prophet Muhammad, did not adopt an explicitly monogenetic theory of procreation. Thus, Delaney's argument in *The Seed and the Soil* that Islam supports monogenesis is controversial. It contradicts the work of B. F. Musallam, who argues in *Sex and Society in Islam* that Islamic procreation models are explicitly duogenetic in nature. Delaney's work has also been directly challenged by Egyptian anthropologist Hania Sholkamy in "Procreation in Islam." Sholkamy also challenges my rendering of Egyptian monogenesis, but under the mistaken assumption that I support Delaney's argument for an *Islamically derived* monogenetic model, which I do not.
25. See Inhorn, *Quest for Conception*, pp. 70–76.
26. See Lane, "Television Minidramas."
27. See Devroey et al., "Do We Treat the Male or His Gamete?"; Gerris, "A Comparative Investigation in the Real Efficacy of Conventional Therapies Versus Advanced Reproductive Technology in Male Reproductive Disorders"; and Kamischke and Neischlag, "Conventional Treatments of Male Infertility in the Age of Evidence-Based Andrology."
28. See Inhorn, *Infertility and Patriarchy*, for a detailed discussion of the social relational problems faced by infertile women in Egypt.
29. See Festinger, *A Theory of Cognitive Dissonance.*
30. See Inhorn, "Sexuality, Masculinity, and Infertility in Egypt."
31. Many feminist critics of the new reproductive technologies have pointed out that the new reproductive technologies effectively "bypass" sex in the making of a baby. See Thompson, "Fertile Ground."
32. See Inhorn, "Sexuality, Masculinity, and Infertility in Egypt."
33. See Rapp, "Moral Pioneers."
34. See Inhorn, *Quest for Conception*, particularly Part III, "Biogynecology," for a detailed discussion of doctor-patient relations between Egyptian gynecologists and poor infertile women.
35. At the time of my 1996 study, none of my informants, including elites, reported obtaining information about infertility and its treatment off the Internet. It is my impression that relatively few of my informants owned home computers, and the Internet industry in the country was still in its infancy.
36. There are innumerable popular health books of this nature in the United States, written specifically for in-

fertile audiences. One of the most comprehensive is Turiel's *Beyond Second Opinions.*
37. See Reame, "Making Babies in the 21st Century."
38. See Lane, "Television Minidramas."
39. Many Arabic-speakers from other countries report their fondness for Egyptian films and the Egyptian dialect of Arabic, which they learn from those films. Thus, most Arabs understand Egyptian Arabic, even though they may speak quite a different dialect.
40. See Shafik, "Prostitute for a Good Reason," p. 711.
41. In addition to Armbrust's work on mass media and popular culture in Egypt and Lane's work on televised health messages, Lila Abu-Lughod has been studying Egyptian soap operas as a cultural form. See, for example, Abu-Lughod, "Movie Stars and Islamic Moralism in Egypt" and "The Interpretation of Culture(s) After Television." However, there is little other cultural studies work that focuses on the Egyptian media. The need for such studies is noted in Ahmed and Donnan, "Islam in the Age of Postmodernity."
42. See Lane, "Television Minidramas."
43. Ibid., p. 167.
44. Ibid.
45. During the period of my 1996 study, Dr. Yehia made efforts to introduce me to a *Nus id-Dunya* reporter, so that the results of my previous research on infertility in Egypt, as well as my current presence in the Nozha Hospital IVF center, would become known to the Egyptian public. However, this meeting never materialized, for reasons that were not clear to me.
46. See Bharadwaj, "How Some Indian Baby Makers Are Made" and "Conception Politics."
47. However, not all "publicity" is completely positive. According to one of my informants, one newspaper article reported how Dr. Mohamed Yehia turned away a forty-two-year-old woman as a potential ICSI patient, given her "advanced" age and the low likelihood of success. My informant considered such information very demoralizing to older Egyptian women with infertile husbands.
48. To my knowledge, an adhesive material to improve the chances of nidation (implantation) is not currently available in any IVF clinic, including in Israel.
49. According to Ragone in *Surrogate Motherhood*, by 1992, four states in the United States had laws effectively banning surrogacy: Arizona banned surrogacy contracts, while Kentucky, Michigan, and Utah banned payment to surrogates. However, I am unable to determine whether this particular story of a Michigan couple wanting "one child only" is true or was created for Egyptian TV for the purposes of entertainment.
50. See Armbrust, *Mass Culture and Modernism in Egypt.*

Chapter 4: Religion

1. Cousin marriage, including among first cousins, is widely practiced among all social classes in Egypt and most Middle Eastern Muslim countries, where patrilineal parallel cousin marriage is the preferred type. For an in-depth discussion of cousin marriage in Egypt, see Inhorn, *Infertility and Patriarchy.*
2. In a famous case reported in the American media, an infertility doctor was discovered to have used his own sperm to impregnate patients whose husbands suf-

fered from male infertility. His patients began to suspect this when many of their offspring appeared to resemble the physician rather than their own husbands. The doctor was eventually questioned by police authorities and admitted what he had done. He was tried and imprisoned for his medically unethical practices.

3. A version of this story also appears in Inhorn, "Money, Marriage, and Morality."

4. In fact, many religious communities in the United States have taken stands on the new reproductive technologies, although their official positions may not have affected the actual practices of the medical profession. For a fascinating discussion of official American religious discourse on the new reproductive technologies, see Brody, "Current Religious Perspectives on the New Reproductive Techniques."

5. This is the name of the aforementioned PBS television special, which aired in 2001.

6. Orientalism refers to the continuing prejudice, stereotypes, and caricatures created of Islam by the West and was first articulated by Edward Said in his book *Orientalism*. Thus, for a Middle Eastern scholar to be called an "Orientalist" is a distinct insult. However, according to Ahmed and Donnan in "Islam in the Age of Postmodernity" (p. 5): "Said's position has created serious intellectual problems, principally because of the manner in which it has been received and applied. It has led to a cul-de-sac. 'Orientalism' itself has become a cliché, and third world literature is now replete with accusations and labels of Orientalism being hurled at critics and at one author by another at the slightest excuse. This has had a stultifying affect on the dispassionate evaluation of scholarship."

7. In "Gender and Health: Abortion in Egypt," Lane shows how Egyptian abortion law is derived from the French penal code and is thus a "remnant of colonial influence" (p. 215). In *Sex and Society in Islam*, Musallam shows how Muslim jurists have argued that the fetus becomes a human being after the fourth month of pregnancy (120 days), when "ensoulment" occurs. Thus, historically, the majority of jurists have believed that abortion should be legalized before ensoulment and prohibited abortion after that stage. Or, as noted by Musallam, "on the whole, abortion was religiously tolerated" (p. 59). Today, early abortions continue to be tolerated in Egypt, despite their illegality. For discussions of the "gap" between official discourses and actual abortion practices, see Lane, "Gender and Health"; and Huntington, "Abortion in Egypt."

8. See MacLeod, *Accommodating Protest.*

9. See Abu-Lughod, "The Marriage of Feminism and Islamism in Egypt," p. 429.

10. Ibid. See also Shafik, "Prostitute for a Good Reason."

11. See Gellner, "Foreword."

12. For an excellent review of studies on religion and health in the West, see Chatters, "Religion and Health: Public Health Research and Practice." Although research in this area is becoming increasingly visible in the social, behavioral, and health sciences, Chatters also points in her review to the ongoing resistance of many researchers toward serious scholarly engagement in this subject.

13. See Gammeltoft, "Between 'Science' and 'Superstition.'"

14. See Rapp, *Testing Women, Testing the Fetus.*

15. For "traditional" approaches to bioethical issues surrounding the new reproductive technologies see, for example, Veatch, *Medical Ethics;* Herz, "Infertility and Bioethical Issues of the New Reproductive Technologies"; and Seibel and Crockin (eds.), *Family Building Through Egg and Sperm Donation.* More recently, a number of more "critical" (especially feminist) bioethical approaches to reproductive technologies have been forthcoming. These would include, for example, Bartels et al., *Beyond Baby M;* Holmes, *Issues in Reproductive Technology;* and Wolf, *Feminism and Bioethics.*

16. See Kleinman, "Anthropology of Bioethics."

17. Ibid., p. 47.

18. Ibid.

19. Ibid., pp. 48–49.

20. Ibid., p. 45.

21. See Brody, "Current Religious Perspectives on the New Reproductive Techniques."

22. Ibid., pp. 47–48.

23. See Kleinman, "Anthropology of Bioethics."

24. See Serour, Aboulghar, and Mansour, "Bioethics in Medically Assisted Conception in the Muslim World."

25. Lane and Rubinstein, "The Use of *Fatwas* in the Production of Reproductive Health Policy in Egypt."

26. Ibid.

27. I use the term "his" followers, because Muslim religious authorities who issue *fatwas* are always male.

28. See Lane and Rubinstein, "The Use of *Fatwas* in the Production of Reproductive Health Policy in Egypt." This information was updated for me in 2002 by Dr. Mohamed Yehia.

29. See Lane and Rubinstein, "The Use of *Fatwas* in the Production of Reproductive Health Policy in Egypt."

30. Ibid.

31. See Serour, El Ghar, and Mansour, "In Vitro Fertilization and Embryo Transfer."

32. Since the late 1980s, Serour has been first or second author on articles with these titles: "In Vitro Fertilization and Embryo Transfer, Ethical Aspects in Techniques in the Muslim World"; "Some Ethical and Legal Aspects of Medically Assisted Reproduction in Egypt"; "Infertility—a Health Problem in Muslim World"; "Bioethics in Artificial Reproduction in the Muslim World"; "Medically Assisted Conception: Dilemma of Practice and Research—Islamic View"; "Islam and the Four Principles"; "Bioethics in Medically Assisted Conception in the Muslim World"; "Bioethics in Reproductive Health: A Muslim's Perspective." See the Bibliography for complete citations.

33. See Serour, ed., *Proceedings of the First International Conference on Bioethics in Human Reproduction Research in the Muslim World, 10–13 December, 1991,* and Serour and Omran, *Ethical Guidelines for Human Reproduction Research in the Muslim World.* For a fascinating discussion of how these bioethical guidelines came into being in Egypt, see Lane, "Research Bioethics in Egypt."

34. See Serour, Aboulghar, and Mansour, "Bioethics in Medically Assisted Conception in the Muslim World," p. 561. See also Inhorn, *Infertility and Patriarchy,* for an extended discussion of the importance of childbearing and motherhood for women in Egypt.

35. See Serour, "Bioethics in Reproductive Health"; and Serour, Aboulghar, and Mansour, "Bioethics in Medically Assisted Conception in the Muslim World."

36. See Serour, "Medically Assisted Conception: Dilemma of Practice and Research—Islamic View," p. 237.
37. Dr. H. Michael Fakih, personal communication.
38. See Serour, "Medically Assisted Conception: Dilemma of Practice and Research—Islamic View," p. 237.
39. Ibid., p. 238.
40. Ibid.
41. Ibid.
42. See Meirow and Schenker, "The Current Status of Sperm Donation in Assisted Reproduction Technology." See also Blank, "Regulation of Donor Insemination," which cites Egypt and Libya as Middle Eastern Muslim nations "prohibiting" donor insemination; indeed, in Libya, donor insemination is a criminal offense, subject to imprisonment under Libya's criminal code.
43. See Meirow and Schenker, "The Current Status of Sperm Donation in Assisted Reproduction Technology," p. 134.
44. See Macnaughton, "Medically Assisted Conception: Dilemma of Practice and Research—Global View," p. 229.
45. See Meirow and Schenker, "The Current Status of Sperm Donation in Assisted Reproduction Technology," p. 134. See also Nicholson and Nicholson, "Assisted Conception in Latin America."
46. See Kahn, *Reproducing Jews.*
47. As noted, however, donor technologies are now being practiced by Shi'ite Muslims in Iran, and perhaps among other Shi'ite populations in the Middle East.
48. For more detailed discussions of religious theodicies among infertile Egyptian women, see Inhorn, *Quest for Conception.*
49. See, for example, Becker, *The Elusive Embryo*; Franklin, *Embodied Progress*; Greil, *Not Yet Pregnant*; and Sandelowski, *With Child in Mind.*
50. See Greil et al., "Why Me?," p. 214.
51. Relatively little is know about the implications of sperm donation for either sperm donors themselves or men who have accepted donor sperm in order to build a family. Only a few studies have been carried out in the West, and even fewer in the non-Western world. For the West, see Daniels and Haimes, *Donor Insemination*; Daniels, "Artificial Insemination Using Donor Semen and the Issue of Secrecy"; and Becker, "Deciding Whether to Tell Children About Donor Insemination." For a fascinating account of why donor insemination is offered, but rarely practiced, in the West African country of Cameroon, see Savage, "Artificial Donor Insemination in Yaounde"; and Ngwafor, "Childlessness in Cameroon."
52. See Sonbol, "Adoption in Islamic Society."
53. Ibid., p. 49.
54. See Kahn, *Reproducing Jews.*
55. See Sonbol, "Adoption in Islamic Society."
56. See Brody, "Current Religious Perspectives on the New Reproductive Techniques."
57. See Humphrey and Humphrey, "A Fresh Look at Genealogical Bewilderment."
58. For an in-depth discussion of adoption in Egypt, including the many cultural prohibitions on its practice, see Inhorn, *Infertility and Patriarchy.* See also Sonbol, "Adoption in Islamic Society"; and Rugh, "Orphanages in Egypt."
59. Rugh, "Orphanages in Egypt."
60. Sonbol, "Adoption in Islamic Society," p. 60.
61. When I showed some of my informants pictures of my own multiracial family, several of them asked me, a light-skinned white woman, why I would have married someone *asmar*, or brown, and they "thanked God" that my infant son looked like me (racially) and not my husband.
62. Juan Cole, personal communication; see also Cole, *Sacred Space and Holy War.*
63. Dr. H. Michael Fakih, personal communication.
64. Ibid.
65. At a loss for an answer, I told her to ask Dr. Yehia himself. I don't know if she did, and I never asked him directly about this case after it happened.
66. See Robertson, "Legal Troublespots in Assisted Reproduction."
67. See Kahn, *Reproducing Jews.*
68. See Shore, "Virgin Births and Sterile Debates," p. 301.
69. See Franklin and Ragone, "Introduction," p. 9.
70. See Strathern, *Reproducing the Future.* See also Edwards et al., *Technologies of Procreation*; and Franklin, *Embodied Progress.*
71. See Kahn, *Reproducing Jews.*
72. See Franklin, *Embodied Progress*, p. 68.
73. See Starrett, *Putting Islam to Work.*
74. See Schleifer, *Motherhood in Islam.*

Chapter 5: Providers

1. See Inhorn, *Infertility and Patriarchy.*
2. See Kahn, *Reproducing Jews.*
3. See Bennett, McPake, and Mills, *Private Health Providers in Developing Countries.*
4. See World Health Organization, *The World Health Report 2000.*
5. See World Bank, *Financing Health Services in Developing Countries* and *Investing in Health.*
6. See Bennett, McPake, and Mills, "The Public/Private Mix Debate in Health Care," p. 2.
7. For an interesting study comparing government to other kinds of nongovernmental health clinics in Palestine, see Cousins, *Ideology and Biomedicine in the Palestinian West Bank.*
8. See McPake, "The Role of the Private Sector in Health Service Provision."
9. Ibid., p. 35.
10. See Mechanic and Meyer, "Concepts of Trust Among Patients with Serious Illness."
11. See Stephens, "Fertile Ground."
12. Ibid.
13. Ibid.
14. I met one such Egyptian physician, a gynecologist whose wife was in need of IVF, in the United States. He had visited Dr. Aboulghar while still living in Egypt, and described to me how Dr. Aboulghar was well-respected among Egyptian gynecologists for his "skill in IVF."
15. However, as described later in the chapter, Dr. Abdulla cancelled this scheduled visit, resulting in dashed hopes for this cohort of ICSI patients.
16. See Mead and Bower, "Patient-Centredness."
17. See Mechanic and Meyer, "Concepts of Trust Among Patients with Serious Illness."
18. See Mead and Bower, "Patient-Centredness."
19. See Stewart et al., *Patient-Centered Medicine.*
20. See Mead and Bower, p. 1090.

21. Ibid., 1091.
22. See Inhorn, *Quest for Conception*.
23. See Falkum and Forde, "Paternalism, Patient Autonomy, and Moral Deliberation in the Physician-Patient Relationship."
24. See Abdel-Tawab and Roter, "The Relevance of Client-Centered Communication to Family Planning Settings in Developing Countries."
25. Ibid., p. 1364.
26. Ibid.
27. See Mechanic and Meyer, "Concepts of Trust Among Patients with Serious Illness."
28. Ibid.
29. See Mead and Bower, "Patient-Centredness."
30. See Mechanic and Meyer, "Concepts of Trust Among Patients with Serious Illness," p. 666.
31. With the exception of my own work (*Quest for Conception*) and that of El-Mehairy (*Medical Doctors*), contemporary doctor-patient relationships have not been well studied in Egypt.
32. Most Egyptian physicians hold office consultations in the evening hours, usually beginning around 7 P.M. and sometimes continuing well after midnight.
33. See Inhorn, *Quest for Conception*.
34. See Falkum and Forde, "Paternalism, Patient Autonomy, and Moral Deliberation in the Physician-Patient Relationship."
35. Ibid., p. 293.
36. According to one physician I interviewed, most rural Egyptian physicians refer their infertile patients to the Egyptian IVF-ET Center, which is the oldest and best known in the country as a whole.
37. See Alubo, "Debt Crisis, Health and Health Services in Africa."
38. See Inhorn, *Quest for Conception*; and Sonbol, *The Creation of a Medical Profession in Egypt*, for extensive discussions of British colonial impact on Egyptian medical services and education.
39. See Stephens, "Fertile Ground."
40. See Aboulghar, Aboul Serour, and Mansour, "Some Ethical and Legal Aspects of Medically Assisted Reproduction in Egypt," p. 265.
41. See Mansour, Aboulghar, and Serour, "In Vitro Fertilization and Embryo Transfer," p. 24.
42. See Nicholson and Nicholson, "Assisted Reproduction in Latin America."
43. See Reame, "Making Babies in the 21st Century."
44. See Okonofua, "The Case Against New Reproductive Technologies in Developing Countries."
45. See Serour, El Ghar, and Mansour, "In Vitro Fertilization and Embryo Transfer," "Infertility," and "In Vitro Fertilization and Embryo Transfer in Egypt."
46. See Aboulghar, Aboul Serour, and Mansour, "In Vitro Fertilization and Embryo Transfer," p. 265.
47. See Serour, El Ghar, and Mansour, "In Vitro Fertilization and Embryo Transfer in Egypt," p. 49.
48. See Aboulghar, Aboul Serour, and Mansour, "In Vitro Fertilization and Embryo Transfer," p. 266.

Chapter 6: Efficacy

1. Huda is mistaken about this. Even in the best centers in the West, success rates are never more than 40 percent, and usually between 20 and 30 percent.
2. See Serour, El Ghar, and Mansour, "Infertility: A Health Problem in Muslim World."
3. For discussion of success rates, see Sciarra, "Infertility: An International Health Problem"; Turiel, *Beyond Second Opinions*; Van Balen and Gerrits, "Quality of Infertility Care in Poor-Resource Areas and the Introduction of New Reproductive Technologies"; and Van Balen and Inhorn, "Introduction—Interpreting Infertility: A View from the Social Sciences."
4. See Becker, *The Elusive Embryo*, Chapter 7.
5. See Turiel, *Beyond Second Opinions*, Chapter 3.
6. Ibid., p. 63.
7. Ibid.
8. Selective reduction procedures are a form of abortion of one or more fetuses in a high-order multiple pregnancy. The desire is to achieve a less risky pregnancy, usually of twins.
9. See Turiel, *Beyond Second Opinions*, p. 63.
10. Ibid., p. 64.
11. Ibid.
12. Ibid., p. 60.
13. Ibid., p. 65.
14. Ibid.
15. Ibid.
16. See Reame, "Making Babies in the 21st Century," p. 152.
17. Ibid., pp. 154–155.
18. For a discussion of these problems in the United States, see Becker, *The Elusive Embryo*; and Reame, "Making Babies in the 21st Century."
19. AIH may be justified for relatively "mild" cases of male subfertility, as well as so-called cervical-factor infertility, where cervical antibodies form a barrier to successful sperm penetration.
20. Informed consent forms are now a standard practice in Egyptian government hospitals, where they must be signed (if not always read by illiterate patients) before any invasive procedure or operation.
21. See Becker, *The Elusive Embryo*; Franklin, *Embodied Progress*; Greil, *Not Yet Pregnant*; and Sandelowski, *With Child in Mind*.
22. See Franklin, *Embodied Progress*, p. 192.
23. See Becker, *The Elusive Embryo*, Chapter 7.
24. Ibid., p. 129.
25. For descriptions of Egypt's lengthy medical history, see Inhorn, *Quest for Conception*; and Sonbol, *The Creation of a Medical Profession in Egypt, 1800–1922.*
26. See Kandela, "Oversupply of Doctors Fuels Egypt's Health-Care Crisis."
27. See Rubinstein, " 'Breaking the Bureaucracy.' "
28. See Becker, *The Elusive Embryo*; and Franklin, *Embodied Progress*.
29. See Inhorn, *Quest for Conception*.
30. See Franklin, *Embodied Progress*, Chapter 4.
31. See Sandelowski, "Compelled to Try."
32. See Scholz et al., "Problems of Multiple Births After ART."
33. See Population Reference Bureau, 2001, "World Population Data Sheet."
34. Even uneducated poor urban couples now express a desire for only two children, given the high expenses associated with raising children in urban areas.
35. A strong cultural preference for sons persists in the Middle East, although most women also desire at least one daughter. See Inhorn, *Infertility and Patriarchy*; and Obermeyer, "Fairness and Fertility" on son preference.
36. See Becker, *The Elusive Embryo*.

37. Laparoscopy is an invasive surgical technique that aids diagnosis of female infertility through the visualization of the reproductive organs themselves.

Chapter 7: Embodiment

1. No Egyptian IVF centers at the time were offering psychological counseling services. These were tried at both the Nozha and Nile Badrawi IVF centers, and most patients refused to be counseled in this way, for reasons that will become clear in Chapter 9.
2. A "borderline" pregnancy means that the pregnancy hormone, beta-hCG, is detected through a very early blood test, but at levels that are lower than anticipated. Such borderline pregnancies are usually either false-positives or are pregnancies that are destined to fail.
3. See van der Ploeg, "Hermaphrodite Patients."
4. See Lorber, "*In Vitro* Fertilization and Gender Politics" and "Choice, Gift, or Patriarchal Bargain?"
5. See Kandiyoti, "Bargaining with Patriarchy."
6. See Lorber, "Choice, Gift, or Patriarchal Bargain?," p. 30.
7. Ibid., pp. 23–24.
8. See Inhorn, *Quest for Conception.*
9. See Joseph, "Connectivity and Patriarchy Among Urban Working-Class Arab Families in Lebanon" and "Brother-Sister Relationships: Connectivity, Love, and Power in the Reproduction of Patriarchy in Lebanon."
10. See Van der Ploeg, "Hermaphrodite Patients," p. 461.
11. Ibid., pp. 461–462.
12. See Inhorn, " 'The Worms Are Weak' " and "Sexuality, Masculinity, and Infertility in Egypt."
13. See Inhorn, "The 'Local' Confronts the 'Global,' " p. 271.
14. See Lloyd, "The Language of Reproduction."
15. See Lloyd, "Condemned to Be Meaningful."
16. See Bourdieu, *Outline of a Theory of Practice.*
17. See Early, "The Logic of Well Being" and "Catharsis and Creation in Informal Narratives of Baladi Women of Cairo."
18. There is only one school of public health in Egypt (one of two in the entire Middle Eastern region) and only a few departments of community medicine where epidemiology is taught. Because of the dearth of trained epidemiologists in the country, the Centers for Disease Control and Prevention (CDC) in Atlanta has entered into a cooperative arrangement with the Egyptian Ministry of Health to offer a Field Epidemiology Training Program (FETP) in the country, teaching Egyptian physicians how to engage in disease investigation and surveillance.
19. See Beck, *Risk Society.*
20. See Furedi, *Culture of Fear.*
21. See Freudenberg, "Perceived Risk, Real Risk."
22. However, diet clinics catering to elites are increasingly prevalent in urban areas of Egypt. See Basyouny, *Just a Gaze—Female Clientele of Diet Clinics in Cairo.*
23. See Amin, "The Epidemiologic Transition in Egypt."
24. See Lock, *Encounters with Aging.*
25. Ibid., p. xxi.
26. See Inhorn, "The Risks of Test-Tube Baby Making in Egypt."
27. See Turiel, *Beyond Second Opinions.*

28. See Klein and Rowland, "Hormonal Cocktails."
29. Ibid., p. 345.
30. Ibid., p. 346.
31. Ibid., p. 345.
32. See Inhorn, *Quest for Conception.*
33. Unexplained, or idiopathic, infertility is a residual category describing couples who have not conceived but have no detectable or known cause for the infertility. Whereas many couples once fell into this category, the percentage of unexplained infertility cases continues to decline as diagnostic procedures evolve and more couples can be categorized.
34. See McConnell, "Diagnosis and Treatment of Male Infertility"; and Wood, *Dynamics of Human Reproduction.*
35. See Howards, "Treatment of Male Infertility"; and Irvine, "Epidemiology and Aetiology of Male Infertility."
36. See Daniels, "Between Fathers and Fetuses"; and Howards, "Treatment of Male Infertility."
37. See Bentley, "Environmental Pollutants and Infertility," p. 136.
38. Ibid.
39. See Bell and Thomas, "Effects of Lead on Mammalian Reproduction"; and Shahara et al., "Environmental Toxicants and Female Reproduction."
40. See Hopkins, Mehanna, and el-Haggar, *People and Pollution*; and Stephens, "Fertile Ground."
41. See Thonneau et al., "Occupational Heat Exposure and Male Fertility."
42. See Curtis et al., "Effects of Cigarette Smoking, Caffeine Consumption, and Alcohol Intake on Fecundability."
43. Ibid.
44. See "Egypt Sets Objectives Through 'Healthy People' Plan," in the March 2002 issue of *The Nation's Health.*
45. See Amin, "The Epidemiologic Transition in Egypt."
46. See Howards, "Treatment of Male Infertility."
47. See Yeboah et al., "Etiological Factors of Male Infertility in Africa."
48. See World Health Organization, *WHO Manual for the Standardized Investigation and Diagnosis of the Infertile Couple.*
49. See Howards, "Treatment of Male Infertility," p. 314.
50. Ibid.
51. See Gerris, *A Comparative Investigation in the Real Efficacy of Conventional Therapies Versus Advanced Reproductive Technology in Male Reproductive Disorders*; and Kamischke and Neischlag, "Conventional Treatments of Male Infertility in the Age of Evidence-Based Andrology."
52. Only four women in this study, mostly from lower- to middle-class backgrounds and/or rural areas, had encountered such treatments on visits to gynecologists. These same women had also been encouraged by family and community members to try traditional remedies, of the kind described at length in my book *Quest for Conception.*
53. See Turiel, *Beyond Second Opinions*, p. 45.
54. See also Lock, *Encounters with Aging*, for a useful comparison of why Japanese women fear the powerful effects of hormonal replacement therapy for menopause.
55. See DeClerque et al., "Rumor, Misinformation and Oral Contraceptives"; and Early, *Baladi Women of Cairo: Playing with an Egg and a Stone.*

56. See Turiel, *Beyond Second Opinions.*
57. Actually, by 1996, there were already ten IVF centers in operation or development in Saudi Arabia, according to Dr. Mohamed Yehia.
58. See Turiel, *Beyond Second Opinions.*
59. Traditionally, plump, voluptuous physiques have been considered a sign of female beauty in Egypt, although this may be slowly changing, particularly among elites.
60. See Mamdani, "Early Initiatives in Essential Drugs Policy."
61. See Rubinstein, "'Breaking the Bureaucracy.'"
62. Ibid.
63. Ibid.
64. See Mamdani, "Early Initiatives in Essential Drugs Policy," p. 3.
65. Ibid., p. 4.
66. Ibid., p. 5.
67. See Inhorn, *Quest for Conception.*
68. See Freeman, *High Tech and High Heels in the Global Economy.*
69. See Kahn, *Reproducing Jews,* for a description of these stages as she observed them in IVF centers in Israel.
70. In my study, numbers of embryos transferred ranged from one, in cases where only one viable embryo emerged after fertilization or microscopic injection, to six in a number of older women whose chances of successful implantation were considered to be low. However, in most cases, either three or four embryos were transferred.
71. See Foucault, *Discipline & Punish.*
72. However, the health effects of prolonged bed rest in an otherwise uneventful pregnancy are unclear.
73. See Bittles and Matson, "Genetic Influences on Human Infertility."
74. Ibid., pp. 46–47.
75. Because of the relatively high prevalence of endogamous marriage, genetic problems of offspring are known to most Egyptians, who have viewed televised health education messages on this subject. For a fascinating account of religious explanations for genetic disorders in Saudi Arabian offspring of consanguineous marriages, see Panter-Brick, "Parental Responses to Consanguinity and Genetic Disease in Saudi Arabia."
76. One infant was delivered early, at thirty-six weeks, because of gestational hypertension in the mother. Another child developed a bilirubin problem after birth and had to be transfused. However, neither of these problems was related in any way to the father's health or the means of ICSI conception.
77. See Kleinman and Kleinman, "Suffering and Its Professional Transformation."
78. See Rubinstein, "'Breaking the Bureaucracy,'" p. 1487.
79. See Van Balen and Inhorn, "Introduction."

Chapter 8: Gender

1. A version of this story can also be found in Inhorn, "The 'Local' Confronts the 'Global.'"
2. Studies on the gender-specific responses to infertility and its treatment in the United States include Abbey, Andrews, and Halman, "Gender's Role in Responses to Infertility"; Berg, Wilson, and Weingartner, "Psychological Sequelae of Infertility Treatment"; Daniluk, "Infertility: Intrapersonal and Interpersonal Impact";

Greil, Leitko, and Porter, "Infertility: His and Hers"; Nachtigall, Becker, and Wozny, "The Effects of Gender-Specific Diagnosis on Men's and Women's Response to Infertility"; and Webb and Daniluk, "The End of the Line."
3. See Kandiyoti, "Bargaining with Patriarchy."
4. See Inhorn, *Infertility and Patriarchy,* for a fuller discussion of marital ideals, expectations, and realities in Egypt.
5. See Greil, Leitko, and Porter, "Infertility: His and Hers."
6. In "The Uses of a 'Disease': Infertility as Rhetorical Vehicle," Sandelowski and de Lacey describe the ways in which infertile Western couples have been "used" as a vehicle for "commercial and academic exchange."
7. For examples of this feminist literature, see Andrews, *The Clone Age;* Corea et al., *Man-Made Women;* Farquhar, *The Other Machine;* Hartouni, *Cultural Conceptions;* Klein, *Infertility;* Lublin, *Pandora's Box;* McNeil, Varcoe, and Yearley, *The New Reproductive Technologies;* Overall, *The Future of Human Reproduction;* Ratcliff, *Healing Technology;* Raymond, *Women as Wombs;* Rowland, *Living Laboratories;* Rothman, *Recreating Motherhood;* Scutt, *The Baby Machine;* Spallone and Steinberg, *Made to Order;* Squier, *Babies in Bottles;* Stanworth, *Reproductive Technologies;* and Van Dyck, *Manufacturing Babies and Public Consent.*
8. See Becker, *Healing the Infertility Family;* and Greil, *Not Yet Pregnant.*
9. See Gadalla, *Is There Hope?;* Ibrahim, "State, Women, and Civil Society"; and Stycos et al., *Community Development and Family Planning.*
10. See Population Reference Bureau, 2001, "World Population Data Sheet."
11. See Obermeyer, "Fairness and Fertility"; and Van Balen and Inhorn, "Son Preference, Sex Selection, and the 'New' New Reproductive Technologies."
12. See Inhorn, *Infertility and Patriarchy.*
13. Ibid.
14. See Joseph, *Intimate Selving in Arab Families,* "Brother/Sister Relationships," and "Connectivity and Patriarchy Among Urban Working Class Arab Families in Lebanon."
15. See Ghoussoub and Sinclair-Webb, *Imagined Masculinities,* p. 8.
16. See Lindisfarne, "Variant Masculinities, Variant Virginities."
17. See Cornwall and Lindisfarne, *Dislocating Masculinity;* and Ghoussoub and Sinclair-Webb, *Imagined Masculinities.*
18. See Connell, *Masculinities,* p. 37.
19. See Kandiyoti, "The Paradoxes of Masculinity," p. 199.
20. See Ali, "Making 'Responsible' Men" and "Notes on Rethinking Masculinities."
21. See Kandiyoti, "The Paradoxes of Masculinity"; Peteet, "Male Gender and Rituals of Resistance in the Palestinian Intifada"; and Sinclair-Webb, "Our Bulent Is Now a Commando."
22. See Ali, "Making 'Responsible' Men" and "Notes on Rethinking Masculinities"; Lindisfarne, "Variant Masculinities, Variant Virginities"; and Ouzgane, "Masculinity as Virility in Tahar Ben Jelloun's Fiction."
23. See Ouzgane, "Masculinity as Virility in Tahar Ben Jelloun's Fiction," p. 3.
24. Ghoussoub and Sinclair-Webb's recent edited collection on Middle Eastern masculinity is entitled *Imag-*

ined Masculinities: Male Identity and Culture in the Modern Middle East—a title intended to convey how little is actually known about this subject.

25. See Inhorn, "'The Worms Are Weak'" and "Sexuality, Masculinity, and Infertility in Egypt."

26. See Omran and Roudi, "The Middle East Population Puzzle."

27. Singerman and Ibrahim, "The Cost of Marriage in Egypt."

28. See Ali, "Making 'Responsible' Men" and "Notes on Rethinking Masculinities"; and Inhorn, *Infertility and Patriarchy.*

29. See Baron, "The Making and Breaking of Marital Bonds in Modern Egypt."

30. See Abu-Lughod, "The Marriage of Feminism and Islamism in Egypt," p. 437.

31. See Inhorn, *Infertility and Patriarchy.*

32. See Becker, *Healing the Infertile Family*; Greil, *Not Yet Pregnant*; and Greil, Leitko, and Porter, "Infertility: His and Hers."

33. See Jenkins, "Childlessness, Adoption, and *Milagros de Dios* in Costa Rica"; and Riessman, "Positioning Gender Identity in Narratives of Infertility."

34. In *Embodied Progress*, Franklin critically assesses the discourses surrounding these "hope technologies"—technologies that, in fact, have very low chances of success.

35. See Kalb, "Should You Have Your Baby Now?" The international edition of *Newsweek* is sold in Egypt and may be read by educated elites.

36. In *The Elusive Embryo*, Becker examines how the age of forty serves as a key "cutoff" point in most infertility clinics in the United States. As a result, many infertile American women are distressed as they approach this age.

37. See Lane, "Gender and Health"; and Huntington, "Abortion in Egypt."

38. See Browner, "Situating Women's Reproductive Activities"; Rapp, *Testing Women, Testing the Fetus*; and Rothman, *The Tentative Pregnancy.*

39. See Singerman and Ibrahim, "The Cost of Marriage in Egypt."

40. Ibid.

41. Ibid.

42. Ibid.

43. Ibid.

44. Diane Singerman, personal communication.

45. See Singerman and Ibrahim, "The Cost of Marriage in Egypt."

46. See Greil, Leitko, and Porter, "Infertility: His and Hers," p. 185.

47. Ibid., p. 182.

Chapter 9: Stigma

1. See Greil, "A Secret Stigma."

2. See Goffman, *Stigma*, p. 3.

3. See Whiteford and Gonzalez, "Stigma," p. 29.

4. Ibid.

5. See Greil, "A Secret Stigma."

6. See Becker, "Deciding Whether to Tell Children About Donor Insemination."

7. See Webb and Daniluk, "The End of the Line," p. 15.

8. See Inhorn, "*Umm Il-Ghayyib*, Mother of the Missing One."

9. See Scambler, "Perceiving and Coping with a Stigmatizing Condition."

10. *Ma'alish* is a common Egyptian expression, equivalent to the English phrase, "No use crying over spilled milk." It is usually meant to convey comfort—to tell a person not to worry—when something has gone wrong. *Haram*, however, means sin and all that is forbidden. Egyptians often use the expression to admonish those, including children, who have actually done something wrong. Thus, *haram* implies volition, whereas *ma'alish* may or may not.

11. See Greil, "A Secret Stigma."

12. See Handwerker, "The Politics of Making Modern Babies in China."

13. Irving Leon, a practicing psychotherapist and adjunct professor of obstetrics and gynecology at the University of Michigan, has told me that many of his infertile female patients experience feelings akin to *hasad*, or envy, and he often gives them "permission" as their therapist *not* to participate in activities where other "happy families" with children will be present.

14. See Stephens, "Fertile Ground."

15. For recent examples of this disclosure literature, see Freeman, "The New Birth Right?"; Landau, "The Management of Genetic Origins"; Nachtigall, "Secrecy"; Nachtigall et al., "The Disclosure Decision"; Nachtigall et al., "Stigma, Disclosure, and Family Functioning Among Parents of Children Conceived Through Donor Insemination"; and Shenfield and Steele, "What Are the Effects of Anonymity and Secrecy on the Welfare of the Child in Gamete Donation?"

16. See Becker, "Deciding Whether to Tell Children About Donor Insemination"; Nachtigall et al., "The Disclosure Decision"; and Nachtigall et al., "Stigma, Disclosure, and Family Functioning Among Parents of Children Conceived Through Donor Insemination."

17. See Becker, "Deciding Whether to Tell Children About Donor Insemination."

18. See Lane, "Research Bioethics in Egypt," p. 891.

19. See Becker, "Deciding Whether to Tell Children About Donor Insemination."

20. See Van Balen, "The Psychologization of Infertility"; Boivin, Scanlan, and Walker, "Why Are Infertile Patients Not Using Psychosocial Counselling?"; and Greil, "Infertility and Psychological Distress."

21. See Van Balen, p. 92.

22. See Becker, *The Elusive Embryo.*

23. See Van Balen, "The Psychologization of Infertility."

24. Dwairy and Van Sickle have also argued that many of the basic concepts and techniques of Western psychotherapy—for example, the emphasis on individualism and the goal of "self-actualization"—are at odds with the core beliefs of "traditional Arab societies." See Dwairy and Van Sickle, "Western Psychotherapy in Traditional Arab Societies."

25. See Bharadwaj, "How Some Indian Baby Makers Are Made" and "Conception Politics"; see also Handwerker, "The Politics of Making Modern Babies in China."

26. See Lock and Kaufert, "Introduction," pp. 19–20.

27. See Becker, "Deciding Whether to Tell Children About Donor Insemination," p. 120.

28. See Lock and Kaufert, "Introduction," p. 21.

Chapter 10: Conclusion

1. See Inhorn, *Quest for Conception* and *Infertility and Patriarchy.*
2. For example, in the last decade, ethnographies on Egyptian poor or working-class communities have included Early's *Baladi Women of Cairo: Playing with an Egg and a Stone*; Homa Hoodfar's *Between Marriage and the Market: Intimate Politics and Survival in Cairo*; Arlene MacLeod's *Accommodating Protest: Working Women, the New Veiling, and Change in Cairo*; Soheir Morsy's *Gender, Sickness, and Healing in Rural Egypt: Ethnography in Historical Context*; Nedoroscik's *The City of the Dead: A History of Cairo's Cemetery Communities*; van Nieuwkerk's *"A Trade Like Any Other": Female Singers and Dancers in Egypt*; Watson's *Women in the City of the Dead*; Wikan's *Tomorrow, God Willing: Self-Made Destinies in Cairo*; and Zuhur's *Revealing Reveiling: Islamist Gender Ideology in Contemporary Egypt.* Only two ethnographies, Gaffney's *The Prophet's Pulpit: Islamic Preaching in Contemporary Egypt* and Starrett's *Putting Islam to Work: Education, Politics, and Religious Transformation in Egypt*, are not situated explicitly within lower-class communities.
3. See Scheper-Hughes, *Death Without Weeping.*
4. The case of Saad Eddin Ibrahim, a well-known Egyptian sociologist and director of the Ibn Khaldun Center who was sentenced to a seven-year jail term for attempting to monitor Egyptian elections and promote minority (i.e., Coptic Christian) rights, provides an example of how even intellectual elites in Egypt are always "at risk" in an authoritarian society.
5. See Sandelowski, Harris, and Black, p. 282.
6. See Ehrenfeld, "Infertility."
7. See Fishel, Dowell, and Thornton, "Reproductive Possibilities for Infertile Couples."
8. Ibid., p. 17.
9. See Okonofua, "The Case Against New Reproductive Technologies in Developing Countries."
10. See Inhorn, *Quest for Conception* and *Infertility and Patriarchy.*
11. See Cambrosio, Young, and Lock, "Introduction," p. 11.
12. Ibid., p. 12.
13. See Aboulghar, Serour, and Mansour, "Some Ethical and Legal Aspects of Medically Assisted Reproduction in Egypt"; Sciarra, "Infertility"; and Serour, El Ghar, and Mansour, "In Vitro Fertilization and Embryo Transfer," "Infertility," and "In Vitro Fertilization and Embryo Transfer in Egypt."
14. See Collet et al., "Infertility in Central Africa"; and World Health Organization, "Infections, Pregnancies, and Infertility."
15. See Serour, El Ghar, and Mansour, "Infertility"; Inhorn, *Quest for Conception*; and Inhorn and Buss, "Infertility, Infection, and Iatrogenesis."
16. See Dixon-Mueller and Wasserheit, *The Culture of Silence.*
17. At a recent University of Michigan conference on "The Epidemiologic Transition Among Arab Popula-

tions: Local-Global Connections," the Dean of the High Institute of Public Health in Egypt denied that Egypt or the rest of the Muslim Middle East has an HIV/AIDS problem. His statement generated an interesting discussion among both the Middle Eastern and American audience members. Other Middle Eastern health officials present argued that the time has come for more "honesty" about this growing problem, including the issue of heterosexual HIV transmission in the Middle East.
18. See World Health Organization, *Reproductive Health Research.*
19. See Irvine, "Epidemiology and Aetiology of Male Infertility."
20. See Boerma and Mgalla, *Women and Infertility in Sub-Saharan Africa.*
21. See Mundigo, "The Role of Men in Improving Reproductive Health."
22. My study, supported by Fulbright and National Science Foundation grants, is titled "Middle Eastern Masculinities in the Age of New Reproductive Technologies." It seeks to compare the experience of male infertility in Lebanon, Syria, and "Arab Detroit."
23. See Rapp and Ginsburg, "Relocating Reproduction, Generating Culture."
24. See Bledsoe, Guyer, and Lerner, "Introduction"; and Browner, "Situating Women's Reproductive Activities."
25. See Ginsburg and Rapp, "Introduction"; and Rapp and Ginsburg, "Relocating Reproduction, Generating Culture." Ginsburg and Rapp have argued forcefully in these two essays that reproduction is now at the center of social theory in anthropology, and they have reviewed the recent scholarly literature in this area to support this claim.
26. See Lock and Kaufert, "Introduction."
27. See Brodwin, *Biotechnology and Culture.*
28. See Becker, "Deciding Whether to Tell Children About Donor Insemination."
29. See Rugh, "Orphanages in Egypt."
30. Ibid.
31. Dale Huntington, personal communication.
32. See Rugh, "Orphanages in Egypt," p. 139.
33. See Steinberg, "A Most Selective Practice."
34. See Thompson, "Fertile Ground," for an excellent discussion of the shifts in feminist thinking on this subject.
35. This is not to say that Egyptian patriarchy itself—which leaves women with few other options besides pursuing motherhood—does not need to be unseated. See Inhorn, *Infertility and Patriarchy*, for an extended discussion of patriarchy in the lives of Egyptian women.
36. See Fishel, Dowell, and Thornton, "Reproductive Possibilities for Infertile Couples."
37. See Nicholson and Nicholson, "Assisted Reproduction in Latin America."
38. Ibid., p. 443.
39. Ibid.
40. See Hess, "Parallel Universes," p. 16.
41. See Inda and Rosaldo, "Introduction," p. 4.

Bibliography

Abbey, Antonia, Andrews, Frank M., and L. Jill Halman. 1991. "Gender's Role in Responses to Infertility." *Psychology of Women Quarterly* 15:295–316.

Abdel-Tawab, Nahla, and Debra Roter. 2002. "The Relevance of Client-Centered Communication to Family Planning Settings in Developing Countries: Lessons from the Egyptian Experience." *Social Science & Medicine* 54:1357–1368.

Aboulghar, M. A., Aboul Serour, G. I., and R. Mansour. 1990. "Some Ethical and Legal Aspects of Medically Assisted Reproduction in Egypt." *International Journal of Bioethics* 1:265–268.

Abu-Lughod, Lila. 2002. "The Marriage of Feminism and Islamism in Egypt: Selective Repudiation as a Dynamic of Postcolonial Cultural Politics." In *The Anthropology of Globalization: A Reader*, ed. Johnathan Xavier Inda and Renato Rosaldo, 428–451. Malden, MA: Blackwell.

———. 1997. "The Interpretation of Culture(s) After Television." *Representations* 59:109–134.

———. 1995. "Movie Stars and Islamic Moralism in Egypt." *Social Text* 42:53–67.

———. 1990. "The Romance of Resistance: Tracing Transformations of Power Through Bedouin Women." *American Ethnologist* 17:41–55.

Adams, Richard H. 2000. "Evaluating the Process of Development in Egypt, 1980–97." *International Journal of Middle Eastern Studies* 32:255–275.

Ahmed, Akbar S., and Hastings Donnan. 1994. "Islam in the Age of Postmodernity." In *Islam, Globalization and Postmodernity*, ed. Akbar S. Ahmed and Hastings Donnan, 1–20. London: Routledge.

Ali, Kamran Asdar. 2000. "Making 'Responsible' Men: Planning the Family in Egypt." In *Fertility and the Male Life-Cycle in the Era of Fertility Decline*, ed. Caroline Bledsoe, Susana Lerner, and Jane I. Guyer, pp. 119–143. Oxford, England: Oxford University Press.

———. 1996. "Notes on Rethinking Masculinities: An Egyptian Case." In *Learning About Sexuality: A Practical Beginning*, ed. Sondra Zeidenstein and Kirsten Moore, pp. 98–109. New York: The Population Council International Women's Health Coalition Network.

Alubo, S. Ogoh. 1990. "Debt Crisis, Health and Health Services in Africa." *Social Science & Medicine* 31:639–648.

Amin, Ezzat. 2001. "The Epidemiologic Transition in Egypt." Paper presented at a conference on "The Epidemiologic Transition Among Arab Populations: Local-Global Connections," University of Michigan, May 10.

Andrews, Lori B. 1999. *The Clone Age: Adventures in the New World of Reproductive Technology*. New York: Henry Holt and Company.

Appadurai, Arjun. 1996. *Modernity at Large: Cultural Dimensions of Globalization*. Minneapolis: University of Minnesota Press.

Armbrust, Walter. 1996. *Mass Culture and Modernism in Egypt*. Cambridge, England: Cambridge University Press.

Assaad, Ragui, and Malik Rouchdy. 1998. "Poverty and Poverty Alleviation Strategies in Egypt." Report Submitted to the Ford Foundation, Cairo, Egypt.

Baron, Beth. 1991. "The Making and Breaking of Marital Bonds in Modern Egypt." In *Women in Middle Eastern History: Shifting Boundaries in Sex and Gender*, ed. Nikki R. Keddie and Beth Baron, 275–291. New Haven, CT: Yale University Press.

Bartels, Dianne M., Priester, Reinhard, Vawter, Dorothy E., and Arthur L. Caplan, eds. 1990. *Beyond Baby M: Ethical Issues in New Reproductive Technologies*. Clifton, NJ: Humana Press.

Basyouny, Iman Farid. 1997. *Just a Gaze: Female Clientele of Diet Clinics in Cairo: An Ethnomedical Study*. Cairo: The American University in Cairo Press.

Beck, Ulrich. 1992. *Risk Society: Towards a New Modernity*. London: Sage.

Becker, Gay. 2001. "Deciding Whether to Tell Children About Donor Insemination: An Unresolved Question in the United States." In *Infertility Around the Globe: New Thinking on Childlessness, Gender, and Reproductive Technologies*, ed. Marcia C. Inhorn and Frank van Balen, 119–133. Berkeley: University of California Press.

———. 2000. *The Elusive Embryo: How Women and Men Approach New Reproductive Technologies*. Berkeley: University of California Press.

———. 1997. *Healing the Infertile Family: Strengthening Your Relationship in the Search for Parenthood*. Berkeley: University of California Press.

Bell, John U., and John A. Thomas. 1980. "Effects of Lead on Mammalian Reproduction." In *Lead Toxicity*, ed. R. L. Singhal and J. A. Thomas, 169–185. Baltimore: Urban & Schwarzenberg.

Bennett, Sara, McPake, Barbara, and Anne Mills, eds. 1997. *Private Health Providers in Developing Countries: Serving the Public Interest?* London: Zed Books.

Bennett, Sara, McPake, Barbara, and Anne Mills. 1997. "The Public/Private Mix Debate in Health Care." In *Private Health Providers in Developing Countries: Serving the Public Interest?*, ed. Sara Bennett, Barbara McPake, and Anne Mills, 1–18. London: Zed Books.

Bentley, Gillian R. 2000. "Environmental Pollutants and Fertility." In *Infertility in the Modern World: Present and Future Prospects*, ed. Gillian R. Bentley and C. G. Nicholas Mascie-Taylor, 85–152. Cambridge, England: Cambridge University Press.

Berg, Barbara J., Wilson, John F., and Paul J. Weingartner. 1991. "Psychological Sequelae of Infertility Treatment: The Role of Gender and Sex-Role Identification." *Social Science & Medicine* 33:1071–1080.

Bharadwaj, Aditya. 2002. "Why Adoption Is Not an Option in India: The Visibility of Infertility, the Secrecy of Donor Insemination, and Other Cultural Complexities." *Social Science & Medicine*, in press.

———. 2001. "Conception Politics: Medical Egos, Media Spotlights, and the Contest Over Testtube Firsts in India." In *Infertility Around the Globe: New Thinking on Childlessness, Gender, and Reproductive Technologies*, ed. Marcia C. Inhorn and Frank van Balen, 315–333. Berkeley: University of California Press.

———. 2001. *Conceptions: An Exploration of Infertility and Assisted Conception in India.* Ph.D. thesis, University of Bristol, England.

———. 2000. "How Some Indian Baby Makers Are Made: Media Narratives and Assisted Conception in India." *Anthropology & Medicine* 7:63–78.

Bill, James A. 1972. "Class Analysis and the Dialectics of Modernization in the Middle East." *International Journal of Middle East Studies* 3:417–434.

Birke, Lynda, and Rosalind Whitworth. 1998. "Seeking Knowledge: Women, Science, and Islam." *Women's Studies International Forum* 21:147–159.

Bittles, A. H., and P. L. Matson. 2000. "Genetic Influences on Human Infertility." In *Infertility in the Modern World: Present and Future Prospects*, ed. Gillian R. Bentley and C. G. Nicholas Mascie-Taylor, 46–81. Cambridge, England: Cambridge University Press.

Blank, Robert. 1998. "Regulation of Donor Insemination." In *Donor Insemination: International Social Science Perspectives*, ed. Ken Daniels and Erica Haimes, 131–150. Cambridge, England: Cambridge University Press.

Bledsoe, Caroline, Guyer, Jane I., and Susana Lerner. 2000. "Introduction." In *Fertility and the Male Life-Cycle in the Era of Fertility Decline*, ed. Caroline Bledsoe, Susana Lerner, and Jane I. Guyer, 1–26. Oxford, England: Oxford University Press.

Boerma, J. Ties, and Zaida Mgalla, eds. 2001. *Women and Infertility in Sub-Saharan Africa: A Multi-Disciplinary Perspective.* Amsterdam, The Netherlands: Royal Tropical Institute, KIT Publishers.

Boerma, J. Ties, and Mark Urassa. 2001. "Associations Between Female Infertility, HIV and Sexual Behaviour in Rural Tanzania." In *Women and Infertility in Sub-Saharan Africa: A Multi-Disciplinary Perspective*, 175–187. Amsterdam, The Netherlands: Royal Tropical Institute, KIT Publishers.

Boivin, J., Scanlan, L. C., and S. M. Walker. 1999. "Why Are Infertile Patients Not Using Psychosocial Counselling?" *Human Reproduction* 14:1384–1391.

Bouhdiba, Abdelwahab. 1985. *Sexuality in Islam.* London: Routledge & Kegan Paul.

Bourdieu, Pierre. 1977. *Outline of a Theory of Practice.* Translated by Richard Nice. New York: Cambridge University Press.

Brodwin, Paul E., ed. 2000. *Biotechnology and Culture: Bodies, Anxieties, Ethics.* Bloomington: Indiana University Press.

Brody, Baruch. 1990. "Current Religious Perspectives on the New Reproductive Technologies." In *Beyond Baby M: Ethical Issues in New Reproductive Technologies*, ed. Dianne M. Bartels, Reinhard Priester, Dorothy E. Vawter, and Arthur L. Caplan, 45–63. Clifton, NJ: Humana Press.

Browner, C.H. 2000. "Situating Women's Reproductive Activities." *American Anthropologist* 102:773–788.

Browner, C. H., and Carolyn F. Sargent. 1996. "Anthropology and Studies of Human Reproduction." In *Medical Anthropology: Contemporary Theory and Method*, ed. Carolyn F. Sargent and Thomas M. Johnson, 219–234. Westport, CT: Praeger.

Cambrosio, Alberto, Young, Alan, and Margaret Lock. 2000. "Introduction." In *Living and Working with the New Medical Technologies: Intersections of Inquiry*, ed. Margaret Lock, Alan Young, and Alberto Cambrosio, 1–16. Cambridge, England: Cambridge University Press.

Cates, W., Farley, T. M. M., and P. J. Rowe. 1985. "Worldwide Patterns of Infertility: Is Africa Different?" *The Lancet* (September 14): 596–598.

Ceballo, Rosario. 1999. "'The Only Black Woman Walking the Face of the Earth Who Cannot Have a Baby': Two Women's Stories." In *Women's Untold Stories: Breaking Silence, Talking Back, Voicing Complexity*, ed. Mary Romero and Abigail J. Stewart, 3–19. New York: Routledge.

Chatters, Linda M. 2000. "Religion and Health: Public Health Research and Practice." *Annual Review of Public Health* 21:335–367.

Claeson, Bjorn, Martin, Emily, Richardson, Wendy, Schoch-Spana, Monica, and Karen-Sue Taussig. 1996. "Scientific Literacy, What It Is, Why It's Important, and Why Scientists Think We Don't Have It: The Case of Immunology and the Immune System." In *Naked Science: Anthropological Inquiry into Boundaries, Power, and Knowledge*, ed. Laura Nader, 101–116. New York: Routledge.

Cliquet, Robert, and Kristiaan Thienpont. 1995. *Population and Development: A Message from the Cairo Conference.* Dordrecht, The Netherlands: Kluwer.

Cole, Juan. 2002. *Sacred Space and Holy War: The Politics, Culture and History of Shi'ite Islam.* London: I. B. Tauris.

Colen, Shellee. 1995. "'Like a Mother to Them': Stratified Reproduction and West Indian Childcare Workers and Employers in New York." In *Conceiving the New World Order: The Global Politics of Reproduction*, ed. Faye D. Ginsburg and Rayna Rapp, 78–102. Berkeley: University of California Press.

Collet, M., Reniers, J., Frost, E., Gass, R., Yvert, F., Leclerc, A., Roth-Meyer, C., Ivanoff, B., and A. Meheus. 1988. "Infertility in Central Africa: Infection Is the Cause." *International Journal of Gynecology and Obstetrics* 26:423–428.

Collins, John A., Bustillo, Maria, Visscher, Robert D., and Lynne D. Lawrence. 1995. "An Estimate of the Cost of in Vitro Fertilization Services in the United States in 1995." *Fertility and Sterility* 64:538–545.

Condit, Celeste Michelle. 1994. "Hegemony in a Mass-Mediated Society: Concordance About Reproductive Technologies." *Critical Studies in Mass Communication* 11:205–230.

Connell, R. W. 1995. *Masculinities.* Berkeley: University of California Press.

Corea, Gena, Klein, Renate Duelli, Hanmer, Jalna, Holmes, Helen B., Hoskings, Betty, Kishwar, Madhu, Raymond, Janice, Rowland, Robyn, and Robert Steinbacher. 1987. *Man-Made Women: How New Reproductive Technologies Affect Women*. Bloomington: Indiana University Press.

Cornwall, Andrea, and Nancy Lindisfarne, eds. 1994. *Dislocating Masculinity: Comparative Ethnographies*. London: Routledge.

Cousins, Andrew. 2000. *Ideology and Medicine in the West Bank of Palestine*. Ph.D. thesis, Emory University, Atlanta, Georgia.

Crapanzano, Vincent. 1973. *The Hamadsha: A Study in Moroccan Ethnopsychiatry*. Berkeley: University of California Press.

Curtis, K. M., Savitz, D. A., and T. E. Arbuckle. 1997. "Effects of Cigarette Smoking, Caffeine Consumption, and Alcohol Intake on Fecundability." *American Journal of Epidemiology* 146:32–41.

Cussins, Charis. 1996. "Ontological Choreography: Agency Through Objectification in Infertility Clinics." *Social Studies of Science* 26:575–610.

Daniels, Cynthia R. 1997. "Between Fathers and Fetuses: The Social Construction of Male Reproduction and the Politics of Fetal Harm." *Signs: Journal of Women in Culture and Society* 22:579–616.

Daniels, Ken R. 1988. "Artificial Insemination Using Donor Semen and the Issue of Secrecy: The Views of Donors and Recipient Couples." *Social Science & Medicine* 27:377–383.

Daniels, Ken, and Erica Haimes, eds. 1998. *Donor Insemination: International Social Science Perspectives*. Cambridge, England: Cambridge University Press.

Daniluk, Judith C. 1988. "Infertility: Intrapersonal and Interpersonal Impact." *Fertility and Sterility* 49:982–990.

Datt, Gairav, Jolliffe, Dean, and Manohar Sharma. 1998. "A Profile of Poverty in Egypt." FCDN Discussion Paper No. 49. Food Consumption and Nutrition Division. Washington, DC: International Food Policy Research Institute.

DeClerque, J., Tsui, A. O., Abul-Ata, M. F., and D. Barcelona. 1986. "Rumor, Misinformation and Oral Contraceptive Use in Egypt." *Social Science & Medicine* 23:83–92.

Delaney, Carol. 1991. *The Seed and the Soil: Gender and Cosmology in Turkish Village Society*. Berkeley: University of California Press.

Devroey, P., Vandervorst, M., Nagy, P., and A. Van Steirteghem. 1998. "Do We Treat the Male or His Gamete?" *Human Reproduction* 13(Suppl 1): 178–185.

Dixon-Mueller, Ruth, and Judith Wasserheit. 1991. *The Culture of Silence: Reproductive Tract Infections Among Women in the Third World*. International Women's Health Coalition Report.

Dwairy, Marwan, and Timothy D. Van Sickle. 1996. "Western Psychotherapy in Traditional Arabic Societies." *Clinical Psychology Review* 16:231–249.

Early, Evelyn A. 1993. *Baladi Women of Cairo: Playing with an Egg and a Stone*. Boulder, CO: Lynne Rienner.

———. 1985 "Catharsis and Creation in Informal Narratives of Baladi Women of Cairo." *Anthropological Quarterly* 58:172–181.

———. 1982. "The Logic of Well Being: Therapeutic Narratives in Cairo, Egypt." *Social Science & Medicine* 16:1491–1497.

Edwards, Jeannette, Franklin, Sarah, Hirsch, Eric, Price, Frances, and Marilyn Strathern. 1999. *Technologies of Procreation: Kinship in the Age of Assisted Conception*, 2nd ed. New York: Routledge.

Egyptian Fertility Care Society. 1995. *Community-Based Study of the Prevalence of Infertility and Its Etiological Factors in Egypt: (1) The Population-Based Study*. Cairo: The Egyptian Fertility Care Society.

Ehrenfeld, Temma. 2002. "Infertility: A Guy Thing." *Newsweek* (March 25): 60–61.

Eickelman, Dale F. 1998. *The Middle East and Central Asia: An Anthropological Approach*, 3rd ed. Upper Saddle River, NJ: Prentice Hall.

Eickelman, Dale F., and James Piscatori. 1990. *Muslim Travellers: Pilgrimage, Migration, and the Religious Imagination*. London: Routledge.

El-Mehairy, Theresa. 1984. *Medical Doctors: A Study of Role Concept and Job Satisfaction, the Egyptian Case*. London: E. J. Brill.

Ericksen, K., and T. Brunette. 1996. "Patterns and Predictors of Infertility Among African Women: A Cross-Sectional Survey of Twenty-Seven Nations." *Social Science & Medicine* 42:209–220.

Falkum, Erik, and Reidun Forde. 2001. "Paternalism, Patient Autonomy, and Moral Deliberation in the Physician-Patient Relationship." *Social Science & Medicine* 52:239–248.

Farquhar, Dion. 1996. *The Other Machine: Discourse and Reproductive Technologies*. New York: Routledge.

Favot, I., Ngalula, J., Mgalla, Z., Klokke, A. H., Gumodoka, B., and J. T. Boerma. 1997. "HIV Infection and Sexual Behavior Among Women with Infertility in Tanzania: A Hospital-Based Study." *International Journal of Epidemiology* 26:414–419.

Feldman-Savelsberg, Pamela. 2001. "Is Infertility an Unrecognized Public Health and Population Problem? The View from the Cameroon Grassfields." In *Infertility Around the Globe: New Thinking on Childlessness, Gender, and Reproductive Technologies*, ed. Marcia C. Inhorn and Frank van Balen, 215–232. Berkeley: University of California Press.

———. 1999. *Plundered Kitchens, Empty Wombs: Threatened Reproduction and Identity in the Cameroon Grassfields*. Ann Arbor: University of Michigan Press.

Fernea, Elizabeth Warnock, ed. 1995. *Children in the Muslim Middle East*. Austin: University of Texas Press.

Festinger, Leon. 1957. *A Theory of Cognitive Dissonance*. Evanston, IL: Row, Peterson.

Fishel, S., Dowell, K., and S. Thornton. 2000. "Reproductive Possibilities for Infertile Couples: Present and Future." In *Infertility in the Modern World: Present and Future Prospects*, ed. Gillian R. Bentley and C. G. Nicholas Mascie-Taylor, 17–45. Cambridge, England: Cambridge University Press.

Fluehr-Lobban, Carolyn. 1994. *Islamic Society in Practice*. Gainesville: University Press of Florida.

Foucault, Michel. 1977. *Discipline & Punish: The Birth of the Prison*. Translated by Alan Sheridan. New York: Vintage.

Frank, Arthur W. 1995. *The Wounded Storyteller: Body, Illness, and Ethics*. Chicago: University of Chicago Press.

Franklin, Sarah. 1997. *Embodied Progress: A Cultural Account of Assisted Conception*. New York: Routledge.

———. 1991. "Deconstructing 'Desperateness': The Social Construction of Infertility in Popular Representations of New Reproductive Technologies." In *The*

New Reproductive Technologies, ed. M. McNeil, I. Varcoe, and S. Yearley, 200–229. London: Macmillan.

Franklin, Sarah, and Helena Ragone. 1998. "Introduction." In *Reproducing Reproduction: Kinship, Power,
and Technological Innovation*, ed. Sarah Franklin and
Helena Ragone, 1–14. Philadelphia: University of
Pennsylvania Press.

Freeman, Carla. 1999. *High Tech and High Heels in the
Global Economy: Women, Work, and Pink-Collar Iden-
tities in the Caribbean*. Durham, NC: Duke University
Press.

Freeman, Michael. 1996. "The New Birth Right? Identity
and the Child of the Reproductive Revolution." *The
International Journal of Children's Rights* 4:273–297.

Freudenburg, William R. 1988. "Perceived Risk, Real
Risk." *Science* 242:44–49.

Furedi, Frank. 1997. *Culture of Fear: Risk-Taking and the
Morality of Low Expectation*. London: Cassell.

Gadalla, Saad M. 1978. *Is There Hope? Fertility and Family
Planning in a Rural Egyptian Community*. Cairo:
American University in Cairo Press.

Gaffney, Patrick D. 1994. *The Prophet's Pulpit: Islamic
Preaching in Contemporary Egypt*. Berkeley: University of California Press.

Gammeltoft, Tine. 2002. "Between 'Science' and 'Superstition': Moral Perceptions of Induced Abortion Among
Urban Youth in Vietnam." *Culture, Medicine and Psychiatry* 26, in press.

Gellner, Ernest. 1994. "Foreword." In *Islam, Globalization
and Postmodernity*, ed. Akbar S. Ahmed and Hastings
Donnan, xi–xiv. London: Routledge.

Gerris, J. M. R. 1997. *A Comparative Investigation in the
Real Efficacy of Conventional Therapies Versus Ad-
vanced Reproductive Technology in Male Reproductive
Disorders*. Antwerpen: Universiteit van Antwerpen.

Gerrits, Trudie. 2001. "Infertility and Mahilineality: The
Exceptional Case of the Macua of Mozambique." In
*Infertility Around the Globe: New Thinking on Child-
lessness, Gender, and Reproductive Technologies*, ed.
Marcia C. Inhorn and Frank Van Balen, 233–246.
Berkeley: University of California Press.

———. 2000. "Studying Infertility and STDs Among the
Macua in Montepuez, Mozambique: A Multidiscipli-
nary Challenge?" In *Social Science Research on Child-
lessness in a Global Perspective: Proceedings of the
Conference 8–11 November 1999, Amsterdam, The
Netherlands*, ed. Frank van Balen, Trudie Gerrits, and
Marcia Inhorn, 166–174. Amsterdam: SCO-Kohnstam
Instituut, University of Amsterdam.

Ghoussoub, Mai, and Emma Sinclair-Webb, eds. 2000.
*Imagined Masculinities: Male Identity and Culture in
the Modern Middle East*. London: Saqi Books.

Ginsburg, Faye D., and Rayna Rapp. 1995. "Introduction:
Conceiving the New World Order." In *Conceiving the
New World Order: The Global Politics of Reproduction*,
ed. Faye D. Ginsburg and Rayna Rapp, 1–18. Berkeley: University of California Press.

Ginsburg, Faye D., and Rayna Rapp, eds. 1995. *Conceiving
the New World Order: The Global Politics of Reproduction*. Berkeley: University of California Press.

Goffman, Erving. 1963. *Stigma: Notes on the Management
of Spoiled Identity*. Englewood Cliffs, NJ: Prentice-
Hall.

Good, Mary-Jo DelVecchio. 1980. "Of Blood and Babies:
The Relationship of Popular Islamic Physiology to
Fertility." *Social Science & Medicine* 14B:147–156.

Greenwood, Bernard. 1981. "III(a) Perceiving Systems:
Cold or Spirits? Choice and Ambiguity in Morocco's
Pluralistic Medical System." *Social Science & Medicine*
15B:219–235.

Greil, Arthur L. 2001. "Infertile Bodies: Medicalization,
Metaphor, and Agency." In *Infertility Around the
Globe: New Thinking on Childlessness, Gender, and Re-
productive Technologies*, ed. Marcia C. Inhorn and
Frank van Balen, 101–118. Berkeley: University of
California Press.

———. 1997. "Infertility and Psychological Distress: A
Critical Review of the Literature." *Social Science &
Medicine* 45:1679–1704.

———. 1991. *Not Yet Pregnant: Infertile Couples in Contemporary America*. New Brunswick, NJ: Rutgers University Press.

———. 1991. "A Secret Stigma: The Analogy Between Infertility and Chronic Illness and Disability." *Advances
in Medical Sociology* 2:17–28.

Greil, Arthur L., Leitko, Thomas A., and Karen L. Porter.
1990. "Infertility: His and Hers." *Gender & Society*
2:172–199.

Greil, Arthur L., Porter, Karen L., Leitko, Thomas A., and
Catherine Riscilli. 1989. "Why Me? Theodicies of Infertile Women and Men." *Sociology of Health & Illness*
11:213–229.

Haddad, Lawrence, and Ahmed A. Akhter. 2000. "Poverty
Dynamics in Egypt: 1997–1999." Washington, DC:
International Food Policy Institute.

Handwerker, Lisa. 2001. "The Politics of Making Modern
Babies in China: Reproductive Technologies and the
'New' Eugenics." In *Infertility Around the Globe: New
Thinking on Childlessness, Gender, and Reproductive
Technologies*, ed. Marcia C. Inhorn and Frank van
Balen, 298–314. Berkeley: University of California
Press.

———. 1995. "The Hen That Can't Lay an Egg ('Bu Xia
Dan de Mu Ji'): Conceptions of Female Infertility in
Modern China." In *Deviant Bodies*, ed. Jacqueline
Urla and Jennifer Temy, 358–386. Bloomington: Indi-
ana University Press.

Hannerz, Ulf. 1996. *Transnational Connections: Culture,
People, Places*. London: Routledge.

Harding, Sandra. 1991. *Whose Science? Whose Knowledge?
Thinking from Women's Lives*. Ithaca, NY: Cornell
University Press.

Hartouni, Valerie. 1997. *Cultural Conceptions: On Reproductive Technologies and the Remaking of Life*. Minneapolis: University of Minnesota Press.

Hatem, Mervat. 1986. "The Enduring Alliance of Nationalism and Patriarchy in Muslim Personal Status Laws:
The Case of Modern Egypt." *Feminist Issues* 6:19–43.

———. 1986. "The Politics of Sexuality and Gender in
Segregated Patriarchal Systems: The Case of Eigh-
teenth- and Nineteenth-Century Egypt." *Feminist
Studies* 12:251–274.

Herz, Elisabeth K. 1989. "Infertility and Bioethical Issues
of the New Reproductive Technologies." *Psychiatric
Clinics of North America* 12:117–131.

Hess, David. 1994. "Parallel Universes: Anthropology in the
World of Technoscience." *Anthropology Today* 10:16–18.

Holmes, Helen Bequaert, ed. 1992. *Issues in Reproductive
Technology: An Anthology*. New York: Garland.

Hoodfar, Homa. 1996. *Between Marriage and the Market:
Intimate Politics and Survival in Cairo*. Berkeley: University of California Press.

Hopkins, Nicholas S., Mehanna, Sohair R., and Salah el-Haggar. 2001. *People and Pollution: Cultural Constructions and Social Action in Egypt*. Cairo: American University in Cairo Press.

Howards, Stuart S. 1995. "Treatment of Male Infertility." *New England Journal of Medicine* 332:312–317.

Humphrey, Michael, and Heather Humphrey. 1986. "A Fresh Look at Genealogical Bewilderment." *British Journal of Medical Psychology* 59:133–140.

Huntington, Dale. 2001. "Abortion in Egypt: Official Constraints and Popular Practices." In *Cultural Perspectives on Reproductive Health*, ed. Carla Makhlouf Obermeyer, 175–192. Oxford, England: Oxford University Press.

Ibrahim, Saad Eddin. 1997. "State, Women, and Civil Society: An Evaluation of Egypt's Population Policy." In *Arab Society: Class, Gender, Power & Development*, ed. Nicholas Hopkins and Saad Eddin Ibrahim, 85–104. Cairo: The American University in Cairo Press.

———. 1982. "Social Mobility and Income Distribution in Egypt, 1952–1977." In *The Political Economy of Income Distribution in Egypt*, ed. Gouda Abdel Khalek and Robert Tignor, 375–434. New York: Holmes and Meier.

Inda, Jonathan Xavier, and Renato Rosaldo. 2002. "Introduction: A World in Motion." In *The Anthropology of Globalization: A Reader*, ed. Jonathan Xavier Inda and Renato Rosaldo, 1–34. Malden, MA: Blackwell.

Inhorn, Marcia C. 2003. "The Risks of Test-tube Baby Making in Egypt." In *Risk, Culture and Health Inequality: Shifting Perceptions of Danger and Blame*, ed. Barbara Herr Harthorn and Laury Oaks. Westport, CT: Greenwood, in press.

———. 2003. "'The Worms Are Weak': Male Infertility and Patriarchal Paradoxes in Egypt." *Men & Masculinities*, 5:238–258.

———. 2002. "Global Infertility and the Globalization of New Reproductive Technologies: Illustrations from Egypt." *Social Science & Medicine*, in press.

———. 2002. "Sexuality, Masculinity, and Infertility in Egypt: Potent Troubles in the Marital and Medical Encounters." *The Journal of Men's Studies* 10:343–359.

———. 2001. "The 'Local' Confronts the 'Global': Infertile Bodies and New Reproductive Technologies in Egypt." In *Infertility Around the Globe: New Thinking on Childlessness, Gender, and Reproductive Technologies*, ed. Marcia C. Inhorn and Frank van Balen, 263–282. Berkeley: University of California Press.

———. 2001. "Money, Marriage, and Morality: Constraints on IVF Treatment Seeking Among Infertile Egyptian Couples." In *Cultural Perspectives on Reproductive Health*, ed. Carla Makhlouf Obermeyer, 83–100. Oxford, England: Oxford University Press.

———. 1996. *Infertility and Patriarchy: The Cultural Politics of Gender and Family Life in Egypt*. Philadelphia: University of Pennsylvania Press.

———. 1994. *Quest for Conception: Gender, Infertility, and Egyptian Medical Traditions*. Philadelphia: University of Pennsylvania Press.

———. 1991. "*Umm Il-Ghayyib*, Mother of the Missing One: A Sociomedical Study of Infertility in Alexandria, Egypt." Ph.D. thesis, University of California, Berkeley.

Inhorn, Marcia C., and Kimberly A. Buss. 1994. "Ethnography, Epidemiology, and Infertility in Egypt." *Social Science & Medicine* 39:671–686.

———. 1993. "Infertility, Infection, and Iatrogenesis in Egypt: The Anthropological Epidemiology of Blocked Tubes." *Medical Anthropology* 15:1–28.

Inhorn, Marcia C., and Frank Van Balen, eds. 2001. *Infertility Around the Globe: New Thinking on Childlessness, Gender, and Reproductive Technologies*. Berkeley: University of California Press.

Irvine, D. S. 1998. Epidemiology and Aetiology of Male Infertility. *Human Reproduction* 13(Suppl):33–44.

Janzen, John M. 1978. *The Quest for Therapy in Lower Zaire*. Berkeley: University of California Press.

Jenkins, Gwynne L. 2001. "Childlessness, Adoption, and *Milagros de Dios* in Costa Rica." In *Infertility Around the Globe: New Thinking on Childlessness, Gender, and Reproductive Technologies*, ed. Marcia C. Inhorn and Frank van Balen, 171–189. Berkeley: University of California Press.

Joseph, Suad, ed. 1999. *Intimate Selving in Arab Families: Gender, Self, and Identity*. Syracuse, NY: Syracuse University Press.

———. 1994. "Brother/Sister Relationships: Connectivity, Love, and Power in the Reproduction of Patriarchy in Lebanon." *American Ethnologist* 21:50–73.

———. 1993. "Connectivity and Patriarchy Among Urban Working-Class Arab Families in Lebanon." *Ethos* 21:452–484.

Kahn, Susan Martha. 2001. "Rabbis and Reproduction: The Uses of New Reproductive Technologies Among Ultraorthodox Jews in Israel." In *Infertility Around the Globe: New Thinking on Childlessness, Gender, and Reproductive Technologies*, ed. Marcia C. Inhorn and Frank van Balen, 283–297. Berkeley: University of California Press.

———. 2000. *Reproducing Jews: A Cultural Account of Assisted Conception in Israel*. Durham, NC: Duke University Press.

Kalb, Claudia. 2001. "Should You Have Your Baby Now?" *Newsweek* (August 13), 40–48.

Kamischke, A., and E. Neischlag. 1998. "Conventional Treatments of Male Infertility in the Age of Evidence-Based Andrology." *Human Reproduction* 13(Suppl 1):62–75.

Kandela, Peter. 1998. "Oversupply of Doctors Fuels Egypt's Health-Care Crisis." *The Lancet* 352:123.

Kandiyoti, Deniz. 1994. "The Paradoxes of Masculinity: Some Thoughts on Segregated Societies." In *Dislocating Masculinity: Comparative Ethnographies*, ed. Andrea Cornwall and Nancy Lindisfarne, 197–213. London: Routledge.

———. 1991. "Islam and Patriarchy: A Comparative Perspective." In *Women in Middle Eastern History: Shifting Boundaries in Sex and Gender*, ed. Nikki R. Keddie and Beth Baron, 23–42. New Haven, CT: Yale University Press.

———. 1988. "Bargaining with Patriarchy." *Gender & Society* 2:274–290.

Kangas, Beth. 2002. "Therapeutic Itineraries in a Global World: Yemenis and Their Search for Biomedical Treatment Abroad." *Medical Anthropology*, 21:35–78.

———. 2002. *The Lure of Technology: Yemenis' International Medical Travel in a Global Era*. Ph.D. Thesis, University of Arizona.

Khattab, Hind, Younis, Nabil, and Huda Zurayk. 1999. *Women, Reproduction, and Health in Rural Egypt: The Giza Study*. Cairo: American University in Cairo Press.

King, Leslie, and Madonna Harrington Meyer. 1997. "The Politics of Reproductive Benefits: U.S. Insurance Coverage of Contraceptive and Infertility Treatments." *Gender & Society* 11:8–30.

Kitzinger, Celia, and Jo Willmott. 2002. "'The Thief of Womanhood': Women's Experience of Polycystic Ovarian Syndrome." *Social Science & Medicine* 54: 349–361.

Klein, Renate. 1989. *Infertility: Women Speak Out About Their Experiences of Reproductive Medicine.* London: Pandora Press.

Klein, Renate, and Robyn Rowland. 1989. "Hormonal Cocktails: Women as Test-Sites for Fertility Drugs." *Women's Studies International Forum* 12:333–348.

Kleinman, Arthur. 1995. "Anthropology of Bioethics." In *Writing at the Margin: Discourse Between Anthropology and Medicine,* 41–65. Berkeley: University of California Press.

———. 1995. *Writing at the Margin: Discourse Between Anthropology and Medicine.* Berkeley: University of California Press.

———. 1992. "Local Worlds of Suffering: An Interpersonal Focus for Ethnographies of Illness Experience." *Qualitative Health Research* 2:127–134.

———. 1988. *The Illness Narratives: Suffering, Healing, and the Human Condition.* New York: Basic Books.

Kleinman, Arthur, Das, Veena, and Margaret Lock, eds. 1997. *Social Suffering.* Berkeley: University of California Press.

Kleinman, Arthur, and Joan Kleinman. 1991. "Suffering and Its Professional Transformation: Toward an Ethnography of Interpersonal Experience." *Culture, Medicine, and Psychiatry* 15:275–301.

Landau, Ruth. 1998. "The Management of Genetic Origins: Secrecy and Openness in Donor Assisted Conception in Israel and Elsewhere." *Human Reproduction* 13:3268–3273.

Lane, Sandra D. 1997. "Television Minidramas: Social Marketing and Evaluation in Egypt." *Medical Anthropology* 11: 164–182.

———. 1997. "Gender and Health: Abortion in Urban Egypt." In *Population, Poverty, and Politics in Middle East Cities,* ed. Michael E. Bonine, 208–234. Gainesville: University Press of Florida.

———. 1994. "Research Bioethics in Egypt." In *Principles of Health Care Ethics,* ed. Raanan Gillon, 885–894. Chichester, England: John Wiley.

Lane, Sandra D., and Robert A. Rubinstein. 1991. "The Use of *Fatwas* in the Production of Reproductive Health Policy in Egypt." Paper presented at the 90th Annual Meeting of the American Anthropological Association, Chicago, Illinois.

Laqueur, Thomas. 1990. *Making Sex: Body and Gender from the Greeks to Freud.* Cambridge, MA: Harvard University Press.

Larsen, U. 2000. "Primary and Secondary Infertility in Sub-Saharan Africa." *International Journal of Epidemiology* 29:285–291.

———. 1994. "Sterility in Sub-Saharan Africa." *Population Studies* 48:459–474.

LaTowsky, Robert J. 1984. "Egyptian Labor Abroad: Mass Participation and Modest Returns." *MERIP Reports* 14:11–18.

Leonard, Lori. 2001. "Problematizing Fertility: 'Scientific' Accounts and Chadian Women's Narratives." In *Infer-*

tility Around the Globe: New Thinking on Childlessness, Gender, and Reproductive Technologies, ed. Marcia C. Inhorn and Frank van Balen, 193–214. Berkeley: University of California Press.

Liamputtong, Pranee. 2000. "A Barren Body: The Cultural Interpretation of Infertility Among Hmong Women in Australia." In *Social Science Research on Childlessness in a Global Perspective: Proceedings of the Conference 8–11 November 1999, Amsterdam, The Netherlands,* ed. Frank van Balen, Trudie Gerrits, and Marcia Inhorn, 140–145. Amsterdam: SCO-Kohnstamm Instituut, University of Amsterdam.

Lindisfarne, Nancy. 1994. "Variant Masculinities, Variant Virginities: Rethinking 'Honour and Shame.'" In *Dislocating Masculinity: Comparative Ethnographies,* ed. Andrea Cornwall and Nancy Lindisfarne, 82–96. London: Routledge.

Lloyd, Mike. 1997. "The Language of Reproduction: Is It Doctored?" *Qualitative Health Research* 7:184–201.

———. 1996. "Condemned to Be Meaningful: Non-Response in Studies of Men and Infertility." *Sociology of Health & Illness* 18:433–454.

Lock, Margaret. 1998. "Perfecting Society: Reproductive Technologies, Genetic Testing, and the Planned Family in Japan." In *Pragmatic Women and Body Politics,* ed. Margaret Lock and Patricia Kaufert, 206–239. Cambridge, England: Cambridge University Press.

———. 1994. *Encounters with Aging: Menopause in the United States and Japan.* Berkeley: University of California Press.

Lock, Margaret, and Patricia A. Kaufert. 1998. "Introduction." In *Pragmatic Women and Body Politics,* 1–27. Cambridge, England: Cambridge University Press.

———. eds. 1998. *Pragmatic Women and Body Politics.* Cambridge, England: Cambridge University Press.

Lorber, Judith. 1989. "Choice, Gift, or Patriarchal Bargain? Women's Consent to in Vitro Fertilization in Male Infertility." *Hypatia* 4:23–36.

———. 1988. "In Vitro Fertilization and Gender Politics." *Women & Health* 13:117–133.

Lublin, Nancy. 1998. *Pandora's Box: Feminism Confronts Reproductive Technology.* Lanham, MD: Rowman and Littlefield.

MacLeod, Arlene E. 1991. *Accommodating Protest: Working Women, the New Veiling, and Change in Cairo.* New York: Columbia University Press.

Macnaughton, Malcolm. 1992. "Medically Assisted Conception: Dilemma of Practice and Research—Global Views." In *Proceedings of the First International Conference on "Bioethics in Human Reproduction Research in the Muslim World,"* ed. Gamal I. Serour, 229–33. Cairo: International Islamic Center for Population Studies & Research, Al-Azhar University.

Mamdani, Masuma. 1992. "Early Initiatives in Essential Drugs Policy." In *Drugs Policy in Developing Countries,* ed. Najmi Kanji, Anita Hardon, Jan Willem Harnmeijer, Masuma Mamdani, and Gill Walt, 1–23. London: Zed Books.

Mansour, R. T., Aboulghar, M. A., and G. I. Serour. 1988. "In Vitro Fertilization and Embryo Transfer: Report of the Egyptian IVF-ET Centre." *Journal of the Egyptian Society of Obstetrics and Gynecology* 14:17–28.

Martin, Emily. 1991. "The Egg and the Sperm: How Science Has Constructed a Romance Based on Stereotypical Male-Female Roles." *Signs* 16:485–501.

Mattingly, Cheryl. 1998. *Healing Dramas and Clinical Plots: The Narrative Structure of Experience.* New York: Cambridge University Press.

Mattingly, Cheryl, and Linda C. Garro, eds. 2000. *Narrative and the Cultural Construction of Illness and Healing.* Berkeley: University of California Press.

McConnell, John D. 1993. "Diagnosis and Treatment of Male Infertility." In *Textbook of Reproductive Medicine,* ed. Bruce R. Carr and Richard E. Blackwell, 453–468. Norwalk, CT: Appleton & Lange.

McNeil, Maureen, Varcoe, Ian, and Steven Yearley, eds. 1990. *The New Reproductive Technologies.* London: MacMillan.

McPake, Barbara. 1997. "The Role of the Private Sector in Health Service Provision." In *Private Health Providers in Developing Countries: Serving the Public Interest?,* ed. Sara Bennett, Barbara McPake, and Anne Mills, 21–39. London: Zed Books.

Mead, Nicola, and Peter Bower. 2000. "Patient-Centredness: A Conceptual Framework and Review of the Empirical Literature." *Social Science & Medicine* 51:1087–1110.

Mechanic, David, and Sharon Meyer. 2000. "Concepts of Trust Among Patients with Serious Illness." *Social Science & Medicine* 51:657–668.

Meirow, D., and J. G. Schenker. 1997. "The Current Status of Sperm Donation in Assisted Reproduction Technology: Ethical and Legal Considerations." *Journal of Assisted Reproduction and Genetics* 14:133–138.

Moghadam, Valentine M. 1993. *Modernizing Women: Gender and Social Change in the Middle East.* Boulder, CO: Lynne Rienner.

Mogobe, Keitshokile. 2000. "Traditional Therapies for Infertility: Implications for the Brokerage Role of the Nurse in Botswana." In *Social Science Research on Childlessness in a Global Perspective: Proceedings of the Conference 8–11 November 1999, Amsterdam, The Netherlands,* ed. Frank van Balen, Trudie Gerrits, and Marcia Inhorn, 111–117. Amsterdam: SCO-Kohnstam Instituut, University of Amsterdam.

Mohanty, C. T., Russo, A., and L. Torres, eds. 1991. *Third World Women and the Politics of Feminism.* Bloomington: Indiana University Press.

Morsy, Soheir A. 1993. *Gender, Sickness & Healing in Rural Egypt: Ethnography in Historical Context.* Boulder, CO: Westview Press.

Mundigo, Axel. 1998. "The Role of Men in Improving Reproductive Health: The Direction Research Should Take." In *Reproductive Health Research: The New Directions—Biennial Report, 1996–1997,* 124–131. Geneva: World Health Organization.

Musallam, B. F. 1983. *Sex and Society in Islam: Birth Control Before the Nineteenth Century.* Cambridge, England: Cambridge University Press.

Nachtigall, Robert D. 1993. "Secrecy: An Unresolved Issue in the Practice of Donor Insemination." *American Journal of Obstetrics and Gynecology* 168:1846–1851.

Nachtigall, Robert D., Becker, Gay, Quiroga, Seline Szkupinski, and Jeanne M. Tschann. 1998. "The Disclosure Decision: Concerns and Issues of Parents of Children Conceived Through Donor Insemination." *American Journal of Obstetrics and Gynecology* 178:1165–1170.

Nachtigall, Robert D., Becker, Gay, and Mark Wozny. 1992. "The Effects of Gender-Specific Diagnosis on Men's and Women's Response to Infertility." *Fertility and Sterility* 54:113–121.

Nachtigall, Robert D., Tschann, Jeanne M., Quiroga, Seline Szkupinski, Pitcher, Linda, and Gay Becker. 1997. "Stigma, Disclosure, and Family Functioning Among Parents of Children Conceived Through Donor Insemination." *Fertility and Sterility* 68:83–89.

Nader, Laura. 1996. "Introduction: Anthropological Inquiry into Boundaries, Power, and Knowledge." In *Naked Science: Anthropological Inquiry into Boundaries, Power and Knowledge,* ed. Laura Nader, 1–25. New York: Routledge.

Nagi, Saad Z. 2001. *Poverty in Egypt: Human Needs and Institutional Capacities.* Lanham, MD: Lexington Books.

Nation's Health. 2002. "Egypt Sets Objectives Through 'Healthy People' Plan." *The Nation's Health* (March 2002): 12.

Nedoroscik, Jeffrey A. 1996. *The City of the Dead: A History of Cairo's Cemetery Communities.* Westport, CT: Greenwood Press.

Ngwafor, Ephraim N. 1994. "Childlessness in Cameroon: Artificially Assisted Fertility or the Customary Law Solution." *Medicine and Law* 13:297–306.

Nicholson, Roberto F., and Roberto E. Nicholson. 1994. "Assisted Reproduction in Latin America." *Journal of Assisted Reproduction and Genetics* 11:438–444.

Nsiah-Jefferson, Laurie, and Elaine J. Hall. 1989. "Reproductive Technology: Perspectives and Implications for Low-Income Women and Women of Color." In *Healing Technology: Feminist Perspectives,* ed. Kathryn Strother Ratcliff, 93–117. Ann Arbor: University of Michigan Press.

Obermeyer, Carla Makhlouf. 1999. "Fairness and Fertility: The Meaning of Son Preference in Morocco." In *Dynamics of Values in Fertility Change,* ed. Richard Leete, 275–292. Oxford: Oxford University Press.

Okonofua, Friday E. 1996. "The Case Against New Reproductive Technologies in Developing Countries." *British Journal of Obstetrics and Gynaecology* 103: 957–962.

Omran, Abdel Rahim, and Farzaneh Roudi. 1993. "The Middle East Population Puzzle." *Population Bulletin* 48:1–40.

Ouzgane, Lahoucine. 1997. "Masculinity as Virility in Tahar Ben Jelloun's Fiction." *Contagion: Journal of Violence, Mimesis, and Culture* 4:1–13.

Overall, Christine, ed. 1989. *The Future of Human Reproduction.* Toronto, Ontario: The Women's Press.

Panter-Brick, Catherine. 1991. "Parental Responses to Consanguinity and Genetic Disease in Saudi Arabia." *Social Science & Medicine* 33:1295–1302.

Patton, Sandra. 2000. *Birth Marks: Transracial Adoption in Contemporary America.* New York: New York University Press.

Peteet, Julie. 2000. "Male Gender and Rituals of Resistance in the Palestinian Intifada: A Cultural Politics of Violence." In *Imagined Masculinities: Male Identity and Culture in the Modern Middle East,* ed. Mai Ghoussoub and Emma Sinclair-Webb, 103–126. London: Saqi Books.

Population Reference Bureau. 2001. "World Population Data Sheet." Washington, DC: Population Reference Bureau.

———. 1999. "World Population Data Sheet: Demographic Data and Estimates for the Countries and Regions of the World." Washington, DC: Population Reference Bureau.

Ragone, Helena. 1994. *Surrogate Motherhood: Conception in the Heart.* Boulder, CO: Westview Press.

Rapp, Rayna. 1999. *Testing Women, Testing the Fetus: The Social Impact of Amniocentesis in America.* New York: Routledge.

———. 1988. "Moral Pioneers: Women, Men and Fetuses on a Frontier of Reproductive Technology." In *Embryos, Ethics, and Women's Rights: Exploring the New Reproductive Technologies,* ed. Elaine Hoffman Baruch, Amadeo F. D'Adamo, Jr., and Joni Seager, 101–16. New York: Haworth Press.

Rapp, Rayna, and Faye D. Ginsburg. 1999. "Relocating Reproduction, Generating Culture." Paper presented at the Annual Meeting of the American Anthropological Association, Chicago.

Ratcliff, Kathryn Strother, ed. 1989. *Healing Technology: Feminist Perspectives.* Ann Arbor: University of Michigan Press.

Raymond, Janice G. 1993. *Women as Wombs: Reproductive Technologies and the Battle over Women's Freedom.* San Francisco: Harper.

Reame, Nancy King. 2000. "Making Babies in the 21st Century: New Strategies, Old Dilemmas." *Women's Health Issues* 10:152–159.

Reproductive Health Outlook. 2002. "Infertility." Online. www.rho.org.

Riessman, Catherine Kohler. 2001. "Positioning Gender Identity in Narratives of Infertility: South Indian Women's Lives in Context." In *Infertility Around the Globe: New Thinking on Childlessness, Gender, and Reproductive Technologies,* ed. Marcia C. Inhorn and Frank van Balen, 152–170. Berkeley: University of California Press.

———. 2000. "Stigma and Everyday Resistance Practices: Childless Women in South India." *Gender & Society* 14:111–135.

———. 1993. *Narrative Analysis.* Qualitative Research Methods Series, No. 30. Newbury Park, CA: Sage.

Robertson, John A. 1996. "Legal Troublespots in Assisted Reproduction." *Fertility and Sterility* 65:11–12.

Rothman, Barbara Katz. 1993. *The Tentative Pregnancy: How Amniocentesis Changes the Experience of Motherhood.* New York: Norton.

———. 1989. *Recreating Motherhood: Ideology and Technology in a Patriarchal Society.* New York: W.W. Norton.

Rowe, P. J. 1999. "Clinical Aspects of Infertility and the Role of Health Care Services." *Reproductive Health Matters* 7:103–111.

Rowe, P. J., and T. M. M. Farley. 1988. "Prevention and Management of Infertility." In *World Health Organization Special Programme of Research Development and Training in Human Reproduction: Research in Human Reproduction—Biennial Report, 1986–1987,* 265–296. Geneva, Switzerland: World Health Organization.

Rowland, Robyn. 1992. *Living Laboratories: Women and Reproductive Technology.* London: Octopus Publishing.

Rubinstein, Robert A. 1997. "'Breaking the Bureaucracy': Drug Registration and Neocolonial Relations in Egypt." *Social Science & Medicine* 46:1487–1494.

Rugh, Andrea. 1995. "Orphanages in Egypt: Contradiction or Affirmation in a Family-Oriented Society." In *Children in the Muslim Middle East,* ed. Elizabeth Warnock Fernea, 124–141. Austin: University of Texas Press.

Said, Edward W. 1978. *Orientalism.* New York: Vintage Books.

Samucidine, M., Barreto, J., Folgosa, E., Mondlane, C., and S. Bergstrom. 1999. "Infertile Women in Developing Countries at Potentially High Risk of HIV Transmission." *African Journal of Reproductive Health* 3:98–102.

Sandelowski, Margarete. 1993. *With Child in Mind: Studies of the Personal Encounter with Infertility.* Philadelphia: University of Pennsylvania Press.

———. 1991. "Compelled to Try: The Never-Enough Quality of Conceptive Technology." *Medical Anthropology Quarterly* 5:29–47.

Sandelowski, Margarete, and Sheryl de Lacey. 2001. "The Uses of a 'Disease': Infertility as Rhetorical Vehicle." In *Infertility Around the Globe: New Thinking on Childlessness, Gender, and Reproductive Technologies,* ed. Marcia C. Inhorn and Frank van Balen, 33–51. Berkeley: University of California Press.

Sandelowski, Margarete, Harris, Betty G., and Beth Perry Black. 1992. "Relinquishing Infertility: The Work of Pregnancy for Infertile Couples." *Qualitative Health Research* 2:282–301.

Savage, Olayinka Margaret Njikam. 1992. "Artificial Donor Insemination in Yaounde: Some Socio-Cultural Considerations." *Social Science & Medicine* 35:907–913.

Scambler, G. 1984. "Perceiving and Coping with a Stigmatizing Condition." In *The Experience of Illness,* ed. R. Fitzpatrick, J. Hinton, S. Newman, G. Scambler, and J. Thompson, 203–226. New York: Tavistock.

Scheper-Hughes, Nancy. 1992. *Death Without Weeping: The Violence of Everyday Life in Brazil.* Berkeley: University of California Press.

Schleifer, Aliah. 1986. *Motherhood in Islam.* Cambridge, England: Islamic Academy.

Scholz, T., Bartholomaus, S., Grimmer, I., Kentenich, H., and M. Obladen. 1999. "Problems of Multiple Births After ART: Medical, Psychological, Social and Financial Aspects." *Human Reproduction* 14:2932–2937.

Sciarra, J. 1994. "Infertility: An International Health Problem." *International Journal of Gynecology & Obstetrics* 46:155–163.

Scutt, Jocelynne. A., ed. 1990. *The Baby Machine: Reproductive Technology and the Commercialisation of Motherhood.* London: Merlin Press.

Seibel, Machelle M., and Susan L. Crockin, eds. 1996. *Family Building Through Egg and Sperm Donation: Medical, Legal, and Ethical Issues.* Sudbury, MA: Jones and Bartlett.

Serour, Gamal I. 1996. "Bioethics in Reproductive Health: A Muslim's Perspective." *Middle East Fertility Society Journal* 1:30–35.

———. 1994. "Islam and the Four Principles." In *Principles of Health Care Ethics,* ed. Raanan Gillon, 75–91. Chichester, England: John Wiley.

———. 1992. "Medically Assisted Conception: Dilemma of Practice and Research—Islamic Views." In *Proceedings of the First International Conference on "Bioethics in Human Reproduction Research in the Muslim World,"* ed. Gamal I. Serour, 234 -242. Cairo: International Islamic Center for Population Studies and Research, Al Azhar University.

————. 1992. "Bioethics in Artificial Reproduction in the Muslim World." Paper presented at the Inaugural Congress of the International Association of Bioethics, Amsterdam, The Netherlands.

Serour, Gamal I., ed. 1992. *Proceedings of the First International Conference on "Bioethics in Human Reproduction Research in the Muslim World."* Cairo: International Islamic Center for Population Studies and Research, Al-Azhar University.

Serour, Gamal I., Aboulghar, Mohamed A., and Ragaa T. Mansour. 1995. "Bioethics in Medically Assisted Conception in the Muslim World." *Journal of Assisted Reproduction and Genetics* 12:559–565.

Serour, G. I., El Ghar, M., and R. T. Mansour. 1991. "Infertility: A Health Problem in Muslim World." *Population Sciences* 10:41–58.

————. 1991. "In Vitro Fertilization and Embryo Transfer in Egypt." *International Journal of Gynecology and Obstetrics* 36:49–53.

————. 1990. "In Vitro Fertilization and Embryo Transfer, Ethical Aspects in Techniques in the Muslim World." *Population Sciences* 9:45–54.

Serour, Gamal I., and A. R. Omran, eds. 1992. *Ethical Guidelines for Human Reproduction Research in the Muslim World.* Cairo: International Islamic Center for Population Studies and Research, Al-Azhar University.

Shafik, Viola. 2001. "Prostitute for a Good Reason: Stars and Morality in Egypt." *Women's Studies International Forum* 24:711–725.

Shahara, F., et al. 1998. "Environmental Toxicants and Female Reproduction." *Fertility and Sterility* 70:613–622.

Shenfield, F., and S. J. Steele. 1997. "What Are the Effects of Anonymity and Secrecy on the Welfare of the Child in Gamete Donation?" *Human Reproduction* 12:392–395.

Sholkamy, Hania M. 1999. "Procreation in Islam: A Reading from Egypt of People and Texts." In *Conceiving Persons: Ethnographies of Procreation, Fertility, and Growth,* ed. Peter Loizos and Patrick Heady, 139–159. London: Athlone Press.

Shore, Cris. 1992. "Virgin Births and Sterile Debates: Anthropology and the New Reproductive Technologies." *Current Anthropology* 33:295–301.

Sinclair-Webb, Emma. 2000. "'Our Bulent Is Now a Commando': Military Service and Manhood in Turkey." In *Imagined Masculinities: Male Identity and Culture in the Modern Middle East,* ed. Mai Ghoussoub and Emma Sinclair-Webb, 65–102. London: Saqi Books.

Singerman, Diane, and Barbara Ibrahim. 2002. "The Cost of Marriage in Egypt: A Hidden Variable in the New Arab Demography." In *Cairo Papers in the Social Sciences,* Special Issue on the New Arab Family, ed. Nicholas Hopkins. Cairo: American University in Cairo Press.

Sonbol, Amira el Azhary. 1995. "Adoption in Islamic Society: A Historical Survey." In *Children in the Muslim Middle East,* ed. Elizabeth Warnock Fernea, 45–67. Austin: University of Texas Press.

————. 1991. *The Creation of a Medical Profession in Egypt, 1800–1922.* Syracuse, NY: Syracuse University Press.

Spallone, Patricia, and Deborah Lynn Steinberg, eds. 1987. *Made to Order: The Myth of Reproductive and Genetic Progress.* Oxford: Pergamon.

Squier, Susan Merrill. 1994. *Babies in Bottles: Twentieth-Century Visions of Reproductive Technology.* New Brunswick, NJ: Rutgers University Press.

Stanworth, Michelle, ed. 1987. *Reproductive Technologies: Gender, Motherhood and Medicine.* Cambridge: Polity Press.

Starrett, Gregory. 1997. *Putting Islam to Work: Education, Politics, and Religious Transformation in Egypt.* Berkeley: University of California Press.

Steinberg, Deborah Lynn. 1997. "A Most Selective Practice: The Eugenics Logic of IVF." *Women's Studies International Forum* 20:33–48.

Stephens, Angela. 1995. "Fertile Ground." *Egypt Today* (February): 73–114.

Stewart, M., Brown, J., Weston, W., McWhinney, I., McWilliam, C., and T. Freeman. 1995. *Patient-Centred Medicine: Transforming the Clinical Method.* London: Sage.

Strathern, Marilyn. 1992. *Reproducing the Future: Essays on Anthropology, Kinship and the New Reproductive Technologies.* New York: Routledge.

Stycos, J. Mayone, Sayed, Hussein Abdel Aziz, Avery, Roger, and Samuel Fridman. 1988. *Community Development and Family Planning: An Egyptian Experiment.* Boulder, CO: Westview Press.

Sundby, Johanne. 2001. "Infertility and Health Care in Countries with Less Resources: Case Studies from Sub-Saharan Africa." In *Infertility Around the Globe: New Thinking on Childlessness, Gender, and Reproductive Technologies,* ed. Marcia C. Inhorn and Frank van Balen, 247–260. Berkeley: University of California Press.

————. 1997. "Infertility in the Gambia: Traditional and Modern Health Care." *Patient Education and Counseling* 31:29–37.

Thompson, Charis M. 2001 "Fertile Ground: Feminists Theorize Infertility." In *Infertility around the Globe: New Thinking on Childlessness, Gender, and Reproductive Technologies,* ed. Marcia C. Inhorn and Frank van Balen, 52–78. Berkeley: University of California Press.

Thonneau, P., Bujan, L., Multigner, L., and R. Mieusset. 1998. "Occupational Heat Exposure and Male Fertility: A Review." *Human Reproduction* 13:2122–2125.

Turiel, Judith Steinberg. 1998. *Beyond Second Opinions: Making Choices About Fertility Treatment.* Berkeley: University of California Press.

Upton, Rebecca L. 2001. "'Infertility Makes You Invisible': Gender, Health and the Negotiation of Fertility in Northern Botswana." *Journal of Southern African Studies* 27:349–362.

Van Balen, Frank. 2001. "The Psychologization of Infertility." In *Infertility Around the Globe: New Thinking on Childlessness, Gender, and Reproductive Technologies,* ed. Marcia C. Inhorn and Frank van Balen, 79–98. Berkeley: University of California Press.

Van Balen, Frank, and Trudie Gerrits. 2001. "Quality of Infertility Care in Poor-Resource Areas and the Introduction of New Reproductive Technologies." *Human Reproduction* 16:215–219.

Van Balen, Frank, and Marcia C. Inhorn. 2003. "Son Preference, Sex Selection, and the 'New' New Reproductive Technologies." *International Journal of Health Services,* in press.

————. 2001. "Introduction—Interpreting Infertility: View from the Social Sciences." In *Infertility Around* the Globe: New Thinking on Childlessness, Gender, and Reproductive Technologies, ed. Marcia C. Inhorn and Frank van Balen, 3–32. Berkeley: University of California Press.

Van Balen, Frank, and T. C. M. Trimbos-Kemper. 1995. "Involuntary Childless Couples: Their Desire to Have Children and Their Motives." *Journal of Psychosomatic Obstetrics* 16:137–144.

Van der Ploeg, Irma. 1995. "Hermaphrodite Patients: In Vitro Fertilization and the Transformation of Male Infertility." *Science, Technology, & Human Values* 20:460–481.

Van Dyck, Jose. 1995. *Manufacturing Babies and Public Consent: Debating the New Reproductive Technologies.* London: MacMillan.

Van Nieuwkerk, Karin. 1995. *"A Trade Like Any Other": Female Singers and Dancers in Egypt.* Austin: University of Texas Press.

Veatch, Robert M., ed. 1989. *Medical Ethics.* Boston: Jones and Barlett.

Watson, Helen. 1992. *Women in the City of the Dead.* London: Hurst.

Webb, Russell E., and Judith C. Daniluk. 1999. "The End of the Line: Infertile Men's Experiences of Being Unable to Produce a Child." *Men and Masculinities* 2:6–25.

Whiteford, Linda M., and Lois Gonzalez. 1995. "Stigma: The Hidden Burden of Infertility." *Social Science & Medicine* 40:27–36.

Whiteford, Linda M., and Lenore Manderson, eds. 2000. *Global Health Policy, Local Realities: The Fallacy of the Level Playing Field.* Boulder, CO: Lynne Rienner.

Widge, Anjali. 2001. *Beyond Natural Conception: A Sociological Investigation of Assisted Reproduction with Spe-cial Reference to India.* Ph.D. thesis, School of Social Sciences, Jawaharlal Nehru University, New Delhi, India.

Wikan, Unni. 1996. *Tomorrow, God Willing: Self-Made Destinies in Cairo.* Chicago: University of Chicago Press.

Wolf, Susan M., ed. 1996. *Feminism and Bioethics: Beyond Reproduction.* New York: Oxford University Press.

Wood, J. W. 1994. *Dynamics of Human Reproduction: Biology, Biometry, Demography.* New York: Aldine de Gruyter.

World Bank. 1993. *Investing in Health: World Development Report 1993.* Washington, DC: World Bank.

———. 1987. *Financing Health Services in Developing Countries: An Agenda for Reform.* Washington, DC: World Bank.

World Health Organization. 2000. *The World Health Report 2000—Health Systems: Improving Performance.* Geneva: World Health Organization.

———. 1998. *Reproductive Health Research: The New Directions—Biennial Report, 1996–1997.* Geneva: World Health Organization.

———. 1993. *WHO Manual for the Standardized Investigation and Diagnosis of the Infertile Couple.* Cambridge, England: Cambridge University Press.

———. 1987. "Infections, Pregnancies, and Infertility: Perspectives on Prevention." *Fertility and Sterility* 47:964–968.

Yeboah, E. D., Wadhwani, J. M., and J. B. Wilson. 1992. "Etiological Factors of Male Infertility in Africa." *International Journal of Fertility* 37:300–307.

Zuhur, Sherifa. 1992. *Revealing Reveiling: Islamist Gender Ideology in Contemporary Egypt.* Albany: SUNY Press.

Index

Women *(continued)*
  fears of extracorporal pregnancies,
    68
  health-care seeking of, 13–14
  Islam and women's rights, 90
  lack of support for, 258–262
  maternal instinct of, 224
  science literacy and, 62–63
  social stigma of infertility, 10–11,
    245–246, 263
  treadmill effect of IVF treatments,
    172–173, 176
  treatment side effects, 182–185, 190–199,
    201–203
*Women and Infertility in Sub-Saharan
  Africa: A Multi-Disciplinary
  Perspective,* 5
World Bank, 130
World Health Organization (WHO), 3–5,
  130, 270

Yehia, Dr. Mohamed, 24, 26, 28–29, 32, 36,
  41, 46–47, 74–75, 78, 87, 112,
  116–118, 123–125
  biography of, 125–126
  on cesarean delivery, 211
  character of, 128, 135
  clinical practice of, 127–128, 134–135,
    141, 147
  genetic counseling, 212–213
  on multiple gestations, 173
  patient-centered medicine, 136–139
  on patient support, 261
  as private provider of NRT, 128–131, 144,
    151–152
  on success rates, 163–164, 169
Young, Alan, 269

Zaki, Dr. Salah, 24, 28, 39, 57, 133–138, 152,
  156–157, 165, 196

Made in the USA
Middletown, DE
16 December 2016